D0238778

Library

RAWN

MANCHESTER
1824

Manchester University Press

*For Deb*

# Staging the UK

*Jen Harvie*

**Manchester University Press**

Manchester and New York

*distributed exclusively in the USA by Palgrave*

Copyright © Jen Harvie 2005

The right of Jen Harvie to be identified as the author of this work
has been asserted by her in accordance with the Copyright, Designs and Patents Act 1988.

*Published by* Manchester University Press
Oxford Road, Manchester M13 9NR, UK
*and* Room 400, 175 Fifth Avenue, New York, NY 10010, USA
www.manchesteruniversitypress.co.uk

*Distributed exclusively in the USA by*
Palgrave, 175 Fifth Avenue, New York,
NY 10010, USA

*Distributed exclusively in Canada by*
UBC Press, University of British Columbia, 2029 West Mall,
Vancouver, BC, Canada V6T 1Z2

*British Library Cataloguing-in-Publication Data*
A catalogue record for this book is available from the British Library

*Library of Congress Cataloging-in-Publication Data applied for*


ISBN    0 7190 6212 8    *hardback*
EAN    978 0 7190 6212 4
ISBN    0 7190 6213 6    *paperback*
EAN    978 0 7190 6213 1

First published 2005

14  13  12  11  10  09  08  07  06  05        10  9  8  7  6  5  4  3  2  1


Typeset by
D R Bungay Associates, Burghfield, Berks

Printed in Great Britain
by Bell & Bain Ltd, Glasgow

**Coventry University**

# Contents

LIST OF FIGURES       *page* vi

ACKNOWLEDGEMENTS       viii

1   Introduction: staging the UK       1

2   Policy paradigms: regional, metropolitan, and national arts and 'creative industries'       16

3   Remembering the nations: site-specific performance, memory, and identities       41

4   The Edinburgh festivals: globalisation and democracy       74

5   The UK and Europe: genealogies and futures of performance       112

6   Bollywood in Britain       156

7   Re-imagining the imperial metropolis       192

REFERENCES       219

INDEX       238

# Figures

**1, 2** and **3** British Council posters, c. 1998: comedians, Benny Hill and Rowan Atkinson; actresses, Julie Christie and Kate Winslet; and playwrights, William Shakespeare and Tom Stoppard. Reproduced by permission of the British Council — *pages* 26 & 27

**4** *It's Your Film* by Stan's Cafe. Photo: Ed Dimsdale. Reproduced by permission of Ed Dimsdale and Stan's Cafe — 29

**5** *Show Off*, Ursula Martinez. Photo: Hugo Glendinning. Reproduced by permission of Ursula Martinez and Hugo Glendinning — 29

**6** Clifford McLucas, *Gododdin* (Brith Gof, 1988) at the old Rover car factory, Cardiff. Reproduced by permission of Brith Gof, Mike Pearson, Alison Woods, and Margaret Ames and with the support of Nick Kaye. Brith Gof's archives are housed at the National Library of Wales — 48

**7** Brith Gof's *Gododdin* (1988). Reproduced by permission of Mike Pearson — 48

**8** Detail of Amanda Montgomery's canteen installation for *convictions* (Tinderbox Theatre Company, 2001) at the Crumlin Road Courthouse, Belfast. Reproduced by permission of Amanda Montgomery — 55

**9** Crumlin Road Courthouse, Belfast. Reproduced by permission of the Culture and Arts Unit, Economic Initiatives Section, Development Department, Belfast City Council (www.belfastcapitalcity.com) — 56

**10** Detail of Amanda Montgomery's hallway installation for *convictions* (Tinderbox Theatre Company, 2001) at the Crumlin Road Courthouse, Belfast. Reproduced by permission of Amanda Montgomery — 63

**11** Fringe Sunday 2001 on the Meadows, Edinburgh. Reproduced by permission of the Edinburgh Festival Fringe — 83

**12** Free street performance outside the Royal Scottish Academy, Edinburgh. Reproduced by permission of the Edinburgh Festival Fringe — 84

**13** Edinburgh International Festival programme, 2001. Photo credit: Edinburgh International Festival, Douglas Corrance (photographer), Still Moving Picture Company, and Tayburn Design — 93

**14** Frank (John Stahl) and Eddie (Paul Thomas Hickey) in the 2002 Traverse Theatre touring production of Gregory Burke's *Gagarin Way*. Photo: Douglas Robertson. Reproduced by permission of the Traverse Theatre — 96

15 Wendy Houstoun, Lauren Potter and Dale Tanner in DV8 Physical
   Theatre's stage production of *Strange Fish* (1992). Photo: Chris Nash.
   Reproduced by permission of DV8 Physical Theatre            132

16 Lauren Potter and Jordi Cortes Molina in DV8 Physical Theatre's
   stage production of *Strange Fish* (1992). Photo: Jeff Baynes.
   Reproduced by permission of DV8 Physical Theatre            133

17 Simon McBurney in Complicite's *Mnemonic*. Photo: Sebastian Hoppe.
   Reproduced by permission of Complicite and Sebastian Hoppe  139

18 *Mnemonic*, Complicite. Photo: Sebastian Hoppe. Reproduced by
   permission of Complicite and Sebastian Hoppe                140

19 Prem (Pushpinder Chani) and Nisha (Mala Ghedia) in Tamasha Theatre
   Company's 2001 production of *Fourteen Songs, Two Weddings and a Funeral*.
   Photo: Charlie Carter. Reproduced by permission of Tamasha Theatre
   Company                                                     173

20 Tamasha Theatre Company's 2001 production of *Fourteen Songs,
   Two Weddings and a Funeral*. Photo: Charlie Carter. Reproduced by
   permission of Tamasha Theatre Company                       173

21 Akaash (Stephen Rahman-Hughes) in *Bombay Dreams*. Bombay Dreams
   TM © 2002 RUG Ltd. Photo: James Bareham                     177

22 Shanti (Adlyn Ross) in *Bombay Dreams*. Bombay Dreams TM
   © 2002 RUG Ltd. Photo: James Bareham                        178

23 Rani (Sophiya Haque) in *Bombay Dreams*. Bombay Dreams TM
   © 2002 RUG Ltd. Photo: James Bareham                        178

24 London Underground *Visit the Empire* posters by Ernest Michael Dinkel
   1933. Reproduced by permission of London's Transport Museum 196

25 Two posters in Transport for London's 'You ♥ London' campaign
   (2003). Reproduced by permission of M & C Saatchi       198 & 199

26 Still from Steve McQueen, *Caribs' Leap* (2002). Reproduced by
   permission of Steve McQueen and Artangel                    203

27 Still from Steve McQueen's *Western Deep* (2002). Reproduced by
   permission of Steve McQueen and Artangel                    204

# Acknowledgements

I am grateful to many teachers, colleagues, and friends who have helped me to develop my thinking on the cultural articulations, effects, and potentials of theatre and other cultural practices, and who have supported me in completing this project.

Thanks to my teachers and mentors, especially: Harry Anderson, Anne McDougall, and Denis Salter (at McGill University); Alan Filewod, Ric Knowles, Harry Lane, and Ann Wilson (at the University of Guelph); and John Caughie, Annette Kuhn, Jan McDonald, and the late Alasdair Cameron (at the University of Glasgow). Thanks also to many supportive colleagues and friends, including (in a sort of chronological order): Patrick Thoburn, Nora Jaffary, Andrew Botterell, Julie Crawford, Stephanie McNamara, Angela Alston, Nadine Sivak, Robyn Laba, Peter Gillis, Susan Bennett, Julie Light, Leslie Hill, Minty Donald, Nick Millar, Tom Arah, Andrew Hurst, Liza Yukins, Gillian Horn, Annabel Leech, Jacky Bratton, Helen Paris, Janette Dillon, Paul Allain, Andy Lavender, Tricia Reid, Claire Timms, Lucy Richardson, David Annen, Nick Ridout, Brian Singleton, Michael McKinnie, Adrian Heathfield, Paul Rae, Karen Fricker, and David Williams. Thanks especially to my colleagues at the Roehampton University: Marcel Bancroft, Gianna Bouchard, Charlotte Burt, Sarah Gorman, Susanne Greenhalgh, Adrian Kear, Valerie Lucas, Susan Painter, Ginny Pavey, Alan Read, Shobha Sait, Robert Shaughnessy, Neil Taylor, Sylvia Vickers, Graham White, and Lee White, plus others mentioned below.

I owe particular thanks to those who have helped me secure funding for this project, and who have supported it editorially: Maggie Gale, Maria Delgado, David Bradby, Peter Reynolds, Simon Shepherd, Morag Shiach, and the School of Arts at Roehampton University. I am grateful to the Arts and Humanities Research Council, which funded this project through a Small Grant in the Creative and Performing Arts and a Research Leave award.

I am also grateful to those who have helped me secure images for this book, and to institutions that have provided other valuable resources and support. Thanks to: Margaret Ames, Ophelia Byrne, Seamus Deane, Ed Dimsdale, Hugo Glendinning, Nick Kaye, Ursula Martinez, Amanda Montgomery, Mike Pearson, and Alison Woods. Thanks also to staff at: the British Library, the National Library of Scotland, Edinburgh Central Library, Glasgow University Library, the Linen Hall Library (Belfast), Queen's University Library (Belfast), Trinity College Library (Dublin), Cardiff Central Library, University of Wales Cardiff Library, the Digby Stuart Learning Resource Centre at Roehampton University, the British Council, Stan's Cafe, Tinderbox Theatre Company, Belfast City Council, the Edinburgh Festival, the Edinburgh Festival Fringe, the Traverse Theatre, DV8 Physical Theatre, Complicite, Tamasha Theatre Company, the Really Useful Group, London's Transport Museum, M & C Saatchi (London), and Artangel.

A version of Chapter 2 was published as 'Nationalizing the "creative industries"' in *Contemporary Theatre Review* 13:1 (2003). Parts of Chapter 4 were published in my article 'Cultural effects of the Edinburgh International Festival: elitism, identities, industries' in *Contemporary Theatre Review* 13:4 (2003). Thanks to the Taylor and Francis Group (www.tandf.co.uk) for permission to reproduce this material. Thanks to London's Transport Museum for permission to reproduce the London Underground rondel. And thanks to staff at Manchester University Press for your much appreciated support, help, and good-humour.

This work has been developed partly through teaching and public presentation. My thanks to my students at the Roehampton University, the University of Nottingham, Glasgow University, and Goldsmiths College, Royal Holloway, and Queen Mary (all University of London). And thanks to audiences at: the Association for Theatre in Higher Education, Philadelphia, 2002, the International Federation for Theatre Research, Amsterdam, 2002, Roehampton University, Royal Holloway, Queen Mary, and University College London.

I am very grateful to the friends and colleagues who have generously read and commented on parts of this book as it developed. Thanks to: Lynette Goddard, Sophie Nield, Máire níFhlathuín, Fiona Wilkie, and anonymous readers for *Contemporary Theatre Review*. Thanks especially to Erin Hurley, Dan Rebellato, and Joe Kelleher for reading and commenting extensively on draft work-in-progress: your feedback and support has been invaluable.

I am especially grateful to two old friends, Jane Sillars and Julia Blazdell. You have taught me so much through your own exemplary intellectual practice, as well as much more, and you have helped to make this place my home.

Finally, I am grateful to my family, who have always supported me. Love and thanks to: my mum, Judy Harvie, and my dad, the late Eric A. Harvie; my sister, Juju Vail, and her family, David, Orillia and Quinte Vail; and to Barbara Rowe. Love and thanks also to: Pat Harvie and George Garlock, Peter and Tess Harvie, Peter and Lorraine Aykroyd, Elizabeth Burrows, Ann, John, Charlotte, Hannah, Joe, and Frank Robinson, Frank Kilbride, Francis Kilbride, Rosemary Kilbride, and Ray Maciocia.

My biggest thanks, for your love and support, go to Deb Kilbride.

# I

# Introduction:
# staging the UK

This book is about how performance has produced national and related identities in the United Kingdom, focusing on the period from the 1980s into the twenty-first century. It is concerned with national identities because their long-standing profile as some of the most pervasively felt and socially potent forms of identity has been both accentuated and fundamentally disturbed by radical changes to national configurations in the UK's recent history. In 1997, after eighteen years of Conservative rule including eleven years of Thatcherism, Tony Blair's New Labour government was elected proclaiming the advent of a 'New Britain'. The 1999 acts of devolution redistributed national power throughout the UK by restoring a parliament in Scotland and launching assemblies in Wales and Northern Ireland. Cities and regions of the UK have been strengthened under New Labour through moves towards establishing regional English governments and through the restoration of elected mayors in many cities where Thatcher had eradicated them (including greater London). At the end of June 1997, near-final vestiges of the UK's empire were dismantled as Hong Kong was handed over to China. Despite this enactment of the 'end of empire', ongoing 'race'-related violence within the UK has indicated the resilience of imperial power relations: the mishandled murder inquiry of black South London teenager Stephen Lawrence in 1993 led to a diagnosis of 'institutional racism' in the Metropolitan Police; 'race'-related rioting occurred in Oldham, Burnley, and Bradford in the North of England in summer 2001; and racist – as distinct from sectarian – violence was reported in Belfast in late 2003. European unification has accelerated, with the launch of a common currency in 2002; but it has also been tested, most notably by the UK's decision to join the USA in a war against Iraq in 2003, despite the vehement objections of France and Germany. Finally, growing awareness of global issues to do with war, climate, religions, and economies – of labour, commodities, capital, culture, and so on – have transformed 'globalisation' from what was once a specialist term to one with a currency that is everyday and possibly global – but not yet total, as long as nations endure as fundamental to the ways people experience the world and our place within it. In Benedict Anderson's still-resonant formulation from 1983: 'nation-ness is the most universally legitimate value in the political life of our time'.[1]

This book focuses on national identities because of their extreme topicality but also – more importantly – because they produce and distribute power, power that can be both oppressive and enabling. As the examples above indicate, national identity can be oppressive when, for example, it is seen as homogeneous, superior, and/or unchanging and it acts to exclude or oppress minorities or perceived 'others' or to restrict cultural change. It can be enabling when it helps develop community identities. Often it is simultaneously, in different degrees, both oppressive and enabling. This book aims not so much to detail the national changes that have occurred to and within the UK in the last two decades as to assess these changes' ambivalent cultural effects: what kinds of community they form; which communities they benefit or hinder and how; what kinds of community expression they encourage or discourage; what tensions exist between conflicting cultural formulations; how those tensions are negotiated; and so on.

In order to scrutinise these national identities and their configurations of power this book examines contemporary UK performance practices. A founding principle here is that national identities are neither biologically nor territorially given; rather, they are creatively produced or staged. I am not arguing, wilfully, that political acts, legislation and the material conditions of geography have no influence on national identities. But it is necessary in this context to distinguish between a state and a nation. A state is a political authority that asserts power; but a nation is a *sense* that people share a culture, a culture that may or may not be coterminous with the state's borders.[2] As Benedict Anderson proposed most influentially in his book *Imagined Communities: Reflections on the Origin and Spread of Nationalism*, a person's sense of his or her nation is based largely on participation in shared cultural practices such as reading newspapers, listening to the radio, watching television, and reading novels.[3] Few people may ever read the legislation that constitutes them as citizens of a particular state, and probably none will ever traverse the state's whole topography and meet all their fellow nationals. But most people will have a sense of a shared national identity through shared cultural practices that are both everyday or 'banal' as Michael Billig puts it[4] – eating food, dressing, talking, listening to the radio, watching television – and 'special' – celebrating holidays, participating in festivals and major sports events, and so on. Through their cultural activities, people will imagine their communities. And one of the ways they will do so is through performance.

Anderson's premise has at least three very important implications for understanding the functioning of national identities and attending to their effects of power. First, if national identities are creatively imagined, that means they are dynamic. In this understanding, 'the UK' is not a stable, universally and timelessly agreed entity; rather, it and its meanings are constantly conceived in many different ways. For example, for Northern Irish Republicans and others, 'the UK' may be an imperialist and assimilating imposition. For others, it may be a focus for national pride. For many, it may be an umbrella term within which there reside numerous different and, for them, possibly more important identities – local, urban, rural, national, regional, ethnic, diasporic, and so on. Furthermore, many people may perceive the UK in a variety of these different ways, both coincidentally and serially. I certainly do not take the UK's meanings as stable or given. This book's title indicates my founding understanding of national identities, including UK identity, as staged, culturally produced, dynamic, and – to use a term invoked by feminist philosopher Judith Butler – inherently troubled.[5]

Second, if national identities are dynamic, they can be changed, and such change might contribute to social improvement – or decline. Xenophobic jingoism, for example, may exist in any nation, but its purchase will never be comprehensive or entirely secure. It might be destabilised – or it might be reinforced. It is cultural practice that will enact both outcomes, and it is partly the function of the kind of cultural criticism that I aim to practise in this book, therefore, both to analyse that cultural practice and to work *as* cultural practice, staging and influencing national and other identities.

Third, if national identities are creatively imagined by numerous people and not just by legislators, authority is necessarily dispersed from the formal centres of state power. Instead of seeing national identity as strictly a tool of state control, a means for the state to define and manage its citizens, Anderson's premise suggests that national identity can be a tool of dispersed, democratic empowerment. By giving 'power to the people', this may have some very positive effects. But it may also mask the risk that the power is more apparent than real. Many argue this is the case in the dominant neo-liberal market economy, where a sense of proliferating consumer choice masks the possibility that there is no meaningful choice. And the same might be said of many liberal democracies, where apparent voter choice – for example, in the UK, between Conservatives and New Labour – may sometimes feel like little choice. Further, there is no guarantee that 'the people' will use their cultural power benevolently; they could, for example, commit racist acts, whether through the insidious operations of institutional racism or through more obvious acts of physical violence.

As these examples indicate, Anderson's premise likewise has important implications for social criticism and analysis: it makes examining cultural practice a political imperative. It locates the lived, social effects of national change not just in the major acts of nations' political institutions – the legislation of devolution and European unification, for example – but in the various cultural activities and structures people engage in, from reading newspapers, to shopping, to making or watching theatre performance. Anderson's premise makes it necessary to examine cultural practices to explore what identities and power dynamics they produce, and not just through their narratives, but also in their forms and institutional structures.[6]

## Devolving UK theatre studies

So while *Staging the UK* is concerned with national identities, it seeks to explore them not in acts of parliament but rather in the cultural practices of performance, especially but not strictly theatre performance. This critical approach responds partly to the political imperative of Anderson's premise and partly to a desire to enhance UK theatre studies' critical focus on how theatre produces relationships of power. While the disciplines of drama and theatre studies are frequently organised into national categories such as British, Irish, or American drama, it is often the case that these categories are not substantially interrogated and are implicitly treated as effectively politically neutral. A recent spate of publications is radically changing and challenging this tendency, and this book aims to join them in so doing.[7] In response to the diverse national configurations and cultural practices this book looks at, it deploys multiple apposite critical insights and approaches derived from diverse fields, including studies of national identity, cultural policy, cultural memory, globalisation, diasporic identities, imperialism, and postcolonialism. This multi-faceted approach is motivated by my desire not to produce – or impose – a single critical schema, and by my interest in exploring the resonances that are produced by juxtaposing these different critical approaches.

Further, this book aims not only to explore how thinking about performance can help us understand the workings of national identities but also the inverse: how thinking about national identities can help us understand the workings of performance. There is a growing body of scholarship that foregrounds contemporary UK theatre's social power dynamics; for example, the ways it represents and constitutes communities of gender, 'race', sexuality, and nation, and how it has been affected by its political and economic contexts.[8] *Staging the UK* aims to contribute to this developing analysis and debate as well.

As my analysis of identity is informed by multiple critical practices, my analysis of performance is likewise informed by at least three critical practices: materialism, historicism, and performance studies' theorisation of the ephemeral quality of performance. Instead of looking strictly at dramatic texts and performance events, this book examines a broader range of cultural practices related to performance. This is in response to the openness suggested by Anderson's metaphor of imagining, which might be practised through innumerable cultural activities. But it also articulates a materialist understanding of artistic practice as never only abstract ideas but always also material practice enacted in – and constituted by and constituting – networks of social relations. Thus, alongside dramatic texts and more conventional performance events such as musicals, this book examines government cultural policy, funding patterns, theatre institutions and companies, major events such as festivals, and particular performance practices including site-specific theatre, physical theatre, and installation art. And it aims to situate these practices in their social contexts. In historical range, the book concentrates on the recent past. This is partly because of the enormous scale of national change that has recently occurred in the UK and partly to facilitate extrapolation of analyses and arguments to the present – to work towards both diagnosis of and intervention in the state of things now and in the future. Although the book concentrates on the recent past, it repeatedly places its analyses in deeper historical context in recognition of the contingent relationships of any period to its pasts. Related to the materialism and historicism of my approach is an understanding of performance practice as ephemeral – temporary, unrepeatable (even when repeated), and therefore unrecordable, because to record it is fundamentally to change it.[9] My aim in this book is to give a sense of particular performance events that recognises this contingency but is strong enough to support analysis. I do this through a variety of means: gathering witnesses', critics', and participants' responses to the work, building a useful critical and historical context in which to assess the work's effects, and juxtaposing examples to produce a dialectical resonance.

By examining a broad range of cultural practices in a variety of sites through multiple research resources and critical strategies, this book aims not to be comprehensive, providing a filled-in, linear history of recent UK theatre. Rather, it aims to be indicative, using resonant selected case studies of particular institutions, events, or practices to develop detailed analysis of those particular cases and to demonstrate critical approaches appropriate for examining both those cases and the issues related to national and other identities they raise. The structure of the book is designed to facilitate thinking about performance practices across a range of forms, both institutional and generic, while allowing for focused study of particular, important objects. Paralleling the diversity of contemporary UK identities, the case studies have been selected to represent both a formal and a socio-geographical range of UK performance, and in part to gather dispersed archival resources that may have been neglected by scholarship that has historically focused on particular kinds of theatre practice in England, predominantly London. While the book is selective in the objects it examines, as well as necessarily partial in its overview of recent British performance practice, it aims to propose questions and develop critical tools that are transferable and might be applied to other institutions, events, practices, and aspects of identity not extensively discussed in this book. For example, I do not consider gender or sexual identities in detail here but I believe – as the foregoing reference to Judith Butler suggests – that critical practice developed here could be partially transferred to thinking about these topics, as well as, for example, religious and class identities. Finally, *Staging the UK* aims to be dialectically resonant, producing echoes and dialogues across the various practices discussed in different chapters.

## Devolving the UK

As the book examines a range of performance practices, it also examines a range of national identity formations. There are two points of clarification I would like to make on my deployment of the term national here. First, 'national' does not necessarily mean nationalist. National identity is sometimes articulated as patriotic, self-promoting, even jingoistic, and eager to present the nation as stable and good. But it is worth re-emphasising that, as Anderson suggests, national identities are not fixed. They may be celebratory and nationalist sometimes, but probably more often they are at least ambivalent and even self-critical. This book explores how performance in the UK primarily since the late 1980s has contributed to the dynamic articulation of national identities.

Second, while 'national' usefully invokes the nation, I want to bring into play other related formations of identity as well, fundamentally because identities are formed not in isolated, discrete categories but in dynamic, overlapping networks.[10] Certainly, some of the articulations of identity considered here are most usefully understood as national, not least because the book's temporal scope coincides latterly with the devolution of state powers to Scotland, Wales, and Northern Ireland in 1999. But this book also looks at configurations that share features with national identities but complicate how we have to think about those identities. Some of these configurations are internal to the nation – for example, identities that are regional and metropolitan – and others extend beyond the UK – for example identities that are global, European, and diasporic, especially black and Asian diasporic identities. As I hope the foregoing discussion makes clear, this book does not aim to assimilate these multiple identities into one coherent UK identity, and nor does it aim to segregate 'us' and 'them' or 'self' and 'other'. What it does aim to do is to acknowledge that UK identities are multiple, mutually contingent, and mutually embedded – simultaneously holding in tension multiple determinants, from affinities with locale, region, and nation to affinities with Europe, global subjectivity, and diasporic communities. As the book aims to produce a dialectical resonance in relation to performance practices across its various chapters, it aims to produce a similar resonance in relation to these diverse and overlapping identities, evoking the contingency of their relationships with each other and underlining the nation's intrinsic and dynamic hybridity.[11]

## Imagined communities/staged identities

*Staging the UK* takes its organising principle from the first two words of Anderson's book title: 'imagined' and 'communities'. Each chapter explores how an imaginative, cultural, or performance practice works to produce a form or forms of community identity, and it focuses this exploration through one or more case studies of particular institutions, practices, events, performances, texts, and/or places.

Chapter 2 looks at how government cultural policy has influenced a range of community identities: regional, metropolitan, and national. It focuses this analysis in two parts. The first analyses the policies and practices of the Arts Council of Great Britain from after the Second World War up to the mid-1970s, exploring the ways they have produced hierarchically organised regional and metropolitan identities. The second part analyses three aspects of New Labour's cultural policy: its promotion of a 'New Britain', its devolution of power to the nations, and its attempt to industrialise the arts and design by branding them 'creative industries'. It explores how 'New Britain' and Scotland are configured through the support and export practices of, respectively, the British Council and the Scottish National Theatre planned by the Scottish Executive. It addresses the risks of cultural commodification presented by New Labour's emphasis on the 'creative industries', but it argues, that despite these risks, the national identities produced resist wholesale commodification and present suggestively complex national imaginaries.

Carrying over this concern with the 'small nations', Chapter 3 explores how the timely production of site-specific performance by Brith Gof in Wales and Tinderbox Theatre Company in Belfast contributed to 'remembering' and constituting national identities in particularly important ways. Its arguments regarding Brith Gof's performance of *Gododdin* (1988–90) are twofold. First, it claims that the production variously celebrated and interrogated Welsh histories – distant and recent, literary and industrial. Second, it argues that the production constituted Wales not – as disparaging treatments of Wales as a mere principality of the UK do – in a diminished relationship to a superior UK but rather in a relationship of dynamic equality within Europe. Its examination of Tinderbox's *convictions* (2001) focuses on the show's intervention in the 'post-Troubles' culture of Belfast and Northern Ireland after the Good Friday Agreement of 1998. It recognises that the production importantly helped to negotiate citizens' relationships to the Troubles. However, it also emphasises how the production worked to challenge the Troubles and religion as uniquely constitutive of Northern Irish identity and to diversify understandings of that identity as formed also by other conditions, especially of class and gender.

Chapter 4 examines the ever-growing Edinburgh festivals in the context of globalisation. As in Chapter 2, this context provokes a concern with cultural commodification and ensuing cultural standardisation, particularly according to national paradigms usually seen as neither British nor Scottish but American. Using models of cultural practice suggested by the corporate operations of two American companies, this chapter evaluates the potential 'McDonaldization' and 'Disneyfication' of the Edinburgh festivals, especially the burgeoning Fringe. While acknowledging that these festivals and their host city do not escape all of globalisation's deleterious effects, I propose that they do challenge and resist many of them – the Edinburgh International Festival partly through an entrenched elitism that implicitly excludes the popular culture more usually seen as producer and product of globalisation, and the Edinburgh Festival Fringe through the maintenance (despite neo-liberal market forces) of a pervasive heterogeneity, especially in performance practices. What is fundamentally at stake here is the potential for democratic expression, and I conclude the chapter by returning to a related older debate about cultural democracy and the contested cultural function of carnival. In Bakhtin's famous analysis, carnival produces an opportunity for democratic cultural expression. However, in the analysis of his critics, carnival is an opportunity for an agent of authority such as a state government to reinforce its power by duping the masses into believing they have temporarily usurped authority. I acknowledge the tensions in this debate. But I propose that by conceiving the Edinburgh festivals as carnival – as well as, possibly, global market – we can reframe the question of the authority exercised by the force of globalisation, thereby de-emphasising globalisation's dangers, and foregrounding the festivals' democratic carnival potential.

Chapter 5 is composed of two parts, both of which examine the UK's contested relationship to Europe. The first part analyses how dominant practices of British theatre historiography work to imagine British theatre as uniquely literary and therefore fundamentally autonomous and potentially anti-theatrical, as well as many of the things anti-theatricality implies: dismissive of the material body and its meanings, anti-expressive and misogynist. The first part of the chapter then proposes one alternative historiography of mid- to late twentieth-century theatre in Britain to explore how it might be neither entirely unique and isolated nor comprehensively anti-theatrical. The second part of the chapter examines the influence in Britain of physical theatre practices predominant in Germany and France in particular through close analysis of DV8 Physical Theatre's *Strange Fish* (1992) and Complicite's *Mnemonic* (1999–2003). It explores these productions' complex negotiations of British/European identities through form, narrative, and features of practical realisation such as casting and touring. Through close analysis of *Mnemonic*, it also interrogates the putative universality of physical theatre's physical expression, arguing instead for a recognition of that expression's historical and cultural specificity as, precisely, European.

Chapter 6 examines two stage examples of the Bollywood musical in Britain to explore their production of diasporic British Asian identities in particular and hybridised British identities more broadly. After examining the contested social value of Bollywood cinema itself, the chapter analyses Tamasha Theatre Company's *Fourteen Songs, Two Weddings and a Funeral* (1998 and 2001) and *Bombay Dreams* (2002), partially conceived by the English musical impresario Sir Andrew Lloyd Webber. It proposes that both shows addressed and articulated hybrid, diasporic British identities but to varying degrees and with different effects. *Fourteen Songs'* observation of many Bollywood conventions offered British-Indian audiences cultural affirmation in a context of some potential racial and imperial oppression as a minority community in the UK. Further, while *Fourteen Songs* produced a familiar Bollywood optimism which some critics have derided as typically deluded Bollywood utopianism, this diasporic context offered a rationale of political and emotional expediency for 'indulging' such a consoling fiction. My analysis of *Fourteen Songs* also proposes that the production offered a timely interrogation – through what Homi Bhabha has identified as postcolonial mimicry – of the fantasy of British racial purity staged in *Fourteen Songs'* near-namesake, the blockbuster British film *Four Weddings and a Funeral* (1994). While *Bombay Dreams* also observed many of Bollywood's conventions and so also produced some British-Indian cultural affirmation, its demonstrable ambivalence about Bollywood – as a form to be joyfully indulged but simultaneously disavowed as embarrassing – undermines the effectiveness of this affirmation and legitimates critical responses to the production as opportunistically exploitative and part of a long tradition of Orientalist representation.

Chapter 7 returns to the topic of metropolitanism addressed explicitly in Chapter 2's analysis of the hierarchical metropolitan/regional identities reinforced by long-standing Arts Council policy, and implicitly throughout the book in my efforts at least partially to redress the entrenched metropolitanism of British theatre and British theatre historiography. As in those cases, this chapter likewise acknowledges the problematics of the metropolis's hegemonic assumption of enormous power, but it aims also to complicate that analysis, recognising that hegemonic control is never complete and always unstable. First, by examining elements of the built and signed environment of inner London – especially monuments and Tube posters – the chapter identifies the metropolis as a site of not merely power but, specifically, imperial power. The chapter then turns to examine in detail a site-specific installation by black British filmmaker Steve McQueen, *Caribs' Leap / Western Deep*, shown at the then-disused Lumière Cinema in central London in 2002. It explores how the piece worked to transform audiences' relationships to the metropolis – and especially to the metropolis's abiding fantasy of imperial power –

by citing Africa (Western Deep, South Africa) and the Caribbean (Caribs' Leap, Grenada) as two corners of the triangular slave trade and inviting its audience to join the dots to the imperial centre. Like Chapter 6, it again explores diasporic identity and it positions British cultural identities more broadly as inherently hybrid, rather than – as imperial fantasies might wish – pure-bred.

## Dialectical resonance

As outlined above, individual chapters are designed to provide detailed analysis of particular practices and to develop critical approaches for focused analysis of those practices' stagings of national and related identities and relationships of power. By returning to particular issues – of, for example, 'small' national identities (Chapters 2 and 3), European identities (Chapters 3 and 5), and global diasporic identities (Chapters 4, 6, and 7) – the book seeks also to establish a dialectical resonance arcing across the chapters. Its aim is not so much to develop a single linear narrative across the book as to produce echoes and correspondences between its chapters, as between different rooms in an architecture, or different nations in a single state. This aim to produce a resonance applies to themes of national and related identities and their multiple genealogies and futures, but also to at least three other themes that I would like briefly to draw attention to here. These are: cultural commodification, democracy, and hybridity.

The risks of contemporary cultural practice's marketisation and commodification arise most visibly in my discussions of New Labour's 'creative industries' policy (Chapter 2), the Edinburgh festivals' potential globalisation (Chapter 4), and the industry of Bollywood cinema (Chapter 6). In all three cases I identify the risks of this trend but also strong evidence of resistance to them. Nevertheless, this trend's potential hazards indicate that its persistence and development bear ongoing scrutiny. The marketisation of culture is further related to the second recurrent theme, democracy, addressed most explicitly in Chapter 4 on the Edinburgh festivals and Chapter 7 on the metropolis of London, but also throughout the book, especially in Chapter 2's analysis of government agencies' ability to enable the widest and greatest expressive participation in cultural practice. What arises in these repeated encounters with issues of democracy is an implicit tension in its current practice as liberal democracy in the UK, a tension which Chantal Mouffe has identified as a product of the ambivalent drives within the two key terms which 'liberal democracy' binds together. Where a liberal tradition emphasises the *individual*'s human rights (including the right to a free market in which to trade in one's own interests), a democratic tradition emphasises equality and *group* rights.[12] Much cultural practice in the UK seems to be re-producing this tension, at once aiming to make possible individual opportunity – even when one person's access to opportunity may directly diminish another person's – but also trying to protect group or community rights. This tension between individual and community can be seen also as a microcosm of the tension between multiple communities within the UK and the UK as a whole. Current cultural practice in the UK seems to be balancing out in greater support of liberal democracy's democratic interests than its liberalism – but this tension, too, bears ongoing observation.

Democracy's concern with the community is protected partly through a recognition of the *internal* diversity of the community, a recognition, in other words, of the group's hybridity and inherent otherness to itself. The hybridity of UK cultural identities resonates in every chapter of the book, one of the reasons why I propose that while it is instructive in different chapters to examine discrete aspects of identity – such as national or European identity – it is necessary to read these chapters dialectically in recognition of these identities' mutual contingency and hybrid combination. To recognise the fundamental hybridity of any identity works towards a development of early intercultural performance analyses which often identified a binary opposition between an oppressed 'other' and an oppressive, powerful 'self'. While critically constructive in their original contexts, these analyses need development for the purposes of assessing intercultural encounter where it is more difficult to specify a primary, let alone solitary, location of power, or where the 'us' and 'them', 'self' and 'other' exist within the same community and/or within the same person.[13]

## Motivations

This emphasis on hybrid identities and my earlier emphasis on multiple disciplinary practices and identity formations might sound as though this book potentially lacks commitment to particular identities or arguments. I do not intend this to be the case. Certainly I argue that UK identities are hybrid, multiple, and produced in diverse ways by numerous material and cultural practices of performance. And I acknowledge my personal investment – as a Canadian immigrant to first Scotland and then England – in an understanding of the UK as hybrid. But specifying, as I aim to do in each chapter, what the UK's multiple identities and practices are, in particular grounded circumstances of time and place, is necessary to track just what configurations of power these identities and practices produce and how they do so. These practices and identities are not infinitely diverse, but they are complex. And it is this complexity of cultural identities and practices, of the power dynamics they produce, and of the interconnections between these three terms – identities, practices, and power – that *Staging the UK* explores.[14]

## Notes

1 Benedict Anderson, *Imagined Communities: Reflections on the Origin and Spread of Nationalism* (London: Verso, [1983] 2nd edn, 1991), p. 3.

2 Ernest Gellner, *Nations and Nationalism* (Oxford: Basil Blackwell, 1983), pp. 4–7.

3 Anderson, *Imagined Communities*, pp. 32-6. I acknowledge that there are nuances of Anderson's argument – for example, his emphasis on the sense of simultaneity produced by certain cultural practices, such as reading newspapers and novels – that I do not pursue in detail in this book. I am principally interested here in exploring his central idea – of the cultural construction of community identities – within the context of theatre practices. Of the scores of volumes that the study of national identities has generated, some key, helpful texts include: Homi K. Bhabha (ed.), *Nation and Narration* (London: Routledge, 1990); Gopal Balakrishnan (ed.), *Mapping the Nation* (London: Verso, 1996); and Geoff Eley and Ronald Grigor Suny (eds), *Becoming National: A Reader* (Oxford: Oxford University Press, 1996).

4 Michael Billig, *Banal Nationalism* (London: Sage, 1995).

5 Judith Butler, *Gender Trouble* (London: Routledge, tenth anniversary edn, 1999). Because I see the meanings of national names as provisional and, in the case of the UK and Britain, often overlapping, I do not distinguish rigorously throughout the book between the terms UK (which technically stands for the political entity of Great Britain and Northern Ireland) and Britain or British. I mobilise these names as inherently unstable, not definitive or defining. I do not aim to elide the implicit tension between the terms, but to allow its articulation and to explore it.

6 Jonathan Culler, 'Anderson and the novel', *diacritics* 29:4 (1999), 20-39, p. 39.

7 Selected examples include: David Adams, *Stage Welsh: Nation, Nationalism and Theatre: The Search for Cultural Identity* (Llandysul: Gomer, 1996); Ophelia Byrne, *The Stage in Ulster from the Eighteenth Century* (Belfast: Linen Hall Library, 1997); Alan Filewod, *Performing Canada: The Nation Enacted in the Imagined Theatre* (*Textual Studies in Canada* 15) (Kamloops, BC: University College of the Cariboo, 2002); Bill Findlay (ed.), *A History of Scottish Theatre* (Edinburgh: Polygon, 1998); Helen Gilbert, *Sightlines: Race, Gender, and Nation in Contemporary Australian Theatre* (Ann Arbor: University of Michigan Press, 1998); Guillermo Gómez-Peña, *Dangerous Border Crossers: The Artist Talks Back* (London: Routledge, 2000); John J. Joughin (ed.), *Shakespeare and National Culture* (Manchester: Manchester University Press,

1997); Loren Kruger, *The National Stage: Theatre and Cultural Legitimation in England, France, and America* (Chicago: University of Chicago Press, 1992); Helka Mäkinen, S. E. Wilmer, and W. B. Worthen (eds), *Theatre, History and National Identities* (Helsinki: Helsinki University Press, 2001); Jeffrey D. Mason and J. Ellen Gainor (eds), *Performing America: Cultural Nationalism in American Theatre* (Ann Arbor: University of Michigan Press, 1999); D. Keith Peacock, *Thatcher's Theatre: British Theatre and Drama in the Eighties* (New York: Greenwood Press, 1999); Lionel Pilkington, *Theatre and the State in Twentieth-Century Ireland* (London: Routledge, 2001); Simon Shepherd and Peter Womack, *English Drama: A Cultural History* (Oxford: Blackwell, 1996); Randall Stevenson and Gavin Wallace (eds), *Scottish Theatre Since the Seventies* (Edinburgh: Edinburgh University Press, 1996); Anna-Marie Taylor (ed.), *Staging Wales* (Cardiff: University of Wales Press, 1997); and S. E. Wilmer, *Theatre, Society and the Nation: Staging American Identities* (Cambridge: Cambridge University Press, 2002).

8  These include, for example: on gender and 'race', Gabriele Griffin, *Contemporary Black and Asian Women Playwrights in Britain* (Cambridge: Cambridge University Press, 2003); on gender, Elaine Aston and Janelle Reinelt (eds), *The Cambridge Companion to Modern British Women Playwrights* (Cambridge: Cambridge University Press, 2000); on 'race', A. Ruth Tompsett (ed.), *Black Theatre in Britain (Performing Arts International* 1:2) (Amsterdam: Harwood Academic, 1996); on sexuality, Nicholas de Jongh, *Not in Front of the Audience: Homosexuality on Stage* (London: Routledge, 1992); and on political and economic contexts, Baz Kershaw, 'Discouraging democracy: British theatres and economics, 1979–1999', *Theatre Journal* 51:3 (1999), 267–83, and Aleks Sierz, 'British theatre in the 1990s: a brief political economy', *Media, Culture and Society* 19 (1997), 461–9.

9  On this quality of performance see Peggy Phelan, *Unmarked: The Politics of Performance* (London: Routledge, 1993).

10  Jonathan Rutherford, 'A place called home: identity and the cultural politics of difference', in Rutherford (ed.), *Identity: Community, Culture, Difference* (London: Lawrence and Wishart, 1990), pp. 9-27.

11  The dynamic hybridity and instability of the nation is attracting increasing critical attention. See, for example: David Bennett (ed.), *Multicultural States: Rethinking Difference and Identity* (London: Routledge, 1998); and Pheng Cheah and Bruce Robbins (eds), *Cosmopolitics: Thinking and Feeling Beyond the Nation* (Minneapolis: University of Minnesota Press, 1998).

12  Chantal Mouffe, *The Democratic Paradox* (London: Verso, 2000), pp. 2ff.

13  Much recent continental European philosophy in particular has argued for understandings of community as formed through the individual's recognition that the other's perceived radical otherness is akin to one's own radical otherness to oneself. See, for example: Alphonso Lingis, *The Community of Those Who Have Nothing in Common* (Bloomington and Indianapolis: Indiana University Press, 1994); Jean-Luc Nancy, *Being Singular Plural*, trans. Robert D. Richardson and Anne E. O'Byrne (Stanford: Stanford University Press, [1996] 2000).

14  My previous publications have also been concerned with intersections between identity formations (especially national and gender identities), performance practices and cultural power. This work includes: on Scots translations of Quebec playwright Michel Tremblay, Jennifer Harvie, 'The real nation?': Michel

Tremblay, Scotland, and cultural translatability', *Theatre Research in Canada* 16:1/2 (1995); on the diverse cultural claims on the work of Quebec director Robert Lepage and the circus company Cirque du Soleil, Jennifer Harvie and Erin Hurley, 'States of play: locating Québec in the performances of Robert Lepage, Ex Machina, and the Cirque du Soleil', *Theatre Journal* 51:3 (1999); specifically on the cultural politics of Lepage's work, Jennifer Harvie, 'Transnationalism, orientalism, cultural tourism: *La Trilogie des dragons* and *The Seven Streams of the River Ota*', in Joseph I. Donohoe and Jane M. Koustas (eds), *Theater sans Frontières: Essays on the Dramatic Universe of Robert Lepage* (East Lansing: Michigan State University Press, 2000), and Jennifer Harvie, 'Robert Lepage', in Joseph Natoli and Hans Bertens (eds), *Postmodernism: The Key Figures* (Oxford: Blackwell, 2002); on economies of international touring, Jen Harvie, 'DV8's *Can We Afford This*: the cost of devising on site for global markets', *Theatre Research International* 27:1 (2002); on feminist art and performance, Jen Harvie, 'Being her: presence, absence, and performance in the art of Janet Cardiff and Tracey Emin', in Maggie B. Gale and Viv Gardner (eds), *Auto/Biography and Identity: Women, Theatre and Performance:* 2004 (Manchester: Manchester University Press, forthcoming); and on globalisation and theatre, a special issue of *Contemporary Theatre Review* co-edited with Dan Rebellato (forthcoming 2005).

# 2

# Policy paradigms: regional, metropolitan, and national arts and 'creative industries'

Benedict Anderson's choice of the word 'imagined' to describe national identities as 'imagined communities' is resonant in at least two ways that I would like to address in more detail here.[1] First, Anderson's word choice emphasises that people's sense of community is produced through cultural practices that are creative and artistic, such as Anderson's own main example, the imaginative practice of reading fiction.[2] Second, Anderson's phrase conveys the impression that the practice of imagining is largely or even entirely volitional – that we each have individual agency to pursue the creative practices we want to in order to produce the national identities we want.

To a certain extent, both of these suggested – and optimistic – meanings are true.[3] But they must also be understood within a broader framework. Creative and artistic practice is never realised in a hypothetical 'blue-skies thinking' bubble where anything is possible. Instead, it happens in a real world riddled with both material and ideological constraints: limited time and finance, built theatre spaces that are finite in their adaptability, and things such as government policies and promoters' categories that may encourage or impose certain practices and inhibit or censor others. 'Non-artistic' contexts and structures such as these can drastically affect artistic practice. As these examples also indicate, although people may have some individual agency over their own artistic practice, it too will inevitably be affected – even determined – by contexts.

This chapter's primary function, therefore, is to examine some of the contexts and structures that have affected how theatre in Britain is produced and how that in turn affects the imagining of particular identities. In other words, it looks at some of the structural contexts of theatre production to see who gets to perform how, making what kinds of identities. Because of their profound and inescapable influence, the contexts it focuses on are government policy and practice.[4]

To establish a historical context and a sense of some of the enduring effects of policy-making over the longer term, the first part of the chapter summarises important fluctuations in postwar government arts policy, how these affected theatre funding and the ways in which this produced particular patterns of theatre practice and cultural understanding.[5] It argues that, despite drastic changes in government arts policy over the course of Britain's postwar twentieth century, theatre practice has consistently been conceptualised and organised through a series of ideological and geographical paradigms pitting the regions against the metropolis and producing several potentially damaging outcomes. Prioritising the centrally located national arts institutions, the metropolitan model has limited democratic cultural expression by being elitist and neglecting those outside the metropolis, and it has denigrated the regional by setting it up as the metropolis's devalued binary opposite. While ostensibly more democratic, the regional model has potentially masked an enduring paternalistic metropolitanism as governments have endeavoured to 'professionalise' – or 'raise' to metropolitan standards – regional practice.

The second part of the chapter concentrates on the contemporary scene since New Labour's election in 1997 and on two aspects of this government's arts and cultural policy. Examining New Labour's prioritisation of the 'creative industries', it considers some of the problems inherent in this fundamental commercialisation of the arts, but it also proposes how this might nevertheless be seen as a welcome change after decades of government neglect when the arts were perceived as worthy but irrelevant because rarely financially profitable.[6] Finally, it examines the mixed effects of New Labour's paradigm shift from the long-standing regional/metropolitan models of analysis and funding to a new model which emphasises – and rebrands – the nations, whether that is the overarching new 'Cool Britannia' or the smaller nations of Northern Ireland, Wales and Scotland who hold greater responsibility for their own arts policies and budgets since 1999 when devolved Welsh and Northern Irish assemblies were established and a devolved Scottish parliament was re-established after a hiatus of nearly three hundred years. It argues that this paradigm shift holds the potential to break down enduring and oppressive postwar models of funding and to help stimulate new ways of conceiving changing British identities, but that it also produces new risks. New Labour's short-lived 'Cool Britannia' was roundly derided in the UK, both because it too shamelessly commodified culture and because it seemed probably optimistic and certainly opportunistic, conjuring images of a delighted Tony Blair perched ludicrously on the coat-tails of bands such as Oasis and artists such as Damien Hirst. However, its effects seem to be more mixed than this cartoon scenario suggests. An examination of some of the recent policy and practice of the most important government-funded arm for promoting UK culture world-wide, the British Council, suggests that Cool Britannia's rebranding pos-itively motivated support for innovative, postmodern UK theatre practice even as it risked producing that as a new norm and distributing it through a kind of neo-imperialism. Finally, an examination of the Scottish Executive and the Scottish Arts Council's plans to establish a highly flexible, non-building-based Scottish National Theatre demon-strates the real potential of this shift in emphasis to the nation to cele-brate the nation and so to empower it, but also to have the confidence to see it as shifting, heterogeneous, and, ultimately, not a set identity – let alone a commodity – but a dynamic social practice.

## 'Few, but roses': metropolitanism after the Second World War

Divisions and disparities between British regional and metropolitan theatre certainly predate the end of the Second World War, but with the postwar expansion of government support for the arts[7] and the formation of the Arts Council of Great Britain they were enforced institutionally in new and significant ways, bringing with them associations of superiority and elitism for the metropolis and inferiority for the regions. In the imme-diate postwar period, public policy aimed initially to get 'the best to the most',[8] maintaining the regional distribution of theatre set up during the war. Despite the Arts Council's initial good intentions, however, this aim was first compromised by market forces which public policy failed to chal-lenge, and then was effectively abandoned by the Arts Council in a radi-cal revision in policy to support 'few, but roses', with the roses in question being located, not surprisingly, in and around the metropolis.

The Arts Council of Great Britain was created out of the Council for the Encouragement of Music and the Arts (CEMA), formed during the war to provide entertainment and to foster arts practice in Britain. Initially, the Arts Council maintained CEMA's complementary aims to distribute the arts widely and to decentralise arts provision,[9] especially through providing support to a handful of regional repertory theatres.[10] Although the organisational model adopted by the Arts Council would prove to be influential – defining regions, channelling limited resources, and effectively permitting or preventing arts practice in any given area – the Council did not devise its own purpose-built model. Instead, it rather passively adopted CEMA's model, with a headquarters in London and twelve regional offices distributed throughout the UK according to a plan devised during the war for the purposes not of arts provision, of course, but of civil defence.

While not purpose-built, this model of regional provision was presumably better for supporting theatre practice distributed throughout the UK than no model at all would have been. However, what it could provide – and therefore its ability to challenge associations of the regional with inferiority and the metropolitan with superiority – was compromised by a variety of economic factors that the Arts Council did little to alter. Although the Council ensured the presence of regional theatre, it did not ensure that this theatre would be informed by and responsive to its local audiences – or that it would, in other words, facilitate pluralist, demo-cratic expression. For many reasons, much postwar theatre throughout Britain was fairly conservative, investing in tried, tested, and somewhat standardised productions dominated by metropolitan tastes. In his book on British culture in the Cold War, Robert Hewison argues that postwar Britons' hunger for culture and their nostalgia for a time before the war meant that, in the theatre, they were fed a steady diet of revivals.[11] Conservative, standardised programming was further enhanced by censorship (which lasted until 1968), a few managements' near-monop-oly control of theatres and their production,[12] and a 10 per cent enter-tainments tax instituted in 1917 to raise war revenue (and reduced in 1948[13] but not abolished until 1958) which raised theatres' costs and intensified the overall economic conservatism already present in the theatre.[14]

Whether these impediments contributed directly or not, the Arts Council soon abandoned its policy of taking 'the best to the most' – a policy that was rather paternalistic in the first place. Generous touring policies quickly declined,[15] the regional offices were gradually closed until all were gone by 1956,[16] and what little investment the Arts Council did make in theatre went increasingly to metropolitan institutions such as the Opera House at Covent Garden, Sadler's Wells, and the Old Vic. By 1948–49, for example, the Opera House took one quarter of the Arts Council's entire annual budget.[17] Defending the Council's change in policy, its Secretary-General William Emrys Williams asked in 1951, 'Might it not be better to accept the realistic fact that the living theatre of good quality cannot be widely accessible and to concentrate our resources upon establishing a few more shrines like Stratford and the Old Vic?'[18] In response to his own rhetorical question, he proposed that the Arts Council 'may decide for the time being … to devote itself to the support of two or three exemplary theatres which might re-affirm the supremacy of

standards in our national theatre'.[19] He summarised this policy in the
phrase '"Few, but roses" – including, of course, regional roses', the final
clause offering little consolation to those any more distant from London
than Stratford.[20] By 1956, this policy of supporting metropolitan arts and
ignoring regional ones was thoroughly entrenched: 'The Arts Council
believe then, that the first claim upon its attention and assistance is that
of maintaining in London and the larger cities effective power houses of
opera, music and drama; for unless these quality institutions can be maintained the arts are bound to decline into mediocrity.'[21] Not by accident,
then, the number of theatres throughout the UK plunged in the 1940s
and 1950s from around one thousand to fewer than five hundred.[22] Seen
by many in this period as nepotistic, unaccountable, and cliquish,[23] the
Arts Council in its first decade entrenched a bias of superiority, priority,
and indeed productivity for the metropolis and one of inferiority and
inactivity for the regions.

### 'The best to the most': regionalism in the 1960s and early 1970s

Throughout the 1960s and into the 1970s, the discourse of arts provision
in Britain shifted its emphasis from 'civilising' – understood to be achieved
by offering select, elite, metropolitan-based culture to a few – to a more
democratic emphasis on socialising – achieved by offering 'the best to the
most'. Practically, this meant the arts received greater government
investment, particularly in order to increase distribution by creating more
regional theatres, especially ones intended to produce their own shows
rather than acting as receiving houses for touring metropolitan work.
Ideologically, the preceding pattern of promoting the metropolis and
denigrating the regions as provincial began to be eroded as a campaign
of regional – especially civic – repertory theatre building spread throughout the UK, responding to and fostering regional civic pride.
Nevertheless, this model of arts provision was not without its weaknesses,
two of which were its inherent paternalism and – given its emphasis on
creating a physical regional theatre infrastructure – its vulnerability to
rising material costs. Thus, while the regional theatres were more thoroughly established throughout the course of this period, their effectiveness in actually facilitating autonomous, devolved cultural practice was
always questionable. By the end of this period, their confidence – and
regional pride with it – was damaged, and the metropolitan/regional
hierarchy, while perhaps temporarily inverted, was not eradicated.

The ideological shift from elitism to socialism that characterised this period was heralded by the Labour appointment of Britain's first Minister for the Arts, Jennie Lee, in 1964. Lee was committed to distributing more art while upholding quality. She 'wanted to level up not down',[24] maintaining grants to existing 'centres of excellence' while fostering the wider diffusion of excellence. She succeeded in persuading government that the Arts Council needed increased subsidy to achieve this aim, trebling the Council's grant in six years to see it rise to £2 million by 1970.[25] As her biographer Patricia Hollis observes, 'Most of Jennie's new money went not into London's national companies, but into Scotland, Wales, and the regions (no one talked about the "provinces" in Jennie's presence)'.[26] Lee's thinking and her ministerial policy clearly influenced the Arts Council's practice, despite her arm's-length relationship to it. From the late 1960s throughout the 1970s, the Council's rhetoric 'repeatedly declar[ed] that "the balance of provision between London and other regions" [was] one of its main concerns'.[27]

The greatest legacy of the rise in theatre funding in this period is the number of theatres it converted and built. This building policy was advocated by the government-commissioned *Housing the Arts in Great Britain* report, published in two parts in 1959 and 1961,[28] and was supported by the government's Capital Fund, established in 1965 'to assist towns in building or renovating theatres'.[29] Critics vary in their estimates of just how many theatres were created in this period, but their statistics point unanimously to a prevailing national 'edifice complex'. Anthony Jackson speculates that, between 1958 and 1970, 'twenty new theatres had been constructed, fifteen of which were designed specifically for repertory'.[30] Other critics, working with broader definitions, conclude that about a hundred new theatres were created from the late 1950s to the mid-1970s.[31] In line with Lee's and the Arts Council's increased emphasis on regional provision, this expansion in theatre building was, as Jackson notes, 'even more a regional than a London phenomenon: no less than thirty-four of the [forty] new theatres [built by 1980] were situated in the English regions, in Scotland and in Wales'.[32] Admittedly, construction finally began on the National Theatre on London's South Bank during this period, but not until as late as 1969. A decade earlier, in 1958, it was a regional theatre, Coventry's Belgrade, which set the pace for theatre building in Britain by becoming the first purpose-built repertory theatre to open in Britain in twenty years.[33] Regional theatre flourished in this period on an unprecedented scale.

Of course that does not mean it facilitated devolved democratic expression. Indeed, Lee's 'best to the most' mission statement bespeaks a government desire to import to regional theatres metropolitan standards at least and, most likely, metropolitan productions and play texts as well. Furthermore, the way regional theatre flourished – in prominent big new buildings – brought its own set of problems. Securing funding for the construction and maintenance of theatre buildings regularly competed with attaining funding for actual theatre practice. Geoff Mulgan and Ken Worpole point out that Britain's local authorities often collectively provide more subsidy to theatre than the Arts Council does and they argue that, in 1963, 'forty-three percent of [local authority] expenditure on "entertainment" was on the upkeep of buildings'. Spending on actual arts provision went first to concerts and art exhibitions and 'Spending on "theatre" came an insignificant fourteenth'.[34] Theatre practice faced another serious problem in 1973–74; namely, the OPEC-led quadrupling of oil prices and, so, of heating costs. Characteristically featuring big windows, spacious, high-ceilinged lobbies, and generously proportioned auditoria, the new regional theatres were particularly vulnerable to this increase in cost, all the more so as inflation continued to rise, reaching over 25 per cent a year by 1975.[35] By this time, 'the increases in annual Arts Council grants were unable to keep pace with inflation' and the press increasingly began to depict the regional theatre complexes as 'white elephants'.[36]

So while Lee and others did much to improve the profile and actual material circumstances of regional theatre throughout this period, they did not necessarily ensure that its productions would provide opportunities for democratic expression and imagining, and they created a theatre that was in some ways hostage to its own fortune, being too dispersed and too accommodatingly spacious to support itself in straightened economic circumstances. The received ideology of regional inferiority and metropolitan superiority prevailed. It is overly schematic to suggest that metropolitanism and regionalism were the only models by which theatre funding was understood by governments before Blair's. Other models already mentioned include, for example, the provincial and the civic. Significantly, though, none of these models appreciably challenged the assumed dominance of the metropolis and the UK-wide hierarchy that dominance underwrote.

### From arts to 'creative industries' at the turn of the millennium

Putting geographical paradigms to one side for the moment, a crucial paradigm shift pursued by the New Labour government since 1997 has entailed a move from conceiving cultural practices through such terms as art and design to marketing them aggressively as 'creative industries'.[37] New Labour has established the Creative Industries Task Force and the Creative Industries Export Promotion Advisory Group (CIEPAG). And it has published two editions of the *Creative Industries Mapping Document* as well as *Creative Britain*, the collected essays of New Labour's first Culture Secretary, Chris Smith.[38] All of these publications spell out the economic benefits of the 'creative industries', reporting, for example, that the performing arts alone earn an annual revenue of half a billion pounds, employ 74,000 people, and produce export income of £80 million,[39] and that is without taking full account of what is generally appreciated to be their immense if incalculable value in the field of 'soft' diplomacy, easing the trade of other, less 'sexy' goods.[40]

By candidly flaunting its economic priorities as well as its preference for the term 'creative industries' over the former 'cultural industries', New Labour's 'creative industries' paradigm raises serious issues about what it will and will not support. Fundamentally, this model's economic emphasis prioritises commercial value over social value and fashions culture as marketable commodities rather than as social acts performed by human agents. It potentially limits the right to artistic expression to those who can make it economically productive. It dangerously conflates objectives of cultural and economic regeneration.[41] It cynically uses 'the aura of culture to attract capital',[42] quite explicitly for organisations such as CIEPAG who advocate using culture to promote the international trade of other British exports, advising, 'The "entertainment" factor should be an essential part of trade weeks, to provide a cultural wrap around for UK plc as the UK itself, [for example] at a launch of a new model in the motor industry'.[43] Its preference for the word 'creative' over 'cultural' has still more damaging implications. While New Labour presumably wants to invoke such 'creative' connotations as dynamism, the contemporary and inventiveness over the potential associations of 'culture' with heritage and conservatism,[44] its choice of term also prioritises the *individual* creative act over *social* cultural activity. The term potentially disempowers people by transforming them from collective audiences and makers into individual and alienated consumers. It celebrates anti-social capitalist commodity fetishism at the expense of social practice.

That said, there are several reasons cautiously to entertain New Labour's emphasis on the 'creative industries'. After years of neglect under consecutive Conservative governments, it at least heralds a renewed interest – and possible investment – in the arts, especially the contemporary arts. Where Major stepped up Conservative attention to the arts in 1992 by establishing a Department for National Heritage, its title alone betrayed its preoccupation with preserving what already existed rather than making new arts. This is not to question the value of preserving existent works of art but to emphasise the value of continuing to make new art expressive of its ever-changing contexts (and to suggest that the Conservative policy was informed by an underlying snobbery). Further, all of the damaging outcomes outlined above are predicated on the expectation that the government's 'creative industries' vocabulary and ideology will actually prevail over real cultural practice, and this may not be the case. Michael McKinnie suggests that tensions within New Labour 'creative industries' discourses and Department for Culture, Media and Sport (DCMS) policies betray New Labour anxiety that British cultural practice may not be doing exactly what they want it to be doing.[45] Indeed, it may be that artists are exploiting renewed government interest in the 'creative industries' to produce some carefully disguised art, even art that is produced socially and not in atomised isolation, that is about practice and not commodity.

### Rebranding the nations

In order to evaluate some of these potentials, the following sections examine two institutions whose current and planned work can be seen as a result of New Labour's emphasis on 'creative industries', as well as its new emphasis on nations. Discourses and structures of regionalism, metropolitanism, and other hierarchical models were not eliminated with Blair's election, but they were dislodged by the shift in perspective to concentrate instead on nations, including the rebranded 'New Britain',[46] as well as Scotland, Wales, and Northern Ireland with their devolved parliament and assemblies and associated powers and budgets. As New Labour's promotion of the 'creative industries' raises concerns, so does this focus on nations. The most obvious risks are that it fosters 'bad' nationalism – nationalism that is xenophobic, jingoistic, exclusive, and falsely homogenising – and that it produces a neo-imperialism, exporting and potentially imposing its cultural models beyond its borders. However, the emphasis on nations may instead help to imagine the UK's parts more equitably than had previously been the case, and to foster a self-reflexive interest in the nations, one that explores and supports their heterogeneity.

The two institutions through which I explore the British Council and its work exporting 'Cool Britann Scottish National Theatre planned by the Scottish Exe Scottish Arts Council. Of course the Arts Councils continue to alter, but I shift from examining them to look at these particul in order to reflect the government's shift in focus to national ide national institutions, and economic aims for the nations' 'creative in tries'. I examine these specific institutions both for their similarities and for their differences. The work of both institutions is partly the result of the government's emphases on nations and the 'creative industries' and is instructive about the results of these emphases. The institutions' differences – in scale, contexts of operation, and effects – are instructive too, however. Where the British Council is supernational (ostensibly representing the UK plus all of the nations that form it), operates in a global context, and indicates some of the risks of the government's new emphases, the Scottish National Theatre is 'small' national, operates primarily in a domestic context, and demonstrates more strongly some of the potentials that can result from the government's paradigm shifts to promoting 'creative industries' and nations.

## The British Council rebrands Britain

Soon after New Labour's 1997 election victory, it launched Panel 2000, a co-ordinated effort by the Foreign Office, the Department of Trade and Industry, the DCMS, and others, to promote the UK and its culture overseas.[47] Represented on Panel 2000 and part-funded by the Foreign Office was the British Council, the main government-related agency for international cultural diplomacy. The British Council claims, 'We build mutually beneficial relationships between people in the UK and other countries and increase appreciation of the UK's creative ideas and achievements'.[48] Despite these admirable aims, the British Council has long been regarded as 'some ancient, obscure, postcolonial organisation'.[49] This profile was obviously not commensurate with the 'Cool Britannia' New Labour wanted to promote and export, and the British Council was quick to get 'on message'. It underwent a 'vision programme',[50] through which it aimed to shed its own outdated image 'as a purveyor of Shakespeare and Jane Austen'.[51] It appointed as its 'impeccably Blairite new chairperson'[52] Baroness Helena Kennedy QC, friend of Blair and Chancellor Gordon Brown and outspoken critic of a variety of aspects of Britain's criminal justice system, especially its treatment of

**1, 2** and **3** British Council posters, c. 1998: comedians, Benny Hill and Rowan Atkinson; actresses, Julie Christie and Kate Winslet; and (facing) playwrights, William Shakespeare and Tom Stoppard

women. And for British Council offices and English-language classrooms overseas, it commissioned a series of twelve new posters designed to demonstrate the continuity and change of Blair's new Britain by marrying old and new images of British creativity, including comedians Benny Hill and Rowan Atkinson, actresses Julie Christie and Kate Winslet, and playwrights Shakespeare and Tom Stoppard (figures 1 to 3).[53]

'Cool Britannia' was widely derided as superficial by the government's critics – indeed, even the government quickly distanced itself from what Chris Smith called 'the flawed phrase' and Helena Kennedy called 'ghastly sloganeering', agreeing that it only swapped one set of reductive clichés for another – or morphed them together, as in the posters.[54] But while the term may have been superficial, reductive, and embarrassingly aspirational, the changes in cultural identity it witnessed, promoted, and/or precipitated may have been more substantial. As the British Council posters indicate, the shift in focus to the present at the very least pulls the focus from the past and promotes current cultural practice – albeit, in these posters, uniformly mainstream cultural practice. Other positive indications are that the British Council seems to have taken seriously certain key words from New

Labour's vocabulary to concentrate on presenting numerous and substantial examples of British work that is creative, culturally diverse, new, dynamic,[55] that is not hijacked by economic priorities and rendered as commodified simulacra, and that is not substantially evacuated and rendered instead as superficial style – the feared result of dreaded New Labour 'spin'.[56] Less optimistically perhaps, it can also be seen to be promoting cultural production characterised by varying degrees of homogeneity and elitism, and to be enacting a dangerous neo-imperialism.

In line with its aim to promote a new version of the UK and its 'creative industries', the British Council has since 1997 altered both how it promotes (or markets) as well as what it promotes, and introduced certain new activities, including international writing workshops. In 1997, it launched the two videos *British Theatre* and *British Dance* and, in 1998, it launched the glossy annual catalogues *British Theatre in Profile* and *British Dance in Profile*, all aimed at overseas promoters.[57] These promotional materials joined the pre-existing website[58] and six-monthly *On Tour: British Drama and Dance* magazine/catalogue produced since 1992 for overseas Council offices. In 1997, the Council increased its exploitation of the Edinburgh Fringe Festival as a shop window for live performance by holding its first week-long British Council Edinburgh Showcase which it describes as 'a unique and concentrated opportunity for promoters and British Council colleagues to see some of the best British theatre currently available for international touring'.[59] Over two hundred international promoters attend this 'snapshot of British creativity', held every two years since its inception.[60] They receive accommodation, show tickets, a guidebook of around thirty productions recommended for touring, and invitations to Council-hosted receptions, parties, and daily breakfast meetings where theatre companies and international promoters can network and broker touring performance contracts.[61] Alongside this work promoting performances, the British

Council Performing Arts Department has also worked to maintain the
high profile of new British theatre writing, especially through its initia-
tion and support of a number of Royal Court activities. For example,
it supported the Royal Court's commission of David Hare to visit
Palestine and Israel and write his response, the one-person show *Via
Dolorosa*, first staged in 1998.[62] And in 1999 it initially invited and then
supported the Royal Court to run a series of new writing seminars in
Russia, promoting the translated work of Sarah Kane, Mark Ravenhill,
and Patrick Marber, and also nurturing new Russian writing.[63] It has
run similar programmes in Brazil, Palestine, and Uganda.[64]

Evident in this brief summary of some of the British Council's activities is a notable and worrying concentration on treating and marketing
performance as exchangeable, exportable commodity. But the relevance
of this Council emphasis is, however, less important socially than what
kind of work it has promoted and how successful that promotion has been
in getting a range of British performance into the public sphere.
Eschewing its image as a 'purveyor' of canonical writing, the British
Council has promoted work that is impressively broad, in both style and
geographical origin. The *British Theatre* video, for example, features fifteen
theatre companies whose work ranges from live art (Bobby Baker) to physical theatre (Frantic Assembly, Improbable Theatre) to puppetry (Stephen
Mottram's Animata) to text-based theatre (Out of Joint, Shared
Experienced). A similar range of text-based, experimental, and physical
theatre is characteristic of the work selected for promotion by the British
Council in any given year since 1997,[65] as well as in the Edinburgh
Showcases. While work promoted comes primarily from the south-east of
England, reinforcing a long-standing metropolitan bias, this emphasis is
by no means exclusive. A recent issue of *On Tour* highlights theatre in
Scotland, Wales, and Northern Ireland,[66] and the *British Theatre* video
includes companies from Bath (Natural Theatre Company), Newcastle
(Northern Stage), Oxford (Stephen Mottram's Animata), Glasgow (nva),
Edinburgh (Communicado), and Swansea (Volcano).[67] Wales, Scotland,
and Northern Ireland are further promoted by the British Council
through arts contacts based in Council offices in Cardiff, Edinburgh, and
Belfast, as well as by a recent (if overdue) shift in the British Council's own
branding to promote the 'UK' and not simply 'Britain' in the poster
campaign launched in 2001. Further, the range and cultural origin of new
theatre the British Council promotes continues to grow. The 2002 *British
Drama in Profile* catalogue included detailed information on 125 theatre
companies and individual artists, many of which come from outside

**4** *It's Your Film* by Stan's Cafe

London and/or are racially mixed or non-white, for example Moti Roti, Tamasha Theatre Company, Tara Arts, Yellow Earth Theatre, and NITRO.[68]

While it is perhaps more difficult to evaluate the success of the British Council's promotion, there are clear indications that it is succeeding in getting a range of British performance work into the market – or, less cynically, the public sphere – and that it is generating income for artists to make further work. For example, as a result of promotion at the 2001 British Council Showcase in Edinburgh, Stan's Cafe and Ursula Martinez both secured extensive touring opportunities. With British Council assistance, Birmingham-based Stan's Cafe, which devises original theatre and installation work, has toured *It's Your Film* (figure 4) to Germany, the Netherlands, the Czech Republic, Ireland, France, Lithuania, Estonia, Croatia, and Portugal.[69] Ursula Martinez, who is based in London and makes hybrid cabaret/live art, toured *Show Off* with its distinctively iconoclastic approach to traditional proscenium arch theatre (figure 5) to

**5** *Show Off*, Ursula Martinez

Australia, the Netherlands, Hong Kong, Hungary, and Estonia, also with Council assistance.[70] On a broader scale, the British Council claims that UK companies earned £1 million worth of work overseas through promotion at the 2000 Edinburgh festivals.[71]

Read positively, the British Council's promotional work is supporting cultural expression that ranges broadly – in form, perhaps most obviously, but also in geographical and cultural origins, fulfilling the British Council Director of Performing Arts John Kieffer's claim, 'We must embrace changes in cultural identity, changes in technology, changes in values and changes in tastes'.[72] In this sense the British Council's work can be seen to support diverse expression and cultural imagining. By helping to displace overseas promoters' and audiences' residual expectations that Britain's theatre export will primarily be based on old texts, grandly staged, performed in a particular style, and costly to import, it is also working to break down prejudices that prevent acceptance of changing, diverse expressions of British national identities. Potentially further supporting diverse cultural expression are the Royal Court writing workshops, where writers in different countries worldwide are facilitated in addressing issues which are particular to – and often urgent within – their local cultural contexts.

Read less optimistically, while the British Council may have moved away from promoting one relatively elitist and homogeneous profile for Britain – featuring 'Shakespeare and Jane Austen' – it may have contributed to developing another profile – featuring postmodern performance art – which some might see as characterised still by elitism and homogeneity. Further, by aiming to export British culture and English language,[73] the British Council has always risked being accused of cultural imperialism. Its current global promotion of what might be seen as a 'house' writing style (Royal Court) and a 'house' performance style (UK postmodern performance art) – as well as global markets in which to sell both – make it vulnerable to this accusation still. Finally, because the British Council only markets a range of British performance and does not directly fund the making of any work, it could be accused of not supporting democratic expression, but rather exploiting an image of Britain as democratic, cynically producing and marketing, in other words, a simulacrum of British democracy.

The actual effects of the British Council's deployment of New Labour's 'creative industries' and 'Cool Britannia' policies probably fall somewhere between these two poles of cultural benefit and loss, but this summary of potential outcomes gives a sense of what is at stake in this deployment of policy.

### Scotland the brand: the National Theatre of Scotland

Like Britain, Scotland and the other small nations have been encouraged to adopt the language of the 'creative industries' and to rebrand themselves in the image of 'New Britain', especially in an international context. Like British government publications, Scottish Executive publications have argued for the economic benefits of the creative industries. The Scottish Executive's *Creating Our Future ... Minding Our Past: Scotland's National Cultural Strategy* (2000) reports that the creative industries 'are estimated to be worth around £5 billion to the Scottish economy each year', that '50,000 are employed in the cultural sector', and, in a significant shift from economic to social considerations, that the creative industries 'make a major contribution to people's quality of life'.[74] It also argues the benefit of investing in Scotland's culture to improve and update its international image in ways familiar from the example of 'New Britain': 'cultural development contributes to the image of Scotland as a modern, dynamic and forward-looking society'.[75] This is an especially crucial factor for the Scottish Executive, given its ambition for Scotland to be the 'most globally connected small nation in Europe'.[76] To fulfil this aim, one of the *Strategy*'s stated priorities is to 'promote international cultural exchange and dialogue' by supporting international travel opportunities for artists, and by building 'upon existing initiatives and joint working by relevant bodies such as SAC [the Scottish Arts Council], the British Council, Scotland Europa, Scottish Enterprise, Scottish Trade International and Scottish Screen to develop opportunities to promote Scotland's culture abroad'.[77]

SAC has fully supported – and in many respects had already anticipated – the Executive's ambitions. 'Scotland's cultural activity and exports', SAC argues, 'are essential tools of national and international dialogue and promotion. They are one of the country's principal marketing tools, equivalent to an advertising spend worth millions of pounds.'[78] The independent Working Group invited by SAC to report on the feasibility of a Scottish national theatre argues, perhaps not surprisingly, that theatre in particular has been especially important in promoting Scotland, implying that it should be supported in continuing to do so. 'In the twentieth century,' the Working Group's final report claims, 'it was theatre which first put distinctively Scottish voices on the cultural map, changed perceptions of Scotland, and operated at the cutting edge of political and social change.'[79]

So, the Scottish Executive, like the British Council, is 'on message' about the value of the creative industries and fully committed to promoting a 'New Scotland' which resembles in key respects the much-touted

'New Britain' – 'modern, dynamic and forward-looking'. However, again, this is neither simply empty rhetoric nor a thin subterfuge claiming interest in the arts while actually undermining them by concentrating primarily on their economic worth. The Scottish Executive has supported a heterogeneous, democratic Scottish theatre, investing not simply in its promotion, as the British Council does, but in its very making, while simultaneously resisting making an autocratic decree about what it should be.

New Labour political discourse about the importance of the creative industries has helped secure much-needed funding for the arts, and particularly for theatre, in Scotland. With a Scottish national opera, ballet, orchestra, chamber orchestra, and gallery already established and with theatre suffering from chronic under-funding, the Executive quickly recognised the need to support Scottish theatre more fully. It made a three-year commitment to allocate Additional Money for Drama (1999–2002)[80] and pledged in its *Strategy* to 'take steps to establish a national theatre for Scotland'.[81] The *Strategy* did not detail what form such a theatre would take, but the final report of the Scottish National Theatre Working Group, published in May 2001, does. It concludes, 'The Scottish National Theatre should be a creative producer which engages with the whole theatre sector as its "production company", working with and through the existing Scottish theatre community to achieve its objectives'.[82]

The Scottish National Theatre thus envisioned will not devour all available public theatre funding, starving existing theatres and theatre work as other National institutions often do – London's Royal Opera House at Covent Garden, mentioned earlier, being a case in point. Nor will it be building-based – potentially limiting what it can produce within one particular set of built constraints,[83] and draining scarce resources into material infrastructures instead of cultural practices, as theatre buildings have previously done (and continue to do) throughout the UK, and as the new Scottish parliament at Holyrood has done, moving from initially projected costs of £40 million to a cost of over £401 million.[84] Nor will this Scottish National Theatre be based in any one location, such as the central belt of Glasgow and Edinburgh, reinforcing a Scottish metropolitanism. Nor will it be about atomised, individuated 'creativity': built on a 'collegiate', collaborative model, it requires co-operation and co-ordination between groups of institutions and people in order to succeed. What it will be is a sponsor and commissioner of a variety of types of work to be produced in a range of working contexts throughout the nation. It will be a devolved national theatre, with power and opportunities for expression distributed to its constituents.

Plans for a Scottish National Theatre have been mooted many times before but, as theatre critic John Fowler notes, 'Where the scheme differs from its predecessors is that it does not aim to create a new theatre company based on any particular theatre (new or old) which would then in a sense demote the rest, but invites all existing companies and creative people to contribute'.[85] In conception at least, this Scottish National Theatre will at once assume the authority of being national while maintaining the confidence to devolve and disperse its powers. It will also work collaboratively, and be adaptable to Scotland's geographical and cultural diversity.[86] It will not impose a uniform Scottish identity or theatre practice, but will facilitate the articulation of different groups' identities, experiences, theatre practices, and, even, different groups' Scotlands. In a sense probably not imagined by New Labour, the Scottish National Theatre will function as a brand – attaching its name (as well as some finance and expertise) to existing theatre companies throughout the nation. It will aim to carry status, but also have the flexibility of a brand. Although it may be a positive outcome of New Labour's ideological investment in the creative industries, its purpose is not simply economic. It is committed to quality, education, and professional development, and to reflecting a sense of identity which is 'inclusive and outward looking', precisely not, as critics of national – or nationalist – institutions might warn, exclusive and inward-looking.[87] Finally, according to plans proposed by the Working Group in 2001, the Scottish National Theatre was to tour internationally as early as 2004/5,[88] fulfilling one of its intended roles as an international ambassador for Scottish culture, and widening the public sphere in which Scottish theatre is performed and Scottish identities are expressed and imagined.

Since initial plans were made, the Scottish Executive has diverted £2 million earmarked for the National Theatre initiative into a new £3.5 million funding package for Scotland's existing theatres, leaving only £1 million in the National Theatre budget for 2003/4, when £1.5 million had originally been proposed.[89] This budget change will certainly set back the timing of the National Theatre initiative, but considering that Scotland's existing theatres were meant to form the basis of the National Theatre in the first place, it might be seen not as a loss to the National Theatre budget but as a shift within it. On the other hand, without adequate capital investment, Blair's cultural capitalism may prove to be unworkable and to be precisely about simulacra rather

than acts, a possibility suggested by many Scottish theatre workers who
see the Scottish Executive's continuing underinvestment in theatre as
indicative of a failure fully and actually to commit to it.[90] As Robert
Hewison warns, 'if the public culture is tied to public policy in the economic sphere, then when the economy suffers, the culture suffers also'.[91]
The future will tell whether this model of what has been officially named
as the National Theatre of Scotland survives or thrives. There is cause
for optimism, with the well-received appointment in July 2004 of former
Paines Plough director Vicky Featherstone as director of the National
Theatre of Scotland and the announcement of £7.5 million in initial
funding, as well as Featherstone's announcement that she intends for
the National Theatre of Scotland to start producing by the end of
2005.[92] The National Theatre of Scotland deserves this kind of investment because it holds out imaginings of Scottish identity which are, in
the Scottish Executive's terms, 'modern, dynamic and forward-looking',
as well as confidently heterogeneous, authoritative, socially purposeful,
and independent. It holds out a progressive, dynamic model of the
nation and a canny interpretation and application of New Labour's
emphasis on 'creative industries' and rebranding.

## Nationalising the 'creative industries'

New Labour's coincidental promotion of the 'creative industries' and the
rebranded nations presents a possible paradox. While New Labour
encourages – or, by force of circumstance, compels – the arts to trade in
the unprotected sphere of private enterprise, it simultaneously demonstrates a desire to maintain national (public) control of them, precisely for
the purpose of manipulating British national identities as commodities.
These urges to privatise and to nationalise, to deregulate and to regulate,
may appear to be antithetical, but they have nevertheless co-existed at
least since 1997 and they bear scrutiny. Perhaps unsurprisingly given their
somewhat paradoxical impetuses, their effects are uneven. They certainly
risk commodifying culture and repressing the expression of cultural
difference by packaging performance into marketable categories and
exploiting it as window dressing to help sell other British products and
clichés of British identity. They risk addressing consumers instead of
audiences. By emphasising export, they risk producing a neo-imperialism,
for example through the international franchising of Royal Court writing
practices. And, by linking cultural practice to financial success, they jeopardise the future of theatre practice.

However, by displacing the historically dominant power-asymmetrical models of metropolitanism and regionalism, they also introduce and enact a more empowering paradigm for imagining the communities that make up the UK. And at their best – as in the sheer range of diverse work promoted by the British Council, and as in the plans for the Scottish National Theatre – they demonstrate that this national imagining can be healthily heterogeneous. New Labour may well be interested in expanding the markets for the knowledge- and service-based economy of 'New Britain' to trade in, and the policy rhetorics through which it advances these interests may be powerful and pervasive and certainly affect how UK artists and audiences imagine their identities. But artists and audiences can at least partially transform New Labour's markets and commodities into public spheres and acts, in and through which ideas and practices can be democratically exchanged and diverse identities can be imagined. Government policy will inevitably affect who can imagine what, how; but as the examples discussed here demonstrate, it need not finally determine that imagining.

## Notes

1  This chapter is a revised and expanded version of Jen Harvie, 'Nationalizing the "Creative Industries"', *Contemporary Theatre Review* 13:1 (2003), 15–32.

2  Benedict Anderson, *Imagined Communities: Reflections on the Origin and Spread of Nationalism* (London: Verso, [1983] 2nd edn, 1991), pp. 25–32.

3  Benedict Anderson explores the globally widespread – and, he suggests, culturally necessary – desire to believe in 'The Goodness of Nations' in the last chapter of his later book, *The Spectre of Comparisons: Nationalism, Southeast Asia, and the World* (London: Verso, 1998), pp. 26 and 360–8.

4  Subsequent chapters consider the influence on theatre practice and analysis of other structural contexts, such as institutions (e.g., the Edinburgh festivals in Chapter 4) and historiographies (e.g., dominant historiographies of British drama and theatre in Chapter 5).

5  Postwar theatre British history has been outlined in detail by many critics, for example: John Elsom, *Post-War British Theatre* (London: Routledge and Kegan Paul, 1979), George Rowell and Anthony Jackson, *The Repertory Movement: A History of Regional Theatre in Britain* (Cambridge: Cambridge University Press, 1984), and Dominic Shellard, *British Theatre Since the War* (New Haven and London: Yale University Press, 1999). For a detailed analysis of the structures of theatre in the UK see Michael Quine, 'The theatre system of the United Kingdom', in H. van Maanen and S. E. Wilmer (eds), *Theatre Worlds in Motion: Structures, Politics and Developments in the Countries of Western Europe* (Amsterdam: Rodopi, 1998), pp. 669–720. I consider postwar British theatre in this context to focus on what patterns of identity it produced and to consider those patterns' long-term ideological effects and legacies.

6 Several recent publications analyse this increasing commodification of culture, a trend which certainly predates New Labour's 1997 election. For a detailed and insightful analysis of recent British theatre's commodification see Baz Kershaw, 'Discouraging democracy: British theatres and economics, 1979–1999', *Theatre Journal* 51:3 (October 1999), 267–83. For a cultural studies emphasis see Timothy Bewes and Jeremy Gilbert (eds), *Cultural Capitalism: Politics After New Labour* (London: Lawrence and Wishart, 2000), and for an emphasis on cultural policy see Clive Gray, *The Politics of the Arts in Britain* (London: Macmillan, 2000).

7 Janet Minihan argues that 'in a single decade, during and after the Second World War, the British Government did more to commit itself to supporting the arts than it had in the previous century and a half'. Janet Minihan, *The Nationalization of Culture: The Development of State Subsidies to the Arts in Great Britain* (London: Hamish Hamilton, 1977), p. 215, quoted in Gray, *The Politics of the Arts*, p. 38.

8 Andrew Sinclair, *Arts and Cultures: The History of the 50 Years of the Arts Council of Great Britain* (London: Sinclair-Stevenson, 1995), p. 62.

9 Simon Trussler, *The Cambridge Illustrated History of British Theatre* (Cambridge: Cambridge University Press, 1994), p. 303.

10 Shellard, *British Theatre Since the War*, p. 6.

11 Robert Hewison, *In Anger: Culture in the Cold War, 1945-60* (London: Methuen, revised edn, 1988), p. 9.

12 Andrew Davies, *Other Theatres: The Development of Alternative and Experimental Theatre in Britain* (London: Methuen, 1987), pp. 138–9.

13 *Ibid.*, p. 148.

14 John Elsom, 'United Kingdom', in Don Rubin (ed.), *The World Encyclopedia of Contemporary Theatre*, Vol. 1, *Europe* (London: Routledge, 1994), pp. 890–920, p. 893.

15 Geoff Mulgan and Ken Worpole, *Saturday Night or Sunday Morning? From Arts to Industry – New Forms of Cultural Policy* (London: Commedia, 1988), p. 20.

16 Robert Hutchison, *The Politics of the Arts Council* (London: Sinclair Browne, 1982), p. 118.

17 Davies, *Other Theatres*, p. 146.

18 *Arts Council Annual Report 1950/51* (London: Arts Council of Great Britain, 1951), p. 34; quoted in Robert Hewison, *Culture and Consensus: England, Art and Politics since 1940* (London: Methuen, revised edn, 1997), p. 80.

19 Quoted in Sinclair, *Arts and Cultures*, p. 88, ellipsis added.

20 *Arts Council Annual Report 1950/51*, p. 34, quoted in Hewison, *Culture and Consensus*, p. 80.

21 *The First Ten Years: Eleventh Annual Report* (London: Arts Council of Great Britain, 1956), quoted in Mulgan and Worpole, *Saturday Night*, p. 20.

22 Elsom, 'United Kingdom', p. 896.

23 Mulgan and Worpole, *Saturday Night*, p. 20.

24 Patricia Hollis, *Jennie Lee: A Life* (Oxford: Oxford University Press, 1997), p. 250.

25 *Ibid.*, p. 250. Theatre's economic fortunes were also improved by its liberation from entertainments tax in 1958 (Elsom, 'United Kingdom', p. 900).

26 *Jennie Lee*, pp. 250–1.

27 Anthony Jackson, '1958–1983: renewal, growth and retrenchment', in Rowell and Jackson, *The Repertory Movement*, pp. 89–129, p. 113. Jackson does not give a

precise reference for the quotation he includes but it is likely an *Arts Council Annual Report*, probably that of 1980/81.

28  *Housing the Arts in Great Britain, Part I: London, Scotland, Wales* (London: Arts Council of Great Britain, 1959), *Housing the Arts in Great Britain, Part II: The Needs of the English Provinces* (London: Arts Council of Great Britain, 1961).

29  Elsom, *Post-War British Theatre*, p. 132.

30  Jackson, '1958–1983', p. 89.

31  Shellard, *British Theatre Since the War*, p. 129; Trussler, *The Cambridge Illustrated History*, p. 336.

32  Jackson, '1958–1983', p. 89.

33  *Ibid.*, p. 89.

34  Mulgan and Worpole, *Saturday Night*, p. 27.

35  Jackson, '1958–1983', p. 96.

36  Shellard, *British Theatre Since the War*, p. 178. The regional theatres pioneered in this era had other shortcomings. Elsom argues that the reliance on grant aid made programming conservative and imitative of metropolitan tastes, as in the postwar era ('United Kingdom', p. 900). While Trussler sees the rise in civic theatres as a positive articulation of civic identity (*The Cambridge Illustrated History*, p. 336), Mulgan and Worpole argue that the civic emphasis of this period supported 'very patrician forms of municipal provision' and resisted what they see as the potentially liberating influences of popular and youth culture (*Saturday Night*, p. 27).

37  The scale of New Labour's promotion of the 'creative industries' was new, but the phrase and its underpinning ideology were not. Economic arguments for the arts and culture were rife throughout the 1980s. See, for example: Mulgan and Worpole, *Saturday Night*; Justin Lewis, *Art, Culture, and Enterprise: The Politics of Art and Cultural Industries* (London: Routledge, 1990); John Myerscough, *The Economic Importance of the Arts in Britain* (London: Policy Studies Institute, 1988); Kershaw, 'Discouraging democracy'; and D. Keith Peacock, *Thatcher's Theatre: British Theatre and Drama in the Eighties* (New York: Greenwood Press, 1999).

38  *Creative Industries Mapping Document* (London: Department of Culture, Media and Sport [DCMS], 1998); *Creative Industries Mapping Document* (London: DCMS, 2nd edn, 2001); Chris Smith, *Creative Britain* (London: Faber and Faber, 1998).

39  *Creative Industries Mapping Document* (2001), pp. 10–12.

40  Ian Black, 'Analysis: cultural diplomacy: no business like show business …', *Guardian* (4 August 1998), p. 13.

41  Lewis, *Art, Culture, and Enterprise*, p. 139.

42  Brian Wallis, 'Selling nations: international exhibitions and cultural diplomacy', in Daniel J. Sherman and Irit Rogoff (eds), *Museum Culture: Histories, Discourses, Spectacles* (Minneapolis: University of Minnesota Press, 1994), pp. 265–81, p. 277.

43  CIEPAG, *Creative Industries: Exports: Our Hidden Potential* (London: DCMS, 1999), p. 46.

44  Michael McKinnie, 'A sympathy for art: the sentimental economies of New Labour arts policy', in Deborah Lynn Steinberg and Richard Johnson (eds), *Labour's Passive Revolution: The Cultural Politics of Blairism* (London: Lawrence and Wishart, forthcoming).

45  *Ibid.*
46  'New Britain' was a prominent phrase in the discourse of New Labour approaching the 1997 general election. In 1996, Tony Blair published his book *New Britain: My Vision of a Young Country* (London: Fourth Estate, 1996), Labour launched its magazine for Party members, *New Labour, New Britain*, and Labour published its guide to policy, *New Labour New Britain: The Guide* (London: Labour Party, 1996). This was not the first time Labour had proclaimed a 'New Britain': it was also pledged by Labour after the Second World War. Hewison, *Culture and Consensus*, p. 66.
47  Richard Brooks, 'Cool Britain flops on the world stage', *Sunday Times* (21 November 1999), p. 7.
48  *British Council*, www.britishcouncil.org/index.htm (accessed January 2004).
49  Helena Kennedy quoted in Mary Riddell, 'Helena Kennedy (Chair of British Council)', *New Statesman* (27 March 2000).
50  Stephen Moss, 'Arts: the man behind Blair plc Michael Johnson is the design guru charged with selling the UK – and the government – to the people', *Guardian* (10 September 1998), p. T9.
51  John Lloyd, 'For the best of Britannia, go to Berlin', *The Times* (6 March 1998), p. 26.
52  Black, 'Analysis: cultural diplomacy'.
53  John Harlow, 'Cook sells Britain's new look abroad', *Sunday Times* (6 September 1998), p. 3; and Moss, 'Arts: the man behind Blair plc'.
54  Smith, *Creative Britain*, p. 5; Kennedy quoted in Black, 'Analysis: cultural diplomacy'.
55  *British Council*, 'Theatre and dance projects overseas', www.britishcouncil.org/arts/drama/dra1.htm (accessed March 2002).
56  See, for example, Stephen Bayley, *Labour Camp: The Failure of Style over Substance* (London: B. T. Batsford, 1998) and Norman Fairclough, *New Labour, New Language?* (London: Routledge, 2000).
57  See *British Council*, 'British Council theatre and dance publications and videos', www.britishcouncil.org/arts/drama/drapub.htm (accessed March 2002). *British Theatre in Profile* became *British Drama in Profile* in 2001.
58  *British Council*, 'Home page: the British Council's theatre and dance UK', theatredance.britishcouncil.org (accessed March 2002).
59  'Edinburgh Showcase 2001', *On Tour* 18 (2001), 26.
60  *Ibid.*
61  'Edinburgh Showcase 2001', *On Tour* 17 (2001), 3, and Alexander Kelly, Borce Nikolovski, and Ken Foster, 'On show', *On Tour* 19 (2002), 14–17, pp. 14 and 16.
62  'A writer's report from the front', *Financial Times* (9 September 1998), p. 20. For more on the Royal Court's British-Council-sponsored activities see Elyse Dodgson, 'International playwrights at the Royal Court Theatre', *On Tour* 16 (July 2000), 2–3, and Sasha Dugdale, 'Revolutions and revelations', *On Tour* 16 (2000), 4.
63  Paul Taylor, 'Russia's new revolution', *Independent* (6 March 2002), p. 9.
64  Mark Espiner, 'All the world on stage', *Guardian Weekend* (23 February 2002), pp. 34–6.
65  To take 1999 as a sample year, the British Council supported some 'old' heritage, for example several Shakespeare productions, including the Royal Shakespeare

Company's *The Taming of the Shrew* and *Troilus and Cressida*, which travelled to Hong Kong and Israel respectively. But not all exported Shakespeare productions were either mainstream or conservative in their modes of production; for example, Steven Berkoff's *Shakespeare's Villains*, which travelled to Argentina, Hong Kong, and India. The Council promoted a great deal of recent writing by Mark Ravenhill, Patrick Marber, Caryl Churchill, and Conor McPherson. And many of the supported companies and makers can be considered avant-garde. To summarise briefly and superficially, these include: physical theatre makers Nigel Charnock, V-Tol, and DV8 Physical Theatre; live artists Franko B and Bobby Baker; postmodern performance companies Forced Entertainment and Desperate Optimists; and visual theatre companies Station House Opera, Improbable, and the David Glass Ensemble. *British Council*, 'A selection of drama and dance events worldwide since January 1999, supported by the British Council'; path: 'Events Review' on 'Home Page: British Council's Theatre and Dance UK', theatredance britishcouncil.org/ (accessed March 2002). See also *On Tour.*

66  See *On Tour* 13 (January 1999).

67  To use 1999 as a sample year again, work promoted came also from Belfast (Dubbeljoint Theatre Company), Nottingham (Nottingham Playhouse), and Scotland. *British Council*, 'A selection of drama and dance events worldwide since January 1999 …'.

68  *British Drama in Profile 2002* (London: The British Council, 2001). I discuss Tamasha's work in more detail in Chapter 6.

69  Email to the author from Stan's Cafe administrator, Emily Dawkes (17 April 2002).

70  *British Drama in Profile 2002*, p. 43, and '(P)Review', *On Tour* 19 (2002), 26–8.

71  'Havergal urges more aid for Scottish theatre', *Herald* (21 August 2001).

72  John Kieffer, 'Let's talk about art, maybe', *Observer* (28 March 1999), p. 33.

73  The British Council outlined its aims in *The British Council. Speeches Delivered on the Occasion of the Inaugural Meeting at St. James's Palace on 2nd July, 1935* (privately printed by the British Council: London, 1935), quoted in Frances Donaldson, *The British Council: The First Fifty Years* (London: Jonathan Cape, 1984), pp. 1–2.

74  Scottish Executive, *Creating Our Future … Minding Our Past: Scotland's National Cultural Strategy* (Edinburgh: Scottish Executive, 2000), www.scotland.gov.uk/ nationalculturalstrategy/docs/cult-03.asp (accessed January 2002).

75  *Ibid.*, www.scotland.gov.uk/nationalculturalstrategy/docs/cult-02.asp (accessed January 2002).

76  Scottish Executive, *A Smart, Successful Scotland: Ambitions for the Enterprise Networks* (Edinburgh: Scottish Executive, 2001), www.scotland.gov.uk/library3/enterprise/sss-00.asp (accessed January 2002). See also Scottish Executive, *Scotland: A Global Connections Strategy* (Edinburgh: Scottish Executive, 2001), www.scotland. gov.uk/library3/enterprise/agcs-00.asp (accessed January 2002).

77  Scottish Executive, *Creating Our Future* www.scotland.gov.uk/nationalcultural-strategy/docs/cult-14.asp (accessed January 2002). Curiously, in this context, the *Strategy* fails to mention Scotland the Brand, an organisation that aims to promote Scottish trade, tourism, culture, and a coherent brand identity and is funded indirectly by the Scottish Executive through Scottish Enterprise. See

*Scotland the Brand*, www.scotbrand.com, and *Scottish Enterprise*, www.scottishenter-prise.com (both accessed January 2002).

78 SAC, *Response to the Consultation on National Cultural Strategy* (Glasgow: Scottish Arts Council, November 1999), pp. 19–20.

79 *Scottish National Theatre: Final Report of the Independent Working Group* (Glasgow: Scottish Arts Council, 2001), p. 6, www.sac.org.uk/nonhtdocs/single-page-pdf (accessed July 2001).

80 SAC, 'News release: a national theatre for Scotland to be proud of' (24 July 2001), www.sac.org.uk/news/news_82.htm (accessed July 2001).

81 Scottish Executive, *Creating Our Future*, www.scotland.gov.uk/nationalcultural-strategy/docs/cult-05.asp (accessed January 2002).

82 *Scottish National Theatre: Final Report of the Independent Working Group*, p. 5.

83 SAC's drama committee chairman, John Scott Moncreiff, argued that 'the lack of a new theatre would give writers, directors and actors greater artistic freedom. He said: "We don't want to stifle them in one building."' Tom Peterkin, 'Holyrood's shadow puts paid to theatre building', telegragh.co.uk (25 July 2001).

84 'Holyrood still on target', *BBC News* (26 January 2004), news.bbc.co.uk/2/hi/uk_news/scotland/3430963.stm (accessed January 2004).

85 John Fowler, 'Theatre and nation', *In Scotland* 3 (2000), 17–21, p. 18. For more on the history of debates about a Scottish National Theatre see: Denis Agnew, 'The Scottish National Theatre dream: the Royal Lyceum in the 1970s; the Scottish Theatre Company in the 1980s', *International Journal of Scottish Theatre*, 2:1 (2001), arts.qmuc.ac.uk/ijost/Volume2_no1/D_Agnew.htm (accessed January 2002); Roger Savage, 'A Scottish National Theatre?', in Randall Stevenson and Gavin Wallace (eds), *Scottish Theatre Since the Seventies* (Edinburgh: Edinburgh University Press, 1996), pp. 23–33; and Donald Smith (ed.), *The Scottish Stage: A National Theatre Company for Scotland* (Edinburgh: Candlemaker Press, 1994).

86 *Scottish National Theatre: Final Report of the Independent Working Group*, pp. 8–9.

87 *Ibid.*, pp. 5 and 9.

88 *Ibid.*, p. 17.

89 Arnold Kemp, 'Scottish National Theatre must wait in wings', *Observer* (3 February 2002). Information on the original budget for the national theatre is from *Scottish National Theatre: Final Report of the Independent Working Group*, p. 4.

90 Mike Wade, 'Cash storm destroys theatre of dreams', *Scotsman* (28 November 2002).

91 Robert Hewison, 'Public policy: corporate culture: public culture', in Olin Robison, Robert Freeman, and Charles A. Riley II (eds), *The Arts in the World Economy: Public Policy and Private Philanthropy for a Global Cultural Community* (Hanover, NH: University Press of New England, 1994), pp. 26–32, p. 31.

92 Tim Cornwell, Dark horse lands top theatre job', *Scotsman* (30 July 2004).

# 3

# Remembering the nations: site-specific performance, memory, and identities

> The core meaning of any individual or group identity, namely, a sense of sameness over time and space, is sustained by remembering ... (John R. Gillis, 'Introduction: memory and identity: the history of a relationship' in *Commemorations: The Politics of National Identity*)

> Of course every culture remembers its past. But how a culture performs and sustains this recollection is distinctive and diagnostic. (Richard Terdiman, *Present Past: Modernity and the Memory Crisis*)

The act of remembering constitutes and produces identity, providing narratives or performances of events and times that are understood to define an individual or a community.[1] But remembering is not an objective act: each instance of remembering constitutes its subject differently and subjectively, eliminating some details and enhancing others as changing conditions demand.[2] Different versions of the 'same' memory serve different social functions and produce different effects of power. Positively, memories may validate identities that have been historically marginalised or oppressed, and they may revise potential imbalances in the power dynamics between communities. Less positively, memories may define other communities as inherently inferior and omit or forget features that trouble the image of itself a community is striving to create. Given these ambivalent potentials, it is important to examine communities' recounted memories to learn what identities they produce – for whose benefit, to whose disadvantage – and how remembering may be a progressive or regressive political act.

Theatre and other forms of performance contribute importantly to the memory work of specific communities – especially, for my purposes here, national communities. They provide versions or stagings of memory through, for example, narrative, scenography, and casting. And they perform those stagings often specifically for an audience that makes up at least part of the community that is remembered, an audience which, as Maureen Hawkins puts it, 'embodies the "national consciousness" the playwright perceives as creating the present with which he or she is concerned and/or as having the power to create the future that he or she desires'.[3] Such performance engages audiences in negotiating, formulating, and changing their relationships to their pasts – and so also their presents and futures.

Site-specific performance can be especially powerful as a vehicle for remembering and forming a community for at least two reasons. First, its location can work as a potent mnemonic trigger, helping to evoke specific past times related to the place and time of performance and facilitating a negotiation between the meanings of those times. As Pierre Nora explores in his multi-volume collaborative work *Les Lieux de mémoire* – which may be translated as the sites or realms of memory – memory is invested in and stimulated by sites.[4] These can be what Nora describes as symbolic sites (such as a minute's silence), functional sites (a reunion), or actual material sites, for example monuments, graveyards, and buildings.[5] When located in a material realm of memory such as a building that evokes significant memories for a community – a building that is a 'haunted house', to adopt Marvin Carlson's resonant phrase – site-specific performance can be exceptionally evocative of those memories and times and, so, especially effective in constituting group identities related to them.[6] Site-specific performance can enact a spatial history, mediating between the past and the present most obviously, but also between the identities of the past and those of the present and future, as well as between a sense of nostalgia for the past and a sense of otherness possibly felt in the present and anticipated in the future. 'Part of what performance knows', writes Peggy Phelan, 'is the impossibility of maintaining the distinction between temporal tenses, between an absolutely singular beginning and ending'.[7] This performance 'knowledge'– informed by its inherent condition of being ephemeral – is enhanced in site-specific work which specifically invokes not only the past/present of its performance but also that of a site resonant with emphatic significations of the past. Second, by being materially and spatially formed and located in ways which differ from performance practice in conventional theatre buildings and spaces, site-specific performance can be especially effective at remembering and constituting identities that are significantly determined by their materiality and spatiality, identities to do with, for example, class, occupation, and gender.[8]

'History plays' – which commonly narrate events in national histories – have been prevalent in Britain and Ireland throughout the twentieth century, perhaps especially following the influence of Brecht's plays and theories. They have also received extensive analysis.[9] Site-specific memory plays have been less prevalent, relatively speaking, and so has their analysis.[10] However, they have been deeply, and perhaps increasingly, influential, especially for their capacities, first, to negotiate the relations between memories or histories and particular sites – what Doreen Massey and other geographers refer to as 'space-time'[11] – and, second, to explore material conditions that have helped to shape communities. A very important relatively early example is 7:84 (Scotland)'s *The Cheviot, the Stag and the Black, Black Oil*, which explored the history of the Scottish Highlands' exploitation by various outsiders and incomers and was performed throughout 1973 around Scotland, often in community centres.[12] At the risk of generalising, a handful of more recent – and diverse – examples might include Bill Bryden's *The Ship* (1990), performed in the Glasgow docks, Bobby Baker's *Kitchen Show* (1991), performed in her kitchen, Forced Entertainment's bus tour, *Nights in the City* (1995), originally produced in Sheffield, and Douglas Maxwell's *Decky Does a Bronco* (2000), performed in a playground, originally in Edinburgh. Site-specific memory performances were the stock in trade of Wales's Brith Gof, as I explore in more detail below, and have also been significant commissions by such organisations as the London-based Artangel and LIFT, the London International Festival of Theatre.[13]

This chapter looks in detail at two site-specific performances that evoked and engaged with their local communities' memories in order to re-constitute those communities' identities. These performances are Brith Gof's *Gododdin* (1988–90), initially produced in a disused Cardiff car factory at a time of significant economic crisis for Wales, and the Northern Irish theatre company Tinderbox's *convictions* (2000), performed in Belfast's also disused Crumlin Road Courthouse two years into the peace process initiated by the 1998 Good Friday Agreement.[14] This chapter aims to assess what identities the performances produced and how their site-specificity – as well as their temporal specificity – particularly affected their meanings. It looks at these two specific shows for a number of reasons. They were effective memory plays in that they strongly evoked locally situated memories and influenced understandings of national identity, in both instances in a 'difficult and conflicted period of transition'.[15] Brith Gof was probably the best-known and most prolific producer of site-specific performance in the UK throughout the 1980s and 1990s, and *Gododdin* was in many respects representative of their work. As a site-specific performance, *convictions* was something of a departure from Tinderbox's usual focus on playwriting, but it made a significant intervention in Belfast's public culture at a time of particular political sensitivity and potential change in Northern Ireland. The two shows offer

for analysis useful points of comparison and contrast, relating to historical, geographical, political, and social contexts, as well as production
methods, aesthetics, and touring practices.

Given Wales's and Northern Ireland's mutual status as historically
marginalised – even colonised – nations in the larger context of the United
Kingdom, both shows, especially *Gododdin*, worked to validate and promote
a sense of these nations' histories and identities. They helped to build and
authenticate identities excluded or oppressed by formerly prevalent practices and discourses and, in so doing, to empower their audiences. Both
shows also, however, worked to interrogate any entirely stable sense of what
the national identity was, preventing one rigid, essentialist understanding
of national identity from simply being replaced by another. Produced in
the context of an unstable peace process, *convictions* was particularly
resistant to providing intractable understandings of Northern Irish history
and identities, but *Gododdin* too was wary of reducing Welsh identity to a
singular identity – especially a romanticised one. Both shows exploited the
potentials of site-specific performance to be especially evocative of
memory and to superimpose multiple histories – including that of their
presents: *Gododdin*'s disused car factory summoned memories of Wales's
particular labour and class histories, and *convictions*' disused courthouse
evoked Northern Ireland's particular histories of conflict, prosecution, and
punishment. In a bid also to 'remember' Wales as European and international, Brith Gof toured *Gododdin* to a series of other, usually non-theatre
venues throughout Europe, losing – or forgetting – some of the very
emphatic memories that its location in Wales had produced for the show
and for Welsh identity. *Convictions*, on the other hand, was only ever produced in a single three-week run in the Crumlin Road Courthouse,
remaining onsite to engage with this very particular building, its history,
and its implications for Northern Irish identities. Specifically located in
time as well as space, *convictions* forced an acknowledgement of its own
obsolescence and of the provisional nature of both its particular version of
Belfast's memories and, by extension, any remembered version of history
and of the nation. Both shows demonstrate the potential of site-specific
performance to explore spatial and material histories and to mediate the
complex identities these histories remember and produce.

## Brith Gof/faint recollections

Brith Gof was probably Wales's internationally best-known performance
company. Established in 1981 by Mike Pearson and Lis Hughes Jones in

Aberystwyth, West Wales, the company made performance featuring Welsh language and performers and ran until the late 1990s, prolifically producing and touring work – reportedly creating forty performances in thirteen countries by 1990.[16] Throughout its long and dynamic production history, Brith Gof was concerned with Welsh cultures, languages, histories, mythologies, and, indeed, memories: 'scattered memories'[17] or, in Pearson's words, 'faint recollections'[18] are translations for its Welsh name. It was Welsh theatre more broadly that Pearson claimed 'might provide a valuable forum for the creating, challenging and changing of identities – artistic, personal, communal and national', but he might easily have described Brith Gof's work in the same terms.[19] Throughout its history, Brith Gof created or adapted its own performance sites. It deemed Wales's relatively few purpose-built theatres as 'problematic in one way or another',[20] not least because, as company co-director Cliff McLucas argued, 'the Welsh-speaking community may see them as "colonial outposts"'.[21] Furthermore, the company preferred what McLucas called 'host sites',[22] places such as Carlson's 'haunted houses' which evoked significant memories and associations for the company's audiences. Initially, Brith Gof made relatively small-scale and often intimate performances in studio spaces and 'found' sites, for example a farm kitchen.[23] With *Gododdin* in 1988, the company moved to large-scale site-specific contexts and works, making a shift in scale that also shifted the company's focus from domestic and potentially more personal and female-dominated sites and concerns to industrial, social and male-dominated ones.

Fundamental to Brith Gof's work, therefore, was a commitment to exploring Welsh identities, first, in the 'real', lived environments where the memories which produced those identities were located – as opposed to purpose-built theatres – and, second, in environments of social, industrial, and economic activity (or forced inactivity) which so significantly constituted many people's – especially men's – experience of Welsh identity at that time of accelerated decline in Wales's mining, steel production, and heavy manufacturing industries.[24] Pearson has compared this theatrical working practice to 'the attractive notion of "deep maps" which combine the geography and natural history of a given location with accounts of the history and lived experience of its inhabitants'.[25]

While Brith Gof was very concerned with making its work for Welsh audiences and taking it to them, it was also concerned to make international work for international audiences. Thus, it toured its work internationally, principally throughout Europe, and it adopted and adapted international performance methods – especially ones pioneered by practitioners from continental Europe, including Grotowski, Barba, and Kantor[26] – to create its own hybrid performance practice featuring extreme physical action as well as a strong emphasis on scenography, music, and text. Brith Gof's campaign to locate and define itself and its methods as international, and especially European, was strongly motivated by its ambition to locate and define Wales likewise. According to Pearson, it was especially appropriate to do this by tracing Welsh theatrical training and influence – or memory – to European sources given that there was no deep theatrical history or orthodoxy in Wales at the time. 'With no mainstream tradition defining what theatre ought to look like, with no national theatre prescribing an orthodoxy of theatrical convention, with no great wealth of playwriting,' Pearson argued, 'then theatre in Wales still has options. It has the chance to address different subject-matters, using different means, in spaces other than the silent and darkened halls of theatre auditoria.'[27] By remembering itself as European, furthermore, Welsh theatre could reject a potential alternative remembering of itself as postcolonial, derivative, and peripheral in its relationship to English theatre. Indeed, Pearson claimed, 'the forms, techniques, preoccupations and placement of a Welsh theatre might bear little relation to those of its English neighbour'.[28] Brith Gof's strategy was to turn what was conventionally seen as a postcolonial disadvantage of having little practice it would recognise as indigenous and not imperially imposed – of having only 'faint recollections' – into the advantage of being able to invent its history and itself.

### *Gododdin*'s narration of memory through contemporary practices

Brith Gof's many imperatives – to speak to and for Welsh and international audiences, in socially situated environments, making social critique – are all manifested in *Gododdin*.[29] Its source text was the elegy, *Y Gododdin*, which Pearson describes as 'one of the earliest surviving examples of Welsh poetry, transcribed in the twelfth century but commemorating an event in the sixth', namely a battle in which an army of Anglo-Saxons a hundred thousand strong, 'who were already consolidating their occupation of much of present-day England', overwhelmingly defeated a warrior-band of three hundred Gododdin from what is now North Yorkshire.[30] Although the Gododdin were not from what is present-day Wales, their shared Celtic ancestry with the people of that area meant

they could – and did – call upon the Welsh to fight with them, and ultimately to die with them. By remembering this text in performance, Brith
Gof's *Gododdin* celebrated the historical depth of Welsh language and
literature and challenged the ways Welsh language especially is marginalised in contemporary British culture. It remembered Welsh identity as
one that stands up to imperial oppression and domination, even in the
face of overwhelming opposition. And it remembered itself in the positive terms of *belonging* to one community – with shared Celtic identity,
languages, history, bravery, and loyalties – rather than the negative terms
of being excluded from and oppressed by another community. To under-
line this orientation, in Brith Gof's *Gododdin*, 'there was no enemy',[31] as
Pearson puts it: the opposing Anglo-Saxons were never 'shown'. It was
only the Gododdin who were represented by performers, not as
triumphant certainly, in this 'lament for loss',[32] but as proud, brave, vigor-
ous, willing, and even heroic in their self-sacrifice.

Although its subject was historical, *Gododdin* was distinctly not atavis-
tic. Its scenography, music, and performance methods were all emphatically contemporary, insisting that the performance was immediately
relevant and that Welsh culture itself was not simply backward-looking,
but up-to-date and participating in and influencing current artistic practice. The scene of battle was represented non-naturalistically in a geomet-
ric arrangement of hundreds of tons of sand, thousands of gallons of
water which eventually flooded part of the performance space, pine trees
suspended from the ceiling (in those venues where there was a ceiling),
banners, rope nets, and the clearly anachronistic details of wrecked cars,
concrete, corrugated iron, and oil drums (see McLucas's scenographic
layout for the production in Cardiff in figure 6). Although the audience
could not enter the performance area, it was free to move around it. Lis
Hughes Jones sang and spoke fragments of *Y Gododdin* in English and
Brythonic (a form of proto-Welsh), boldly combining old, new, and
regional language variations in ways that credited them all as being poetic
and Welsh. Her voice and its text, however, competed for audibility with
acoustic and amplified sound created by the performers (for example, by
crashing shields made from car bonnets), recorded music, and the roar-
ing live music of Brith Gof's collaborators on this project, the industrial
percussion group Test Department. Invoking a Celtic heritage, the four
male actor/performers wore deep-red kilts while the two female
actor/performers wore dresses in the same material. Invoking an industrial present and a countercultural ethos, all the performers wore Dr
Marten boots. Narrative was not told but was physically performed in

task-based sequences that indicated, for example, the Gododdin army's gathering, arming, journey, battle, and lament.[33] While the *Gododdin* performers did not fight against personified Anglo-Saxons, they did fight against the tough and sometimes violent environmental conditions of the performance context – its loud, percussive, and pervasive sound, its slippery, hard, cold, and abrasive surfaces, its enormous, dwarfing space, the tall stacks of oil drums the performers leapt over and crashed into, and the steep incline of the rope net they attempted to climb while being sprayed with strong jets of cold water (figure 7). By presenting its historical or remembered subject through contemporary, often innovative, and certainly energetic methods, Brith Gof presented itself and its Welsh identity as equally contemporary, innovative, and energetic, importantly not defeated despite economic decline and political marginalisation.

### Labouring in the factory: *Gododdin*'s site-specificity

Of course, *Gododdin*'s other obvious contemporary reference was its site of production – in its December 1988 Welsh premiere, this was the disused and somewhat decrepit Rover car factory in the Cardiff dock-

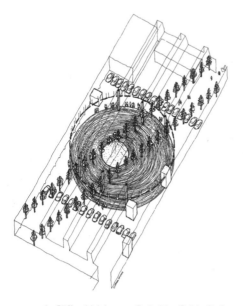

**6** Clifford McLucas, *Gododdin* (Brith Gof, 1988) at the old Rover car factory, Cardiff

**7** Brith Gof's *Gododdin* (1988)

lands. As scenographer Cliff McLucas noted, 'Just by doing it in that building – by doing it in a place where there were no longer cars being manufactured – all kinds of resonances about cultural, economic and regional decline are brought in'.[34] *Gododdin* was to be Brith Gof's 'penultimate manifestation' of a longer and already well-established project inspired by Francisco Goya's eighty etchings, *The Disasters of War*,[35] and reflections on war certainly influenced and were manifested in this production. However, *Gododdin*'s more immediate and urgent stimuli were the industrial and social conditions in South Wales in the mid- to late 1980s – conditions of rapid industrial decline and spreading unemployment which, at 13.6 per cent in 1985, was some thirty per cent higher in Wales than in the UK as a whole.[36] '[T]he impetus to create the performance', Pearson records, 'came with the darkest days of "Thatcherism", a time when Margaret Thatcher herself proclaimed society dead'.[37] The war waged in *Gododdin* was as much against an historic Anglo-Saxon enemy as it was against the contemporary stripping away of Wales's industrial economy.

The factory triggered its audience's living memory of times of greater economic security followed by times of economic decline by offering itself as a palimpsest of the recent past and the present. The building's physical deterioration, coldness (a result and reminder of inactivity), and the very emptiness that allowed it to accommodate the gigantic architecture, expansive movement, and 'big' sound of *Gododdin*, all evidenced its current state of disuse. The show's scenographic feature of eight car bodies, 'distressed with thin white paint and with working headlights',[38] haunted the building, standing painfully inadequately in the place of the cars which had preceded them in this place and which were, by contrast, more plentiful, new, unspoilt, and importantly more economically valuable. Likewise, the show's physical labour – its frenetic activity and ultimately heat-producing energy – 'stood in' for the industrial labour that had animated the building previously, and challenged the inactivity imposed by the Rover branch plant's closure. While *Gododdin*'s text remembered Wales's deep history to celebrate and lament it, therefore, the site remembered Wales's more recent history of rapid de-industrialization and economic decline in order to lament it and to celebrate the Welsh people's strength in the face of it.

*Gododdin* remembered and constituted a strong and often positive narrative of Welsh identity as linguistically and culturally rich, loyal, creative, innovative, and brave, whether in the face of war, environmental onslaught, or economic decline. It did not, however, present an entirely unified sense of national identity that might then be seen as fixed or, indeed, exclusive and xenophobic. McLucas argued, 'The idea of an authentic Welshness which speaks for the heartland is a myth'.[39] Many of *Gododdin*'s makers and performers were Welsh but Welsh nationality was certainly not a prerequisite for participants. Both Pearson and McLucas, for example, came from England, and although Test Department included Scottish members it was based in South London. Further, the performance was not unified or linear, but layered and hybrid, 'entirely opposite to ideas of purity and authenticity', as McLucas put it.[40] This hybridity featured narratives of the Gododdin as both strong *and* defeated, it included both natural and manufactured materials, competing sounds, tumultuous action, and iconographic references to both the past and the present, and it produced both theatre practice and Welsh identities as hybrid. Nick Kaye has observed, 'Rather than look toward a synthesis of elements through performance, the guiding metaphor for the construction of Brith Gof's work ... has been the coexistence of distinct "architectures" inhabiting one another and the site itself without resolution into a synthetic whole'.[41] 'The dominant concern in orthodox theatre is to produce something that is like a well-formed, perfect object, a piece of sculpture', McLucas proposed. 'But everything we do is about hybridisation, about internal fractures within work, bodies of material that coexist rather than unify.'[42] *Gododdin* remembered Welsh history and identities with enough coherence to allow viable analysis and even a degree of celebration of them. But it resisted imposing the kind of coherence that would restrict the hybridity of those identities and limit their potential for future change.

The meanings produced by *Gododdin*'s site-specific performance in Cardiff were, of course, altered when it moved to different sites throughout Europe. Following its Cardiff premiere, *Gododdin* toured to a working sand quarry in Polverigi, Italy; an outdoor site in Hamburg, Germany; an ice hockey stadium in Leeuwarden, Frisland, the Netherlands; and the Tramway, a former tram garage converted to a performance and exhibition venue in Glasgow.[43] This movement added to *Gododdin* significations of adaptability, a capacity to look and speak outward as well as inward, and, importantly, an identity constituted as European as well as Welsh. It also showed an interest in revising dominant, even clichéd narratives of Welsh identity for both Welsh and European audiences. But by continuing to use Welsh language and Brith Gof's own hybrid performance aesthetic, *Gododdin* maintained its distinctiveness and resisted assimilating itself – and the Welsh identity it conveyed – to a *generic*, pan-European commodity. As Pearson says, 'I do think that this cultural specificity means that our work is often very problematic in, kind of, "Euro-theatrical" terms. I think we often consciously use naivete and all sorts of "non-U" techniques which are problematic in relation to air-brushed "Euro-products" that can move anywhere.'[44] The show produced itself as Welsh – but not conventionally Welsh – and European – but also distinctively Welsh.

While Brith Gof was able to choose its Cardiff site of production and to determine some of the show's site-specific references there, McLucas noted that, 'After that, when we did re-stagings of *Gododdin*, the sites chose us.'[45] In this process, *Gododdin* lost some of the Rover car factory's particular references and acquired some new – and sometimes unwelcome – ones. The biggest loss was the original show's references to a recent past marked by labour and post-industrial decline, key elements of the version of contemporary Welsh identities which the show aimed to remember and which it triggered so effectively by situating itself in a decommissioned car factory. Transplanted from the Cardiff site of enforced inactivity and arrested productivity to sites of active labour (the Italian sand quarry) and leisure (the Dutch hockey stadium), *Gododdin* certainly diminished – and potentially undermined – this aspect of its remembering of Welsh identities. As a former tram depot, Glasgow's Tramway shared with Cardiff's car factory a capacity to evoke memories of work, urban expansion, and mechanised transport. But the site took on different connotations in its then-recent and ongoing conversion into an international arts venue that, for Alasdair Cameron among others, was comparable to 'many other prestigious European theatre buildings like the Bouffes du Nord or the Cartoucherie de Vincennes in Paris and the Mercat dels Flors in Barcelona'.[46] As Cameron persuasively argued, the large Tramway can be credited as 'a catalyst for experimentation and the exploration of new forms of staging and theatre' in Scotland after its opening in 1988.[47] However, the venue's very similarity to a host of other industrial chic European venues suggests it might also be accused of succumbing to the kind of generic European commodity market that Pearson disparages, above. *Gododdin*'s contextualisation within such an 'established theatrical estate',[48] to borrow Baz Kershaw's phrase, might again displace memories of local labour pools and industrial decline with new associations and memories of consumption rather than production, the international rather than the local, and gentrification. Certainly, there were ironies to be read in the paradoxical placement of *Gododdin* and its memories of industrial decline within these new sites of work, leisure, and international art consumption; nevertheless, the show lost some of the resonance of recent Welsh post-industrial decline that it so effectively evoked in the site of memory of the disused Cardiff docklands car factory.

In transferring this site-specific piece to other sites – and, indeed, markets – Brith Gof risked not only losing certain memories but also summoning other unwelcome ones. This was a particular problem in Germany, 'the one place that the show didn't work', according to Pearson.[49] At three weeks' notice, Brith Gof was informed that it was not permitted to present in the large hall it had been planning for and would have to move the show outside. Here, Pearson suggests, aspects of *Gododdin*'s scenography unwittingly evoked memories of the Holocaust: 'when you get semi-naked men and fire in Germany it means one thing. And that's where our problems lay.'[50] McLucas suggested further that Wales's history of oppression framed the show's potentially nationalist rhetoric as benign, whereas Germany's history of expansionist and aggressive nationalism framed it as malignant.

> The central problem is that a piece of work within Wales which is about 'nationalism' takes on entirely different meanings when transported into Germany. It's a different kind of nationalism. If we're talking about a defensive nationalism, a kind of nationalism which comes from centuries of abuse[,] and move that into a place where there was actually an expansionistic, destructive kind of nationalism – it's the same word, but not the same thing.[51]

Brith Gof's experiences in moving and showing *Gododdin* around Europe seem at least partially to reinforce a claim Pearson has made about site-specific performances: 'They are inseparable from their sites, the only context within which they are readable.'[52] In Cardiff's disused Rover car factory, *Gododdin* was distinctly readable as a performance remembering an enduring Welsh language, culture, bravery, history of oppression, sense of European identity, and sense of loss – in war, but also and immediately in industry and economic livelihood. It was also readable as a performance constituting a hybrid national identity, not immortalised and stuck in the past, but dynamic and changing in the present. It realised the potential of site-specific theatre to explore spatial and material histories and identities – particularly ones that were crucially important in the contexts of postcolonialism and industrial decline in the late 1980s in Wales. In its production in different sites throughout Europe, many of these meanings were still resonant and some, like the sense of European identity, were enhanced. However these new sites' specificity brought new 'memories' and invoked different histories, potentially diminishing what was a very important emphasis on Wales's then-current experience of economic decline. Recognising some of the problematics of touring site-specific performance, Brith Gof subsequently concentrated less on international touring and more on producing work specifically for communities sited throughout Wales. Increasingly uneasy with addressing such 'grand narratives' as nationalism,[53] Mike Pearson gradually shifted focus to smaller, more personal performance, eventually leaving Brith Gof to form, in 1997, Pearson Brookes with *Gododdin* collaborator Mike Brookes.[54]

## Tinderbox's *convictions*

Unlike *Gododdin*, *convictions* was only ever produced over a three-week period in a single site for a local community. It was produced for the Belfast at Queen's Festival in the autumn of 2000 by Tinderbox Theatre Company in the then-disused Crumlin Road Courthouse. Decommissioned in 1998 after the Good Friday Agreement, the Courthouse had been the site of some of the most notorious trials in the history of Northern Ireland's Troubles. *Convictions* aimed to examine issues of justice and was composed of a series of installations and seven short plays by playwrights from or settled in Northern Ireland.[55] Through a variety of formal, narrative and site-specific strategies, it acknowledged but also in some ways de-authorised hegemonic memories and understandings of Belfast in particular and Northern Ireland more broadly, especially understandings which foregrounded these places' sectarian and colonial pasts and presents. It also built alternative understandings of Belfast and Northern Irish identities, identities defined, for example, not only by conventionally recognised and enforced colonial, political, and religious memories and relationships but also by class and gender. It did not create definitive new meanings and identities, but meanings and identities that disrupted and destabilised those of the past, proposed alternatives, and empowered audiences by demonstrating the potential for social change.

## *Convictions*' dialogic narratives

*Convictions*' punning title begins to indicate how the production both acknowledged and undermined the baggage of identity that Belfast and Northern Ireland carry. It played on the multiple meanings of 'conviction' as both 'belief' and 'sentence', conflating them as the Courthouse did when it sentenced prisoners for actions committed out of allegiance to their beliefs, whether they were Catholic or Protestant, nationalist or unionist, republican or loyalist, or something else again. Pluralised and not capitalised, *convictions* recognised the multiple and often complex beliefs that exist in Belfast and undermined the stability that the singular, capitalised 'Conviction' might suggest. The plural form invited audiences to consider not only the religious and political convictions which so dominate Belfast's and Northern Ireland's public discourses, but also other social and cultural beliefs held by the Northern Irish and forming their identities. Finally, by taking on the names of the places where they were performed, the seven short plays which made up the whole event gave varying signals, invoking the objectivity of clinical description but also the irony of contrast, juxtaposing the austerity of 'Court No. 1' by Owen McCafferty with the 'piss take' of 'Male Toilets' by Daragh Carville. From its very choice of titles, *convictions* acknowledged the enormous influence and importance of both belief and the law in Northern Ireland, even as it compelled an understanding of both as plural, complex and, to at least some degree, unstable and subjective.

*Convictions*' title is indicative of the show's pervasive dialogism and its refusal to uphold any dominant version of the history of the courthouse or Belfast, much less to offer its own definitive version. Dialogism, one of the key terms pioneered by Russian literary critic Mikhail Bakhtin,[56] describes a discourse that does not aim to impose a unified, coherent, even official version of events but instead admits and articulates differences and indeterminacy. Like polyphony, another concept developed by Bakhtin, dialogism includes but does not assimilate many and often contradictory voices and opinions. *Convictions* was dialogic because it incorporated but did not synthesise a range of voices, genres, and media. Characters included those who ruled the Courthouse, like the Judge of Damian Gorman's 'seethingly corrosive'[57] 'Judge's Room'; those who were ruled by it, like the inmate Mad Dog Brannigan in Gary Mitchell's 'Holding Room'; and those whose positions were literally liminal, like the ghost Victim in 'Court No. 1'. Generically, *convictions*' individual plays took on a variety of attitudes and styles, from the reverent to the satirical. 'Holding Room' was a brief, poignant realistic scene in which Mad Dog Brannigan, just sentenced and on his way from courthouse to gaol via Crumlin Road's notorious tunnel, railed with macho bravado against his guard until left alone in the dark of a holding cell where the audience could hear him '*whimpering, sobbing*'.[58] Marie Jones's 'Court No. 2', by contrast, was a 'knockaround comedy'[59] involving two consultants and a '*passionate, arrogant, undiscovered genius*'[60] musician, all charged with transforming the Courthouse into an interactive heritage centre. Both serious and irreverent, neither impression was necessarily prioritised in the audience's experience of *convictions* because the audience – or more precisely audiences – encountered individual plays in different orders. With a total capacity of eighty, *convictions* accommodated the audience as a whole for only three plays out of seven, including in Court No. 2 at the beginning and in the Main Hall at the end.[61] For the intervening plays, the audience was arbitrarily divided into four groups of twenty and led through different itineraries of the building, its plays, and its takes on the Courthouse's and Belfast's past, present and future.[62]

*Convictions*' media, too, were diverse and often unsynthesised and included the short plays, a sound score, art installations including video, the printed programme (with interviews, photographs, and all the plays' texts), and the textuality of the building itself. Like its individual play texts, *convictions*' dialogic media acknowledged dominant historical and social narratives of the building and of Belfast and destabilised those narratives, especially by presenting alternatives that have otherwise been marginalised or silenced. Artist Amanda Montgomery's installations of floating women's hats, violently scattered broken crockery (figure 8), and a child's

**8** Detail of Amanda Montgomery's canteen installation for *convictions* (Tinderbox Theatre Company, 2001) at the Crumlin Road Courthouse, Belfast

toy plane circling the post room also included video and Neil Martin's sound compositions but no coherent narrative voice or explanation besides her few comments recorded in the programme.[63] They assumed a meaningful silence, directly indicating the stories that had been silenced by the Courthouse – especially the stories of women and children whose lives the Courthouse had so significantly affected. Indirectly, they acknowledged the many memories of Belfast and the Troubles that have not been told.

Although the audience was not led down the underground tunnel connecting courthouse and gaol, Montgomery's installations included some video footage of the tunnel, co-created with filmmaker Hugh McGrory, in which she aimed 'to recreate the damp dark last walk'.[64] This video significantly differed from the audience's most likely former media relationship to the Courthouse – through television news reports, generically composed to produce particular narratives of justice. 'It was never off the news', notes *convictions* composer Neil Martin, 'that infamous focus-pull from barbed wire to scales' on the statue of Justice atop the building (see figure 9).[65] For Mark Lawson, 'the Crumlin Road Courthouse became infamous in the 1970s when the barbed wire attached to the top of its elegant walls was featured in news reports on the

**9** Crumlin Road Courthouse, Belfast

committals or trials of the numerous people accused there of terrorism'.[66] Such widespread public media representations reinforced the Courthouse's authority by focusing on the public, official façade of the building. By linking the barbed wire with the façade and its statue, they also potentially reinforced the building's conflation of physically coercive control with justice. Montgomery's video literally undermined this official media narrative of the building, focusing on its underground tunnel as a site of containment, isolation, and suppression. I discuss the textuality of the building itself in more detail below, but it is worth noting here that the production's diverse and sometimes conflicting literary texts included the building's pervasive, unavoidable and often threatening graffiti inscribed by a range of Belfast's citizens.[67]

*Convictions* was also disruptive in its narrative remembering of the past, foregrounding the inevitable subjectivity of any representation of the past, warning against glorifying the past, and notably avoiding direct reference to certain infamous – or, for some, famous – aspects of the Courthouse's history. Marie Jones's opening play, 'Court No. 2', was explicit in its depiction of the subjectivity which informs various memories of the Courthouse. '[C]orporate' Karen, whose job it is '*to oversee the new project of turning the site into a heritage centre*', naively imagines that the Courthouse's history was neutral and unbiased, and that its present representation should reflect that. '[O]verly enthusiastic' Claire, who is charged with realising the centre, has different ideas. For her, the 'criminal' is 'leering, unrepentant, showing no remorse'. For musician Fabian, however, the 'victim' is 'a proud man, upright, no signs of caving in, proud, a soldier, a fighter, a zealot ... he should look like [the film star] George Clooney'.[68]

Several of the plays were scathing in their indictment of current desires to romanticise and glorify the Courthouse's victims and the Troubles. The Photographer in Carville's 'Male Toilets' speaks ruefully of the days when the Troubles gave Belfast 'an internationally recognised brand-name', and suggests that the city might still need 'Just the odd wee bomb' to 'Make Belfast – a boom-town again'.[69] In Damian Gorman's 'Judge's Room', Mr Justice Colin Wellblood tries to drum up support for his Troubles Opera Trust – or 'TOT' – premiere production of '*Der NordIrischeKriegZyklus – The Ulster War Cycle*', a production he calls 'a kind of Wagnerian *Riverdance* for the Troubles' and which is epitomised for him not by the citizens who experienced the war but by his poster image of a German soprano 'arising helmeted and majestically-breasted from the blackened ruins of Belfast'.[70] These plays acknowledged residual yearnings for the Troubles – for their apparent certainties, their passions, and indeed their celebrity and attendant 'glamour'. But they also mocked these yearnings as misdirected, perverse, and even cruel, warning against nostalgic, lionising memorialisations of the Troubles.

Significantly, although Montgomery played back some audio recorded facts about some of the Courthouse's most famous trials in her installation in Courtroom 6,[71] none of *convictions'* individual plays 'touched on Diplock, Supergrasses or the Butchers',[72] the most famous aspects of the Courthouse's Troubles' history. Perhaps because those stories are already so authoritative and so deeply embedded in the public consciousness of Belfast, the playwrights – and Montgomery, in most of her installations – told other, less sensational, or more common stories. The plays told of a man jailed for domestic murder (Martin Lynch's 'Main Hall'), a schoolteacher shot dead while coaching his students in badminton ('Court No. 1'), and a woman whose father was murdered ('Judge's Room'). They also told not about the past but about the present, about what it means to be living 'post-Troubles' ('Court No. 2', 'Male Toilets', and 'Judge's Room'). And they told about the mundane and daily cruelty of the Courthouse, its horrible but unspectacular effects on incarcerated prisoners ('Holding Room') and the routine intimidation of jurors (Nicola McCartney's 'Jury Room'). *Convictions'* relationship to hegemonic narratives of the Courthouse's high-profile past was by turns explicitly subjective, ironically irreverent, and wilfully dismissive. It highlighted the vested interests at stake in glorious portrayals of the Courthouse and heroic portrayals of its former players. By refusing explicitly to acknowledge the Courthouse's most well known, sensational, and uncontested history, it perhaps acknowledged a fatigue with remembering and with trusting in apparent certainties, especially in the context in which it was produced, with the peace process following the Good Friday Agreement injured but limping on towards no faction's triumphant finish line. As playwright Martin Lynch put it, 'we haven't gone from war to peace, from conflict to resolution', and 'some of the pieces accurately reflect that'.[73]

*Convictions* was pervasively disruptive and dialogic. It displaced the audience's conventional relationship to the Crumlin Road Courthouse and its history, decisively undermining a hegemonic remembering of the building as evidence of Northern Ireland's irreducible and sole basis in sectarianism, as representative of an uncomplicated understanding of justice, and as a site of strictly official discourse. *Convictions* offered its audience no single, comfortable position from which to relate to either the building itself or the events that happened there. However, it did offer multiple, varied, and often previously marginalised or silenced per-spectives on the Courthouse and its activities. By suggesting some of the other concerns besides religion and politics that inform life in Northern Ireland, *convictions* began to acknowledge the complexity of a term like 'justice' and the variety of ways it could be interpreted by different par-ties in different contexts, and it accommodated instead of oppressing the voices and stories of the marginalised, including the Courthouse's convicted and the women who worked, visited, and were also tried and sentenced there.

### Entering, occupying, and installing in the Courthouse: *convictions*' site-specificity

As with *Gododdin*, *convictions*' specific social contexts of production, in time and space, were crucial to its meaning. Temporally, *convictions*' production in the autumn of 2000 placed it in the context of a breakthrough in the history of the Troubles in Northern Ireland, coming after approval of the Good Friday Agreement in 1998, and the commencement of devolution and establishment of the Northern Ireland assembly in 1999. Also coming after violent events such as the Real IRA bombing in Omagh which killed twenty-nine people, after repeated temporary suspensions of devolution and the reimposition of direct rule from London, and more immediately after a particularly violent marching season in summer 2000 and a rocket attack on MI6's London headquarters by dissident republi-cans in September 2000,[74] *convictions*' production context was also extremely unstable politically. As performer Vincent Higgins wrote, the temporal context for the production was 'where we are now, in this no winners, post-troubles society'.[75] For the editors of *Politics and Performance in Contemporary Northern Ireland*, this context of diminished *armed* struggle remains a context in which 'Symbolic struggle is especially important', and the symbolic acts of staged performance bear exceptional political potential.[76]

The physical context for the production was 'one of Belfast's most infamous buildings',[77] the Crumlin Road Courthouse. Closed in 1998 as the peace process rendered it redundant, the Courthouse was notorious nevertheless for 'having been for decades an epicentre of the Troubles in the city'.[78] Surrounded by sites of sustained and often intense violence, with North Belfast flanking it to the north, and the legendary Shankill and Falls roads less than a mile to the south, the Courthouse had been a place of reckoning for both republican and loyalist communities. 'Everyone who was anyone in republican and loyalist organisations stood in the dock here', claims the *Independent*'s reviewer, political writer David McKittrick.[79] It was the site of the trials of many of the Troubles' most infamous accused, including the Shankill Butchers. It was notorious for its freewheeling approaches to justice signalled by its juryless Diplock trials adopted in 1973[80] as well as its notorious 'supergrasses', unnamed 'converted terrorists'[81] who testified against – or 'grassed' – those they claimed were their former associates. And it was ominously 'partnered by means of a subterranean passage to the grim and forbidding [Crumlin Road] Gaol across the road.'[82] McKittrick conjectures that 'more than 10,000 republicans, loyalists and others were tried by the Diplock non-jury courts' at the Courthouse, and hazards a 'rough guess' that 'the judges who heard these cases handed down sentences that totalled more than a quarter of a million years'.[83] As a site of memory, therefore, the Crumlin Road Courthouse was enormously resonant for the Troubles, for Belfast, for Northern Ireland, and for *convictions'* audiences.

By entering, occupying, and installing work in the Courthouse, *convictions* challenged the site's dominant position in the social memory of Belfast, as well as the physical, intellectual, and emotional topography of the city. It undermined the Courthouse's assumption of authority by challenging the obedience the building enforced in Belfast's citizens and it destabilised the extraordinary power assumed by the Courthouse by filling it with the ordinary and everyday and acknowledging its banal unpleasantness. Not triumphant in its occupation of the Courthouse – a tactic which would have risked only inverting instead of dismantling the Courthouse's former hierarchical ordering of power – *convictions* nevertheless intervened in the Courthouse's history, adding its own stories to those that had gone before, and altering the terms in which the Crumlin Road Courthouse, Belfast, and Northern Ireland might subsequently be remembered and understood.

The writings of French sociologist Henri Lefebvre help to elucidate how the Courthouse historically assumed an apparently inviolable dominance in the social memory and physical landscape of Belfast. Lefebvre argued that space instructs and prohibits, coercively producing particular social practices and power dynamics.[84] 'Activity in space', he writes, 'is restricted by that space; space "decides" what activity may occur ... Space lays down the law because it implies a certain order ... Space commands bodies, prescribing or proscribing gestures, routes and distances to be covered.'[85] The authority space produces frequently works in the interests of the state since it is often the state that has produced or 'dominated'[86]

the space. However, the benefits to the state – and the coercion or control
of the state's citizens – may not themselves be immediately obvious
because the organisation of space is made to seem collectively agreed
upon and favourable. 'Repressive space', Lefebvre argues, 'wreaks repression and terror even though it may be strewn with signs of the contrary
(of contentment, amusement, or delight)'[87] – or, in the Courthouse's case,
of composure, peacefulness, balance, and justice. 'Monumentality, for
instance,' writes Lefebvre, 'always embodies and imposes a clearly intel-
ligible message. It says what it wishes to say – yet it hides a good deal more:
being political, military, and ultimately fascist in character, monumental
buildings mask the will to power and the arbitrariness of power beneath
signs and surfaces which claim to express collective will and collective
thought'[88] – and, in the case of a courthouse, collective good, justice, and
belief.

Through its monumental occupation and organisation of space, the
Crumlin Road Courthouse (figure 9) unilaterally laid down its own laws
imbued with what conservation architect Dawson Stelfox describes as
'Victorian moral self-righteousness'.[89] '[R]aised on a tall plinth and looking imperiously down', featuring 'overscaled classical orders' and a 'giant
portico', the Courthouse, Stelfox argues, 'was designed to impress all who
entered with the power and status of the law'.[90] Its monumental, regal,
and even fortress-like authority commanded Belfast's citizens to respect
and remember both its rule and its boundaries and to keep out – unless
invited or ordered to enter. Both *convictions'* composer Neil Martin and
installation artist Montgomery record that despite living in close proximity to the Courthouse, and despite Martin's confessed curiosity about the
place, neither of them had ever entered the building until commissioned
to work on *convictions*.[91] The same is conceivably true for many of *convictions'* other makers, as well as its audiences. Despite the Belfast at Queen's
Festival's perceived elitism, these audiences probably came from across
the sectarian divide given the mixed constituency of the show's makers
and the Courthouse's proximity to North Belfast, where Catholics and
Protestants live in multiple, small, adjacent communities spatially segre-
gated by the euphemistically named 'peace walls'.[92] By inviting these
participants into the Courthouse, *convictions* bade them transgress the '*lived
obedience*'[93] they had – likely unwittingly – learned to adopt in the face
of Belfast's many spatial regulations, including those which enforced the
Courthouse's enormous (UK) state authority.

After crossing the threshold, *convictions'* challenge to the spatial logic
of the Courthouse continued throughout the building. The audience's

itineraries led them through the building's formerly public spaces – its
Main Hall, courtroom galleries, and dining room – but also through its
formerly restricted spaces, both those which aggrandised the judiciary,
such as the relatively spacious upstairs Judge's Room, and those which
kept other Courthouse visitors 'in their place', including the ground-floor
Jury Room and the cramped, windowless basement prisoners' Holding
Room.[94] Importantly, although *convictions'* audiences were able to enter
and travel through the Courthouse, they were not allowed to forget the
spatial authority the building formerly commanded. After the first play,
guides costumed as guards divided the audience into four groups of
twenty, arbitrarily separating groups of friends and family who had come
to the show together, and reproducing – if only temporarily and relatively
mildly – the experience of separation the Courthouse had previously
occasioned for so many families, friends, and associates. Installations
inserted in the spaces between plays compelled audiences to remember
the building's repressive history, including its imperial history. Having
learned that Queen Victoria gave the Irish £2,500 after the famine but
also that she was a 'patron of Battersea dogs' home and had given a large
sum of money to them',[95] Montgomery made a plaster dog's head (fitted
with a real cow's tongue) and positioned it so that its gaze locked with that
of a large, long-standing, and centrally placed statue of Queen Victoria.
The installation subverted the statue's memorialisation of Victoria as
benevolent and authoritative, first, by suggesting that she was possibly
more generous towards dogs than to the Irish, and, second, by placing her
in an ocular stand-off with a dog whose appetite might have seemed all
too real given its flesh-and-blood tongue.

Other installations remembered and made present the building's
historical violence – spatial, emotional, and physical. They exposed the
violence the Courthouse masked with evenness and order by rendering
its surfaces uneven, whether cluttered with broken crockery and knives as
in the dining room (figure 8), or with hundreds of keys, barely visible in a
dark corridor and 'janglin'' like hundreds of mini-repetitive threats',[96] as
the character Ghost says in Lynch's 'Main Hall'. Various missiles made
the Courthouse's headspaces treacherous, with 'prison documents and
statements flying off walls on air currents'[97] (figure 10), hats suspended at
various heights down a corridor, and, in the 10 by 8 foot post room, a
child's toy plane circling the ceiling, screaming 'fire, fire'.[98] Knives stabbed
the dining room floor and letters pierced the post room walls, ceiling, and
floor, suggesting both the threat of violence posed *by* the building and a
felt violence *towards* the building.

10 Detail of Amanda Montgomery's hallway installation for
*convictions* (Tinderbox Theatre Company, 2001) at the
Crumlin Road Courthouse, Belfast

*Convictions* further highlighted the Courthouse's apparent duplicity –
its claim to represent justice and its perceived injustice – simply by drawing
attention to the building's sheer discomfort, both emotional and physical.
*Irish Theatre Magazine* editor Karen Fricker succinctly summarises the felt
hypocrisy of the Courthouse: 'For many, the Courthouse and its sister
structure across the road, the Crumlin Road Goal, represent not justice but
the breakdown of justice – the failure of societal structures to deal with the
hatred and violence that have plagued the North for many decades.'[99]
*Convictions* acknowledged that the Courthouse itself provided some of the
most resonant material metaphors for its own hypocrisy and brutality.
While, externally, the building familiarly enacted its own monumental

(state) authority, inside, it was 'crumbling', 'rotting', and 'freezing'.[100]
*Fortnight* reviewer Mairtín Crawford observed:

> Booking information recommended wrapping up warm and to wear
> boots. The place is freezing, damp, dark and decidedly unfriendly. There
> is paint and wallpaper peeling from the walls, floorboards missing, holes
> in the walls and windows, water dripping from the ceiling—a ready
> made house of horrors replete with its own ghosts. The atmosphere
> is stifling but fascinating and the set designers have done a marvellous
> job in working with the grim interior.[101]

In a detailed, insightful article on *convictions*, Michael McKinnie
observes that by reminding 'the audience that the building was once the
place of the British state', *convictions*' emphasis on the building's 'disrepair
was a commentary on that state's heavily circumscribed legitimacy in
contemporary Northern Ireland'.[102]

*Convictions*' plays and installations further worked to undermine the
assumed authority and elitism of the Courthouse by displacing its self-
authored history of extraordinary officialdom with the everyday vernacular – vernacular scenes, languages, and objects. None of the plays
presented a court case or even a judge with any authority; instead, they
presented random victims of the Troubles, Courthouse 'support staff',
journalists, project planners, and a few convicted criminals – all characters who were excluded and often oppressed by the Courthouse's ruling
elite. Instead of Received Pronunciation English and legal jargon, most
of the plays used recognisably local language and slang. And the installations' objects were icons not of elite authority – gavels and wigs – but
rather of the everyday and, sometimes, mass-production – cafeteria
crockery, keys, a child's toy, and letters. Repeatedly, the installations
referred to how the Courthouse was experienced not by the judiciary but
by prisoners, their families, and 'support staff' – especially women,
numerous but marginalised in this male-dominated realm. The
suspended ladies' hats referred to a memory recounted by Jimmy Boyd,
a shorthand writer at the Courthouse from 1948 to 1998.

> When I started they were all male shorthand writers, but then through
> the years all the men eventually left or died. Women came in and the
> women had to wear hats. They actually got an income tax allowance
> in those days of £145 per year for having to buy hats for to wear in
> court. It was like Ascot with them trying to outdo each other, and some
> of them had these big flowing things.[103]

The residual smell of boiled cabbage conjured by Montgomery in the kitchen referred to the food prepared by some of the Courthouse's other female workers, the cooks. As Montgomery notes, food prepared in this kitchen would have been eaten by all of the Courthouse's visitors, regardless of their status – 'lawyers, accused, victims, families',[104] loyalists, Irish nationalists, and others. Indeed, as one-time Courthouse Catering Manager Mary O'Donnell records in her interview, the same food was sometimes presented under different names to assuage different sensibilities: what was Irish Fry and Irish stew one day was Ulster Fry and mince steak stew another.[105]

The letters in the post room evoked the private writings of the inmates, their families, and friends, writings the Courthouse censored but – the installation suggested – nevertheless found secret ways to slip through the walls. And the toy plane referred to the fact that, 'When a parent on trial was to be sentenced children were not allowed to be present in the courtroom. Instead, a child could send or give their mother or father a toy or another reminder of them.'[106] These installation objects remembered and demonstrated the Courthouse's unofficial uses, functions, and histories, especially those experienced by people who were neither its judiciary and law enforcers or its accused but simply 'those passing through this building over the years',[107] people who were the families and friends of the accused or for whom the Courthouse was a daily workplace.

*Convictions* witnessed and memorialised understandings of the past, but restrained that memorialisation from nostalgically romanticising and fixing the past. To do this, it first added its own, present-day meanings to the history of the Courthouse, not erasing the Courthouse's past but decentring and recontextualising it in acknowledgment of the present and future. Second, the performance was knowingly – perhaps wilfully – ephemeral, working in some ways as a counter-monument, which Jeanette R. Malkin defines as 'an interactive, mobile, mutable, and self-effacing monument that act[s] as a provocation rather than a sanctified representation of the past'.[108] *Convictions* required its audiences to encounter it as mobile and transient by making them walk throughout the building from play to play. Its installations too were mobile – flying through the air – and literally superficial – covering surfaces. As a site-specific performance, the length of its access to the Courthouse necessarily limited *convictions'* run and it could and would not be remounted. Its temporary intervention produced a potential parallel with other events in the Courthouse's history and indicated the finiteness this event shared with particular trials, particular conflicts, and, even, the Troubles. This sense of finiteness or built-in obsolescence was enhanced by the Courthouse itself, now 'decommissioned', usually deserted, visibly crumbling, and moving towards its own uncertain future. Fricker succinctly identified the significance that the building's transitional state had for the show.

> Deserted since 1998, the future of the Courthouse is uncertain. Some argue it should be preserved for its historical significance, while others dispute that the history it contains bears preserving, and say the only thing for it is to tear it down. The genius of Tinderbox Theatre Company's *Convictions* project ... was its full exploitation of the Courthouse's metaphoric potential as a symbol of Northern Ireland itself, poised between a difficult but inescapable past and an uncertain future. With *Convictions* the Courthouse became a site for the staging of imagined pasts and futures; it was not a project about answers or solutions, but rather opened up a space for consideration of the issues involved.[109]

*Convictions* remembered the Crumlin Road Courthouse in ways that recognised people's awe and even hatred of it, but also constituted their power over it. The performance acknowledged that the Courthouse had posed as state-controlled, inviolable, and hierarchical, but showed too that, in some ways, it had also been controlled by all the people who populated it, ate in it, and visited it. The Courthouse was dangerous and violent, yes, but it was also banal. *Convictions* acknowledged the patterns of identity that the Troubles had made available – or, in some respects, mandatory – for the citizens of Belfast and, more broadly, Northern Ireland over the preceding thirty years. It acknowledged the pervasive and deeply embedded influence of sectarianism, the violence it both faced and engendered, and the pain the Troubles had produced, especially for Northern Ireland's least powerful citizens. But it did not glorify the Troubled past, and it emphasised that Belfast had multiple, dialogic histories. It remembered Belfast and Northern Ireland as constituted, indeed, by political and religions identities, but also by identities such as gender and class that the North's relentless cultural focus on the Troubles had marginalised. Perhaps most importantly, *convictions* remembered the Courthouse and its significations as ephemeral – one Belfast site of memory in a long line before and to follow. *Convictions* acknowledged the immense and inevitable significance of the past for the citizens of Belfast and Northern Ireland, but it presented that past as not monolithic or set and therefore, within limits, as available for reinterpretation.

## Now remember

Both *Gododdin* and *convictions* engaged their communities in remembering and reconstituting their national identities in socially constructive – but not dogmatic – ways. Both exploited the potentials of site-specific performance to be especially evocative of memory, and both demonstrated the significance of the temporal and physical contexts of production to exploring memories and identities that are profoundly influenced by their material conditions. Differences between the production histories of the two shows demonstrate that the *social* specificity of the location and timing of site-specific performance potentially matters profoundly. Brith Gof's touring allowed it to produce itself as a nomadic, European brand but this came partly at the expense of *Gododdin*'s Cardiff-based emphases on the significance of the decline of industrial labour to current Welsh identities.[110] *Convictions*' time-limited and singularly sited production demonstrated the effective but knowingly provisional kind of intervention that site-specific performance concerned with social memory and identities can make in places and times of acute, immediate cultural significance.

## Notes

1 John R. Gillis, 'Introduction: memory and identity: the history of a relationship', in Gillis (ed.), *Commemorations: The Politics of National Identity* (Princeton: Princeton University Press, 1994), pp. 3–24, p. 3; and Richard Terdiman, *Present Past: Modernity and the Memory Crisis* (Ithaca: Cornell University Press, 1993), p. 3.

2 Tradition is invented and often repeatedly and even coincidentally reinvented, especially in the interests of sustaining strong national imaginaries. Eric Hobsbawm and Terence Ranger (eds), *The Invention of Tradition* (Cambridge: Cambridge University Press, 1983).

3 Maureen S. G. Hawkins, 'Brenton's *The Romans in Britain* and Rudkin's *The Saxon Shore*: audience, purpose, and dramatic response to the conflict in Northern Ireland', in John P. Harrington and Elizabeth J. Mitchell (eds), *Politics and Performance in Contemporary Northern Ireland* (Amherst: University of Massachusetts Press, 1999), pp. 157–73, p. 157.

4 Pierre Nora (ed.), *Les Lieux de mémoire* (Paris: Editions Gallimard, 1984).

5 Pierre Nora, 'Between memory and history: *Les Lieux de mémoire*', *Representations* 26 (1989), 7–25, p. 19.

6 Marvin Carlson, *The Haunted Stage: The Theatre as Memory Machine* (Ann Arbor: University of Michigan Press, 2001), pp. 131ff.

7 Peggy Phelan, 'Introduction: the ends of performance', in Peggy Phelan and Jill Lane (eds), *The Ends of Performance* (New York: New York University Press, 1998), pp. 1–19, p. 8.

8  Live performance's ability to explore somatic aspects of memory such as space, scent, and sound can be especially effective in stimulating memory. Peter Middleton and Tim Woods, *Literatures of Memory: History, Time and Space in Postwar Writing* (Manchester: Manchester University Press, 2000), p. 152.

9  See, for example, D. Keith Peacock, *Radical Stages: Alternative History in Modern British Drama* (New York: Greenwood Press, 1991), Christopher Murray, *Twentieth-century Irish Drama: Mirror up to Nation* (Manchester: Manchester University Press, 1997), and Richard H. Palmer, *The Contemporary British History Play* (Westport, CT: Greenwood Press, 1998).

10  Although they do not focus particularly on memory, several works do look in some detail at site-specific performance. These include Nick Kaye, *Site-specific Art: Performance, Place and Documentation* (London: Routledge, 2000), Mike Pearson and Michael Shanks, *Theatre/Archaeology* (London: Routledge, 2001), and Fiona Wilkie, 'Mapping the terrain: a survey of site-specific performance in Britain', *NTQ: New Theatre Quarterly* 18:2 (70, 2002), 140–60.

11  See, for example, Doreen Massey, 'Places and their pasts', *History Workshop Journal* 39 (1995), 182–92, pp. 188ff.

12  John McGrath, *The Cheviot, the Stag and the Black, Black Oil* (London: Eyre Methuen, 1981), pp. 81–2. Wilkie provides more detail on the history of the form in Britain in 'Mapping the terrain'.

13  LIFT's commissions include Deborah Warner's *The St. Pancras Project* (1995) and *The Tower Project* (1999), and Artangel's include Neil Bartlett and Robin Whitmore's *The Seven Sacraments of Nicolas Poussin* (1997), performed at the Royal London Hospital, John Berger and Simon McBurney's *The Vertical Line* (1999), performed in the disused Aldwych Tube station in central London, and Janet Cardiff's audio walk, *The Missing Voice (Case Study B)*, available from the Whitechapel Library in East London since 1999. I discuss Artangel's commission by Steve McQueen, *Caribs' Leap/Western Deep* (2002), in detail in Chapter 7.

14  Because Tinderbox does not capitalise *convictions* in its published version of the text, I do not capitalise the title either, except where I quote others who do capitalise it.

15  Gillis, 'Introduction: memory and identity', p. 20.

16  Charmian C. Savill, 'Dismantling the wall', *Planet* 79 (1990) 20–8, p. 22. As David Adams notes, the company is also internationally well known within academic communities because of its members' prolific publishing. See David Adams, *Stage Welsh: Nation, Nationalism and Theatre: The Search for Cultural Identity* (Llandysul: Gomer, 1996), p. 55.

17  Elan Closs Stephens, 'A century of Welsh drama', in Dafydd Johnston (ed.), *A Guide to Welsh Literature, c.1900–1996* (Cardiff: University of Wales Press, 1998), pp. 233–70, p. 266.

18  Pearson in Pearson and Shanks, *Theatre/Archaeology*, p. xi.

19  Mike Pearson, 'Special worlds, secret maps: a poetics of performance', in Anna-Marie Taylor (ed.), *Staging Wales: Welsh Theatre, 1979–1997* (Cardiff: University of Wales Press, 1997), pp. 85–99, p. 85. For more information on Brith Gof see, for example: Kaye, *Site-specific Art*, pp. 52ff; Cliff McLucas and Mike Pearson (Brith Gof), interview with Nick Kaye in Nick Kaye, *Art into Theatre: Performance Interviews and Documents* (Amsterdam: Harwood Academic Publishers, 1996), pp. 209–34;

Pearson and Shanks, *Theatre/Archaeology*; Charmian C. Savill, 'Brith Gof', in Taylor (ed.), *Staging Wales*, pp. 100–10; and Geraldine Cousin, 'An interview with Mike Pearson of Brith Gof', *Contemporary Theatre Review* 2:2 (1994), 37–47.

20  Pearson in McLucas and Pearson in Kaye, *Art into Theatre*, p. 209.

21  McLucas in Clifford McLucas and Mike Pearson, interview, in Gabriella Giannachi and Mary Luckhurst, *On Directing: Interviews with Directors* (London: Faber and Faber, 1999), pp. 78–89, p. 83.

22  McLucas in McLucas and Pearson in Kaye, *Art into Theatre*, p. 213.

23  Savill, 'Brith Gof', p. 100.

24  Throughout the twentieth century and into the twenty-first, Wales has relied heavily on industrial manufacturing to provide a considerable proportion of its GDP. But this base has proved repeatedly vulnerable to worldwide fluctuations in oil and steel prices – particularly after the 1973 oil crisis and into the 1980s – as well as to branch plant closures, over which Wales can operate little or no control when the parent company is not based in Wales. Calvin Jones, 'Comparative disadvantage?: the industrial structure of Wales', in Jane Bryan and Calvin Jones (eds), *Wales in the 21st Century: An Economic Future* (Basingstoke: Macmillan, 2000), pp. 11–23, pp. 12–15.

25  Mike Pearson, 'Theatre/archaeology', *The Drama Review*, 38:4 (T144, 1994), 133–61, p. 151.

26  See Pearson, 'Special worlds', p. 98 especially, as well as Savill, 'Brith Gof', p. 101, and David Hughes, 'The Welsh National Theatre: the avant-garde in the diaspora', in Theodore Shank (ed.), *Contemporary British Theatre* (Basingstoke: Macmillan, [1994] revised edn, 1996), pp. 139–51, especially pp. 143–4.

27  Pearson, 'Special worlds', p. 85. David Adams similarly portrays professional Welsh theatre history as quite short, claiming that 'while performance has been part of Welsh culture for longer than most other European nations, the provision of professional theatre in Wales is actually less than thirty years old'. Adams, *Stage Welsh*, p. 21.

28  Pearson, 'Special worlds', p. 85.

29  No play text or complete video version of Brith Gof's *Gododdin* has been published; however, sections of performance in different sites are shown in the video *Gododdin*, directed and produced by Mike Parker and Martin McCarthy (Green Eye Productions for HTV, 1990), and it is described in some detail in Pearson and Shanks, *Theatre/Archaeology*, pp. 101–10, and in Savill, 'Dismantling the wall', pp. 20–2.

30  Pearson in Pearson and Shanks, *Theatre/Archaeology*, pp. 101–2.

31  *Ibid.*, p. 105.

32  Mike Pearson in Swithin Fry, 'Mike Pearson', in 'Profiles and Features', *Theatre in Wales*, www.theatre-wales.co.uk/people/mmikep.htm (accessed July 2001), originally printed in the *Western Mail* (5 February 1998).

33  Pearson in Pearson and Shanks, *Theatre/Archaeology*, p. 103.

34  McLucas in McLucas and Pearson in Kaye, *Art into Theatre*, p. 212.

35  Pearson in Pearson and Shanks, *Theatre/Archaeology*, p. 102.

36  Jones, 'Comparative disadvantage?', p. 13.

37  Pearson in Pearson and Shanks, *Theatre/Archaeology*, p. 102. As the first of Brith Gof's major large-scale works to be sited in a disused industrial site, *Gododdin* was followed by many others, including *Haearn* (Iron), performed in 1993 at the Old

British Coal Works in Tredegar, Wales (see Kaye, *Art Into Theatre*, p. 209), and *Prydain: The Impossibility of Britishness*, performed in 1996 in 'a chilly warehouse in Cardiff Bay' (Pauline McLean, 'Funky beat in Bay as band backs Brith Gof', *Western Mail* 28 February 1996, p. 12).

38  Pearson in Pearson and Shanks, *Theatre/Archaeology*, p. 104.

39  McLucas quoted in Savill, 'Dismantling the wall', p. 28.

40  *Ibid.*, p. 28.

41  Kaye, *Site-specific Art*, p. 53.

42  McLucas in McLucas and Pearson in Giannachi and Luckhurst, *On Directing*, p. 84.

43  McLucas's floor plans for three of these sites are reproduced in McLucas and Pearson in Kaye, *Art Into Theatre*, p. 214 (Italy), pp. 216 and 217 (the Netherlands), and in Savill, 'Dismantling the wall', p. 21 (Glasgow).

44  Pearson in *ibid.*, p. 219

45  McLucas in *ibid.*, p. 215.

46  Alasdair Cameron, 'Experimental theatre in Scotland', in Shank (ed.), *Contemporary British Theatre*, pp. 123–38, p. 125.

47  *Ibid.*, p. 125. For more on the Tramway's social and production history and its potential see Alasdair Cameron, 'Glasgow's Tramway: little Diagilevs and large ambitions', *Theatre Research International* 17:2 (1992), 146–55.

48  Baz Kershaw, *The Radical in Performance: Between Brecht and Baudrillard* (London: Routledge, 1999), p. 74.

49  Pearson in McLucas and Pearson in Kaye, *Art Into Theatre*, p. 215.

50  *Ibid.*, p. 215.

51  McLucas in *ibid.*, p. 219.

52  Mike Pearson and Cliff McLucas, 'The host and the ghost: Brith Gof's site-specific works' (no further bibliographic information given), quoted in McLucas and Pearson in Kaye, *Art Into Theatre*, p. 211. As Fiona Wilkie suggests, this approach to site-specific work suggests it might also be considered 'site-exclusive'. Wilkie, 'Mapping the terrain', p. 149.

53  Mike Pearson, 'From memory: or other ways of telling', *New Welsh Review* 30 (1995), 77–83, p.78.

54  'Pearson Brookes', *Theatre in Wales*, www.theatre-wales.co.uk/companies/company_details.asp?ID=24 (accessed July 2001).

55  Tinderbox's publication *convictions* collects the project's play texts, photographs from the Courthouse, statements from some of its artists, and further information. Ophelia Byrne (ed.), *convictions* (Belfast: Tinderbox Theatre Company, 2000). Further contextual information, extracts from reviews, and an excerpt from Owen McCafferty's play 'Court No. 1' are provided in Ophelia Byrne (ed.), *State of Play? The Theatre and Cultural Identity in 20th Century Ulster* (Belfast: The Linen Hall Library, 2001), pp. 138–41. Tinderbox's website provides information on the company and the show: www.tinderbox.org.uk (accessed October 2003). And Margaret Llewellyn-Jones's *Contemporary Irish Drama and Cultural Identity* (Bristol: Intellect, 2002) provides more useful context on contemporary Irish drama with some reference to *convictions* (pp. 160–1).

56  See, for example: Mikhail M. Bakhtin, *The Dialogic Imagination*, trans. Caryl Emerson and Michael Holquist, Holquist (ed.) (Austin: University of Texas Press,

1981); Bakhtin, *Problems of Dostoevsky's Poetics*, ed. and trans. Caryl Emerson (Minneapolis: University of Minnesota Press, 1984); and Bakhtin, *Rabelais and His World*, trans. Hélène Iswolsky (Bloomington: Indiana University Press, 1984).

57 Ian Shuttleworth, 'Escorted through the courthouse', review of *convictions*, *Financial Times* (20 November 2000).

58 Gary Mitchell, 'Holding Room', in Byrne (ed.), *convictions*, pp. 45–8, p. 48.

59 Mic Moroney, 'Court in the act', review of *convictions*, *Guardian* (1 November 2000).

60 Marie Jones, 'Court No. 2', in Byrne (ed.), *convictions*, pp. 9–12, p. 9.

61 Moroney, 'Court in the act'; David Grant in David Grant, 'Tim Loane in conversation with David Grant', in Lilian Chambers, Ger FitzGibbon, and Eamonn Jordan (eds), *Theatre Talk: Voices of Irish Theatre Practitioners* (Dublin: Carysfort Press, 2001), pp. 264–76, p. 268. Tim Loane is one of the founders, and a former Artistic Director, of Tinderbox Theatre Company.

62 Jocelyn Clarke, review of *convictions*, *Sunday Tribune* (26 November 2000); Karen Fricker, review of *Convictions*, *Irish Theatre Magazine* 2:8 (2001), 60–3, p. 61.

63 Amanda Montgomery, '*convictions* visual art installations', in Byrne (ed.), *convictions*, p. 13. The installations are described and illustrated in Amanda Montgomery, '*Convictions* at the Crumlin Road Courthouse', *Art Bulletin* 18:97 (2001), 16–18; and described in Mairtín Crawford, 'Convicted in the Crum', *Fortnight* (December 2000), 20–1, p. 20.

64 Montgomery, '*Convictions* at the Crumlin Road Courthouse', p. 18.

65 Neil Martin, 'The Crum', in Byrne (ed.), *convictions*, p. 49. A photograph of the Courthouse's statue of Justice, her scales noticeably now absent, appears on the cover of the *convictions* publication (Byrne [ed.]).

66 Mark Lawson, interview with Martin Lynch, *Front Row*, BBC Radio 4 (7 November 2000).

67 The insistent presence of the Courthouse's graffiti comes across in the numerous times it is mentioned in reviews and articles about the event. See, for example: Montgomery, '*Convictions* at the Crumlin Road Courthouse'; Lawson's interview with Martin Lynch on *Front Row*; Moroney, 'Court in the act'; and Vincent Higgins, 'Time well spent', *Fortnight* (December 2000), 22. John Baucher's photograph shows an example in Byrne (ed.), *convictions*, p. 32.

68 Jones, 'Court No. 2', pp. 9 11, ellipsis original.

69 Daragh Carville, 'Male Toilets', in Byrne (ed.), *convictions*, pp. 33–7, pp. 36 and 37.

70 Damian Gorman, 'Judge's Room', in Byrne (ed.), *convictions*, pp. 39–43, pp. 39 and 40.

71 Montgomery, '*Convictions* at the Crumlin Road Courthouse', p. 17.

72 Higgins, 'Time well spent'.

73 Lynch in interview with Lawson, *Front Row*.

74 An extensive chronology of the Troubles is included in David McKittrick and David McVea, *Making Sense of the Troubles* (Belfast: The Blackstaff Press, 2000), pp. 243–320, and they provide more detail on the period 1997–2000 in their penultimate chapter, titled 'Breakthrough' (pp. 215–29).

75 Higgins, 'Time well spent'.

76 John P. Harrington and Elizabeth J. Mitchell, Introduction, in Harrington and Mitchell (eds), *Politics and Performance in Contemporary Northern Ireland*, pp. 1–6, p. 1.

77  Higgins, 'Time well spent'.
78  David McKittrick, 'Courthouse takes centre stage as actors revisit horrors of Belfast', *Independent* (15 November 2000).
79  McKittrick, 'Courthouse takes centre stage'.
80  Clarke, review of *convictions*.
81  Byrne (ed.), *State of Play?*, p. 86.
82  *Buildings of Belfast*, www.belfast.city.gov/heritage/posters/Panel13.pdf (accessed December 2003). Conservation architect Dawson Stelfox recounts a brief architectural history of the building in 'Conviction', in Byrne (ed.), *convictions*, p. 50.
83  McKittrick, 'Courthouse takes centre stage'.
84  Henri Lefebvre, *The Production of Space*, trans. Donald Nicholson-Smith (Oxford: Blackwell, 1991), pp. 142 and 137.
85  *Ibid.*, p. 143, ellipses added.
86  Lefebvre argues that '*dominated* (and dominant) space' is 'a space transformed – and mediated – by technology, by practice', he cites 'Military architecture, fortifications and ramparts' as examples, and he claims that 'dominant space is invariably the realization of a master's project'. *Ibid.*, pp. 164–5.
87  *Ibid.*, p. 144.
88  *Ibid.*, p. 143.
89  Stelfox, 'Conviction'.
90  *Ibid.*
91  Martin, 'The Crum'; Amanda Montgomery, '*Convictions* at the Crumlin Road Courthouse', p. 16.
92  Mark Phelan, 'A new light on Northern culture?', *Irish Theatre Magazine* 3:11 (2002), 12–20, p. 13.
93  Lefebvre, *The Production of Space*, p. 143, emphasis original.
94  Aspects of the Courthouse's spatial organisation are conveyed in the building's ground plans reproduced in Byrne (ed.), *convictions*, pp. 6–7 and 30–1.
95  Montgomery, '*Convictions* at the Crumlin Road Courthouse', p. 16.
96  Lynch, 'Main Hall', p. 18.
97  Montgomery, '*Convictions* at the Crumlin Road Courthouse', p. 17.
98  *Ibid.*, p. 18.
99  Fricker, review of *Convictions*, p. 60.
100  Higgins, 'Time well spent'.
101  Crawford, 'Convicted in the Crum', p. 20. The site's discomfort was further highlighted by treacherous installation features and by references within the plays themselves – 'It's freezin' in here. There's a terrible draught', says the Man in Nicola McCartney's 'Jury Room' (in Byrne (ed.), *convictions*, pp. 25–9, p. 25).
102  Michael McKinnie, 'The state of this place: *Convictions*, the Courthouse, and the political geography of performance in Belfast', *Modern Drama* 46:4 (2004).
103  Jimmy Boyd, interview with Laura Haydon, 'Courthouse interviews', in Byrne (ed.), *convictions*, pp. 52–5, p. 52.
104  Montgomery, '*Convictions* at the Crumlin Road Courthouse', p. 16.
105  Mary O'Donnell, interview with Haydon, 'Courthouse interviews', p. 55.
106  Montgomery, '*convictions* visual art installations'.
107  *Ibid.*

108 Jeanette R. Malkin, *Memory-Theater and Postmodern Drama* (Ann Arbor: University of Michigan Press, 1999), p. 12.

109 Fricker, review of *Convictions*, p. 60, ellipsis added.

110 Miwon Kwon considers the commodity status of internationally touring site-specific artwork in more detail in 'One place after another: notes on site specificity', in Erika Suderburg (ed.), *Space, Site, Intervention: Situating Installation Art* (Minneapolis: University of Minnesota Press, 2000), pp. 38–63, especially pp. 47–51, and in chapter 2 of Miwon Kwon, *One Place After Another: Site-specific Art and Locational Identity* (Cambridge, MA: MIT Press, 2002).

# 4

# The Edinburgh festivals:
# globalisation and democracy

What is Edinburgh if not a Classical and Romantic, Apollonian and Dionysian, theme park? (Priscilla Boniface, 'Theme park Britain: who benefits and who loses?', in J. M. Fladmark (ed.), *Cultural Tourism*)

It is increasingly like shopping in a cultural hypermarket. (Michael Billington, 'Why I hate the Fringe', *Guardian*, 25 July 2002)

The great pleasure of the Fringe is that it is a glorious mongrel. (Lyn Gardner, 'Never mind the length, feel the quality', *Guardian*, 30 July 2001)

Since their inception in 1947, the collective Edinburgh festivals have never been particularly small or lacking in controversy, but they have grown exponentially in the intervening years and with them has grown debate – especially debate concerned precisely with their phenomenal growth. The central point of dispute focuses on how the festivals' quantitative changes have affected them qualitatively. On one hand, commentators such as Boniface and Billington suggest that where the Edinburgh festivals were once 'high' cultural events characterised by profound artistic expression and experience, recently they have become 'low' cultural events characterised by superficial (theme-park-style) economic (hypermarket-style) activity, offering a spectre of difference and choice but an experience of homogenising sameness and repetition.[1] On the other hand, critics such as Gardner argue that the unfettered proliferation of the Edinburgh Festival Fringe in particular allows it to offer hybrid new choices and improved opportunities for greater expression to a broader spectrum of participants. At base, critics dispute precisely how changes to the festivals affect democratic participation in them, understanding participation as being a meaningful opportunity to engage in the event, whether through performing, being a member of an audience, or otherwise.

These questions about the Edinburgh festivals' cultural effects – whether they are 'high or 'low', profound or superficial, homogenising or hybridising, artistic or commercial, and elitist or democratic – are the kinds of questions that might be asked about a large number of cultural forms. But they are increasingly urgent within the contexts of globalisation because it accelerates culture's distribution to more sites and audiences. Globalisation describes the relatively recent changes to worldwide material circumstances that produce a sense of compressed time and space, a sense that objects, people, cultures, ideas, information, and capital move great distances very rapidly – even instantaneously.[2] Optimistic readings of these changing conditions view globalisation as producing extra opportunities, more broadly dispersed, for widespread democratic participation in culture. More sceptical readings, however, warn that the balance of cultural distribution under globalisation is uneven, that the West (and the USA in particular) continues to dominate 'the rest' culturally and economically, and that culture under globalisation does not experience diversification but, rather, commodification, commercialisation, and homogenisation, often according to American models.

Questions about the Edinburgh festivals' cultural effects are more urgent for recent festivals because the festivals themselves look suspiciously as if they are increasingly becoming objects and agents of globalisation. The Edinburgh festivals bear the distinctive features of a global marketplace in that they bring together hundreds of different shows, people, cultures, and economies for a brief period of time in the compressed space of one city. Further, the phenomenal growth of the Edinburgh festivals can be directly attributed to globalisation: the import of performance work and audiences to Edinburgh is funded by globalisation's mobile capital, realised by its cheaper, faster air travel, and administratively smoothed by its quicker electronic communication and the proliferation of English as a *lingua franca*. While there is a fair amount of evidence suggesting that the Edinburgh festivals are experiencing globalisation, however, what is less clear – and what grounds the debate between *Guardian* colleagues Billington and Gardner – is what the cultural effects of the Edinburgh festivals' globalisation might be. Are they proliferating and democratising culture, or homogenising and limiting it?

This chapter assesses what is at stake, culturally, in the globalisation of the Edinburgh festivals, concentrating on how audiences' and makers' meaningful democratic participation in the event is encouraged or limited by conditions of globalisation. To do this, it evaluates the degree to which some of the strongest criticisms of globalisation's cultural effects pertain to what is happening at the Edinburgh festivals. One of the most virulent criticisms of globalisation, indicated above, is that its apparent

compression of time and space – the sense that it 'opens up' the world –
is not evenly experienced around the globe. Rather, it is argued, this
compression allows certain powerful communities that are privileged
primarily by wealth to invade other, more vulnerable communities. As
John Beynon and David Dunkerley point out, globalisation 'is widely
attacked as heralding in a new and voracious phase of Western capitalism and the imposition of Americanized culture'.[3] This standpoint
argues that while globalisation may appear to support democracy by
diminishing the authority and even, sometimes, the tyranny of geo-political borders, it actually and coercively erodes democracy by erecting less
visible but very powerful borders – of ideology, class, and capital. It
argues further that, under globalisation, the neo-liberal capitalist market
prevails over other potential modes of organisation, such as the welfare
state. In this context, standardising models of (American) market organisation proliferate. Hence the rise of what critics have dubbed
'McDonaldization' and 'Disneyfication', market models that not only
threaten to standardise products – as epitomised by the McDonald's
hamburger – but, worse yet, threaten to homogenise cultures – as manifested in the themed 'lands' of Disney's parks.

This chapter begins by considering in more detail how it might be
appropriate to consider the Edinburgh festivals as 'globalised'. Then it
adopts some of the above mentioned terms to evaluate the festivals' globalisation. It considers whether the festivals are driven by principles of the
neo-liberal capitalist market and with what effects. It asks whether globalisation means Americanisation and the adoption of specifically
American models of commercial practice as epitomised by McDonald's
and Disneyland. And it considers whether the Fringe is 'McDonaldized',
whether Edinburgh is 'Disneyfied', and whether other nations as well as
Scotland risk cultural homogenisation through participation in the festivals. It argues that while critics such as Billington are right to warn about
the deleterious effects of the festivals' proliferation under globalisation,
we should assume neither that such effects are inevitable or irresistible,
nor that more positive effects are not also possible. Certainly, the
Edinburgh festivals have responded to globalisation by, in part, reproducing some of its worst effects; but they also negotiate and resist some of
those effects. Given globalisation's apparently voracious capacity to grow
and spread, along with arguments that its effects are even more pernicious
elsewhere – in the Third World, for example[4] – it is especially worth iden-
tifying the opportunities for negotiating and defending democratic participation in cultural practice that either are made possible in the context of

globalisation or can be mounted in the face of it. Thus identified, these opportunities can then best be developed and extended.

### From modern to global? The growing Edinburgh festivals

Popularly known as the 'Edinburgh Festival', the enormous cultural bonanza that has taken place in Edinburgh each August since 1947 is, more accurately, some of the Edinburgh festivals. Ever since 1947, August festivals have included the Edinburgh International Festival (EIF) and nascent forms of the Edinburgh Festival Fringe (Fringe), the Edinburgh International Film Festival and the Edinburgh Military Tattoo. The Edinburgh Book Festival officially joined the August festivities in 1983 (although various writers' conferences had preceded it), and the 'Longest-running jazz festival in the UK', the Edinburgh International Jazz and Blues Festival, began in 1980.[5] While this chapter concentrates on the theatre provision of the EIF and Fringe, because many people experience Edinburgh in August as one large festival, it also occasionally considers cultural conditions in Edinburgh in the festival season more broadly.

As the Edinburgh International Festival's name suggests, it has always understood itself as international; so how has it – and how have its fellow Edinburgh festivals – evolved from being international to global? In brief, early Edinburgh festivals differ from recent festivals – including their programmes, their budgets, and their audiences – in that the latter are several times bigger and attract many more participants from numerous different countries but they are not much longer in duration, so they are more compressed. In 1947, the EIF offered opera, music, dance, and two theatre companies, one English and one French, presenting four plays, also English and French.[6] In 2001, it offered the same complement of art forms, including a still relatively modest programme of ten theatre productions coming from a – less modest – range of at least seven countries.[7] But while the scale of the EIF's programme may have changed little, its budgets and audiences have roughly doubled. In 1947, public donations and funding to the EIF amounted to £61,791 (which would have had the 'buying power' of less than £1.5 million in 2001).[8] In 2001, public funding amounted to £2,182,418, with a total income of £7,508,050.[9] First-year ticket sales of 180,000 across all art forms in 1947 more than doubled to 400,000 in 2001.[10] In financial scale, at least, the EIF seems to be experiencing globalisation's compression.

Changes to the EIF have been conceptual and geo-political as well as quantitative, and the relationship of these changes to globalisation is less clear. At its inception, the EIF had an explicit international – if primarily European – agenda conceived in a spirit of postwar reconstruction: to provide a forum in which European artists whose own cities had been devastated by war could continue to perform; and to reconsolidate a valued sense of European identity by bringing together the best of European talent.[11] As the EIF's first theatre programme indicates, however, its working definition of 'European' noticeably excluded Scotland. This is unsurprising given that its inventors had no particular cultural commitment to Scotland: they conceived the idea for the Festival in Glyndebourne, in south-eastern England; they tried first to site it elsewhere in England but were unsuccessful; they ultimately chose Edinburgh as much for its beauty as for pragmatic reasons, including that it had not suffered bomb damage during the war; and they were frequently insensitive to the cultural differences of their Scottish collaborators.[12] The EIF's initial exclusion of Scottish drama and theatre does, however, indicate that early EIFs did not operate democratically even within the relatively narrow domain of European representation.

As postwar conditions faded into memory, as European unification became ever more institutionally enshrined,[13] and as EIF organisers appreciated the political folly of excluding Scottish work, the EIF's initial aims became increasingly redundant and were altered accordingly. In recent years, a commitment to bringing the best international work to Scottish audiences and the best Scottish work to international audiences has prevailed.[14] This appears to shift the EIF's focus from Europe to Scotland and to the international or global. Interestingly, however, as I consider in more detail below, the EIF's working definition of 'the best international theatre' continues to prioritise continental European theatre. Thus, although the exponential growth of the EIF's budgets and audiences suggests it has experienced globalisation, its programming suggests this has not resulted in either its increased democratisation or the kind of Americanisation generally associated with globalisation.

The Fringe has expanded even more dramatically than the EIF, and its programming does appear to have been at least somewhat Americanised. In the EIF's inaugural year of 1947, the fringe theatre event (it would not accrue the name Fringe for another year) included eight theatre companies presenting nine stage plays and some puppet plays. All of the companies were Scottish and English but the programme included plays by writers from the United States, Russia, and Sweden, as well as Scotland and England, already representing a greater range of nations than the EIF's first theatre programme did.[15] In 2002, the Fringe offered 20,342 performances of 1,491 shows, the greatest number of which – over five hundred – were theatre performances.[16] The Fringe first sold more tickets than the EIF in 1974 and has continued to do so ever since.[17] The Fringe's growth continues: in 2002 it sold 918,509 tickets, worth over £7.1 million; in 2003, ticket sales rose to one million, valuing £10 million; in 2004 the Fringe sold over 1.2 million tickets, worth almost £10.8 million.[18] As these spiralling figures indicate, the Fringe is unquestionably experiencing globalisation's compression.

Expansions to the Fringe's programming, like the EIF's, have also been geographical. Non-UK companies started participating in the Fringe as early as 1949, when the Scottish Community Drama Association brought over companies from Canada, Norway, and France.[19] The United States was first represented by the University of Southern California School of Performing Arts Drama Department Festival Theatre as late as 1966,[20] but it has subsequently established itself as the most highly represented non-UK country on the Fringe. By 2001, companies came from forty-nine countries and, in 2002, overseas countries' shows made up twenty-four per cent of the Fringe total.[21] This growth in foreign – and particularly American – programming suggests that the Fringe is experiencing the Americanisation associated with globalisation, although perhaps not to the degree that the term 'Americanisation' might seem to imply. Indeed, given the growth in English companies' representation at the Fringe – they made up over fifty per cent of the total in 1996[22] – it might be more accurate to see the Fringe as Anglicised, a possibility that holds similar if distinct implications of insidious neo-imperialism in this Scottish context.

Finally, the Fringe has altered ideologically. The first Fringe festivals were not organised according to any collective agenda; however, many participants did share a commitment to offering material that was distinctly alternative to what was on offer at the official Festival.[23] While the EIF offered companies that were metropolitan, English and French, plays that were old, and productions that were relatively expensive, the Fringe offered companies that were predominantly Scottish, plays that were new and selected from a broader international corpus, and productions that were sometimes amateur and almost certainly less expensive. Thus the Fringe represented less dominant communities, offered more affordable work to broader audiences, and chose material that was non-canonical and both more international and more local. It was certainly more committed to democratic representation than early EIFs were. While some of these alternative agendas may still hold for some companies performing on the Fringe, it is safe to assume that they do not hold for all of the Fringe's many hundreds of productions. Further, for some critics, including Billington, the proliferation of non-alternative work on the Fringe risks overwhelming both its less numerous alternative shows and its very function as alternative. And the increasing dominance of American work on the Fringe risks producing Americanised culture rather than some idealised, democratically diverse culture.

The EIF and Fringe have grown, making them – as well as the city they occupy and the global world they might seem to represent – a 'more compressed place'.[24] But the fact of growth and compression does not inevitably produce globalisation's effects, either as they are positively conceived (producing democratisation) or as they are negatively conceived (producing homogenisation). The crucial question is not simply whether the Edinburgh festivals have been affected by globalisation or not, but what cultural effects the festivals' globalisation has produced.

## A market of elitist exclusion at the EIF

The greedy maw of Beynon and Dunkerley's 'voracious' capitalism and its neo-liberal market ideology appear in criticisms of the Edinburgh International Festival in claims that it is an over-expensive, elitist market, accessible only to those with the high financial and cultural capital required to cross its threshold.[25] The EIF has been plagued by charges of elitism virtually from its inception, partly because participation is strictly by invitation of the Festival Director only (unlike the Fringe, which has a 'come-all' policy). These allegations of elitism have recently thrived under the long term of EIF Director Brian McMaster (1992–), who is committed to programming 'difficult' work that might not otherwise get staged.[26] In his insightful analysis of McMaster's eighth season, in 1999, Ric Knowles argues that the EIF continues to be elitist because, like many other major international festivals, it maintains 'a strong trace of [its] origins in post-war modernism', visible in its preference for 'inscrutable, high modernist' shows. Typically for this kind of nostalgic modernist festival, Knowles observes, theatre at the 1999 EIF was 'dominated by exquisitely crafted and self-consciously high-cultural avant-garde offerings from Holland, Germany and Poland, almost all of which were subtitled, slowly paced, bleak, brilliantly performed and sparsely attended'.[27] As Knowles indicates, the programming was primarily European, producing a resistance to 'globalised' 'Americanisation', even if it did reinforce a European elitism, even snobbery. Thus, while the EIF's programming may resist globalisation and some of its worst effects, it is nevertheless anti-democratic because it maintains an 'Old World', European bias and reproduces First World privilege.

The EIF's standards of high cultural capital generally translate in practical terms into expenses of high financial capital, most of which are passed on to government funding agencies (and taxpayers) and to audiences through ticket prices. In 2002, the EIF broke the £100 price barrier for tickets to Wagner's *Parsifal* directed by Peter Stein, conducted by Claudio Abado, and coproduced by the EIF and the Osterfestspiele, Salzburg – although one hundred seats per show were reserved for sale at £5 each on the day.[28] The top price for a theatre ticket was more reasonable, but dear nevertheless, at £26 for the Vienna Burgtheater's production of Schiller's *Maria Stuart* directed by Andrea Breth. The EIF defended its prices as reasonable because comparable to ticket prices in London or Salzburg;[29] nevertheless, tickets at this price in any of these cities would be beyond the means of many.

Certainly, the EIF operates according to market principles that limit democratic access, but it also pursues both economic and cultural strategies for extending access beyond a strictly elite clientele. In 2002, for example, it offered tickets at £5 to a series of classical concerts in a bid designed precisely 'to open the festival to a wider audience';[30] theatre ticket prices extended as low as £4. It also offers free events, such as access to the enormously popular fireworks concert on its final Saturday.[31] In a 1991 survey of 349 UK arts festivals, the EIF was one of only five that reported attendance of over a hundred thousand at free events.[32] The EIF and Director Brian McMaster are unapologetic about the high cultural capital of EIF programming, but they are also committed to extending accessibility by offering opportunities for new audiences, especially children, to develop their own cultural capital through education and outreach programmes that operate year-round. The EIF's main outreach programme of 2000, for example, aimed to 'celebrat[e] the role of music in our lives' and included a production of playwright Zinnie Harris's and composer Marian Adamia's *Gravity* that toured to audiences of adults and young people.[33] Free 'Insight' lunchtime lectures and conversations throughout the 2002 programme aimed to provide background and context for performances.[34]

The EIF may be ruled by market forces, but these forces are not those of globalisation, and nor are their effects wholly malignant. The EIF's elitism prevents it from being 'globalised' and, thereby, reproducing some of globalisation's worst effects; however, it also means that it is at least partially anti-democratic because of the high financial and cultural capital it requires of its audiences. This anti-democratic elitism is not absolute, however. The EIF recognises that providing free and inexpensive education and outreach events is in its (market) interests because they develop future audiences/consumers. Benefit falls not only to the EIF as a business, though, but also to audiences, as education and outreach events develop audiences' cultural capital and, in so doing, extend a sense of cultural entitlement and a fluency in cultural discourse – including cultural criticism – to a wider community. The EIF's own defence for offering high cultural events is not only that they are intrinsically worthy but also that more popular events are adequately provided by the Fringe. The strength of this defence requires closer consideration of the Fringe and its operation as a market.

### The 'free' market of the Fringe

For many observers, Beynon and Dunkerley's 'voracious' capitalism and its market ideology are much less apparent at the EIF than they are at the self-proclaimed largest arts festival in the world, the Edinburgh Festival Fringe.[35] For some, the Fringe operates a benign capitalism, offering a welter of choice at relatively affordable prices, especially when compared with the EIF. For others, the Fringe offers only a spectre of choice because it is a 'hypermarket', where production values and audience choice are undemocratically determined and standardised by neo-liberal market forces rather than artistic ones. Thus, relative to the EIF, the Fringe may be democratically accessible; worryingly, however, the Fringe's democracy risks being colonised by neo-liberal market values.

Certainly, the Fringe is almost always more affordable financially than the EIF, especially, of course, when it is free. The Fringe's many free events include Fringe Sunday (on the Meadows in figure 11), an outdoor extravaganza where performers present extracts from their shows to audiences of around two hundred thousand.[36] Free too is *The Edinburgh Evening News* Festival Cavalcade on the opening Sunday of the Fringe, in which hundreds parade down Princes Street with an estimated two hundred thousand spectators watching.[37] Free street performance has long been part of the Fringe, especially on Parliament Square, near the Fringe Society box office, and in front of the Royal Scottish Academy at the bottom of the Mound on Princes Street (see figure 12). Since 1999, eight safe street performance spaces have been demarcated near the Fringe

Society box office on the High Street.[38] Even when they are not free, Fringe prices are still relatively low. Criticised for raising its prices in 2002, the Fringe pointed out that, at £7.77, the average ticket price was up by only 18p from the previous year.[39] Further, forty-four per cent of tickets cost £5 or less, and ten per cent of tickets were free.[40] Fringe organisers boasted that even the 'hottest ticket' on the 2002 Fringe, *The Guys*, was reasonably priced at £15.[41] Though they may have been relatively inexpensive, these tickets were nevertheless rare. In Anne Nelson's off-Broadway hit *The Guys*, a journalist helps a firefighter compose eulogies for colleagues killed in the events of 11 September 2001. Edinburgh's staged readings of the play starred Hollywood couple Oscar-winning Susan Sarandon and Oscar-nominated Tim Robbins, were only performed three times, and sold out in three days.[42] Thus, while the Fringe may look like a hypermarket offering choice that is virtually unlimited and very affordable, choice is in fact often strictly limited by product scarcity – by market forces, in other words, rather than artistic ones.

More ominous than the example of limited ticket availability to one show is the suggestion that certain kinds of programming are not even getting to the Fringe, or are getting edged out, because it operates as a neo-liberal market. The Fringe Society may be genuinely committed to operating as an open festival, permitting any company that wants to mount a show the right to do so provided it is able to secure a venue and

11 Fringe Sunday 2001 on the Meadows, Edinburgh

12 Free street performance outside the Royal Scottish Academy, Edinburgh

pay a relatively small fee to be listed in the Fringe programme.[43] But many other forces – chief among them, market forces – limit this openness in crucial ways. It is widely suspected, for example, that the Fringe's prolif-erating comedy schedule is elbowing out its theatre provision, a situation notable by its reported reversal in 2001. *Guardian* correspondent Fiachra Gibbons argued that, after a decade of being criticised as overblown and overhyped, the Fringe was back on form thanks to 'a spectacular renais-sance in theatre, for so long the Cinderella to comedy's swaggering Loadsamoney'.[44] It is probably fair to criticise the Fringe for hyping *The Guys* as evidence of its commitment to making the 'best' work accessible to wide audiences, but blaming it for limiting choice by allowing comedy to elbow out theatre is less defensible. The powerful impression that comedy dominates the Fringe is probably less an effect of its actual programming than it is of comedy's profuse, high-profile advertising, its dominance by stars, the media attention it generates through its annual Perrier Awards, and its after-Fringe-life spent touring and on television. Because, while the Fringe does offer many comedy shows – 340 in 2002 – what it offers most of is theatre – over five hundred shows in the same year.[45] Indeed, comedy is not even its second largest offering: music is.[46] Further, even if comedy is proliferating on the Fringe, this does not mean it will kill off theatre. Gardner suggests that, on the contrary, comedy's survival depends on theatre because theatre programming can bring venues much-needed revenue during comedy's graveyard hours. 'The big venues couldn't operate cost-effectively without their theatre programmes', she argues. 'Even such comedy darlings as Rich Hall or Alan Davies wouldn't get many takers at 10 in the morning.'[47] The relationship between theatre and comedy in the market of the Fringe is not, in other words, strictly adversarial but in important respects symbiotic, with each not only surviving in the market but supporting the other there.

Another claim made against the capitalist market conditions of the Fringe, perhaps more ominous again, is that its intense competitiveness sacrifices quality as performers make 'safe' work to ensure a guaranteed return in order to meet their growing expenses – of agents' fees, advertising, venue hire, and so on. Competition has long been a prominent aspect of the Fringe, both in its relationship with the EIF and within its own programming. Lord Harewood, EIF Artistic Director from 1961 to 1965, indicates the historic wariness that has marked the EIF's attitude towards the Fringe as a drain on potential audiences. 'I had no grudge whatsoever against the Fringe,' he claims, 'but when I arrived it was officially very much frowned on, as taking money that could be spent [by audiences] on Festival tickets.'[48] It could be argued, though, that competition between the EIF and Fringe is not threatening to standards because it provides instead some healthy incentive to save the EIF from the worst excesses of elitism. Michael Billington, for example, claims there was a time when he liked the Fringe, particularly because it was useful 'as a stick with which to beat the international festival', highlighting, by contrast, the EIF's conservatism.[49] It could also be argued that there is no effective competition between the two festivals, as Brian McMaster suggests in his claim that the EIF and Fringe simply offer different fare, satisfying different markets.

Fierce – and potentially damaging – competition does, however, exist on the Fringe itself. In 2002, for example, the Fringe ran for twenty-three days and offered 20,342 performances of 1,491 shows. As previously mentioned, the greatest number of these – over five hundred – were theatre performances.[50] Some tickets are, of course, pre-booked after the Fringe programme is published in June, but many are sold during the course of the festival, whether through direct advertising strategies such as leafleting or through good press. Accordingly, the streets of Edinburgh in August become swathed in posters, carpeted with leaflets, and deluged with performers, all hustling to attract audiences to particular shows. Companies compete for good press amidst the thousands of column inches, radio and television minutes, and web pages generated by the

Fringe and the two thousand journalists who attend it. And they compete for sponsorship and for the opportunity of being spotted and picked up by one of the five hundred scouts who attend the Fringe, whether representing an agency, a production company, or a government agency such as the British Council.[51]

Amid the Fringe's enormous welter of choice, companies are eager to find means of gaining competitive advantage. One such (dubious) advantage is to hire a promotion company such as Avalon, which represents so many comedians in particular that it reportedly 'imports an entire London office to Edinburgh' for the duration of the festival.[52] But the advantage of doing this is mitigated when virtually all the competition is doing it too, and when the promotional fees are so high that performers claim they cannot make a profit.[53]

Another – again dubious – advantage is to perform in a venue which is a known quantity to audiences and which supplements the promotion guaranteed by listing in the Fringe Society programme by publishing its own programme, as many theatres regularly do. In 2002, for example, the *Scotsman* Assembly Rooms, the Gilded Balloon, the Pleasance, and the George Square Theatre published a 136-page brochure listing hundreds of shows.[54] 'Super venues' like these have existed – and dominated the Fringe – for decades. The Assembly was established first, in 1981, and the Circuit with its 'supertent' was founded in 1982.[55] The Circuit is now defunct, but in 1982, '24% of the Fringe [was] housed in one or other of the eight Circuit/Assembly spaces', and this kind of super venue control persists.[56] The Assembly Rooms, for example, reportedly sold 160,000 tickets in 2002 and nearly £2 million worth of tickets in 2004 – nearing twenty per cent of the Fringe's total ticket sales in both these years.[57]

One problem with the dominance of these clustered super venues is that they may impose or produce a house style or brand across a range of performance. Nominally offering great choice, they effectively standardise the Fringe's fare and produce a condition Naomi Wolf has identified in the proliferation in Western cities of clusters of brand-name coffee shops: 'a loss of meaningful choices'.[58] This problem is potentially exacerbated by most Fringe venues' adoption of the standard two-hour slot per show, a measure designed to maximise scheduling and box-office potential that has had the corollary effect of virtually eliminating any show longer than two hours.[59] Another problem with the super venues is that because they are able to charge such high rents – for their high-profile names, exclusive marketing, and central locations – they financially straitjacket performance companies into producing saleable fare.[60] Rents at the

Assembly Rooms and the Pleasance in particular are reportedly 'so astro-nomical that the companies feel obliged to play it safe'.[61]

A third putative advantage is to find private subsidy, usually through a venue; Beck's beer, for example, supported the Spiegeltent venue in 1998, and Smirnoff supports the Smirnoff Underbelly, a venue located in the vaults under the Central Library.[62] But signing up to a product name, like signing up to a venue name, means that performance compa-nies risk being coerced into a predetermined brand identity, a standardi-sation which may be reinforced by what Ric Knowles sees as the 'reductive review and assessment discourses' that the Fringe generates in media commentators eager to get their responses to so much work presented over such a short space of time into the public domain as quickly as possible.[63]

While the Fringe's free market conditions certainly militate against unbounded innovation, however, by no means do they eradicate it. Branding, for example, is not inevitably oppressive, bad, or even uniform. Trendy international alcoholic products do seem to dominant the spon-sorship market but other sponsors include the local Scottish Bible Society[64] and the fair-trade coffee company Cafédirect. The latter has its British distribution centre in Edinburgh and aims precisely to prevent some of the worst effects of global capitalism by maintaining a commit-ment to 'a better deal for Third World producers' while nevertheless bringing to market a high-quality product.[65]

This company sponsored the Cafédirect Aurora Nova mini-festival of international theatre and dance organised by the Komedia company in its St Stephens and Theatre Workshop venues in 2002. As well as team-ing up with a relatively ethical sponsor, the Komedia is pioneering ways of limiting the financial risk for international companies that participate in its Aurora Nova programme by guaranteeing every one a share of the mini-festival's entire takings. In 2001, the first year the Komedia ran Aurora Nova, 40 per cent of the box office revenue for each individual company performing at the mini-festival went to that company; the rest went to a pool to be divided equally by all companies performing in Aurora Nova. This made it more feasible for international companies to come to the Fringe in the first place, and it allowed them to be more inno-vative once there. 'It takes the potential financial catastrophe out of the Fringe for international companies', argued Komedia's Edinburgh direc-tor, Tim Hawkins. 'The reason we haven't seen much good international work on the fringe in recent years', he proposed, 'is that the risk is too great. This set-up takes away a lot of the risk. We only need a few shows selling quite well to ensure that all the companies in Aurora Nova will at least cover their costs.'[66] Komedia-style 'good companies' – as opposed to 'super venues' – may not yet dominate the Fringe, but the example of the Komedia's Cafédirect Aurora Nova demonstrates both that sponsorship need not hyper-standardise the entire Fringe and that it is possible to maintain market competitiveness without sacrificing innovation.

Innovation is also encouraged more broadly by *The Scotsman* Fringe First awards for the best British or world premieres at the Fringe. [67] The Fringe Society recognised as early as the beginning of the 1970s that the expansion of the Fringe threatened to standardise its programme, as audiences sought more familiar work in a bewilderingly extensive selection, and it suggested that *The Scotsman* should establish these awards. Duly founded in 1973, the Fringe Firsts have since been regarded as successful in encouraging companies to produce entirely new work at the Fringe. In 1994, for example, 296 new plays were premiered, making up almost twenty per cent of the Fringe's annual total of 1,432 shows that year.[68]

Finally, despite the extreme competitiveness of the Fringe market, and despite the presence there of much familiar, bland, or even poor work, many companies continue to take the risk of being innovative. An energetic advocate of the Fringe, Lyn Gardner enumerates the companies, directors, and writers she admires who have recently broken through on the Fringe in a list that reads like an ode to contemporary, innovative UK theatre: Frantic Assembly, Theatre O, Ridiculusmus, Spymonkey, Grid Iron, A B & C, and Signal to Noise, directors Ben Harrison and Chris Goode, and writers David Greig and Abi Morgan.[69] Further, she credits the Fringe – rather than London theatre – for introducing her to the work of, among others, directors Deborah Warner, Polly Teale, and Sean Matthias, writer/directors Steven Berkoff and Dario Fo, UK companies including The Right Size, Unlimited Theatre, and Complicite, and foreign companies including Derevo, Do/Fabrik, Circus Oz, Dublin's Abbey Theatre, and many companies from South Africa.[70]

Despite the best ambitions of the Fringe Society to make the Fringe equally accessible to all would-be participating companies, the putatively 'free' market of the Fringe cannot be completely open since it operates in and as a market-driven economy. Competition amongst companies and between genres of performance breeds expense, anxiety, and pressure to accept 'branding' through sponsorship or signing up to a super venue. Some companies may respond to these pressures by not coming to the Fringe or by making performance that 'plays it safe' or appears standardised according to brand 'rules'. But even if we accept that individual brands are standardising, there are certainly differences amongst the brands at the Fringe. Venues such as Komedia's St Stephens are pioneering ways of helping companies to take creative risks in safer financial conditions. And incentives – especially awards – continue to encourage innovation. Finally, the market of the Fringe cannot afford to be exclusive; variety is, in some respects, its own brand identity, and it allows venues to attract a range of audiences. But what is this variety? Is it genuine or apparent? Does it avoid standardisation only to produce a new standard, one that fetishises novelty?[71] And how else is it affected by the Fringe's commercialisation? Does it, for example, bear the features of specifically American commercialisation?

## Is globalisation 'Americanisation'?

English companies present the highest proportion of performance on the Fringe, at over 52 per cent in 1996.[72] Although debate continues about why Scotland is not more highly represented at the EIF, in both its most senior staffing and its programming,[73] Scotland has always been well represented in these areas on the Fringe. Scottish performance provided roughly 75 per cent of the Fringe's fare in 1947, and almost 30 per cent in 1996.[74] The USA is the most highly represented non-UK nation at the Fringe, and has been for a number of years. In 2000, for example, work from the United States made up 58 per cent of the Fringe's non-UK drama, theatre and performance provision.[75]

American companies' dominant appearance on the Fringe can be explained by a number of factors, including their relative mobility, competence in the dominant language of the Fringe, and ability to meet expenses. American companies have political mobility because, while all foreign performers' access to the Fringe is eased somewhat by the fact that they do not require work permits, usual UK visa requirements stand.[76] With passports from a First World nation – for Rustom Bharucha, 'the ultimate sign of global privilege'[77] – American performers do not require visas and so avoid this hurdle. In 2001 a company from Sierra Leone due to perform at Aurora Nova was stopped at this obstacle when its ten actors were denied visas on the grounds that 'they might claim political asylum once they arrived'.[78] American performers are linguistically mobile because the *lingua franca* of the Fringe, not to mention much of the world, is English – maybe even American English. Probably most importantly, given the USA's relative wealth, American companies often enjoy a financial advantage over other would-be performers on the Fringe. As well as the costs of securing promotion and hiring a venue for performance, companies must also pay for transport to the Fringe and accommodation in Edinburgh. These costs are particularly high during August, when airlines usually charge relatively high summer fares and the population of Edinburgh swells by an estimated half a million people, temporarily doubling its population size, creating high demand for beds, and pushing up rental prices.[79]

Many observers do not object to the Fringe's American content, as such; indeed, American shows are often widely admired, both by critics who award positive reviews and prizes and by audiences who ensure shows that they like – or anticipate they will like – sell out at the box office.[80] What critics do object to is how 'Americanised' the Fringe is, and how it 'Americanises' Edinburgh. In these contexts, 'Americanised' tends to mean commercialised in ways epitomised by two icons of American culture: the Fringe as a market is seen to be 'McDonaldized' and Edinburgh, as a city, is perceived to be 'Disneyfied'.

## McDonaldized theatre

The 'McDonaldization thesis' pioneered by American sociologist George Ritzer proposes that '*the principles of the fast-food restaurant are coming to dominate more and more sectors of society as well as the rest of the world*'.[81] For Ritzer, these principles have primarily to do with rationalisation – efficiency, calculability, predictability, and control. They aim to guarantee workers and consumers the faster delivery of products of predictable – and often homogenised – quantity and quality and, simultaneously, the elimination of as many risks as possible.[82] Despite the menacing ring to the phrase 'McDonaldization', Ritzer points out some of its benefits: it can extend access to a broader range of customers, improve quality for some, empower consumers to compare products and suppliers more easily and so make better-informed choices, and so on. However, he is mainly concerned with the problems and dangers arising from 'McDonaldization'. These he sees as consequences of the inevitable irrationalities that arise from rational systems and feature, at their worst, the dehumanisation of the conditions of both production and consumption.[83]

The 'McDonaldization' of the Fringe can be seen in measures that the Fringe Society, venues, and performing companies have taken to rationalise their products and delivery to produce an environment where a journalist can observe, 'People are consuming culture as if it was fast food'.[84] The Festival Fringe Society was founded in 1959 'to co-ordinate publicity and ticket sales and offer a comprehensive information service to both performers and audience alike'.[85] It has worked to consolidate its rational distribution of tickets and information throughout its history, setting up its shop-front box office on the centrally located High Street in 1977,[86] launching its www.edfringe.com website in 1995, and introducing online booking in 2000.[87] As mentioned above, venues generally offer companies two-hour performance slots, maximising the number of shows the venues can schedule. Audiences may benefit from these efficiency measures in a number of ways. For example, they can purchase tickets more easily and predict better what kind of show they may see at a particular venue or within a particular Fringe marketing category such as 'musicals and opera' or 'theatre'. Further, they can see more shows in less time, potentially making their visit to Edinburgh (if they are not residents) more economical overall, as they may spend less on accommodation and expenses. The main things these measures sacrifice are performance variety and performance conditions as companies are compelled to tailor work to tight get-in, performance, and get-out schedules, and to accept modest to poor conditions – of, for example, time and material resources – for their show lengths, lighting and set designs, cast sizes, access to dressing rooms, and so on.[88] For some critics, of course, these declining conditions of production ultimately limit the quality of the work that is finally produced.

It is important to recognise, though, that the rationalisation of the Fringe is hardly comprehensive; as Ritzer predicts of all things 'McDonaldized', the Fringe is frequently irrational. This irrationality accounts for some of the Fringe's problems, but also, in this case anyway, offers evidence that the Fringe is not becoming standardised beyond recognition and worth. Audience experience may be somewhat more streamlined than it once was, but it is by no means entirely efficient or predictable. Queues for tickets and shows persist, shows run over schedule, and crossing Edinburgh from show to show remains a challenge amidst the pedestrian, performer, and vehicle traffic generated by the festivals and daily life in the city. More importantly, variety persists – across schedules, venues, and types of performance. Scheduling may be on a relatively strict two-hour slot pattern, but it remains vastly different from regular theatre scheduling. Where UK (and many other Western) theatres usually offer regular evening shows and twice- or once-weekly matinées, the Fringe offers scheduling virtually around the clock, 'from 10 o'clock in the morning through to 5 o'clock the next morning'.[89] It also offers an enormous variety of venues – including tents, streets, hilltops, church halls, bars, black boxes, proscenium arch theatres, cars, caves, a lift[90] – and a huge variety of forms – including revue, stand-up, theatre, physical theatre, dance, musicals, and so on. Opportunity persists, in other words, for audiences to see and performers to make unusual, precisely non-standardised work. And risk persists. Despite pervasive attempts to control performance – for example, discursively, through reviewers' and marketers' categories, physically, through venue restrictions, and temporally, through scheduling constraints – determining whether work will be 'good' or 'bad' maintains a high degree of unpredictability. Finally, to reiterate a point made above, the part-rationalisation of the Fringe has its benefits. Ritzer's thesis has been accused of some elitism in seeming to yearn for a time when there was less choice understood and appreciated by a smaller, more elite, market – precisely the situation cultivated by the EIF.[91] By popularising the Edinburgh festivals, the Fringe certainly extends their access to a broader audience. Further, the cultural expression of that audience may not simply be stifled by the experience, as Marx suggested audiences were when fed bread and circuses – a diet he considered to be filling but uninspiring. Fiachra Gibbons argues that, at least recently, Fringe audiences are voting with their feet and money for challenging, stimulating fare.[92]

### Edinburgh: the Disneyland of the North?

With the classical culture that thrived in Edinburgh in the eighteenth century – and the Grecian follies built then that still grace its skyline – Scotland's capital is often referred to as 'the Athens of the North', a characterisation picked up by Patricia Boniface in her rhetorical question, 'What is Edinburgh if not a Classical and Romantic, Apollonian and Dionysian, theme park?'[93] Scottish novelist Irvine Welsh heartily rejects that elite characterisation of the city in favour of a grittier, more contemporary, but nevertheless impressive profile in his infamous 1993 novel *Trainspotting*. Despite his sympathy for reconceiving Edinburgh in non-classical terms, however, Welsh shares Boniface's sense that the festivals thematically package the city. He pours scorn on what he see as Edinburgh's annual transformation into a 'shortbread Disney',[94] reductively objectified along with Scottish culture more broadly through often crude and clichéd 'it's-a-small-world' narratives and iconographies that bear an ominous resemblance to those developed by Walt Disney for his eponymous theme parks.

As we have seen, the Fringe is packaged by its programmes, the categories of performance those programmes create, and the categories reviewers and commentators employ to analyse performances. More disturbing – because its cultural effects would be more pervasive – is the possibility that the city itself is also systematically packaged during the festivals. Geographically, Edinburgh is charted out in maps conveniently printed in programmes and newspapers and designed to help visitors find venues. Visually, it is summarised in a handful of familiar images featured on brochures, postcards, and tartan tea towels and including such an iconic image of the city as the castle silhouetted against the skyline – the cover image of the EIF's 2001 programme (figure 13). Indeed, the city itself is marketed as a show, one conveniently viewed from a variety of natural lookouts, such as Arthur's Seat and Calton Hill, as well as manufactured ones, such as the Castle and Outlook Tower with its *camera obscura*. For year-round Edinburgh residents, of course, the unavoidable feeling of being a performer in the show of Edinburgh can be invasive and oppressive, 'akin to being a prisoner in the panopticon'.[95] Temporally, Edinburgh is packaged by scheduling – bookended by the

13 Edinburgh International Festival programme, 2001, showing the famous profile of Edinburgh Castle on the Castle Rock

opening cavalcade and the closing fireworks, punctuated by the Tattoo's nightly fireworks, and literally filled with shows – producing a profound, saturated sense of a 'festival city' each August. And culturally, it is packaged in Edinburgh guides provided in newspapers and magazines, in mass-produced books such as *The Rough Guide to Edinburgh* (a shortened version of which was distributed free with copies of *The Independent* in 1993),[96] and on bus tours such as Guide Friday.

'Disneyfication' has some of the same potential effects – both positive and negative – as 'McDonaldization'.[97] Positively, it can help make Edinburgh more accessible to a broader constituency of visitors, both physically and conceptually.[98] More worryingly, of course, it can reduce the city to an apparently culturally homogeneous entity that is seemingly fully understandable through a handful of simplistic categories, images and maps that leave out large swathes of the city, physically and culturally. Festival maps of Edinburgh usually focus on the city centre, for example, leaving out many poorer suburbs such as Leith, one of the key settings for Welsh's fiction. And cultural descriptions tend to focus on an apparently homogeneous tartan Scottish culture, nostalgically fetishising some utopian vision of a culturally harmonious past rather than exploring Scotland's cultural diversity, including, for example, Edinburgh's ethnic minority populations.[99]

As was the case with 'McDonaldization', however, the 'Disneyfication' of Edinburgh diagnosed by Welsh is again only partial, limiting the influence of its potentially most harmful effects. Despite cartographers' best efforts to reduce the city to clearly demarcated streets, areas, parks, and venues, Edinburgh is not an easily navigable theme park. Like Disney's theme parks, it too has a castle at its centre; unlike his theme parks, all roads do not lead to Edinburgh's castle. More accurately, the rock formation the castle sits on actually *obstructs* movement across the city: its steep incline needs traversing going north–south, and its precipice simply halts traffic going east–west. Further, while the Old and New Towns may provide convenient ready-made themed areas eerily akin – at least in name – to Disneyland's Frontierland and Tommorowland, Edinburgh's Old Town in particular is again not easily navigable, with its twisting medieval architecture and multi-layered streets, and neither the Old or the New Town is of course homogeneously old or new in the saturated style of a theme park's 'villages'. Temporally, daily life in Edinburgh continues not only outside of festival time but during it too. This may seem obvious, but the point is that even the noisy, frenzied, attention-grabbing activities of the festival – however reminiscent they may be of the rides and games of a theme park and however all-encompassing and overwhelming they may appear to be – cannot obliterate the obvious evidence of non-festival, non-theme-park activities continuing in Edinburgh. For example, children travel through the city not as at a theme park but wearing school uniforms and carrying backpacks weighted with books, returning to school in mid-August, well before the end of the festivals. Newspapers such as *The Scotsman, The Edinburgh Evening Standard*, and *The Herald*, all of which carry extensive coverage of the festivals, continue to carry other Scottish news. And daily commerce visibly continues as workers travel the city, work there, and occasionally protest the presence of so many visitors.[100]

Finally, the festivals do not irreducibly package the cultures of Edinburgh and Scotland into a very few simple clichés. Like its geography, Edinburgh's diverse populations of course remain there during the festival and they are visibly and audibly in evidence throughout it. Seventeen per cent of the Fringe's performances are by people from Edinburgh, and almost 30 per cent are by people from Scotland.[101] The handbook *How to Do a Show on the Fringe* demonstrates that the Fringe Society is keenly attuned to its Scottish contexts. It includes information about the Scottish curriculum so that companies can make work to suit; information about Scottish laws of defamation (as distinct from English and Welsh laws of slander and libel); and a fair amount of Scottish phrasing and vocabulary, including words such as 'outwith'.[102] Since 1980, the winning illustration in an annual competition for children in Scottish schools has been used as the basis for the Fringe poster, and since 1991 a student of the Edinburgh College of Art has designed the Fringe brochure.[103] Audiences are overwhelmingly Scottish, with people from Scotland making up 57 per cent of the totals for the EIF in 2001, and people from Edinburgh and the surrounding area alone making up 41 per cent of the Fringe's audiences according to a report in 2002.[104] Since 1995, members of Edinburgh's Asian communities have organised the Edinburgh Mela, an arts festival and bazaar that takes place over the first weekend in September (usually at the close of the EIF), featuring Asian music, dancing, and performance.[105]

For Scottish playwright David Greig, the articulation of more varied Scottish voices is positively encouraged – rather than prohibited – by the festivals, even more so than elsewhere. He points out that recent Scottish plays that have achieved success in London, such as adaptations of Welsh's *Trainspotting* and Gregory Burke's *Gagarin Way* (figure 14),

tend to be plays of underclass violence and comedy. This doesn't diminish those plays, but it does suggest to me that the London critics feel
most comfortable with Scottish work when it fits their understanding
of Scots – violent and funny poor people who are slightly frightening.
The softer voices, the poetic voices, and the experimental voices are
met with bemusement, apathy or patronising disdain.[106]

Greig argues that those many, different Scottish voices thrive at the
Edinburgh festivals, especially on the Fringe. As noted above, it has always
offered more opportunities than the EIF has for Scottish performance
and for the exploration – explicit or implicit – of Scottish identities.

The festivals provide cultural benefit to Edinburgh and Scotland
directly by presenting opportunities for dynamic and varied creative
expression. They also provide it indirectly, by generating income to
finance other aspects of Scottish culture, including education and health.
By 1990, the Edinburgh Festivals were already credited with generating
£72 million for the Scottish economy.[107] In 1998/9, the Scottish Arts
Council reported that Edinburgh's ten festivals generated £125 million
in additional spending in the city and supported around 2,500 full-time
jobs.[108] In 2002, Edinburgh City Council leader Donald Anderson

14 Frank (left, John Stahl) and Eddie (Paul Thomas Hickey) in the 2002 Traverse
Theatre touring production of Gregory Burke's *Gagarin Way*

claimed the August festivals earned the city £150 million annually, acknowledging, 'It really has helped to boost our economy. ... We are now the fastest-growing city economy in the UK.'[109] This is value for money because, as Donald Anderson admits, the city earns much more from the festivals than it invests in them. In 2002, Edinburgh gave the Fringe £20,000 and the EIF £1.4 million. Public bodies including the Edinburgh City Council, the Scottish Arts Council and the Scottish Executive subsidised the EIF and Fringe in 2002 to the tune of only £2.5 million and £57,000 respectively.[110] One of the reasons the EIF in particular believes it is so beneficial economically is that it operates efficiently. Public funding to the EIF declined after 1994 and was restored to 1994 levels only in 2002.[111] And compared to some other major international festivals, for example, the EIF's budgets are modest. Iain Crawford notes that while the Salzburg Festival once operated with a permanent staff of 120, the EIF managed at the same time with a staff of only twenty.[112]

The festivals provide financial benefits to Edinburgh and Scotland directly through such things as theatre-makers' salaries and ticket sales, the latter totalling over £2 million for the EIF in 2001 and £10 million for the Fringe in 2004.[113] But these financial benefits result also from indirect expenditure, especially the money spent on food and accommodation by the festivals' non-local, visiting audiences. By 2002, reports claimed that the Edinburgh festivals collectively double the city's usual population of roughly half a million people to one million.[114] Non-local visitors make up roughly 60 per cent of total audiences for both the EIF and the Fringe.[115] Unusually in contexts both British and European, many of these visitors are specifically cultural tourists: attending the festivals is the primary reason for their visit. 'Cultural facilities make up a major part of most tourists' experience of Scotland', the Scottish Arts Council acknowledges, 'but for some, the arts are the reason for their visit. Scotland attracted 200,000 UK arts tourists in 1996 – as many as Greece and almost twice as many as any other destination. Pre-eminent among their destinations is the Edinburgh International Festival.'[116] Fringe visitors spend, on average, £47 a day and stay in Edinburgh for an average of 7.4 nights. Most often, accommodation is paid for – only 27 per cent of these visitors claim to stay with friends or relatives.[117] The EIF estimates that its visitors spend an average of 9.6 nights in Edinburgh, attending an average of five EIF events.[118] All this expenditure in Edinburgh is only part of the picture. Research indicates that 'about forty per cent of the economic impact of the festivals in Scotland as a whole is due to expenditure outside Edinburgh'.[119] Finally, the financial imperative behind the festivals is long-standing and not simply an ominous outcome of globalisation's corrupting influence. In the austerity of the immediate postwar period in which the Edinburgh festivals began, the principal Scottish architect of the EIF's foundation, Harvey Wood, argued:

> If the Festival succeeds, Edinburgh will not only have scored an artistic triumph but laid the foundation of a major industry, a new and exciting source of income. At a time when we need as never before to attract visitors and foreign capital to this country, it would be as senseless to disguise this aspect of the Festival as it is childish to attack it.[120]

Certainly there are critics, like Welsh, who would deem the financial benefits generated in recent years by the festivals as poor recompense for Edinburgh selling itself out to commercial culture as 'shortbread Disney'. Some might also claim that the money generated by the theme park operates simply in the theme park's interests – enabling more consumers to participate and persuading them it is right and 'good' to do so. But, as I have argued above, there is considerable evidence in support of seeing Edinburgh as not having sold out, not having 'McDonaldized' its theatre, and not having turned itself into a Disney-style theme park. And, by Council leader Donald Anderson's own admission, Edinburgh earns far more from the festivals than it invests in them, generating income to invest in other areas. Rather than oppressing Scottish cultures, the festivals provide numerous and welcome opportunities for dynamic and diverse cultural expression. Further, in the context of ongoing change in Scotland's major industries and sources of income, the festivals provide welcome finance.

### Cultural trademarks and mindless multiculturalism

What is more, the festivals provide opportunities for cultural expression and financial gain for visiting companies and countries too. Ric Knowles has warned that visiting companies may be expected to represent reductive 'registered cultural trademarks' for their nations of origin, exoticising or orientalising themselves to attract positive attention and investment at what is effectively a global trade fair rather than a cultural festival.[121] David Graver and Loren Kruger warn further that, as a result of numerous companies and countries bringing shows as 'cultural trademarks', a 'bland multicultural mist' arises at the Edinburgh festivals.[122] For Jean Baudrillard, this is inevitable in a world that has become 'a triumph for Walt Disney, that inspired precursor of a universe where all past or present forms meet in a playful promiscuity, where all cultures recur in mosaic'.[123] As Una Chaudhuri warns, intercultural theatre 'in the frame of globalization risks being an international commodity exchange, another place for consumerism, adventure tourism, and exotic shopping'.[124] What Knowles, Graver, Kruger, Baudrillard, and Chaudhuri imply is that events such as the Edinburgh festivals function like a spectacular mosaic to incorporate many tiny tiles of performance which stand in for easily identifiable cultural difference – in ways that are hopelessly inadequate and dangerously reductive. As Disney put it, it's a small world, after all.

Having acknowledged with Knowles, Graver, and Kruger the dangerous cultural reductionism that the Edinburgh festivals in particular risk producing, it is heartening to note that these critics nevertheless credit the festivals for producing much work which is culturally complex and, for Graver and Kruger, 'pointedly intercultural and international, rather than mindlessly multicultural and hastily universalist'.[125] There remains work that may be culturally reductive, as for example many critics found Teamworks' production of *Yeh Hai Mumbai Meri Jaan* to be in the Traverse Theatre's Fringe offerings in 2002. But there is also much work that articulates complex significations about its cultures of origin. Two brief examples may indicate some of the range of this work. Liz Lochhead's Scots adaptation of Euripides' *Medea* was first produced on the Fringe at the Scotsman Assembly in 2000, was revived in 2001 when it featured in the British Council Showcase, and was widely credited for animating the classic text with robust local language.[126] Volcano's *Lambton, Kent*, at the Traverse in 2001, reversed the common anthropological gaze by showing a black African's study of the strange habits of white Presbyterian inhabitants of rural south western Ontario. International festivals such as those in Edinburgh may also provide the opportunity for artists to develop work in ways that are not encouraged in their domestic contexts; Frédéric Maurin argues Paris's Festival d'Automne served this purpose for Robert Wilson.[127] Such festivals may also foster new kinds of work tailored to and arising out of the particular conditions of festival touring, as Karen Fricker argues is the case with Robert Lepage's peripatetic works-in-progress.[128]

And there is much work at these festivals that explores the complexities of communicating across cultural differences precisely about cultural differences and similarities – work, in other words, that exploits its globalised context to explore some of the conditions of globalisation. This is especially the case with some international co-productions that the EIF –

thanks to its wealth – is able to commission. Although it was not very successful at the box office, the EIF/Abbey Theatre 2000 co-production of Ramón del Valle-Inclán's *Barbaric Comedies*, translated by Frank McGuinness and directed by Calixto Bieito, demonstrated the potential richness of an Irish company exploring the potentials of a Spanish play in Edinburgh. The play's exploration of Catholicism resonated richly with its Irish producers and elicited a suggestive dissonance in a city historically dominated by Protestantism and a country nevertheless marked by sectarian difference and conflict. The 2002 EIF/Berlin Schaubühne Theatre's co-production of the Norwegian Jon Fosse's *The Girl on the Sofa*, translated by Scotsman David Harrower, directed by German Thomas Ostermeier, and cast with British performers, offered a similar opportunity for intercultural exploration of family, memory, and betrayal. Further, productions such as these allow artistic collaboration and opportunities for artistic invention and hybridisation of practices and talents that might otherwise not be possible outside of the contexts of an international festival benefiting from multinational interest and the investment of time and talent as well as money. *The Girl on the Sofa* 'perfectly fulfils one of the main roles of a successful 21st-century festival', Joyce McMillan argued, 'in that it brings together a dazzling combination of talent that might not otherwise have had a chance to work together on the same project'.[129]

Producing work at the Edinburgh festivals is potentially culturally and financially rewarding for visiting companies and countries in other ways as well. The British Council's week-long biennial Showcase of UK performance (discussed in Chapter 2) results in real opportunities for international touring for numerous UK companies. Many of these companies are so small that their preservation and promulgation on the back of a global event represents the triumph of the small and the local in globalised markets rather than the takeover of global 'McDonaldized' or 'Disneyfied' monopolies. Even if one sees Edinburgh as a hopelessly culturally whitewashing theme park, where no visiting culture is ever adequately exposed or contextualised for audiences properly to appreciate its intercultural difference,[130] it can nevertheless serve as a route to contexts of production that are less culturally compromised. Small Fringe companies that attract opportunities for longer touring to other nations independently – that is, not as part of a 'theme park' – may there experience more meaningful intercultural exchange. Furthermore, non-British companies benefit from the British Council's Showcase by 'piggy-backing' it, attending the Fringe in Showcase years in order to expose their work to the agencies attracted to the Showcase. This practice is especially valuable for countries and companies that have much more limited resources for promotion than the UK does. Even in years when the Showcase is not organised, non-British companies recognise the benefits of the festivals as providing opportunities to expose their work to international audiences and producers. The Delhi-based producer and Indian arts activist Sanjay Roy, for example, brought sixteen productions to the 2002 EIF, Fringe, Tattoo and Film Festival precisely to promote them to international markets. 'Edinburgh is the great showcase,' he claimed, 'the world comes to see you. We've had small audiences for some events, but we've ended up with invitations to Australia, Japan and America.'[131]

## Carnival festival

The Edinburgh International Festival and the Edinburgh Festival Fringe are experiencing globalisation but not in equal measure and not with entirely negative effects. Despite exponential growth throughout its history in both audience numbers and budgets, the EIF is not thoroughly 'globalised' because it maintains an anti-populist elitism in its programming. This prevents the EIF from suffering some of the worst of globalisation's commercialising effects and it demonstrates that it is possible to resist globalisation's hegemony, but it also means that the EIF is at least in part anti-democratic because it maintains a financial bias towards wealthier audiences and an aesthetic bias towards modernist European performance. Unapologetic about its elitism, the EIF nevertheless demonstrates some interest in developing more democratic audience access to its programming because it is committed to offering education and outreach opportunities, especially for children, thus extending the franchise of elite cultural capital to a broader audience.

The Fringe does appear to be more thoroughly 'globalised': its shows, audiences and budgets have all mushroomed since its inception; it continues to attract more and more international audiences and performers, especially from the USA; and it appears increasingly to be operating according to neo-liberal market principles and to bear features of 'McDonaldization' and 'Disneyfication'. The neo-liberalisation of the Fringe market does appear to be having some homogenising effects on its programming, as the rule of financial success intimidates some companies out of producing work that is innovative – or simply different. However, this outcome of globalisation is not totalising in its effects.

Innovation continues to thrive on the Fringe – not least in response to the *challenge* of neo-liberalism's economic determinism. Testament to this is the example of the Aurora Nova mini-festival's strategies for helping their international companies simultaneously to innovate and to break even. The commercialisation of the Fringe does also seem to have the effect of rationalising the ways the Fringe is organised and offered to audiences. This has some benefits for audiences in particular, as going to shows on the Fringe becomes potentially easier and, so, physically more accessible. While it does jeopardise performance conditions and quality, the perseverance of risk-taking on the Fringe suggests that quality at least is able to survive and thrive in these conditions. With the proliferation and commercialisation of the Fringe, there is the risk too that its environment – the whole of Edinburgh – will suffer commodification and reduction to a few patronising clichés. However, the cultures of Edinburgh appear to be too robust to allow this to happen. Further, it is possible to argue that the Fringe has long provided – and continues to provide – a context in which Edinburgh and Scottish cultures are nurtured, productively challenged, developed, and distributed, rather than demeaned and diminished. And this seems to be true for many visiting companies and countries besides. Finally, the festivals' indirect cultural benefits to Scotland are considerable, thanks to the financial contribution the festivals make to Scotland's economy.

I have evaluated the Edinburgh festivals *against* some of the more negative effects attributed to globalisation. To emphasize how the festivals resist and challenge some of globalisation's most destructive effects, I will conclude by pointing briefly to how the festivals produce some of carnival's more productive effects. Despite what may appear to be the festivals' at least partial cultural stultification – their transformation into commercialised, 'McDonaldized', predictable programmes, their commodification, and their 'Disneyfication' into the culturally banal – they retain an effect of carnival and of the cultural renewal carnival potentially carries with it. As Dennis Kennedy points out, all tourism is carnivalesque, characterised by its extraordinary dimension, temporal limitation, and absence of responsibility.[132] The Edinburgh festivals' many visitors, including its local ones, may experience the festivals as theme park, but they may also experience them as carnival, with all of the socially constructive attributes that implies. According to Mikhail Bakhtin, carnival is 'time out' from 'official' culture, allowing transgressive behaviour, the interrogation of cultural rules, and opportunities for cultural renewal and reinvention.[133] Juliusz Tyszka and Annette I.

Combrink have argued that theatre festivals in Poland and South Africa have fulfilled just this role of cultural reinvention in their respective contexts.[134] For our purposes here, the carnival event of the Edinburgh festivals may provide opportunities for transgressive, anti-capitalist behaviour, as when they find ways of offering free events, or of maintaining variety and choice in a market which appears to favour simplification and repetition. Critics responding to Bakhtin have sometimes argued that the licensed nature of carnival means that it is 'simply a form of social control of the low by the high and therefore serves the interests of that very official culture which it apparently opposes'.[135] In the face of these conflicting arguments, Peter Stallybrass and Allon White argued, 'The most that can be said in the abstract is that for long periods carnival may be a stable and cyclical ritual with no noticeable politically transformative effects but that, given the presence of sharpened political antagonism, it may often act as a *catalyst* and *site of actual and symbolic struggle*'.[136] The globalisation of the Edinburgh festivals has made them 'affirm' dominant, capitalist culture in numerous ways – sometimes accepting market priorities over artistic or social ones, standardising products, and simplifying cultures, for example. But they have also remained sites of 'actual and symbolic struggle' – challenging market priorities, maintaining product variety, refusing to reduce cultures always to clichéd cartoons, and actively struggling with globalisation's expansion and compression. Certainly the Edinburgh festivals indicate some of globalisation's dangers; but, encouragingly, they also demonstrate that its deleterious effects can be negotiated, resisted and challenged, and they provide a site and an event where people can meet face-to-face to engage in this negotiation. These opportunities provided and demonstrated by the Edinburgh festivals to negotiate globalisation are doubly important, as cultural festivals and globalisation appear to proliferate worldwide.[137]

## Notes

1 Priscilla Boniface, 'Theme park Britain: who benefits and who loses?', in J. M. Fladmark (ed.), *Cultural Tourism* (London: Donhead Publishing, 1994), p. 101.

2 The library on globalisation is enormous and growing. A useful selection is collected in John Beynon and David Dunkerley (eds), *Globalization: The Reader* (London: Athlone Press, 2000). Influential texts include: Mike Featherstone, *Undoing Culture: Globalization, Postmodernism and Identity* (London: Sage, 1995); Michael Hardt and Antonio Negri, *Empire* (Cambridge, MA: Harvard University Press, 2000); and Malcolm Waters, *Globalization* (London: Routledge, 2nd edn, 2001).

3 John Beynon and David Dunkerley, 'General introduction', in Beynon and Dunkerley (eds), *Globalization*, pp. 1–38, p. 2.

4 Rustom Bharucha, *The Politics of Cultural Practice: Thinking Through Theatre in an Age of Globalization* (London: Athlone Press, 2000).

5 'Festivals overview', *Edinburgh Festivals*, www.edinburgh-festivals.com/festivals.cfm (accessed September 2002); Michael Dale, *Sore Throats and Overdrafts: An Illustrated Story of the Edinburgh Festival Fringe* (Edinburgh: Precedent Publications Ltd, 1988), p. 10. Even more Edinburgh festivals occur at other times of the year, including Edinburgh's Hogmanay (December/January), the Scottish International Children's Festival (May/June), the Edinburgh International Science Festival (April), and the Edinburgh Folk Festival (April and November). See The Festival Fringe Society, *How to Do a Show on the Fringe* (Edinburgh: The Festival Fringe Society, 2000), p. 54, and *Edinburgh Festivals*, www.edinburgh-festivals.com (accessed September 2002).

6 The theatre companies were the Old Vic presenting Shakespeare's *The Taming of the Shrew* and *Richard II* and Paris's Compagnie Jouvet de Théâtre de l'Athenée presenting Molière's *L'Ecole des femmes* and Giraudoux's *Ondine*. See Eileen Miller, *The Edinburgh International Festival, 1947–1996* (Aldershot: Scolar Press, 1996), p. 160. Miller provides the most detailed published history of the EIF, including full details of programming from 1947 to 1996 (pp. 159–327). Other sources for information on the EIF include: George Bruce, *Festival in the North: The Story of the Edinburgh Festival* (London: Robert Hale and Company, 1975); and Iain Crawford, *Banquo on Thursdays: The Inside Story of 50 Years of the Edinburgh Festival* (Edinburgh: Goblinshead, 1997).

7 I write 'at least' because some shows were international co-productions. The EIF's theatre shows in 2001 were: Tom Murphy's *Too Late for Logic*, produced by the EIF; Alessandro Baricco's *Novecento*, produced by the Théâtre de Quat'sous, Montreal; Shan Khan's *Office*, co-produced by the EIF and the Soho Theatre Company, London; Agota Kristof's *The Notebook* and *The Proof*, produced by De Onderneming, Antwerp; Carles Santos's *Ricardo i Elena*, produced by the Companyia Carles Santos, Barcelona; Heiner Goebbels's *Hashirigaki*, produced by the Théâtre Vidy-Lausanne; John Cage's *Marcel Duchamp, James Joyce, Erik Satie: An Alphabet*, co-produced by the EIF and seven other organisations from around the world; and Thomas Bernhard's *Alte Meister* (*Old Masters*) and Chekhov's *The Seagull*, produced by the Burgtheater, Vienna.

8 Miller, *The Edinburgh International Festival*, p. 389. The 2001 value (precisely £1,460,257) was calculated using John J. McCusker, 'Comparing the purchasing power of money in Great Britain from 1264 to any other year including the present', *Economic History Services*, 2001, www.eh.net/hmit/ppowerbp (accessed October 2002).

9 'Financial Statements', 'Events in the 2001 Festival', *2001 Edinburgh International Festival Annual Review*, p. 2, *Edinburgh International Festival*, www.eif.co.uk/about (accessed October 2002).

10 Crawford, *Banquo on Thursdays*, p. 14; *2001 Edinburgh International Festival Annual Report* (Edinburgh: Edinburgh International Festival, 2001), p. 7, www.eif.co.uk/about (accessed September 2002).

11  'History', *Edinburgh International Festival*, www.eif.co.uk/about (accessed September 2002). For more analysis of the EIF's early aims and effects see Jen Harvie, 'Cultural effects of the Edinburgh International Festival: elitism, identities, industries', *Contemporary Theatre Review*, 13:4 (2003), 12–26.

12  Miller, *The Edinburgh International Festival*, pp. 1–4.

13  European unification has been institutionalised through bodies such as the European Parliament (established 1979), agreements such as the Maastricht Treaty (1992), and activities such as the launch of a common currency (2002). 'Welcome to the European Parliament', *European Parliament*, www.europarl. eu.int/presentation/default_en.htm (accessed November 2002).

14  'History and background, aims and objectives', *Edinburgh International Festival*, www.eif.co.uk/about (accessed November 2002).

15  Plays in this first fringe were: *Macbeth* (Christine Orr Players, Edinburgh), Gorky's *The Lower Depths* and Robert Maclellan's *The Laird o'Torwatletie* (Glasgow Unity Theatre), *Thunder Rock* (Edinburgh People's Theatre), James Bridie's *The Anatomist* (Edinburgh District Scottish Community Drama Association), Eliot's *The Family Reunion* and *Murder in the Cathedral* (the Pilgrim Players from the Mercury Theatre, London), Strindberg's *Easter* (Edinburgh College of Art), and *Everyman* (sponsored by the Carnegie Trust) (Alistair Moffat, *The Edinburgh Fringe* (London: Johnston and Bacon, 1978), pp. 16–17). Moffat was Fringe Society Administrator from 1976 to 1980 and his *The Edinburgh Fringe* is the most detailed published history of the Fringe's first thirty years. For further information on the Fringe see: Alice Bain, *The Fringe: 50 Years of the Greatest Show on Earth* (Edinburgh: Scotsman Publications, 1996); the Festival Fringe Society's informative *How to Do a Show on the Fringe*; Michael Dale's *Sore Throats and Overdrafts*, based in part on interviews conducted by Dale, who was Fringe Administrator from 1981 to 1985; Marina Garattoni, 'Scottish drama at the Edinburgh Fringe until the seventies', in Valentina Poggi and Margaret Rose (eds), *A Theatre that Matters: Twentieth-century Scottish Drama and Theatre: A Collection of Critical Essays and Interviews* (Milan: Edizioni Unicopli, 2000) pp. 171–87; and *Edinburgh Festival Fringe*, www.edfringe.com (accessed September 2002). Unlike the case of the EIF, little information about early Fringe budgets is in the public domain, partly because the Fringe did not acquire an enduring administrative unit until the formation of the Festival Fringe Society in 1959.

16  'Exclusive: Fringe uses venue for 5000 and uplifting show for one', *Herald* (5 June 2002).

17  Moffat, *The Edinburgh Fringe*, p. 98.

18  'Record-breaking Fringe tops £7m in ticket sales', *Herald* (27 August 2002); Tim Cornwell, 'Festival refuses to be sidelined', *Scotsman* (7 August 2004); 'Fringe tops record with £10.8m of tickets sold', *Edinburgh Evening News* (20 October 2004).

19  Moffat, *The Edinburgh Fringe*, p. 29.

20  *Ibid.*, p. 72.

21  Gardner, 'Never mind the length, feel the quality', *Guardian* (30 July 2001); Alastair Jamieson, 'Record-breaking Fringe sales hit 918,000', *Scotsman* (27 August 2002).

22  Owen Dudley Edwards, 'Cradle on the tree-top: the Edinburgh Festival and Scottish theatre', in Randall Stevenson and Gavin Wallace (eds), *Scottish Theatre Since the Seventies* (Edinburgh: Edinburgh University Press, 1996), pp. 34–48, p. 40.

23 Ric Knowles, 'The Edinburgh Festival and Fringe: lessons for Canada?', *Canadian Theatre Review* 102 (2000), 88–96, p. 90.

24 Beynon and Dunkerley, 'General introduction', p. 2.

25 Pierre Bourdieu, *Distinction: A Social Critique of the Judgement of Taste*, trans. Richard Nice (London: Routledge and Kegan Paul, 1984).

26 Fiachra Gibbons, 'Festival chiefs deny cash crisis: special report: the Edinburgh festival 2000', *Guardian* (19 August 2000); Andrew Clark, 'Maestro with a touch of prejudice', *Financial Times* (3 August 2002); Lynne Walker, 'Edinburgh Festival: each night is an adventure in unknown territory', *Independent* (8 August 2002).

27 Knowles, 'The Edinburgh Festival and Fringe', p. 89.

28 Clark, 'Maestro with a touch of prejudice'.

29 Kirsty Scott, 'Fringe benefits outweighed by high prices', *Guardian* (24 August 2002).

30 Despite the success of this scheme, however, the EIF does not plan to run it again, claiming that it is simply not economically viable. Scott, 'Fringe benefits outweighed'.

31 Donald Reid, *Edinburgh: The Mini Rough Guide* (London: Rough Guides Ltd, 2000), p. 262.

32 527 festivals were sent questionnaires and 349, or 66 per cent, responded (Heather Rolfe, *Arts Festivals in the UK* (London: Policy Studies Institute, 1992), p. 2). One of the other four festivals to attract over one hundred thousand to free events that year was the Edinburgh Festival Fringe (Heather Rolfe, 'Arts festivals', *Cultural Trends* 15 (1992), 1–20, p. 10). Rolfe's 'Arts festivals' article summarises her findings from *Arts Festivals in the UK*.

33 'History and Background', *Edinburgh International Festival*, www.eif.co.uk/about/press.asp?page+2000Two (accessed September 2002).

34 For more developed analysis of the EIF's resistance to elitism see Harvie, 'Cultural effects of the Edinburgh International Festival'.

35 See, for example, the Fringe Society, *How to Do a Show on the Fringe*, and *Edinburgh Festival Fringe*, www.edfringe.com (accessed September 2002).

36 Bain, *The Fringe*, p. 18; 'Outdoors at the Fringe' (1 May 2002), *Edinburgh Festival Fringe*, www.edfringe.com/story/html?id=125&area_id=35 (accessed November 2002). Audience numbers for Fringe Sunday have often proved hard to estimate. Organisers expected five to ten thousand people for the first Fringe Sunday held in the High Street in 1981; forty thousand came (Bain, *The Fringe*, p. 18). Overcrowding forced Fringe Sunday to move to Holyrood Park in 1983 and thence to the Meadows in 2001. Fringe Society, *How to Do a Show on the Fringe*, p. 9; 'Outdoors at the Fringe'.

37 Fringe Society, *How to Do a Show on the Fringe*, p. 9.

38 *Ibid.*, p. 9.

39 Jamieson, 'Record-breaking Fringe sales'.

40 'Exclusive: Fringe uses venue for 5000 and uplifting show for one'.

41 Scott, 'Fringe benefits outweighed'.

42 Angelique Chrisafis, 'Hollywood stars choose fringe for Sept 11 catharsis', *Guardian* (15 August 2002); Jack Malvern, 'Festival's first couple attack Iraq war plans', *The Times* (17 August 2002).

43  In 2002, this fee was £397.16 including VAT. 'What's on? How much will it cost?', *Edinburgh Festival Fringe*, www.edfringe.com/static/how-much.html (accessed November 2002).

44  Fiachra Gibbons, 'Festival's buzz is back as 1m flock to shows', *Guardian* (21 August 2001).

45  'Exclusive: Fringe uses venue for 5000 and uplifting show for one'.

46  Edwards, 'Cradle on the tree-top', p. 40. In 2000, theatre made up 36 per cent of Fringe performance, music 24 per cent, and comedy and revue 20 per cent. In 2001, the figures were: theatre, 40 per cent; music 21 per cent; and comedy and revue 20 per cent. *Edinburgh Festival Fringe Annual Report 2001*(Edinburgh: Edinburgh Festival Fringe, 2002), p. 2, rpt at *Edinburgh Festival Fringe*, www.edfringe.com/uploads/attachments/102035581Fringe_A._RptFinal.pdf (accessed November 2002).

47  Gardner, 'Never mind the length'.

48  Lord Harewood (George Lascelles, 7th Earl of Harewood), *The Tongs and the Bones: The Memoirs of Lord Harewood* (London: Weidenfeld and Nicolson, 1981), p. 187.

49  Michael Billington, 'Why I hate the fringe', *Guardian* (25 July 2002).

50  'Exclusive: Fringe uses venue for 5000 and uplifting show for one'.

51  Angelique Chrisafis, 'A performing duck, a badger, and 20,340 other events: it must be the fringe', *Guardian* (3 August 2002); Knowles, 'The Edinburgh Festival and Fringe', p. 91.

52  Brian Logan, 'Show me the money', *Guardian* (26 August 2002).

53  *Ibid.*

54  Billington, 'Why I hate the fringe'. In a slightly different mapping of the Fringe's power structures, Gardner writes about 'the PR-driven golden triangle of the Traverse, the Pleasance and the Assembly Rooms' ('Never mind the length').

55  Bain, *The Fringe*, p. 34.

56  *Ibid.*, p. 5.

57  Jamieson, 'Record-breaking Fringe sales hit 918,000'; Cornwell, 'Festival refuses to be sidelined'.

58  Naomi Klein, *No Logo* (London: Flamingo, 2000), p. 130.

59  Billington, 'Why I hate the Fringe'.

60  This problem threatens to worsen as Edinburgh property prices continue to rise steeply. Andrea Mullaney, 'High rents set to bring house down for Fringe', *Edinburgh Evening News* (23 August 2002).

61  Lyn Gardner, 'Why I love the Fringe', *Guardian* (25 July 2002).

62  Jamieson, 'Record-breaking Fringe sales hit 918,000'.

63  Knowles, 'The Edinburgh Festival and Fringe', p. 95.

64  Angelique Chrisafis, 'Sermons mounting at the fringe', *Guardian* (6 August 2002).

65  'Fairtrade', *Cafédirect*, www.cafedirect.co.uk/index2.html (accessed October 2002).

66  Quoted in Lyn Gardner, 'Life after debt', *Guardian* (6 August 2001).

67  Moffat, *The Edinburgh Fringe*, p. 95.

68  Edwards, 'Cradle on the tree-top', p. 48.

69  Gardner, 'Never mind the length'.

70  Gardner, 'Why I love the fringe'.

71  Karen Fricker points out the irony that many international theatre festivals'
    emphasis on the new provokes them to market shows as local 'premieres', even
    when the shows may have been touring for years. Karen Fricker, 'Tourism, the
    festival marketplace and Robert Lepage's *The Seven Streams of the River Ota*',
    *Contemporary Theatre Review* 13:4 (2003), 79–93, p. 82.
72  Edwards, 'Cradle on the tree-top', p. 40.
73  All of the EIF directors to 2003 have been English, although two have had
    Scottish fathers, John Drummond (1979–83) and Frank Dunlop (1984–91)
    (Edwards, 'Cradle on the tree-top', p. 48).
74  Edwards, 'Cradle on the tree-top', p. 40.
75  Visiting Arts, *Visiting Arts Guide to the Edinburgh Festivals 2000* (London: Visiting
    Arts, 2000), n.p. Rpt at *British Council*, www.britcoun.org/visitingarts/edinburgh-
    festival (accessed August 2002).
76  Fringe Society, *How to Do a Show on the Fringe*, p. 44.
77  Bharucha, *The Politics of Cultural Practice*, p. 30.
78  The play, *Kpundeh (Crisis)*, was by Inaju Ruben and was to have been performed
    as 'the sole African representation' in the Aurora Nova mini-festival of interna-
    tional theatre at Komedia St Stephens. Fiachra Gibbons, 'African play blocked
    by visa refusals', *Guardian* (7 August 2001).
79  *Time Out Edinburgh Guide* (London: Penguin Books, 1998), p. 32.
80  In 2002, for example, one of the most widely celebrated plays on the Fringe was
    New Yorker C. J. Hopkins's *Horse Country*, presented at the Scotsman Assembly,
    and winner of the Scotsman Best of the Fringe Firsts award. Jackie McGlone,
    'Serious horseplay', *Scotsman* (23 August 2002).
81  George Ritzer, *The McDonaldization of Society: An Investigation into the Changing
    Character of Contemporary Social Life* (Thousand Oaks, CA: Pine Forge Press, 2nd
    edn, 1996), p. 1, emphasis original. Ritzer and others have expanded the thesis
    in, for example: George Ritzer, *The McDonaldization Thesis: Explorations and
    Extensions* (London: Sage, 1998); George Ritzer (ed.), *Mcdonaldization: The Reader*
    (Thousand Oaks, CA: Pine Forge Press, 2002); and Mark Alfino, John S. Caputo,
    and Robin Wynyard (eds), *McDonaldization Revisited: Critical Essays on Consumer
    Culture* (Westport, CT, and London: Praeger, 1998).
82  Ritzer, *The McDonaldization of Society*, pp. 9–12.
83  *Ibid.*, pp. 12–13.
84  Samantha Ellis, 'London calling', *Scotsman* (23 August 2002).
85  Festival Fringe Society, *How to Do a Show on the Fringe*, p. 52.
86  Moffat, *The Edinburgh Fringe*, p. 114.
87  *Edinburgh Fringe Festival Annual Report 2001*, pp. 6–7.
88  Angelique Chrisafis reports that working conditions have worsened for technical
    staff at the Fringe as it has expanded. Chrisafis, 'A performing duck, a badger,
    and 20,340 other events'.
89  Fiona Sturges, 'Edinburgh Festival: how I spent 12 hours showjumping at the
    Fringe', *Independent* (17 August 2002).
90  'Exclusive: Fringe uses venue for 5000 and uplifting show for one'.
91  Martin Parker, 'Nostalgia and mass culture: McDonaldization and cultural elit-
    ism', in Alfino *et al.* (eds), *McDonaldization Revisited*, pp. 1–18.
92  Gibbons, 'Festival's buzz is back as 1m flock to shows'.

93  Boniface, 'Theme park Britain', p. 101.

94  James Morrison, 'Welsh backs rival festival for locals', *Independent* (11 August 2002).

95  Chris Rojek and John Urry, 'Transformations of travel and theory', in Chris Rojek and John Urry (eds), *Touring Cultures: Transformations of Travel and Theory* (London: Routledge, 1997), pp. 1–19, p. 7.

96  *The Independent / Rough Guide to Edinburgh 1993* (London: Rough Guides Ltd, 1993).

97  For analyses of the cultural effects of Disney's cultural industries see the influential early work by Ariel Dorfman and Armand Mattelart, *How to Read Donald Duck: Imperialist Ideology in the Disney Comic*, trans. David Kunzle (New York: International General, 1984), as well as more recent work, including: Alan Bryman, *Disney and His Worlds* (London: Routledge, 1995); Eleanor Bryne and Martin McQuillan (eds), *Deconstructing Disney* (London: Pluto Press, 1999); Henry Giroux, *The Mouse that Roared: Disney and the End of Innocence* (Lanham, MD: Rowman and Littlefield, 1999); Stephen M. Fjellman, *Vinyl Leaves: Walt Disney World and America* (Boulder: Westview Press, 1992); and Eric Smoodin (ed.), *Disney Discourse: Producing the Magic Kingdom* (London: Routledge, 1994).

98  Dennis Kennedy defends this aspect of Disneyfication in 'Shakespeare and cultural tourism', *Theatre Journal* 50:2 (1998), 175–88, p. 180.

99  Figures collected in the 1991 census indicate that Scotland had a minority ethnic population at that time of 62,634. Of this total, 16 per cent, or roughly ten thousand, lived in Edinburgh. *Scottish Executive*, 'Family mediation services for minority ethnic families in Scotland', www.scotland.gov.uk/cru/kd01/purple/mediation-05.htm (accessed October 2002).

100  See, for example, David Stenhouse, 'Edinburgh notebook', *The Times* (26 August 2002).

101  Morrison, 'Welsh backs rival festival for locals'; Edwards, 'Cradle on the tree-top', p. 40.

102  Fringe Society, *How to Do a Show on the Fringe*, pp. 33ff, 41, 44, and *passim*.

103  Bain, *The Fringe*, p. 5.

104  *2001 Edinburgh International Festival Annual Report*, p. 7, www.eif.co.uk/about (accessed October 2002); Morrison, 'Welsh backs rival festival for locals'.

105  See *Edinburgh Mela*, www.edinburgh-mela.co.uk (accessed October 2002).

106  David Greig, 'Reaping the harvest of Scottish theatre', *Independent* (9 August 2002).

107  Matty Verhoef, *European Festivals*, trans. Sam A. Herman (Geneva: European Festivals Association, 1995), p. 106. Some of my material here first appeared in Harvie, 'Cultural effects of the Edinburgh International Festival'.

108  *Scottish Arts Council Annual Report, 1998–99* (Glasgow: Scottish Arts Council, 1999), quoted in Department of Culture, Media and Sport, *Creative Industries Mapping Document* (London: DCMS, 2nd edn, 2001).

109  Donald Anderson quoted in Logan, 'Show me the money'.

110  Brian Ferguson, 'City says no to cash for Fringe', *Edinburgh Evening News* (27 August 2002).

111  'This job? It can change people's lives', *Scotsman* (18 March 2002).

112  He does not specify when this was. Crawford, *Banquo on Thursdays*, p. 7.

113  Tony Thorncroft, 'Corporates join in the party: Edinburgh sponsorship: the festivals would be a pale shadow without support from big companies', *Financial Times* (3 September 2001), p. 14; Cornwell, 'Festival refuses to be sidelined'.

114  Robin Young, 'Record ticket sales for Fringe', *The Times* (27 August 2002). The *Time Out Edinburgh Guide* lists Edinburgh's population as 447,550 in 1995 and roughly one million during August, 1997 (p. 32).

115  *2001 Edinburgh International Festival Annual Report*, p. 7; Morrison, 'Welsh backs rival festival for locals'.

116  Scottish Arts Council, *Response to the Consultation on National Cultural Strategy* (Glasgow: Scottish Arts Council, 1999), p. 20.

117  Allan Brown, 'Cash cow has finally leapt over the moon', *Sunday Times* (12 August 2001).

118  *2001 Edinburgh International Festival Annual Report*, www.eif.co.uk/about.

119  C. Gratton and G. Richards, 'The economic context of cultural tourism', in Greg Richards (ed.), *Cultural Tourism in Europe* (Wallingford: CAB International, 1996), pp. 71–86, p. 83.

120  Henry Harvey Wood in 1947, quoted in Verhoef, *European Festivals*, p. 106.

121  Knowles, 'The Edinburgh Festival and Fringe', pp. 89 and 91.

122  David Graver and Loren Kruger, 'Locating theatre: regionalism and interculturalism at Edinburgh', *Performing Arts Journal* 15:2 (44, 1993), 71–84, p. 71.

123  Jean Baudrillard, *The Illusion of the End*, trans. Chris Turner (Cambridge: Polity Press, 1994), p. 118, quoted in Kennedy, 'Shakespeare and cultural tourism', p. 188.

124  Una Chaudhuri, 'Beyond a "taxonomic theater": interculturalism after post-colonialism and globalization', *Theater* 32:1 (2002), 33–47, p. 39.

125  Graver and Kruger, 'Locating theatre', p. 84.

126  See, for example, the British Council's Showcase 2001 dedicated review page for *Medea*, www.edinburghreview.com/Featured/BCMedea.html, as well as producing company Theatre Babel's website, www.theatrebabel.co.uk/babel.html (both accessed November 2002).

127  Frédéric Maurin, 'Did Paris steal the show for American postmodern directors?', in David Bradby and Maria M. Delgado (eds), *The Paris Jigsaw: Internationalism and the City's Stages* (Manchester: Manchester University Press, 2002), pp. 232–47.

128  Fricker, 'Tourism, the festival marketplace and Robert Lepage's *The Seven Streams of the River Ota*'.

129  Joyce McMillan, 'When Harrower met Fosse', *Scotsman* (22 March 2002).

130  Clive Barker makes this argument about theatre festivals in 'The possibilities and politics of intercultural penetration and exchange', in Patrice Pavis (ed.), *The Intercultural Performance Reader* (London: Routledge, 1996), pp. 247–56, p. 249.

131  Sanjay Roy in Bob Flynn, 'Bollywood meets Holyrood', *Guardian* (22 August 2002).

132  Kennedy, 'Shakespeare and cultural tourism', p. 175.

133  Mikhail M. Bakhtin, *Rabelais and His World*, trans. Hélène Iswolsky (Cambridge, MA: MIT Press, 1968), p. 109.

134  Juliusz Tyszka, 'The school of being together: festivals as national therapy during the Polish "Period of Transition"', trans. Jolanta Cynkutis and Tom Randolph, *NTQ: New Theatre Quarterly* 13:50 (1997), 171–82; Annette I.

Combrink, '"The arts festival as healing force" (Athol Fugard): the role of the two major arts festivals and possible resurgences in South African drama', in Marcia Blumberg and Dennis Walder (eds), *South African Theatre as / and Intervention* (Amsterdam: Rodopi, 1999), pp. 195–205.

135 Peter Stallybrass and Allon White, *The Politics and Poetics of Transgression* (London: Methuen, 1986), p. 13.

136 *Ibid.*, p. 14, emphasis original.

137 On the growth of cultural festivals in the 1990s see Nell Arnold, 'Festival tourism: recognizing the challenges; linking multiple pathways between global villages of the new century', in Bill Faulkner, Gianna Moscardo, and Eric Laws (eds), *Tourism in the 21st Century: Lessons from Experience* (London: Continuum, 2000), pp. 130–62.

# 5

# The UK and Europe:
# genealogies and futures of performance

The search for descent is not the erecting of foundations: on the contrary, it disturbs what was previously considered immobile; it fragments what was thought unified; it shows the heterogeneity of what was imagined consistent with itself. (Michel Foucault, 'Nietzsche, genealogy, history', 1971)

British political culture has a long history of resisting European unification. Two resonant reminders of this in the early twenty-first century have been the UK's failure to adopt the common European currency along with other European Union member states in 2002, and its alliance with the USA against such nations as Germany and France in deciding to go to war in Iraq in 2003. But these are only two of the latest manifestations of the UK's reluctance to integrate and collaborate with Europe. In the nineteenth century, Britain's concentration on empire partly informed a continental policy characterised by 'splendid isolation'.[1] Less than a century later, 'With the Empire lost, naval predominance ended, and the Commonwealth ineffective, Britain was forced, however reluctantly, to become a European power'.[2] Nevertheless, the UK's recalcitrance towards European unification endured, so that while, for example, the Treaties of Rome established the European Economic Community in 1957, the UK did not join until 1973.

The most commonly articulated rationale for keeping the UK out of Europe is that the UK not only stands to gain little from unification, it risks being damaged through unification. From Prime Minister John Major's evangelical promise to the 1992 Conservative Party conference – 'I will never, come hell or high water, let our distinctive British identity be lost in a Federal Europe'[3] – to the five economic tests that New Labour Chancellor Gordon Brown requires the Euro to pass before his government will entertain thoughts of adopting it, the vocabulary is different but the sentiment the same: the UK must be protected from the corrosive effects of European unification.

By conflating economic, political, and cultural arguments and senti-
ments, this reasoning adopts a scientific rationalism to mask its ideological prejudices; namely, its assumptions that UK and European cultures
can be defined and kept autonomous from one another and that, in
crucial respects, UK culture is exceptional, and certainly better than
European culture. All of these assumptions are problematic. Following
Benedict Anderson's arguments about the continuous creative production
of community identities, European and UK identities must be seen as
dynamic; elements can be ascertained, but these will always be partial and
temporary. Identities cannot necessarily be kept autonomous from each
other as communities move, mix, overlap, and go on being – as Foucault
reminds us – heterogeneous.[4] Thus, UK claims to autonomy and superiority can be seen as hopeful, at best, not to say snobbish, xenophobic, and
fundamentally fearful of miscegenation.

Of course, the idea that any community should want to perceive itself
as superior to those around it is not surprising, this practice is hardly
unique to the UK, and it can have beneficial social effects, such as building community identity and confidence. But it risks a lot. To imagine itself
as better, a community necessarily imagines others as worse and poses
both categories as, to some degree, static. In Foucault's terms, the desire
for a reassuring narrative of genealogy leads to its representation as
immobile and consistent with itself, rather than its recognition as heterogeneous. Often this means that conservative – and sometimes reactionary
– understandings of community identity are maintained and change is
resisted and even prohibited.

Fortunately, while these identities may present themselves as secure
and incontrovertible, Anderson reminds us that they are in fact imagina-
tively produced and Foucault reminds us that it is the work of the kind of
critical historiography that I aim to practise in this chapter to explore their
heterogeneity. This chapter examines how British theatre practices have
participated in – but also resisted – imagining British culture as
autonomous from and better than European culture and asks what the
cultural and ideological effects of this participation and resistance have
been and can be. It begins by surveying the ways in which dominant
British theatre historiography has described – and so produced – its object
as uniquely British and autonomous from other traditions and histories
through a narrative which constructs British drama and theatre as
uniquely and consistently literary.[5] Certainly British theatre has enormous and long-standing literary strengths, but paying grossly disproportionate attention to this aspect of British theatre to the neglect of others

produces damaging results for the theatre's development, and therefore for the cultural identities that theatre and performance help to imagine. In crucial ways, the emphasis on British theatre as literary – as words written by a writer and spoken by an actor – diminishes attention to the ways in which British theatre is material – movements performed, scenographies designed, sounds produced, work done. At heart, it is symptomatic of an anti-theatrical – if not an anti-dramatic – prejudice, neglecting aspects of theatre that are material, embodied, physically expressive, and produced through the work of a group. It does not necessarily produce a cliché of British theatre and identities as cerebral and only verbally expressive, but it risks doing so. Furthermore, it conveniently corresponds with opposing clichés of European theatre and identities as more emotional and expressive, reinforcing those clichés.

To challenge these dominant constructions of British theatre as autonomous and uniquely literary, this chapter next draws out the long (repressed) history of mainland European theatre practices' influences on British theatre, especially the British theatre's exposure to and development of traditions of physical theatre. Finally, it analyses the practices of two of the UK's foremost contemporary devising physical theatre companies, DV8 Physical Theatre and Complicite, and two of their exemplary shows, DV8's *Strange Fish* (1992) and Complicite's *Mnemonic* (1999–2003). Both of these are informed by mainland European performance histories and practices, materially engage with continental European culture through casting and touring, and diegetically explore European cultural identities. Far from denigrating or ignoring European culture, these companies and shows demonstrate the creative scope of a healthily heterogeneous, miscegenated theatre genealogy and its benefits as a means of negotiating British identities not as distinct from European ones but precisely *as* – multiple and dynamic – European identities.

## A literary theatre of impeccable pedigree

'[T]he writer defines the Britishness of British theatre', attests Aleks Sierz in the introduction to *In-Yer-Face Theatre: British Drama Today*.[6] British theatre does have a long, strong literary tradition, but the intrinsic literariness of British theatre is taken for granted not only as a result of the theatre itself but also, importantly, because of the critical and material structures surrounding it and the ideological biases they manifest and produce. Through these structures, the apparent truth of British theatre as fundamentally literary is reiterated so frequently and often uncritically that it is reinforced and naturalised, producing potentially damaging effects.

The primary agent that promotes what Claire Armitstead has called the 'traditional textual patriotism' of British theatre is the historiography that describes it.[7] The enormous library of books on twentieth-century British theatre concentrates overwhelmingly on plays and playwrights, perhaps partly because, for many, it is easier to write about static text than about the ephemeral theatre event.[8] Nevertheless, the preponderance of criticism that examines British theatre as writing reinforces its understanding principally as written text rather than integrally as theatre. The myriad of books on single authors aside, there are dozens of books that examine the work of groups of playwrights,[9] and many more whose titles claim to focus on theatre but concentrate more accurately on plays and playwrights.[10] Director Sir Peter Hall's *The Necessary Theatre*, for example, latterly makes a brief case for why he 'believe[s] in verbal theatre' but predominantly assumes that British theatre is its drama and frequently uses drama and dramatist as synonyms for theatre and theatre maker.[11]

The apparent 'truth' of British theatre's fundamentally literary identity is further naturalised by being given an impeccable, deep and unbroken pedigree, 'the sense of an "organic" national tradition',[12] stretching back, inevitably, to Shakespeare. 'The greatest artist of all time is British: Shakespeare', Hall claims.[13] Sierz fills in the lineage:

> What characterizes British theatre during its golden ages of creativity – Elizabethan and Jacobean, Restoration, Edwardian, and postwar – is not its actors, nor its directors, nor its theorists, but its writers. The people you remember are Shakespeare and Webster, Congreve and Wycherley, Wilde and Shaw, Osborne, Pinter, Bond and Stoppard.[14]

For Christopher McCullough, Shakespeare's continuing dominance in Britain helps to account for the text's pre-eminent treatment in British theatre, a situation, he notes, that does not prevail elsewhere in Europe, despite Shakespeare's establishment position in German theatre, for example.[15]

While the British theatre's literary pedigree usually operates to defend its sovereignty from other national theatre practices and traditions, it frequently makes an exception to accommodate Irish drama. Sierz's list of 'British' writers quoted above implicitly assimilates Wilde and Shaw, both of whom were born in Ireland. Hall gamely acknowledges that assimilating like this is presumptuous, but does it anyway: 'The British, without doubt, are the best makers of theatre in history. If I presume to add the great Irish talents to this roll call of dramatists, its record is unmatchable.'[16] This assimilation sadly mimics the imperial history of Britain's relationship with Ireland and suggests that discourses on British theatre are prepared to accommodate other traditions if they are perceived as not only enhancing but also unthreatening because subordinate and colonial. Other European theatre traditions may be less comfortable – or more difficult – to accommodate.

British theatre's 'traditional textual patriotism' is also a product of the material conditions – institutional, professional, financial, architectural, and legal – which have accumulated around it. Institutionally, most theatres are organised and staffed to produce plays by writers, usually well-established writers. Professionally, as Dan Rebellato demonstrates, many other artists in British theatre besides the writer – from actor to director to lighting designer – have been expected to work in the service of letting 'the text speak for itself'.[17] Financial limitations mean that few British theatre companies can afford to devise work over even reasonably lengthy rehearsal periods, and that commissioning new work is risky.[18] Architecturally, most theatres are designed to present picture-framed plays, the 'other theatre' exceptions to this rule being both exceptional and marginal, as their titles acknowledge: Stratford's The Other Place, the Barbican's Pit, and the Royal Court Upstairs. Finally, at least until it was abolished in 1968, censorship legally enhanced the primacy of the written script and made devised or improvised theatre nearly impossible to stage because scripts were required to be submitted for review by the Lord Chamberlain before production.[19]

The truth claim that 'the writer defines the Britishness of British theatre' is discursively and materially overwhelmingly reproduced, as is the corollary implication that British theatre is entirely autonomous, a product of its own impeccable literary genealogy (with a dash of Irish blarney thrown in for good measure). While this situation may not be easily changed, it is worth trying to change because of the problems and limits it produces, both for British theatre and for the identities that theatre helps to imagine.

### Individual creativity, isolationism, and anti-theatricalism

Crucially, this situation limits the British theatre by contributing to its problematic promotion of three things: individual creativity, isolationism, and anti-theatricality. Its prioritisation of the individual expressive writer and his (*sic*) 'speaking-for-itself' text betrays ideological commitments to

the (privileged) individual over the (less privileged) group and to a romanticised sense of expression as spontaneous over recognising it as time-
consuming labour.[20] These ideological commitments are familiar from
New Labour's promotion of the 'creative industries', discussed in Chapter
2, and they maintain a vision of the British theatre industry as not only
romantically naive but also hierarchical and fundamentally resistant to
practices of devising and/or collaborating. This leads to the second major
problem in this construction of British theatre – what critics have called
its 'quintessential parochialism',[21] 'entrenched isolationism', 'purblind
parochialism', and 'theatrical chauvinism'.[22] As Jane Edwardes observes,
'British theatre is often accused of being insular, text-bound and dead
from the neck down'.[23] British theatre has long been fundamentally
limited by its separation from other nations' theatre histories and practices. Reflecting in the early 1990s on his career as a theatre critic in
Britain, Billington remarked,

> The more I travelled in Europe in the seventies, the more I also realised
> how cut off we were from the great French, German, Italian, Spanish
> and Russian classics. The situation has now radically improved, thanks
> largely to the existence of theatres like the Glasgow Citizens and the
> Gate, but internationalism still seems to me a cause worth fighting for.[24]

The kind of theatre Billington indicates he wants Britain to be exposed
to – mainland European 'classics' – remains literary, but is nevertheless
not the autonomous British literary theatre otherwise so widely cultivated.
Further, this continental European theatre has a significantly different
literary tradition – including, for example, German expressionism – that
incorporates not only different dramatic features but different expressive
*theatrical* effects as well. It is also a different *theatre* tradition that places
stronger emphasis on multiple aspects of production, especially direction:
'we distrust the continental power of the director', Billington remarks.[25]
Thus, British theatre's entrenched emphasis on its own literary history
limits it by neglecting theatre's material aspects, especially – for Billington
and McCullough – directing, but also scenography, movement, and
performers' bodies. It produces and reproduces a specifically anti-mate-
rial, anti-phenomenological, anti-*theatrical* prejudice.

In his wide-ranging book *The Antitheatrical Prejudice*, Jonas Barish indicates the variety of forms that anti-theatricalism has historically assumed
in the West. At least as far back as Plato's time, theatre has been suspect
because it is mimetic, it promotes identification, and it stirs audiences'
emotions, impairing their abilities to judge and reason.[26] Theatre is not

to be trusted because it is mimetic – and so is deceitful, unscrupulous, and hypocritical. It is also ostentatious, exhibitionist, and lacks modesty.[27] In Renaissance England, anti-theatricalism was part of a Puritan censure of activities involving pleasure and recreation, especially sexuality, 'this being equated with femininity, with weakness, with the yielding to feeling, and consequently with the destruction of all assured props and boundaries'.[28] In this and other contexts, anti-theatricalism exhibited 'a misogynist tinge'.[29] Sometimes, as in the writings of Ben Jonson, 'there lurks a puritanical uneasiness about pleasure itself, and also a distrust of movement, which connects with … an ideal of stasis in the moral and ontological realm'.[30] There is also a recurrent 'revulsion from the actors' and a 'struggling against the grossness of the physical stage'.[31]

Barish provides many more examples of anti-theatricalism, but this list already resonates with the biases of dominant British theatre historiography. The literary theatre claimed for Britain is resistant to several aspects frequently associated with a more theatrical theatre: exhibitionism, indulgence in feeling, sexuality, femininity, the physicality of the stage and its actors, the company's personified emphasis on community over individuality, and movement. Barish's point that a suspicion of physical movement corresponds to a resistance to ontological and moral change is especially salutary because it draws attention to the moral and ontological conservatism at the heart of anti-theatrical prejudice, and it shows up the fundamental conservatism of claims that British theatre continuously reproduces itself in its own literary image. This anti-theatricalism also produces resistance to different theatre practices, cultures, and ways of being. It reinforces the cliché of British culture as epitomised by the stiff upper lip: modest, undemonstrative, rational, and conventionally masculine (if not macho, which would be exhibitionist). And these features conveniently reinforce opposing clichés of European theatre and identities as exuberant, sexually active and expressive, exhibitionist, irrational, and feminine; in short, more emotionally expressive.

This is not to say that dominant narratives of British theatre describe it as being entirely without feeling. Simon Shepherd and Dan Rebellato have both suggested that much twentieth-century British theatre culture has been hostile to the presumed philosophical bent of French theatre in particular, favouring instead a Leavisite common sense and statement of ostensibly honest feeling. They also, however, illustrate the hazards of this partiality. Shepherd argues that much of putatively 'proper' British drama's focus on 'people' precludes a focus on ideas, argument, and politics. Naturalism persists in postwar British drama 'because it promises that

theatre can be serious without being – precisely by not being – either theoretical or theatrical'.[32] Rebellato identifies the distrust of French theatre
in 1950s Britain as symptomatic of a 'dubious imperial nostalgia', a sense
that 'Britain had suffered by separating its thought and feeling', and a
rejection of what was regarded as the undiluted intellectualism of French
drama.[33] In the historiographic practices identified by Shepherd and
Rebellato, British theatre and identity may be somewhat emotive, but
they are nevertheless anti-intellectual and still organised in opposition to
continental European cultures.

By celebrating individual creativity, seeking isolation, indulging anti-
theatricalism, and maintaining a hostility to theory, dominant British
theatre culture resists collaborative practices, healthy miscegenation, and
a recognition of creativity as labour, material practice, and intellectual
practice. It produces profound limitations for British identities, not least
in an era where changing political contexts might invite Britons to re-
imagine themselves in substantially different ways both within and in relation to a changing Europe.

## A miscegenated theatre

I trace British theatre's dominant literary narrative in order to unpack
some of the limitations and prejudices it produces and naturalises, but I
want also to refute this narrative to show that the genealogy of British
theatre has not been as comprehensively literary, autonomous, xenophobic, and as resistant to collaboration, theatricality, and theoretical
concepts as that narrative presumes.[34] The rest of this chapter explores
how this is so in an alternative British theatre historiography (one which
recognises implicitly that other historiographies again are also possible).
First, I survey a selection of important (if often repressed) instances where
twentieth-century mainland European theatre in particular has been
introduced to and has influenced British theatre. This survey aims to
demonstrate that British theatre culture is not hermetically isolated in a
literary ivory tower, simply reproducing itself in its own conservative
image and promulgating its own biases; rather, it is and has long been
open to theatre practices from beyond its geo-political borders. My aim
is not simply to replace one 'bad', xenophobic narrative with a 'better',
culturally open one that is more politically correct. But I do want to
demonstrate how the latter narrative might at least be read, and to draw
attention to the more progressive ideological possibilities it allows, both
for British theatre and for British identities.

### Brecht in Britain

Probably the least overlooked figure in this history of continental European influence on British theatre is Bertolt Brecht. In what is widely remembered as a turning point in British theatre history, the impresario Peter Daubeny brought Brecht's Berliner Ensemble to the Palace Theatre in London in August 1956, just after Brecht's death, to perform three productions: *Mother Courage*, *The Caucasian Chalk Circle* and *Trumpets and Drums*. 'At the time', notes Ronald Bryden in his Afterword to Daubeny's *My World of Theatre*, this Berliner London mini-season 'seemed a modish teacup furore of Hampstead intellectuals, insignificant beside the native revolution launched by Osborne's *Look Back in Anger*. To appreciate its impact', he argues, 'you have to cast your eye over the whole following decade'.[35] The Berliner's visit to London 'was to unleash prolonged and profound debate about the Brechtian method of acting',[36] as it was to influence countless subsequent theatre makers, especially those seeking a political theatre. Although the Ensemble's 1956 visit was important, however, Brecht's work had already long influenced British theatre and would continue to do so for many years after 1956, especially through British productions of his plays, the return of the Berliner Ensemble in 1969, and the influence of a next generation of British Brechtian and political theatre makers.[37] In *After Brecht: British Epic Theatre*, Janelle Reinelt points out that Brecht's 'legacy' in Britain is twofold, providing and influencing both a body of theatre practice and a critical discourse for understanding political theatre.[38] His influence on British playwriting has been widely examined, fitting as it does with dominant British theatre historiography's logocentrism. However, less attention has been paid to his influence on theatre practice, for example his development of practices of visual theatre through emphasising the *Gestus*, and his stress on the importance of collaboration with other artists, such as the designer Caspar Neher, the composer Kurt Weill, and the actor Helene Weigel. The influence of these visual and collaborative aspects is noticeable in the work of British companies such as Joint Stock and Joan Littlewood's Theatre Workshop.[39]

Brecht's influence on British theatre may be the most notorious, but his was not the only mainland European theatre company to visit and shape British practice. The Comédie Française led by Jean-Louis Barrault appeared at the second Edinburgh International Festival in 1948 and in London in 1951, and suggested a powerful alternative approach to acting. Dominic Shellard argues that 'Audiences were intrigued by the way the

Frenchman employed the whole of his body to express himself, compared to which English actors appeared to be locked in rigor mortis' and to perform 'primarily with the voice'.[40] The example of the Comédie Française was reinforced by other foreign performance that poured in to London in particular, especially from the mid-1950s on.

## Peter Daubeny's World Theatre Seasons

Widely credited for importing this theatre, doing 'much to break down the parochialism of the West End', and playing 'a crucial role in opening up the West End stage to world theatre' from the 1950s until 1973 was Peter Daubeny.[41] He began presenting theatre and dance in London in 1945, from 1951 to 1955 he primarily presented foreign dance companies, and thereafter he presented foreign dance and theatre, including Jean Vilar's Théâtre National Populaire as well as the Berliner Ensemble in 1956, the Moscow Art Theatre in 1958, and the Comédie Française in 1959. This importation of French productions to London was not happening in a vacuum, as French plays were already very popular there. 'In the early fifties', Rebellato observes, 'probably the most successful playwright in Britain was Jean Anouilh'. Giraudoux, several other French writers, and many Italian playwrights besides were also extensively produced in London.[42] In 1964, Daubeny launched his much-celebrated annual World Theatre Seasons at London's Aldwych Theatre. These seasons' duration and make-up varied annually, but they took place in the spring and presented six or seven companies in a total of ten or eleven programmes over two to three months. Alongside the Comédie Française in 1964, Daubeny presented the Moscow Art Theatre and the Abbey Theatre from Dublin. Subsequent years saw the Actors' Studio Theatre from New York (1965), the Nō Theatre of Japan and the Piccolo Theatre of Milan (1967), Sweden's Royal Dramatic Theatre (1968), and the Negro Ensemble Company from New York (1969). The 'world' presented by Daubeny's World Theatre Seasons was unquestionably Eurocentric. But alongside representing Western Europe (France, West Germany, Italy, Ireland, Greece, Sweden, Spain), they also represented Eastern Europe (Poland, the USSR, Czechoslovakia, Turkey), the USA, the Middle East (Israel), and East Asia (Japan).

As high-profile and international as the visiting companies were, the question remains whether these seasons were only another 'modish teacup furore of Hampstead intellectuals' like the one Bryden initially sensed during the Berliner's 1956 visit – affecting a small elite only briefly

– or whether their influence was genuine, broad, and deep. Bryden himself argues the latter: 'there *are* reasons justifying Peter Daubeny's labours, but they are scattered and diffuse, noticeable over the long run of subsequent British theatrical activity'.[43] He credits the Berliner's 1956 visit for influencing John Osborne, John Arden, and 'the whole style and output of the Royal Shakespeare Theatre in the 1960s'. 'The work of a whole generation of British playwrights, directors and actors was radically affected by that three-week season at the Palace Theatre', he argues, concluding, 'the ripples of its influence are still spreading'.[44] He further credits the 1959 and 1964 visits of the Comédie Française for reviving British theatre makers' interest in the 'possibility of farce as a form', various visits for inspiring the National Theatre to expand its European repertoire, the Nō Theatre's 1967 visit for influencing Peter Brook and Edward Bond, Czech designer Josef Svoboda for developing design in Britain, and the Abbey Theatre's 1968 'mockery-free' production of Dion Boucicault's *The Shaughraun* for reviving British interest in melodrama. Most importantly, Bryden argues, Daubeny's World Theatre Seasons demonstrated the value not just of the solitary writer but of permanent ensembles – *companies* where repertoires could be developed and *practices* could be innovated.[45] Bryden is not alone in his praise for Daubeny. 'The magnitude of his work', argues Shellard, 'was such that after his death in 1975 there was nobody able to match his commitment'.[46] '[E]ver since the demise of Peter Daubeny's World Theatre Seasons', write Ralph Yarrow and Anthony Frost, 'we have been looking for a successful way to import the best of world drama on a regular basis'.[47]

### The Royal Shakespeare Company

As Daubeny was importing productions, Peter Brook was importing theories and methods of production in his directing work. Coinciding with the launch of Daubeny's World Theatre Seasons in 1964 was the launch of Brook's and Charles Marowitz's Theatre of Cruelty season under the auspices of the RSC. As its title suggested, the season was inspired by the writings of Antonin Artaud and his advocacy of an expressive, emotive, visual, subjective, 'total' theatre that Brook would later call a theatre 'more violent, less rational, more extreme, less verbal, more dangerous'.[48] This season's most notorious public outcome was Brook's RSC production of Peter Weiss's *The Marat/Sade* at the Aldwych, but many of that first season's principles – of collective creation, emphasising the visual, and pursuing profound emotional expression – persisted through Brook's subsequent work on *US* in 1966, and beyond. Throughout his career, Brook has notoriously sought in other cultures' theatre practices the means of invigorating his own, and certainly this engagement has been contentious, most notably in what has been criticised as his exploitative, imperialist engagement with Hindu traditions in *The Mahabharata* (1985).[49] But his mid-1960s borrowing from continental European theatre practices occurred in a context where differences of cultural power were less uneven, and it certainly animated British theatre with practices that developed its non-verbal, physical, visual, and collaborative aspects in an adaptable black or white box environment that challenged the dominance of proscenium-arch staging. 'It inspired', writes John Elsom, 'a new generation of fringe theatres across the country in which a mixture of French, Polish and American influences all played their parts'.[50] It also influenced the theatrical establishment, placed as Brook was within the RSC.

Brook was not alone in expanding the RSC's repertoire and practices in the early to mid-1960s. Another important figure in this context was Michel Saint-Denis, who was invited by RSC director Peter Hall to join the company, along with Brook, in 1962. For Colin Chambers, Saint-Denis helped to develop the RSC's awareness and practice of theatre as a form that combined many arts and required the input of many collaborating artists. Chambers writes,

> Saint-Denis was a bridge to a rich European tradition going back to the 1920s, which included his own Compagnie des Quinze of acrobatic pioneers ... Saint-Denis founded the RSC's Actors Studio when he joined the Company ... His approach laid great stress on the visual, and he brought into the Company Farrah, the head of design at the Strasbourg School of which Saint-Denis had been director. His work was seen by the leadership as integral to the Company's life – a workshop for actors, directors, writers, designers, and technical staff, to develop singly and together their own craft and imagination, and that of the Company, as a company.[51]

## The Edinburgh festivals

Saint-Denis died in 1971, Brook left for Paris to found his Centre for Theatre Research in 1970, and Daubeny ceased producing his World Theatre Seasons after 1973. Despite the absence of these figures, foreign theatre productions and practices continued to be imported to Britain, not only in London but also elsewhere, most notably Edinburgh. As discussed in the previous chapter, from its inception in 1947, the Edinburgh International Festival has consistently imported productions by major international companies.[52] A selection of early visitors includes: the Compagnie Jouvet de Théâtre de l'Athenée from Paris (1947), the Comédie Française (1948), and Jean Vilar's Théâtre National Populaire as well as the Compagnie de mime Marcel Marceau (1953), the Piccolo Theatre of Milan directed by Giorgio Strehler (1956), and the Compagnie Roger Planchon (1960). The British premiere of Grotowski's Laboratory Theatre was at the EIF in 1968.[53] After presenting shows on the Edinburgh Festival Fringe in 1972, 1973, and 1976, Kantor's Cricot 2 appeared at the EIF in 1980.[54] The Berliner Ensemble appeared in 1984, and the Toho Company of Japan directed by Yukio Ninagawa appeared in 1985 and 1986. Successive World Theatre Seasons in the 1980s featured companies from Scotland and England alongside ones from the USSR, Germany, Ireland, Israel, Japan, New Guinea, and Georgia in 1987; Japan, Canada, South Africa, Italy, France, Belgium, and Germany in 1988; and Italy, Spain, the USA, France, the USSR, Ireland, and Japan in 1989. Fringe companies did not initially come from as far away as did EIF companies (as the last chapter identifies, this would change in years to come), but the Fringe has produced and promoted international plays from its beginnings. Only Scottish and English companies appeared at the first Fringe in 1947, but their repertoires included plays by Gorky, T. S. Eliot, and Strindberg.[55] One of the greatest advocates for international drama on the Fringe is the Traverse Theatre; since opening in January 1963 with plays by Arrabal and Sartre, the Traverse has continued to present and support international drama.[56]

## Glasgow's Citizens and London's Gate

Two other notable companies dedicated to promoting plays and playwriting from abroad commended by Billington, above, are Glasgow's Citizens and London's Gate. Founded in 1943 by James Bridie, the Citizens initially produced a mix of Scottish plays and European classics. Under the direction since 1969 of Giles Havergal, Philip Prowse, and, later, Robert David MacDonald, the theatre's work has been characterised by a 'visual delight and European orientation which bears no relation whatsoever to the great upheavals in British theatre since the mid-1950s'.[57] Since 1969, it has rapidly made its way through a large European repertoire in what Michael Coveney describes as a 'swaggering

cultural crusade designed to knock an audience out of its sense of composure and into a forbidden garden of sensual, aesthetic, intellectual and
moral riot'. In year upon year of ambitious programmes, he continues,
the Citizens has offered

> nods in the direction of the mainstream humanist European post-war
> theatre of Bertolt Brecht, Giorgio Strehler, and Roger Planchon; eclec-
> tic flashbacks to the more Slavic extravagances of Meyerhold and
> Eisenstein; a succession of Goldoni discoveries; rare Coward revivals
> and Wilde melodramas; British premières of Lermontov, Hochhuth,
> Goethe and Karl Kraus; new adaptations of Proust, Tolstoy, de Sade,
> Offenbach and Balzac; and high-voltage, daring assaults on the darker
> recesses of the Jacobean and Restoration repertoire.[58]

In Coveney's estimation, 'the Citizens, engaging responsibly with all
manner of texts over the years, has consistently been our most interesting
centre of dramaturgical endeavour'.[59]

While much smaller and younger, London's Gate Theatre has steadily
introduced new world drama to Britain. Founded in 1982, it aims 'to introduce the work of international playwrights to a British audience' and 'has
always aspired to produce the best of undiscovered world drama, providing a platform for the emerging talents of actors, designers, directors
and translators'.[60] To this end, it produced several thematically organised
seasons – including Women in World Theatre, The Spanish Golden Age,
Six Plays for Europe, Agamemnon's Children, and Storm and Stress – and,
in the 1990s, ran the Gate Biennale, dedicated to presenting 'the newest,
freshest work from our continent'.[61] Designed 'to ask important questions
about Britain's European identity, as well as if there is such a thing as a general European identity, at a time when the issue has never been more sensitive', it aimed also to be 'a celebration, diverse and chaotic, of the most
innovative contemporary work and writers in Europe today'.[62] Other
British theatre companies notable for the work they have done importing
drama and theatre include Glasgow's Tron and Tramway, Manchester's
Royal Exchange Theatre, and the Tricycle,[63] Bush,[64] and Royal Court[65] as
well as numerous other theatres in London.

### LIFT, BITE and the London International Mime Festival

While it may appear that there is no single company importing *theatre* on
the same scale or with the same impact as Daubeny once did, closer
examination of the contemporary scene suggests otherwise. From the

1980s at least, more organisations cumulatively import work more consistently, especially to London; so, perhaps what is gone is not the international content of Daubeny's seasons but the sense of novelty they cultivated in their brief annual outings. Chief of this new generation of organisations is LIFT, the London International Festival of Theatre, founded as a biennial summer event by Lucy Neal and Rose Fenton in 1981 and presenting, in that first year alone, ten companies, 'ranging geographically from Malaysia to Peru',[66] and always ranging across and exploring an enormous variety of forms and practices, from installation, to large-scale community events, to the showing of work-in-progress.[67] As Theodore Shank points out, however, 'The directors of LIFT are not content merely to bring productions to London for the entertainment of audiences, they aim to have an impact on the art of theatre in Britain'.[68] Rejecting the kind of superficial relationship between visitor and site often produced through international touring's usual economy of brief runs and quick turnover, LIFT's directors present dialogues between visiting and local artists, hold after-show discussions for audiences and visiting companies, develop site-specific work, and create opportunities for local artists and audiences to collaborate with visiting artists. They also explicitly ask such questions as, 'What is theatre actually for? ... How many different cultures co-exist in London? What is their relationship with their countries of origin? And how do we make connections between London and the rest of the world?'[69] For Claire Armitstead, LIFT has 'helped to move the markers of British theatre away from its traditional textual patriotism towards an acceptance of different ways of seeing and doing'.[70]

The Barbican International Theatre Event (BITE) is also responsible for importing a vast, diverse range of large- and small-scale international theatre, puppetry, circus, and dance to London, not least since it began presenting work year-round in 2002, when space was freed up by the RSC's decision to stop using the Barbican as its sole winter venue in London.[71] Performances at the annual London International Mime Festival, founded in 1977, are usually staged at much smaller venues (such as the ICA and the Battersea Arts Centre), but this annual two-week long festival nevertheless attracts a large and dedicated audience to a range of work featuring movement, music, and scenography. Work presented comes predominantly from continental Europe (in 2000 this included France, Italy, the Netherlands, Russia, Belgium, Spain and Germany), but also from the UK and beyond (in 2000, Brazil and New Zealand).[72] Other UK festivals that regularly import a variety of forms of theatre and dance

include the Brighton Festival, the Belfast Festival at Queen'
1980s and 1990s, Glasgow's Mayfest.

## Hybridised theatre culture and practices

Clearly, theatre in Britain throughout the latter half of the twentieth
century and into the twenty-first has not been the domain of, simply, the
English literary play. Non-British drama and theatre – including continental European epic, expressionist, circus, and other physical forms of
theatre – have been consistently produced and have made a strong impact
across British theatre practices. The influence of Brechtian epic and other
styles of political theatre has already been explored in some detail by, for
example, Reinelt and McCullough.[73] Other influences – such as that of
Meyerhold, Artaud, Ionesco, Grotowski, Bausch, Barba, Lecoq, and even
Stanislavski – have yet to be fully considered.[74] And other work could of
course be done on the influences of practices from elsewhere around the
world, especially the USA and Asia.

The final sections of this chapter aim to indicate the heterogeneous
European genealogies of two of Britain's outstanding contemporary
theatre companies, DV8 Physical Theatre and Complicite. Both companies have been directly influenced by the practices of prominent continental European theatre and dance practitioners and have pioneered
hybrid, devised, physical theatre. Both promulgate the influence of these
continental genealogies within the UK by becoming, themselves, influential in the development of other theatre companies and practices. And
both further explore the potential of mixing influences by casting mixed-
nationality companies and developing narratives and performance practices that examine experiences of encountering cultural difference. Most
importantly, these companies demonstrate the potential value of this
hybrid theatre – the multiple discourses it can adeptly deploy, its accessibility to audiences of different language communities, and crucially its
openness to a pro-theatricality that may make possible the expression of,
among other things, sexuality, femininity, movement, emotional expression, ideas, and new and changing British/European identities.

## DV8 Physical Theatre's deviant genealogies

DV8 Physical Theatre was established by dancer/choreographer Lloyd
Newson and colleagues in London in 1986 specifically to develop dance
that was '*about* something'.[75] This impetus was partly a reaction to the

predominant dance of the time which Newson felt was primarily abstract and failed to address – or to allow him to express – his feelings as a dancer and a person, not least as a gay man in Thatcher's and Major's Conservative Britain. With a background in sociology and a desire to explore what dance could say about social experiences, he set up DV8 to develop a hybrid dance vocabulary that would deal with real social issues – especially of social relations, initially between gay men, but also between men and women, between predominantly heterosexual men, and between people of different ages, abilities, and body types. The company's physical vocabulary characteristically combines movement inspired by the everyday with that informed by more formal dance training, aiming both to suit the company's social material and to be legible to a broad audience that may not be literate in formal dance languages. Initially setting itself up as iconoclastic, DV8 has achieved enormous popular success, both within Britain and internationally. This success is warranted: DV8's work is characterised by compelling, suggestive, and skilful movement and imagery, an honest, intelligent, and risk-taking commitment to social analysis, a willingness to be self-reflexive about its own thinking and practices, and a wry humour.

Certainly DV8 was and still is at least somewhat iconoclastic in a contemporary dance culture that continues to feature a preponderance of movement characterised by abstract formalism. Further, as Newson emphasises, his company has never slavishly imitated the work of any other practitioner.[76] Nevertheless, it has been strongly influenced by numerous continental European performance traditions. Newson has credited Beckett for the latter's inspiring combination of humour and absurdism,[77] both of which feature in DV8's *Strange Fish*, discussed in more detail below. Newson and others have indicated his debt to the German dancer and choreographer Pina Bausch,[78] particularly: her development of *Ausdruckstanz*, a form of German expressionist dance, to explore and express ideas and feelings, especially loneliness and alienation, frustration and fear, as well as playfulness and love;[79] her invitation to performers to build movement out of their own experiences and everyday movement; and her exploitation of 'theatrical' aspects of production, most notably speech and scenography.[80] And Ana Sanchez-Colberg has presented a strong case for seeing physical theatre in general as fundamentally shaped by body-focused avant-garde theatre and dance practices, including the Theatre of the Absurd of Beckett and Ionesco, the dance of Bausch, and the total theatre of Antonin Artaud.[81] In the face of what he perceived as Western theatre's 'exclusive dictatorship of words', Artaud argued: 'the stage is a tangible, physical place that needs to be filled and it ought to be allowed to speak its own concrete language', its own 'spatial poetry' composed of 'those expressive means usable on stage such as music, dance, plastic art, mimicry, mime, gesture, voice inflexion, architecture, lighting and décor'.[82]

Connecting it to Artaud's total theatre, DV8 calls itself a physical theatre company, committed to movement as well as other aspects of theatre production, including speech, music, and scenic design.[83] Atypically for a performance company with a dance background, DV8's performances have increasingly included speech and written text: in 1993, Newson commented that not to do so was to remain mute, to deny his productions one of the expressive languages at their disposal.[84] DV8's music combines material composed specifically for the particular show with well-known popular music, such as Cher's *Believe* in the suggested club setting of a section of *Can We Afford This* (2000), making direct reference to the music's cultural contexts as well as the social relations produced in those contexts. Similarly, DV8's scenic design combines the relatively abstract with elements that suggest real, socially specific places, such as the gay dance club of *Dead Dreams of Monochrome Men* (1988), the pub of *Enter Achilles* (1995–98), and the domestic spaces of *The Happiest Day of My Life* (1999), helping the productions to make references to specific social situations – such as cruising in a club – and to make more general observations about movement, social behaviour, or emotional feeling. Scenography is not superficial, a pretty place in which to perform; it is an integral part of each show and its spatial meanings.[85] As such, it is often developed prior to choreographing of movement, so the movement can respond to the space and be integrated with it, not simply grafted on top.[86]

Significantly, these continental European influences emphasise many of the features of 'theatricality' Barish found so commonly distrusted in anti-theatrical cultures: emotional expression, actual movement, and the metaphorical movement that is a willingness to engage with the dynamism and hybridity of diverse performance languages and practices, identities and cultures. Further, these influences include an intellectual trajectory – ready to engage with ideas and arguments – as well as some commitment to group-devised practice. These practices of what we might call a 'pro-theatricality' extend in the UK not only to DV8 but also to other companies and practitioners, as well as their inheritors. Several DV8 regulars, including dancers Wendy Houstoun and Nigel Charnock, have formed their own companies, and DV8's work is regularly taught in British curricula, at secondary school level and beyond.[87] Writing in *Dance*

*Theatre Journal* in 2002, Keith Watson argued that, until recently, 'much of the middleground contemporary dance [in the UK] ... has sprung from the [Martha] Graham/[Merce] Cunningham school of thought'. 'But things are changing,' he argues. 'The evidence of a trio of recent works gives encouraging signs that ... the major figures to have emerged in British dance over the past two decades – Lloyd Newson, Lea Anderson and Mark Murphy – are now the key reference points for a whole new generation of dance makers', including Protein, Ersatz, and Jasmin Vardimon, the last of whom Watson identifies as having been particularly strongly influenced by Newson.[88]

## The total theatre of DV8's *Strange Fish*

A closer examination of DV8's *Strange Fish* (1992) will illustrate in detail the company's practice of an Artaud- and Bausch-inspired, emotionally expressive, intellectually engaged total theatre. While this show is now more than a decade old, I have chosen to examine it for two primary reasons. First, it is representative of DV8's work and its relationship to total theatre's practices and expressive aims while also marking a movement for DV8 out of expressing an explicit political agenda towards conveying a greater sense of ambivalence, so that the work more closely resembles Bausch's.[89] Second, its specific historical and social contexts and narrative concerns relate to continental Europe in ways that enhance the critical engagement with European identities and cultural practices already begun through the disciplinary genealogies of DV8's performance practices.[90]

The central social relationships *Strange Fish* explored were between friends and lovers. 'This piece is about friendship', explained Newson, 'and about the search for something or someone to believe in'.[91] Its political critique focused on the power dynamics of personal relationships but it was not dogmatic. Newson remarked: '[the show] questions whether our need for love and intimacy saves or enslaves us'.[92] Characters teamed up and fell out as friendships were struck and tested, outsiders were bullied or seduced, and allegiances were forged and nourished, or neglected and accidentally or wilfully destroyed. The show explored various intimacies, infatuations, commitments, and betrayals as well as the feelings these produce: communion, comfort, security, and love, but also entrapment, alienation, loneliness, disappointment, and despair.

Instead of dance's more conventional bare stage, *Strange Fish*'s set featured 'a brown back wall covered in windows, doors and ledges to produce startling visual surprises', as performers reached through to grab at each other and slipped through to escape.[93] Rocks and water fell down this wall, assaulting the performers. Rough floorboards could be lifted to reveal a pool from which performers emerged, and into which they jumped, fell, or were thrown. Like many of Bausch's settings, this scenography designed by Peter J. Davison allowed the company to invoke both real social contexts and the relationships that are forged or dismantled in them, as well as more abstract, emotive environments. Suggested realistic environments included a chapel, where characters practised or questioned faith and commitment; a bar, where they teased and flirted; and a bedroom, where they tested intimacies and vulnerabilities. Less literally, the setting suggested an inner world – underground, under water or in the unconscious – that might give access to unconscious desires and fears, or might be a place of significant transition, whether in life stages, between life and death, or in evolutionary development (from human to fish or vice versa). With its potential surprises and hazards, the setting produced the kind of combined humour and absurdity, comedy and menace that Newson admired in the work of Beckett.

Sound in *Strange Fish*, too, worked to make both literal and more abstract references. Speech was primarily limited to performer/characters calling each other by name, and a single, striking monologue. Like Bausch's use of direct address, the use of performers' personal names as character names in *Strange Fish* acknowledged their identities as people, and prevented them from being seen simply functionally as dancers. It also bore witness to the fact that, as in all DV8 productions, the performers drew on their own experiences in devising the show and, so, were speaking and dancing for both themselves and their performed personae. As Newson emphasised when speaking about his previous work in 1995, it 'was very much based on the individuals who were involved in the production. The pieces were built around them: their improvisations, their personalities, the way they looked, how they spoke'.[94] Nigel Charnock delivered *Strange Fish*'s most sustained speech in a party scene: 'I love people, you see. I love people. No, I do, I'm a people person ... I collect people, people ... I do, they're my hobby.'[95] Nigel's breathless testimony literally drove the other partygoers away from him and into each others' arms to form temporarily intimate and virtually impregnable partnerships that Nigel, undeterred, attempted to penetrate. Here, speech literally demonstrated the potential instability of protestations of love by showing that claiming to be intimate is not necessarily a performative speech act: neither is the claim necessarily true in the first place, and nor will it necessarily produce what it claims.

*Strange Fish*'s music was deliberately less literal. Melanie Pappenheim
sang doleful, elegiac songs composed in a hybrid language by Jocelyn
Pook. Newson explains that 'In *Strange Fish*, we wanted Melanie to have a
language of her own that people couldn't understand, so a lot of the
words are English sung backwards, or Latin – yet at the same time I think
it's very clear what she's saying'.[96] What is clear is both a social reference
– to devotional music and a specifically Catholic cosmology – and a mood
– one suggesting loss and despair as well as religious passion. Instrumental
music composed by Adrian Johnston ranged from the playful, in scenes
of flirtation, to the harrowing, as Wendy Houstoun punished herself by
rolling on a bed of stones after a failed affair, to the apocalyptic, as in the
final scene, where Wendy ascended a cross to suck the life from Christ-
like Melanie.

Movement too used a dual approach, combining the specific and the
abstract. 'There are no dictionaries for movement like there are for
words', says Newson, 'so I struggle to find what I've called "specific ambiguity" – this can hold the story together and at the same time allow individual audience members to have their own reading of what's
happening.'[97] Everyday vernacular movement informed scenes such as

15  Wendy Houstoun, Lauren Potter and Dale Tanner (left to right) in
DV8 Physical Theatre's stage production of *Strange Fish* (1992)

the party, where Nigel flung his arms out in search of a hug. It also informed Wendy and Lauren Potter's physical vocabularies of flirtation (figure 15), as well as Wendy's stomping irritation with her deserting friends Lauren and Nigel, and it grounded the show in a familiar vocabulary of behaviour that many audiences would recognise from everyday social practices. Combined with this vernacular movement, though, were many more ambiguous sequences of relatively abstract, formal dance which were nevertheless expressive of a range of emotions and social relations. In an extended 'knot' dance where they never unclasped their arms from around one another, Lauren and Jordi Cortes Molina produced 'a

sense of intimacy, but also entrapment, and perhaps dependency as well',[98] a sense illustrated in figure 16. The abstraction of the movement allowed it to indicate specific meanings – such as character intimacy – while maintaining enough semantic openness to articulate the polyphony of that meaning – its inherent ambiguity and its potential to change.

*Strange Fish* deployed the range of expressive media available in a total theatre approach to performance – scenic design, text and sound, and movement – to produce a show marked by Newson's 'specific ambiguity', by complex and dynamic social observation, and by wide-ranging emotional expression around feelings of security, insecurity, faith, and despair.

### The European social history of, and in, *Strange Fish*

This particular DV8 show further explored the relationship of British cultural practices to European identities through its historical and social contexts, other aspects of its practice, and its narrative. *Strange Fish* was produced in 1992, a significant year in British political history. After thirteen years and four consecutive terms of

16 Lauren Potter (left) and Jordi Cortes Molina in DV8 Physical Theatre's stage production of *Strange Fish* (1992)

Conservative rule under Thatcher and Major, many confidently believed that the general election of April 1992 would finally see in a Labour government. Of course, this did not happen: the Conservatives were re-elected with a slim majority of twenty-one seats and their opponents entered a phase of at least partial disaffection with traditional party politics and apparently direct political action. Many left-leaning political artists likewise re-examined their work's effectiveness, questioning attempts to make explicit political arguments and sometimes adopting more abstract approaches. The movement from political explicitness to a greater degree of ambivalence that Sanchez-Colberg has identified in DV8's *Strange Fish* could be seen as symptomatic of this broader transformation in political art in the UK provoked at least in part by the 1992 election and the surrounding political climate.

The year 1992 was also one of debate about the Maastricht Treaty. Many saw ratification of this treaty of European unification as a point of no return, so it acted like a litmus test for attitudes towards unification, both for UK citizens more broadly and notoriously for Conservative politicians in particular. To highlight the year's significance, the most outspoken group of Conservative MPs opposed to unification took it as their name, calling themselves the 1992 Committee.

Despite considerable domestic hostility to European unification in 1992, however, the UK continued to participate in numerous Europe-wide initiatives. It held presidency of the European Union in 1992, a fact it celebrated by hosting a six-month-long European Arts Festival throughout the country.[99] It also participated in EXPO 92, an international trade and cultural fair that ran from April to October in Seville, Andalusia, Spain.[100] The UK's contribution to EXPO 92 was a substantial pavilion used largely to promote British trade and industry,[101] and a programme of music, theatre, and dance events. One of these, co-commissioned by EXPO 92, Britain at EXPO, and Canada's National Arts Centre, was DV8's *Strange Fish*.

*Strange Fish* engaged directly with the political and social contexts of its production for and at EXPO. Newson and Houstoun undertook developmental research for *Strange Fish* not only in London but also in Spain, workshops and auditions were held in London and Barcelona, devising took place in the UK, Spain, and Hungary, the show toured to Hungary, Spain, the UK, and Canada, and the cast was made up of dancers from the UK, Spain, Australia, and New Zealand (Newson himself is from Australia; he moved to Britain in 1980).[102] While it is not unusual for a major dance company to be made up of an international cast, it is unusual for dance significantly to explore its performers' backgrounds. For DV8, such exploration is an explicit aim: 'Our work', says Newson, 'is about individuals, their lives, interactions and personalities'.[103] Nationality is thus part of what *Strange Fish* explored.

*Strange Fish*'s narratives and imagery made reference to its contexts of production to explore the ambivalent feelings produced by social encounter in general and sometimes by encountering apparent European differences in particular. In the video version of *Strange Fish*, this is focused through Wendy's experiences. Early in the show, she pals around with fellow Englishwoman Lauren. Their performance vocabulary is ironic and they mock movement that expresses sensuality or macho bravado (figure 15). Before long, though, Lauren is seduced by Spaniard Jordi Cortes Molina, and goes off to perform the 'knot' dance, a sinuous, sustained duet that expresses sensuality but, as discussed above, not just as a cliché. The narrative suggests that Lauren encounters and embraces a different (dance) discourse and culture, but it does not reduce that culture to stereotype. Wendy, meanwhile, struggles with Lauren's apparent 'conversion', attempts to recruit first a new ironic playmate in Nigel then a lover in Dale Tanner, and ends up violently rejecting the faith represented by Melanie's Christ-figure by effectively murdering her. Certainly part of what is staged is a repressed (English and/or northern European) agnosticism and an expressive (Spanish and/or southern European) Catholicism – not least when loquacious Nigel states in his Northern English accent that 'the Spanish are a very physical people'.[104] In both stage and video versions, *Strange Fish* maintains too much nuance to be suggesting a crude Manichaean struggle between these two identities; Lauren, for example, demonstrates that the identities are not mutually exclusive. However, the show does posit these features as part of cultural difference and part of what has to be negotiated both socially and individually by the performer/characters in their historically and socially situated contexts of performance. In the context of 1992, *Strange Fish* explored both hostility to European unification and openness to the hybridity and pleasures it might produce – in both personal relationships and performance practices.[105]

## Complicite

Complicite is widely recognised as one of the most important and influential theatre companies in the UK.[106] It has produced over thirty shows and revivals since it was founded in 1983 as the Théâtre de Complicité by Annabel Arden, Simon McBurney, Marcello Magni, and Fiona Gordon with a large and constantly evolving membership of theatre makers from around the world, especially continental Europe.[107] Most of the founder members trained in Paris with gurus of mime and physical theatre Jacques Lecoq, Philippe Gaulier, and Monika Pagnieu; McBurney also worked with mime artist Jérôme Deschamps and Dario Fo.[108] The influence of these training backgrounds was vast and varied but key elements include: from Lecoq, emphases on the analysis of movement, the use of movement to convey meaning, and playing; and from Gaulier, the idea of complicity, or connection among performers and between performers and audience.[109]

Like DV8's work, Complicite's is total theatre, characterised by an inventive, suggestive and intelligent deployment of a wide range of theatre media. The most important of these is probably visual, but Complicite's visual media incorporate a large variety of elements, from action to scenography, images, objects, lighting, and video and projections. The company avoids literal representations and aims to produce more poetic, physical means of conveying meaning.[110] In *The Three Lives of Lucie Cabrol* (1994–96), the chaotic movement of wooden boards obliquely represented two characters having sex in a barn. In *Mnemonic* (1999–2003), a broken chair puppet represented the five-thousand-year-old Iceman. And in *The Elephant Vanishes* (2003), the slow, measured cross-stage progress of four empty chairs indicated an elephant's ponderous walk. Continuous ensemble movement produces ever-shifting and overlapping images, unstable but multi-layered meaning, and a phenomenal dexterity in suggesting transitions as well as connections between times, places, characters, and ideas.

While all the company's work is devised, since the early 1990s much of this devising has been based on existent literary texts. Artistic Director McBurney stresses, though, that in good total-theatre style, the company considers all aspects of theatre meaning potentially equally important. All shows begin with a text, he acknowledges, but 'the text can take many forms ... it can equally well be a visual text, a text of action, a musical one as well as the more conventional one involving plot and characters. ... Action is also a text. As is the space, the light, music, the sound of footsteps, silence and immobility.'[111] Shows are developed through workshops that emphasise creative play and aim to produce 'imaginative, disruptive theatre'.[112] They are notoriously funny but also committed to social analysis if not explicit political analysis.[113] Early devised pieces examined grief (*A Minute Too Late*, 1984) and relationships in the family (*Please, Please, Please*, 1986) and in the office (*Anything for a Quiet Life*, 1987–89). More recent devised pieces have explored memory and identity (*Mnemonic*) and the life of composer Dmitri Shostakovich, credited as a genius but condemned by the Soviet regime under which he lived (*The Noise of Time*, a collaboration with the Emerson String Quartet, 2000–2). Complicite's first literary text-based production was of Dürrenmatt's *The Visit* in 1989. Since then, the company has garnered a reputation for working with 'lesser-known Eastern European authors',[114] many of whom, as Helen Freshwater observes, have been 'marginalized and silenced'.[115] These include the Polish Jew Bruno Schulz (*The Street of Crocodiles*, 1992–94), the Russian Daniil Kharms (*Out of a House Walked a Man*, 1994–95), and the Swede Torgny Lindgren (*Light*, 2000). The company has also adapted the writings of John Berger (*The Three Lives of Lucie Cabrol*), Brecht (*The Caucasian Chalk Circle*, 1997), Ionesco (*The Chairs*, 1997–98), the South African J. M. Coetzee (*Foe*, 1996), and the Japanese Haruki Murakami (*The Elephant Vanishes*). Across all this work, Complicite has maintained narrative focus on those who are socially excluded, aiming to emulate their alternative perspectives.

As this short introduction to Complicite's work indicates, the company has taken on multiple European influences through the training and literary texts it has engaged with. Further European influences come through its work with the ideas and practices of other theatre makers, including 'Pina Bausch, the Polish director Kantor, [and] the Russian director Meyerhold'.[116] Even more European influences in Complicite's work come from employing theatre makers from across Europe, including France, Switzerland, Italy, and Greece, and other international influences come from collaborating with artists from elsewhere. As in DV8's work, the effect of this national difference is not superficial. 'What we try to see', explains long-time Complicite collaborator actor Lilo Baur, 'is that each nationality has its own way of expressing a word.' She demonstrates that the meaning of 'to take' resonates differently in various languages and therefore inspires different corresponding physical movements: 'For me, being Swiss, I would say "ley" and "ley" has a long sound, so I would maybe collect it. … You see what the gesture is in each language.'[117] Both Baur and McBurney are motivated by the intrinsic variations in different nationalities' languages to find a universal theatrical language with which to communicate across cultures. 'If theatre is to have power,' says McBurney, 'it is when it manages to touch on what is a primal and universal human need.'[118]

## A universalising theatre? The example of *Mnemonic*

This attitude shared by Baur and McBurney raises one of the most important issues in relation to both physical theatre in general and Complicite's work in particular: the degree to which it universalises gestures and, by extension, languages, attitudes, memories, experiences, and identities. I will explore this issue with close reference to *Mnemonic* because it is in relation to this show that this problem has sustained most scrutiny. First devised and produced in 1999, *Mnemonic* received enormous positive critical response and was subsequently revived in 2002.[119] It tells two interwoven quest stories concerned with identity. One is based on a true account of the 1991 discovery of a five-thousand-year-old corpse in the Austrian Alps and follows scientists and academics as they try to piece together his story: where he came from, what he did, why he died, and whether he was the victim of a violent attack. The second tells the fictional story of a contemporary couple, Virgil (Simon McBurney) and Alice (originated by Katrin Cartlidge and played in the revival, after Katrin's death, by Susan Lynch). Alice has discovered that the father her mother had always told her was dead may still be alive and she has abruptly left Britain to go across mainland Europe in search of him. She has been gone eight months as the play begins, leaving only an answerphone message for Virgil in London by way of explanation. For the first half of the play, Virgil only remembers her; after that, she finally phones him and they have a number of phone conversations. We also see Alice in various scenes throughout Europe – on the Eurostar and several other trains, and in Germany, Poland, Latvia, the Ukraine, and Italy. She discovers that her father was Jewish and her narrative intersects with numerous references to the Holocaust as well as other European episodes of persecution and forced migration.

The play opens with a semi-comic monologue about memory delivered by Simon McBurney as 'himself' and a coup de théâtre that takes us seamlessly from the 'real' into the fictional. In a sustained blackout, McBurney's live speech imperceptibly turns into recorded speech. When the lights come up, he has 'doubled' to now play the fictional Virgil sitting in a theatre listening to McBurney's recorded monologue. Thus, both of the play's central stories are framed by questions of memory and history and how they are produced through attempts at objectivity but also speculation, imagination, and, even, trickery. Further, as well as playing himself and Virgil, McBurney frequently plays the Iceman, as in figure 17, where the Iceman's body is scrutinised by scientists in a laboratory and/or by tourists in a museum. Thus, the two quest narratives are linked through McBurney's often-naked body. And in the play's final scene, (figure 18), all seven performers serially and literally roll in silhouette into the place and pose of the Iceman on the display table and so assume his identity. As the stage directions describe this scene, the performers 'lay themselves down and roll off again, just as generation succeeds generation in a never-ending cycle'.[120]

*Mnemonic* has provoked at least two opposing arguments regarding the possible universalism summed up in this rotating Iceman image of human history and identity as common and continuous. For Helen Freshwater in *New Theatre Quarterly*, *Mnemonic* productively 'asks us how we can move beyond individual reminiscence to explore the conflicted region of our collective past'.[121] Against what she describes as the ethical indeterminacy of the production's take on memory as an act of imagination, Freshwater suggests that *Mnemonic* posits 'the conviction that we are all related however distantly' through an 'emphasis on the body as a collective mnemonic, the lowest common denominator'. By serving 'to remind us of our common humanity', Freshwater suggests, *Mnemonic* provokes the audience to take responsibility for the five-millennia-long history of social persecution that the production 'remembers'.[122] Thus, some of the benefits of theatrically universalising human experience are that issues of timeless and global significance can be addressed. To extend Freshwater's analysis, it could be argued that Complicite uses both narrative and,

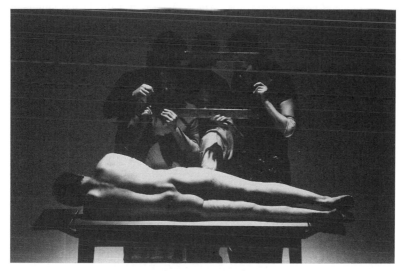

17 Simon McBurney in Complicite's *Mnemonic*

18  Cast rotating onto the Iceman's table in Complicite's *Mnemonic*

importantly, physical imagery across the range of its work to universalise human experience and compel audiences to take responsibility for a variety of ethical issues, including, for example: ethnic persecution here, the oppression of the socially excluded in *Lucie Cabrol*, issues of moral uncertainty in times of crisis in *Light*, and so on.

Janelle Reinelt's analysis of *Mnemonic*'s universalising tendencies is considerably less favourable. First in a 2000 review and subsequently in a longer essay, both for *Theatre Journal*, Reinelt has criticised the show for 'making a "family of man" statement, linking everyone in an image of sameness'.[123] 'The problem', she argues, 'is that white Europeans (for all the characters are white) represent all humans who are, it is implied, essentially similar in their travels, their struggles to survive, their bodiliness.' Reinelt argues that by narrating numerous historical acts of social persecution, the show proposes that 'human history is violent and has always produced massacres'. '[F]inally', she writes, 'the worldview of the play is a return to universalism and even a kind of fatalism.'[124] *Mnemonic* exemplifies for Reinelt some of the great risks of universalism: the arrogant if familiar liberal humanist tendency to privilege the experiences of the already culturally privileged white European (male) and the fatalism of universalising violent behaviour.

I agree with both Freshwater and Reinelt that *Mnemonic* aims to universalise experience in a number of ways, not the least of which is physical performance. However, at the risk of sounding as if I am prevaricating, I think this attempted universalising can simultaneously draw audiences' attention to *both* the benefits that Freshwater identifies and the problems that Reinelt raises. Further, I think that through narrative, movement, and the critical self-reflexivity the show can produce, *Mnemonic*'s attempt to universalise is only partially successful, that what it tries to universalise it produces more specifically as pan-European, and that it nevertheless acknowledges that 'European' may mean many, heterogeneous things.

## A European performance

As Reinelt herself acknowledges, *Mnemonic* may universalise, but it also pays considerable narrative 'attention to cultural specificity and difference':[125] we learn only partial but varied social histories of characters from Britain, Greece, and Eastern Europe; the Italian and Austrian governments assert their national difference by fighting over ownership of the Iceman's body, discovered on their borders; and characters speak a variety of European languages, many of which are not translated, preventing the characters from understanding one another and, perhaps, from being understood by audiences. This discourse on cultural difference is reinforced through analyses of the seventeen different types of wood the Iceman had with him when he died and the distinct properties and purposes they all had.[126] Thus, while *Mnemonic* aims to produce a certain universalism, it nevertheless acknowledges cultural differences (even if it seems determined to position them as a constant source of conflict). Further, if any commonality is produced, it is precisely – not inadvertently – a European one. I agree with Freshwater and Reinelt that the show attempts to demonstrate that cultural experience is shared universally but, to be fair, the overwhelming majority of cultural experiences *Mnemonic* shows are European. This risks generalising European experience – and, as Reinelt importantly points out, omitting non-white European experience. But it perhaps avoids the imperialist gesture of projecting European experiences as universal while, to reduce the breadth of Freshwater's argument, it proposes that Europeans themselves must take particular responsibility for their shared history of social persecution *in Europe*.

The movement and use of bodies in *Mnemonic*, as well as in other physical theatre, may also be less universalising than it at first appears. Again, as this chapter has aimed to demonstrate, we might see the

physical theatre techniques that Complicite uses as themselves culturally specific, part of a distinctive – if heterogeneous – European performance tradition. And while many practitioners within this tradition
– including Baur, McBurney, and Lecoq – see their work as universal
in its meanings, it is possible to read it as originating out of historical,
geographical and social specificity. Stephen Knapper illustrates, for
example, how *Mnemonic* is itself a mnemonic for Complicite's own particular history, a kind of 'taking stock' of its practices, inspirations, and
concerns throughout the 1990s.[127] Similarly, we might read Lecoq's particular practice as a product of the social history of his time and his
travels. As a young man during 'the German occupation of France[,]
he joined with a group of young enthusiasts who sought to use gym-
nastics, mime, movement and dance to express opposition to the prevailing Fascist ideology. This led him on, after the liberation of France,
to develop experimental performance work in which movement and theatre combined.'[128] He learned about bodies and movement as a phys-
iotherapist during the Second World War.[129] He developed an intimate
knowledge of commedia and mask work while living and working in
Italy for eight years from the late 1940s.[130] The student protests of 1968
in France provoked him to modify his training methods to give his students more responsibility for their own work.[131] And although Lecoq
himself saw his work as universal – about 'simply life'[132] – it was deeply
imbued with these experiences of being a Frenchman in postwar
Europe. Set themes for independent student scene-making at his school,
for example, included a day in the life of a French market town and
'The Exodus', which he explained 'was very poignant in the postwar
years' and claimed in the late 1990s 'is now finding new echoes'.[133] The
physical theatre performance practice Lecoq helped to pioneer is
embedded with this distinct material and social history.

Because of its emphasis on the material, the physical theatre practised by Complicite also has the potential to provoke – not universalising
readings – but specific materialist analysis, drawing attention to the ways
social relations are produced by particular material conditions, not by
some inevitable human condition. Reinelt points out that Rush Rehm
drew such an analysis from Complicite's *Lucie Cabrol*. He 'characterized
the work "as a rare case of artistic brilliance and political engagement",
pointing out a link between Berger's critique of consumerism [in the
source text] and Complicite's form of theatre practice: "The company's
theatrical imagination seems to spring from the ground up, or – perhaps
more accurately – up from the grounded body"'.[134] Certainly *Mnemonic*

suggests that migration is produced by material conditions of potential
and actual violence that Reinelt sees as fatalistically universalised in the
piece. But the show also acknowledges that migration can be caused by
other material conditions, such as economics, whether of hardship, for
those such as the character Simonides – who must migrate to seek work
– or of privilege – for those such as Alice and the Americans she meets
who can afford to travel as tourists. Likewise, the show may aim to set up
a universal human body both visually and textually: the Iceman is played
as infinitely exchangeable with all of the performers and – by extension
– everyone else after Alice says, 'Seeing a naked body of any age we
remember our own, putting ourselves in someone else's place, in the gully,
for example, 5,000 years ago'.[135] But I would argue that the performance
draws at least equal, and possibly even more, attention to the very visible
material differences between the different bodies. Even in the show's
frequent use of silhouette, muscular, tattooed McBurney is not inter-
changeable with small, lithe Susan Lynch, and nor, for that matter, does
she exactly replace tall, lean Katrin Cartlidge. The material bodies manifest their differences – of sex, age, ability, injury, style, comfort and
discomfort.[136]

Admittedly, *Mnemonic* invites sentimental engagement with its shared
'family of man' story, especially in McBurney's opening monologue. After
instructing the audience to put on blindfolds and remember their ancestors, McBurney concludes that 'a thousand years ago, if there really were
no kinship ties, that line [of ancestors stretching behind each audience
member] would be longer than all people who have ever been born.
Which, of course, is not possible … but it means that you are related to
everyone sitting in the theatre.'[137] However, the show simultaneously
resists universalising identity because it also provokes critical scrutiny of
master narratives. As Freshwater argues, the production emphasises the
instability and creativity of memory. It also demonstrates that identity is
composed of and by memories. Thus, even in the show's own terms, identity must be at least somewhat unstable and dynamic.

Further, while the show posits certain memories as shared,
McBurney has acknowledged outside the production that people
certainly have different experiences and memories. This may seem obvious, but what he recognises is that those different experiences and memories constitute people in vastly different ways. In an article for the *Guardian*,
he describes some of his own memories of the opening night of
*Mnemonic*'s 2002–3 European tour in Zenica, a Bosnian town where, as he
put it, 'the first refugees arrived from Srebrenica'.

> The audience listens to my voice. ... I have just asked them the ques-
> tion: 'Where were you 10 years ago? Can you remember?' Out of the
> darkness there is a hoarse shout. 'In a cellar with my fucking family!' ...
> [T]he packed audience laugh and murmur. ... In London, when I ask
> the same questions, few remember. Here, memories of 10 years ago
> are all too clear.[138]

McBurney's comment recognises cultural difference, but it also problemati-
cally portrays the memories of 'Zenica' as more meaningful than those of
'London' while nevertheless portraying himself as able to feel the suffering
of those ('European') memories – despite being a Londoner himself. The
risk here is that McBurney (and Complicite) do not challenge and destabilise
the anti-European anti-theatricality of dominant British theatre discourses,
but simply invert those discourses' prejudices by being anti-British.

Finally, it may not have been Complicite's intention for its audiences
to be sceptical about or to reject *Mnemonic*'s arguments, but certainly some
did. Reinelt, for example, responds to McBurney's conclusion 'you are
related to everyone sitting in the theatre' with the observations:

> A utopian sense of connection, yes, and yet, how many people in the
> theatre wanted to imagine holding their parents hands? – or even knew
> who those parents were, or why they had to be so definitely biologi-
> cal and of course heterosexual? In other words, the play began with a
> disarming appeal to 'family', which I found disturbing.[139]

Watching the show first at London's National Theatre in 2001 and at the
Riverside Studios in 2003, I too thought about how McBurney's narrative was both presumptuous and impossible, as did many others with
whom I discussed this scene. The play can invite the audience to share its
vision of a 'family of man', but it cannot guarantee that the invitation
will be accepted.

## British–European theatre futures

In the article in which she discusses *Mnemonic*, 'Performing Europe', Reinelt
seeks in recent British theatre a dramaturgy that can 'stimulate the imagination' and 'work in the subjunctive "what if" and "suppose that"' to
explore the opportunities of what she calls a New Europe that is 'an inclusive, socially responsible, super-democracy'.[140] Alongside *Mnemonic*, she
also looks at David Edgar's *Pentecost* and David Greig's *Europe* (both 1994),
and she is optimistic in her conclusions.

> All of these plays stage, at the level of content, the necessity to think broadly of the peoples located in Europe as European. For a UK audience, where the isolation of the island, the history of empire, and the Anglo-American connection often mitigate against such an identity-leap, this address from the stage to fellow-Europeans is inclusive, possibly even an interpellative invitation in Louis Althusser's sense.

Audiences to all of these shows, she concludes, are narratively interpellated 'as citizens of the new Europe'.[141] But she is more cautious in her analysis of the plays' forms, concluding:

> the challenge is to avoid replacing a deadly verbal text with a physical text that slips into imprecision and political ambivalence. British theatre will need to produce new forms of theatrical representation, perhaps 'Europeanizing' itself by drawing from Artaud and Lecoq without losing its own tradition of engaged political writing and muscular diversity.[142]

Developing such a 'Europeanised', hybrid, critically engaged, physical theatre is precisely what companies such as DV8, Complicite and many more besides have done and continue to do.

The critically engaged physical theatre of DV8 and Complicite presents a confidently hybridised form of theatre that offers both new representational possibilities and provocative examples of British–European creative co-operation and development – for a 'New Europe', for a 'pro-theatrical' theatre, and for cultural and theatrical practice that is open to exploring different ways of doing things. Work such as DV8's and Complicite's may not dominate British theatre, but it is growing, thanks in part to these two companies' influence. Like DV8's collaborators, many of Complicite's, including McBurney, also work outside the company distributing its ideas and practices,[143] and Complicite runs extensive education programmes, offering training in the hybrid creative practices it has developed.[144] Further, there are numerous other contemporary UK companies that emphasise what Lynn Sobieski calls the 'visual and aural score' in the ways DV8 and Complicite do.[145] In her article on such 'performance theatre', Sobieski discusses the People Show, Lumiere & Son and Hesitate and Demonstrate. To name a handful more – while still recognising that they have numerous differences and that this is only a small selection – we might add: Blast Theory, the Clod Ensemble, the David Glass Ensemble, Desperate Optimists, Doo Cot, Forced Entertainment, Frantic Assembly, Neil Bartlett's Gloria company, Grid Iron, Improbable Theatre, Reckless Sleepers, Ridiculusmus, Shared

Experience, Station House Opera, Suspect Culture, Theatre O, Volcano Theatre, and V-Tol.

These companies have not sprung spontaneously from a British theatre culture that was ever fully autonomous. British theatre has long been dynamically engaged with mainland European drama and theatre – not to mention other international drama and theatre – even if this history has been suppressed or neglected. The work of companies such as these demonstrates that the genealogies of contemporary British performance are complex, hybrid, and often strongly connected to – as well as engaged in dynamic relationships with – mainland European practices. It challenges the implicit xenophobia, fear of miscegenation, and anti-theatricalism that informs dominant narratives of British theatre as autonomous. Further, by negotiating hybrid European theatrical practices, it suggests ways of negotiating the changing meanings of European identities. It does not aim to capture and fix ideas of European identity, and nor am I trying to do so here. As Jacques Derrida, John Caughie, Stuart Hall, and many others have argued, European identity is neither stable nor homogeneous, and 'becoming European' is a never-ending process.[146] As Caughie notes, 'That kind of identity, national or supranational, which no longer recognises its own differences and instabilities, an identity which is no longer becoming but *has arrived*, fully achieved, is a dangerous and almost invariably malign thing'.[147] Historical evidence supporting this argument is the example of past European practice that understood and projected its own experiences as universal. These companies do not attempt to define and set Europe's meanings; but they are engaged in negotiating what being European might mean, as well as what and how the UK might mean in relation to and within a changing Europe.

## Notes

1 Alex May, *Britain and Europe since 1945* (London: Longman, 1999), p. 2.

2 John W. Young, *Britain and European Unity, 1945–1999* (London: Macmillan, 2nd edn, 2000), p. 185.

3 John Major quoted in Robert Hewison, *Culture and Consensus: England, Art and Politics since 1940* (London: Methuen, revised edn, 1997), p. 9.

4 Michel Foucault, 'Nietzsche, genealogy, history', in Foucault, *Language, Counter-memory, Practice: Selected Essays and Interviews*, Donald F. Bouchard (ed.), trans. Bouchard and Sherry Simon (Oxford: Basil Blackwell, 1977), pp. 139–64, p. 147.

5 The category 'British theatre', as we shall see, often imperially assimilates the non-British and/or assumes the more authoritative status of calling itself 'British' when it refers more accurately to English theatre. I refer to British theatre here because I want to try to look at theatre that is not only English.

6  Aleks Sierz, *In-Yer-Face Theatre: British Drama Today* (London: Faber and Faber, 2001), p. xi.

7  Claire Armitstead, 'LIFTing the theatre: the London International Festival of Theatre', in Theodore Shank (ed.), *Contemporary British Theatre* (London: Macmillan, revised edn, 1996), pp. 152–65, p. 152.

8  Peggy Phelan provocatively explores the importance of writing about theatre's ephemerality and how to approach doing so in *Unmarked: The Politics of Performance* (London: Routledge, 1993).

9  A not remotely comprehensive sample of examples from 1999 on includes: Elaine Aston and Janelle Reinelt (eds), *The Cambridge Companion to Modern British Women Playwrights* (Cambridge: Cambridge University Press, 2000); David Edgar (ed.), *State of Play: Playwrights on Playwriting* (London: Faber and Faber, 1999); Sierz, *In-Yer-Face Theatre*; and Michelene Wandor, *Post-war British Drama: Looking Back in Gender* (London: Routledge, 2001).

10  See, for example: Michael Billington, *One Night Stands: A Critic's View of Modern British Theatre* (London: Nick Hern Books, 1994); John Bull, *Stage Right: Crisis and Recovery in British Contemporary Mainstream Theatre* (London: Macmillan, 1994); Vera Gottlieb and Colin Chambers (eds), *Theatre in a Cool Climate* (Oxford: Amber Lane Press, 1999); and Sheridan Morley, *Our Theatre in the Eighties* (London: Hodder and Stoughton, 1990).

11  Peter Hall, *The Necessary Theatre* (London: Nick Hern Books, 1999), pp. 51, 16.

12  Terry Eagleton, *Literary Theory: An Introduction* (Oxford: Basil Blackwell, 1983), p. 28.

13  Hall, *The Necessary Theatre*, p. 6.

14  Sierz, *In-Yer-Face Theatre*, p. xi.

15  Christopher McCullough, *Theatre and Europe: 1957–95* (Exeter: Intellect, 1996), p. 29.

16  Hall, *The Necessary Theatre*, p. 16.

17  Dan Rebellato, *1956 and All That: The Making of Modern British Drama* (London: Routledge, 1999), p. 88.

18  This was the rueful situation in Britain in the 1980s and 1990s according to D. Keith Peacock and Theodore Shank. D. Keith Peacock, *Thatcher's Theatre: British Theatre and Drama in the Eighties* (New York: Greenwood Press, 1999), pp. 187ff; Theodore Shank, 'Preface to the 1996 reprint', in Shank (ed.), *Contemporary British Theatre*, pp. vii–ix, p. ix.

19  Ralph Yarrow and Anthony Frost, 'Great Britain', in Yarrow (ed.), *European Theatre, 1960–1990: Cross-cultural Perspectives* (London: Routledge, 1992), pp. 220–37, p. 222.

20  Eagleton, *Literary Theory*, pp. 19–20.

21  Peacock, *Thatcher's Theatre*, p. 204.

22  Billington, 'Britain's theatrical chauvinism', *Guardian* (1 October 1977), rpt in *One Night Stands*, pp.108–13, pp. 110 and 112.

23  Jane Edwardes, 'Directors: the new generation', in Shank (ed.), *Contemporary British Theatre*, pp. 205–22, p. 212.

24  Billington, Foreword, *One Night Stands*, pp. ix–xv, p. xiii.

25  Billington, 'Britain's theatrical chauvinism', p. 109. See also McCullough, *Theatre and Europe*, p. 26.

26 Jonas Barish, *The Antitheatrical Prejudice* (Los Angeles: University of California Press, 1981), pp. 10ff.

27 *Ibid.,* pp. 103, 104, 196, 96, 156, 170, and *passim.*

28 *Ibid.,* p. 85.

29 *Ibid.,* p. 203.

30 *Ibid.,* p. 135, ellipsis added.

31 *Ibid.,* pp. 343 and 349.

32 Simon Shepherd, 'Playing it straight: proper drama', chapter 10 in Shepherd and Peter Womack, *English Drama: A Cultural History* (Oxford: Blackwell, 1996), pp. 275–305, p. 285.

33 Rebellato, *1956 and All That,* pp. 153 and 143. Rebellato elaborates on these ideas in chapter 5 of *1956 and All That,* 'Something English: the repatriation of European drama'.

34 As Robert Young explores in detail, narratives of essentialised cultural autonomy are often actually riven with desire for intercultural encounter and miscegenation. Robert J. C. Young, *Colonial Desire: Hybridity in Theory, Culture and Race* (London: Routledge, 1995).

35 Ronald Bryden, Afterword, in Peter Daubeny, *My World of Theatre* (London: Jonathan Cape, 1971), pp. 335–9, p. 337.

36 Daubeny, *My World of Theatre,* p. 257.

37 On Brecht's influence in Britain before and after 1956 see: Bryden, Afterword, p. 337; Nicholas Jacobs and Prudence Ohlsen (eds), *Bertolt Brecht in Britain* (London: TQ Publications, 1977); Janelle Reinelt, *After Brecht: British Epic Theatre* (Ann Arbor: University of Michigan Press, 1994); and Dominic Shellard, *British Theatre since the War* (New Haven and London: Yale University Press, 1999), pp. 71–80.

38 Reinelt, *After Brecht,* p. 1.

39 Andrew Davies notes that Littlewood was further influenced by Adolphe Appia and the German expressionist movement. See: Andrew Davies, *Other Theatres: The Development of Alternative and Experimental Theatre in Britain* (London: Methuen, 1987), pp. 150–4; Howard Goorney, *The Theatre Workshop Story* (London: Methuen, 1981); Joan Littlewood, *Joan's Book: Joan Littlewood's Peculiar History as She Tells It* (London: Methuen, 1994); Rob Ritchie (ed.), *The Joint Stock Book: The Making of a Theatre Collective* (London: Methuen, 1987).

40 Shellard, *British Theatre since the War,* pp. 20 and 17. Shellard cites Harold Hobson, 'A French actor', *Sunday Times* (12 September 1948).

41 Shellard, *British Theatre since the War,* p. 73. For details of his productions to 1971 see Daubeny, 'List of major productions, companies and seasons presented in London by Peter Daubeny', in Daubeny, *My World of Theatre,* pp. 13–20.

42 Rebellato, *1956 and All That,* pp. 128–9.

43 Bryden, Afterword, p. 336; emphasis original.

44 *Ibid.,* p. 337.

45 *Ibid.,* pp. 337–8.

46 Shellard, *British Theatre since the War,* p. 74.

47 Yarrow and Frost, 'Great Britain', p. 234. See also Simon Trussler, *The Cambridge Illustrated History of British Theatre* (Cambridge: Cambridge University Press, 1994), p. 337.

48  Peter Brook, *The Empty Space* (Harmondsworth: Penguin Books, [1968] 1972), p. 61.

49  Rustom Bharucha is Brook's most outspoken critic in this context. See 'Peter Brook's *Mahabharata*: a view from India', chapter 4 in Bharucha, *Theatre and the World: Performance and the Politics of Culture* (London: Routledge, revised edn, 1993), pp. 68–87. See also David Williams (ed.), *Peter Brook and The Mahabharata: Critical Perspectives* (London: Routledge, 1991).

50  John Elsom, 'United Kingdom', in Don Rubin (ed.), *The World Encyclopedia of Contemporary Theatre*, Vol. 1, *Europe* (London: Routledge, 1994), pp. 890–920, p. 897. Elsom rightly points out that American theatre also had a strong influence on British theatre at this time. Visiting US theatre included: the Living Theatre (1964 and 1971); La Mama (1967 and 1969); the Open Theatre (1967 and 1973); and the Bread and Puppet Theatre (annually from 1968 to 1970). Trussler, *The Cambridge Illustrated History of British Theatre*, p. 344.

51  Chambers, *Other Spaces*, p. 21, ellipses added.

52  Unless otherwise noted, the following details on the EIF's programmes are from Appendix 1, 'Programmes 1947–1996', in Eileen Miller, *The Edinburgh International Festival, 1947–1996* (Aldershot: Scolar Press, 1996), pp. 159–327.

53  Trussler, *The Cambridge Illustrated History of British Theatre*, p. 338.

54  Alistair Moffat, *The Edinburgh Fringe* (London: Johnston and Bacon, 1978), p. 71; Miller, *The Edinburgh International Festival*, p. 103.

55  Moffat, *The Edinburgh Fringe*, p. 16.

56  Joyce McMillan, *The Traverse Theatre Story* (London: Methuen, 1988), p. 105. See also Moffat, *The Edinburgh Fringe*, pp. 53–66.

57  Michael Coveney, *The Citz: 21 Years of the Glasgow Citizens Theatre* (London: Nick Hern Books, 1990), p. 4.

58  *Ibid.*, pp. 4–5. Other featured European playwrights have included Laclos, Anouilh, Behan, Genet, Chekhov, Büchner, Molière, Gogol, Beaumarchais, Cocteau, Toller, Schiller, Ibsen, Racine, Pirandello, Dumas, Koltès, Muller, Beauvoir, Strindberg, and Brecht. For productions before 1990 see Coveney, *The Citz*, pp. 285–95. For subsequent productions, see *Citzsite: The Unofficial Citizens Theatre Website*, members.aol.com/glasgocitz/citz/gcplaysf.htm (accessed July 2003).

59  Coveney, *The Citz*, p. 71. Time will tell if this endeavour persists after the retirement of the Havergal/Prowse/MacDonald triumvirate in 2003/4 and the succession of new Artistic Director Jeremy Raison.

60  *Gate Biennale* (London: Methuen, 1996), n.p..

61  *Ibid.*, n.p.

62  *Ibid.*, n.p.

63  Founded in 1980 and sited in Kilburn, North London, the Tricycle promotes 'work which reflects the cultural diversity of its neighbourhood, in particular, plays by Irish, African-Caribbean, Jewish and Asian writers'. 'About us', *Tricycle*, www.tricycle.co.uk/html/aboutus/ (accessed February 2003).

64  The Bush was founded in 1972 (*Bush Theatre*, www.bushtheatre.co.uk/bushtheatre.html (accessed February 2003)). One-time Bush artistic director Dominic Dromgoole argues that the Bush is 'actually more of a European than a British theatre, in the sense of its understanding of stories. Many theatres are crushed

by the heavy hand of the twentieth-century British tradition; Shaw (more British that the Brits), Maugham, Granville-Barker, Rattigan, Priestley. This is the theatre of thumping "boys-own" plots and big noisy messages. The Bush has always followed the more glancing, oblique, opaque textured styles of Ibsen, Strindberg, Chekhov and Brecht.' Dominic Dromgoole, Introduction, *Bush Theatre Plays* (London: Faber and Faber, 1996), pp. xi–xiii, p. xiii.

65  Noted for its long development of British playwriting, the Royal Court also supports international writing through its international department, links with foreign theatres, translation projects, and writers' workshops (mentioned in Chapter 2). 'International', *Royal Court Theatre*, www.royalcourttheatre.com/ rc_international_into.asp (accessed August 2003); Charlotte Higgins, 'Continental drift', *Guardian* (17 April 2003).

66  Peacock, *Thatcher's Theatre*, p. 204.

67  For examples see LIFT's online archives at *LIFT 1997*, www.liftfest.org/lift97/intro.html, and *LIFT 1999*, www.liftfest.org/lift99/ (both accessed July 2003).

68  Shank, 'Preface to the 1996 reprint', p. vii.

69  Rose Fenton quoted in Michael Billington, 'The year of living dangerously', *Guardian* (6 June 2001), ellipsis added.

70  Armitstead, 'LIFTing the theatre', p. 152.

71  For evidence of BITE's geographical and generic range see, for example, *BITE 02*, www.barbican.org.uk/bite/archive/flash.html (accessed July 2003).

72  *London International Mime Festival 2000*, www.mimefest.co.uk/2000/ (accessed July 2003).

73  Reinelt, *After Brecht*; McCullough, *Theatre and Europe*, pp. 11–12.

74  For some consideration of Grotowski's influence on British theatre see McCullough, *Theatre and Europe*, p. 60. A recent edited collection considers Lecoq's impact in Britain in more detail, though with no sustained examination of Complicite: Franc Chamberlain and Ralph Yarrow (eds), *Jacques Lecoq and the British Theatre* (London: Routledge, 2002). A useful introduction to the European practitioners and practices that have influenced physical theatre's development in the UK is Dymphna Callery, *Through the Body: A Practical Guide to Physical Theatre* (London/New York: Nick Hern Books/Routledge, 2001), pp. 6–16. Space permitting, it would be informative to compare the genealogical hybridity of British theatre with that of other cultural practices, such as sport. See, for example, Andy Smith, '"Grass Roots": Eric Cantona, Jürgen Klinsmann and the Europeanisation of English football', in John Milfull (ed.), *Britain in Europe: Prospects for Change* (Aldershot: Ashgate Publishing Ltd, 1999), pp. 226–47.

75  Lloyd Newson, 'Dance *about* something', in *Enter Achilles* programme, 1995, rpt in 'Press archive', *DV8*, www.dv8.co.uk/press/interviews/danceabout.html (accessed March 2004). Some surveys of DV8's profile and work include: Fiona Buckland, 'Towards a language of the stage: the work of DV8 Physical Theatre', *NTQ: New Theatre Quarterly* 11:44 (1995), 371–80; Lloyd Newson, 'Lloyd Newson in interview with Jo Butterworth', in Butterworth and Gill Clarke (eds), *Dance Makers Portfolio: Conversations with Choreographers* (Bretton Hall: Centre for Dance and Theatre Studies, 1998), pp. 115–25 (rpt on *DV8*, www.dv8.co.uk); Stacey Prickett, 'Profile: Lloyd Newson', *Dance Theatre Journal* 19:1 (2003), 27–31; and

Christopher Winter, 'Love and language: or only connect the prose and the passion', *Dance Theatre Journal* 7:2 (1989), 10–13.

76 Lloyd Newson, 'DV8: ten years on the edge' (partly based on an interview with Mary Luckhurst), in *Bound to Please* programme, 1997; rpt on *DV8*, www.dv8.co.uk.

77 Nadine Meisner, Introduction to Lloyd Newson, '*Strange Fish*: Lloyd Newson talks to *Dance and Dancers* about his new work', *Dance and Dancers* (July 1992), 11–13, p. 12.

78 See: Buckland, 'Towards a language of the stage', p. 371; Jen Harvie, 'DV8's *Can We Afford This*: the cost of devising on site for global markets', *Theatre Research International* 27:1 (2002), 68–77, p. 70; Josephine Leask, 'The silence of the man: an essay on Lloyd Newson's physical theatre', *Ballett International* 8–9 (1995), 48–53, p. 50; Judith Mackrell, *Reading Dance* (London: Michael Joseph, 1997), p. 114; Lloyd Newson, interview, in Gabriella Giannachi and Mary Luckhurst, *On Directing: Interviews with Directors* (London: Faber and Faber, 1999), pp. 108–14, p. 113; and Libby Snape, 'Lloyd on love: Lloyd Newson talks to Libby Snape', *Dance Theatre Journal* 15:2 (1999), 8–12, p. 12.

79 For more detail see, for example: Malve Gradinger, 'Pina Bausch', in Martha Bremser, *Fifty Contemporary Choreographers* (London: Routledge, 1999), pp. 25–9; and 'Pina Bausch', in Paul Allain and Jen Harvie, *The Routledge Companion to Theatre and Performance* (London: Routledge, forthcoming).

80 Scenically, Bausch and her collaborators must be credited with leading a revolution in stage design for dance. Eschewing dance's oft-preferred 'empty space', Bausch's stages are consistently and literally covered in dead leaves (*Blue Beard*, 1977), chairs (*Café Müller*, 1978), a carpet of carnations (*Nelken*, 1982), ankle-deep water (*Arien*, 1985), and a pit of earth (*Viktor*, 1986).

81 Ana Sanchez-Colberg, 'Altered states and subliminal spaces: charting the road towards a physical theatre', *Performance Research* 1:2 (1996), 40–56.

82 Antonin Artaud, *The Theatre and Its Double*, trans. John Calder (London: John Calder, [1964] 1977), pp. 27–9.

83 Newson notes, 'DV8 was the first company in Britain to call their work physical theatre, which is a Grotowski-based term', but he adds, 'Now it's a term I'm hesitant to use because of its current overuse in describing almost anything that isn't traditional dance or theatre'. Newson, 'DV8: ten years on the edge'.

84 Gary Carter, 'In the plush hush of the mainstream: Gary Carter talks to DV8's Lloyd Newson', *Dance Theatre Journal* 10:4 (1993), 6–9 and 53, p. 9.

85 Newson emphasises, 'Set design has become more integral to my work. I'm interested in the relationship between architecture and the body.' Newson in Giannachi and Luckhurst, *On Directing*, p. 111.

86 Newson, 'Lloyd Newson in interview with Jo Butterworth', p. 123. Extending this logic, DV8 developed material from *Can We Afford This* into *Living Costs* (2003), a site-specific promenade performance for Tate Modern, London.

87 'I think we've had a strong influence on dance and on some theatre in England', says Newson. 'Acting schools now incorporate physical theatre practitioners into their courses, and the Royal Shakespeare Company have a stronger physical component in their training these days.' Newson, interview, in Giannachi and Luckhurst, *On Directing*, p. 113.

88  Keith Watson, 'Under the influence', *Dance Theatre Journal* 18:1 (2002), 32–5, p. 32, ellipsis added.

89  Sanchez-Colberg, 'Altered states and subliminal spaces', p. 52.

90  I aim primarily to discuss the stage performance of *Strange Fish* but refer also to the video version produced also in 1992. David Hinton (director), *Strange Fish* (DV8 Films Production for the BBC in association with RM Arts, 1992).

91  *Strange Fish* press release 1992. Rpt on *DV8*, www.dv8.co.uk/strangefish/fish.folder.html (accessed March 2004).

92  *Ibid.*

93  Meisner, Introduction to '*Strange Fish*', p. 10.

94  Newson, 'Dance *about* something'.

95  Hinton, *Strange Fish*, ellipses added.

96  Newson, '*Strange Fish*: Lloyd Newson talks to *Dance and Dancers*', p. 13.

97  Newson in Giannachi and Luckhurst, *On Directing*, p. 109.

98  Newson, '*Strange Fish*: Lloyd Newson talks to *Dance and Dancers*', p. 11.

99  Michael Church, 'Stand in line for a triumph of style over substance', *Observer* (17 May 1992).

100  Edward Owen, 'Expo '92 ends with late rush of visitors', *The Times* (12 October 1992).

101  For more information see: Colin Davis, *British Pavilion, Seville Exposition 1992. Nicholas Grimshaw and Partners* (London: Phaidon, 1992); Adela Gooch, 'High-tech Britain is making an exhibition of itself abroad', *Independent on Sunday* (19 April 1992); and Kenneth Powell, 'Building up to a fiesta or siesta?' *Daily Telegraph* (16 April 1992).

102  'Cast and crew and press release', *Strange Fish*, *DV8*, www.dv8.co.uk/strange-fish/fish.folder.html (accessed March 2004); Newson in Giannachi and Luckhurst, *On Directing*, p. 108.

103  Newson, 'Dance *about* something'.

104  Hinton, *Strange Fish*.

105  Other DV8 shows have also explored national and international identities and relationships. *Enter Achilles* invited consideration of Juan Kruz Diaz de Gariao Esnaola's implied sexual, ethnic, and national identity within the pub culture of a community of predominantly English men. *Can We Afford This* engaged with global identities and cultural relations through multinational casting, references to the 2000 Sydney Olympics and the Olympic Arts Festival in which it was first produced, and international touring. And the site-specific piece partly developed from *Can We Afford This*, *Living Costs* (2003), scrutinised the commodification of dance art and dancers in the context of a major international art gallery, London's Tate Modern.

106  See, for example, Lyn Gardner, quoted in 'About us, Reviews', *Complicite*, www.complicite.org/about/review.html?id=55 (accessed August 2003).

107  The company adopted a French name because McBurney originally anticipated working in France, but it has been based in London throughout its career and simplified its name in 2000. For further information about Complicite see, for example: *Complicite*, www.complicite.org/about; Hilary Taylor, 'Language in their gesture: Théâtre de Complicité', *The European English Messenger* 2:2 (1993), 39–42; Jane Edwardes, 'Directors: the new generation', in Shank (ed.),

*Contemporary British Theatre*, pp. 205–22; and Simon McBurney, interview, in Polly Irvin, *Directing for the Stage* (Mies, Switzerland: RotoVision SA, 2003), pp. 72–83. Three of the company's plays (*The Street of Crocodiles*, *The Three Lives of Lucie Cabrol* and *Mnemonic*) have been published in Complicite, *Complicite Plays 1* (London: Methuen, 2003).

108 Edwardes, 'Directors', p. 212; Simon McBurney, interview, in Giannachi and Luckhurst, *On Directing*, pp. 67–77, p. 75.

109 Edwardes, 'Directors', p. 212; Taylor, 'Language in their gesture', p. 40.

110 McBurney in 'Reviews', *Complicite*, www.complicite.org/about/message.html (accessed August 2003), ellipsis added.

111 McBurney in 'Reviews', *Complicite*, www.complicite.org/about/message.html (accessed August 2003).

112 'About Complicite', *Complicite*, www.complicite.org/about/ (accessed August 2003).

113 Janelle Reinelt claims the company has never 'been strongly political in any traditional sense' although she acknowledges its projects' organisation 'around social relations'. Janelle Reinelt, 'Performing Europe: identity formation for a "new" Europe', *Theatre Journal* 53:3 (2001), 365–87, p. 374; rpt in Helka Mäkinen, S. E. Wilmer, and W. B. Worthen (eds), *Theatre, History, and National Identities* (Helsinki: Helsinki University Press, 2001), pp. 227–56.

114 Dominic Cavendish, 'Dominic Cavendish, 2003', 'About us, reviews', *Complicite*, www.complicite.org/about/review.html?id=57 (accessed August 2003).

115 Helen Freshwater, 'The ethics of indeterminacy: Theatre de Complicite's *Mnemonic*', *NTQ: New Theatre Quarterly* 17:3 (67, 2001), 212–18, p. 216.

116 Sir Richard Eyre in Dominic Cavendish, 'Dominic Cavendish, 2003', 'About us, reviews', *Complicite*, www.complicite.org/about/review.html?id=57 (accessed August 2003).

117 Lilo Baur in Alan Wade, 'A *Theatre Annual* interview with Theatre de Complicite's Lilo Baur and Marcello Magni', *Theatre Annual* 53 (2000), 69–78, p. 74, ellipsis added. Lecoq uses the same example in Jacques Lecoq, in collaboration with Jean-Gabriel Carasso and Jean-Claude Lallias, *The Moving Body*, trans. David Bradby (London: Methuen, [1997] 2000), p. 49.

118 McBurney in Giannachi and Luckhurst, *On Directing*, p. 70.

119 *Mnemonic* was originally coproduced with the Salzburg Festival and toured, in 1999–2000, to Huddersfield, Cambridge, Newcastle, Oxford, Salzburg, and London's Riverside Studios. Revived in 2001, it played London's Royal National Theatre, Barcelona, Paris, and New York. Revived again in 2002–3, it appeared in Sarajevo, Thessaloniki, Munich, Warsaw, Helsinki, Strasbourg, Lyon, Paris, and London, at the Riverside Studios. 'Productions', *Mnemonic*, *Complicite*, www.complicite.org/productions/detail.html?id=1#toured (accessed August 2003).

120 Complicite, *Mnemonic* (London: Methuen, revised edn, 2001), p. 75.

121 Freshwater, 'The ethics of indeterminacy', p. 212.

122 *Ibid.*, p. 218.

123 Reinelt, 'Performing Europe', p. 376. See also Janelle Reinelt, review of *Mnemonic*, Complicite, Riverside Studios, London, 1999, in *Theatre Journal* 52:4 (2000), 578–9.

124  Reinelt, 'Performing Europe', p. 376.
125  *Ibid.*, p. 376.
126  Complicite, *Mnemonic*, pp. 39–41.
127  Stephen Knapper, 'The theatre of memory: Theatre de Complicité's *Mnemonic*', *TheatreForum* 17 (2000), 28–32, p. 31.
128  Lecoq, *The Moving Body*, p. xi. This is not to suggest that physical theatre was not also coincidentally practised by Fascists, although it is to suggest that these practices might have been different, and were certainly informed by different impetuses.
129  Simon McBurney, Foreword, Lecoq, *The Moving Body*, pp. ix–x, p. ix.
130  Lecoq, *The Moving Body*, p. 6.
131  McBurney, Foreword, p. ix.
132  Lecoq, *The Moving Body*, p. 46.
133  *Ibid.*, p. 92.
134  Reinelt, 'Performing Europe', p. 374. Reinelt quotes Rush Rehm, 'Lives of resistance: Theatre de Complicite, an appreciation', *TheatreForum* 6 (1995), 88–92.
135  Complicite, *Mnemonic*, pp. 74–5.
136  Writing on British performance art more broadly (although citing Complicite as a prime example), Tony Dunn argues that 'this theatre always foregrounds the human body, often naked, and the sequences, by now a convention, of bruising physical encounter emphasise its material existence'. Tony Dunn, 'Sated, starved or satisfied: the languages of theatre in Britain today', in Shank (ed.), *Contemporary British Theatre*, pp. 19–38, p. 24.
137  Complicite, *Mnemonic*, p. 7, ellipsis original.
138  Simon McBurney, 'You must remember this', *Guardian* (1 January 2003), ellipses added.
139  Reinelt, 'Performing Europe', p. 376.
140  *Ibid.*, pp. 372 and 365.
141  *Ibid.*, p. 384. Reinelt cites Louis Althusser, *For Marx*, trans. Ben Brewster (New York: Pantheon Books, 1969), p. 233.
142  Reinelt, 'Performing Europe', p. 385.
143  For example: Baur and Magni have worked with the RSC and the New Globe Theatre, London (Wade, 'A *Theatre Annual* interview'); and McBurney directed a stage show for comedians Dawn French and Jennifer Saunders in 2000, as well as a 2002 New York production of *The Resistible Rise of Arturo Ui* starring Al Pacino.
144  See 'Education', *Complicite*, www.complicite.org/education/ (accessed August 2003). Further training in physical theatre and 'new mime' is available in the UK through numerous other schools such as the Ecole Philippe Gaulier and the School of Physical Theatre, both in London. Callery, *Through the Body*, pp. 217–18.
145  Lynn Sobieski, 'Breaking the boundaries: the People Show, Lumiere & Son and Hesitate and Demonstrate', in Shank (ed.), *Contemporary British Theatre*, pp. 89–106, p. 91.
146  See, for example: Stuart Hall, 'European cinema on the verge of a nervous breakdown', and John Caughie, 'Becoming European: art cinema, irony and

identity', both in Duncan Petrie (ed.), *Screening Europe: Image and Identity in Contemporary European Cinema* (London: BFI, 1992); Jacques Derrida, *The Other Heading: Reflections on Today's Europe*, trans. Pascale-Anne Brault and Michael B. Naas (Bloomington and Indianapolis: Indiana University Press, 1992); Jan Nederveen Pieterse, 'Unpacking the West: how European is Europe?', in Ali Rattansi and Sallie Westwood (eds), *Racism, Modernity and Identity: On the Western Front* (Cambridge: Polity Press, 1994); and Stephanie Jordan and Andrée Grau, Introduction, in Andrée Grau and Stephanie Jordan (eds), *Europe Dancing: Perspectives on Theatre Dance and Cultural Identity* (London: Routledge, 2000).

147  Caughie, 'Becoming European', p. 35, emphasis original.

# 6

## Bollywood in Britain

Around the turn of the millennium, Bollywood erupted in Britain like …
an all-singing, all-dancing opening number in a Bollywood movie. In
January 2001, a Bollywood version of Puccini's *Turandot* premiered at
London's Royal Opera House. From April to November 2002, the British
Film Institute ran an 'ImagineAsia' season. Throughout May 2002, the
upmarket Selfridges department store on London's Oxford Street
adopted a Bollywood theme. Channel 4 broadcast a 'Bollywood Women'
season in August 2002. The exhibition 'Cinema India: The Art of
Bollywood' ran at the Victoria and Albert Museum from June to October
2002. And in June 2002, Sir Andrew Lloyd Webber – composer of *Cats*
and *The Phantom of the Opera* and one of the founding fathers of the late-
twentieth-century British megamusical – premiered his new production
and firm indication of the direction he thought British musicals needed
to go to survive and thrive in this new millennium: the homage to
Bollywood cinema, *Bombay Dreams*.[1]

Of course, it is entirely wrong to suggest that popular Hindi cinema
from Mumbai (colonial name, Bombay) – commonly known as
Bollywood cinema – had little to no presence in Britain before the new
millennium as it had already long enjoyed the reliable patronage of
British Asian communities.[2] Writing in *Sight and Sound* in 1998, Heather
Tyrrell argued that Bollywood cinema had been screened commercially
in England at least since the 1950s, that by '1980 UK Asians were the
world's first mass video audience' with 'up to 20 Bollywood video shops
in most British cities, and a phenomenal 45 in Leicester', and that, by the
time of her article, four Asian cable channels delivered 'Bollywood direct
to 90 per cent of British Asian homes'.[3] The change that occurred around
the turn of the millennium was that Bollywood cinema suddenly became
an object of enormous fascination not just within British Asian communities but also beyond them, in British cultural contexts that were more
mainstream and, as that term implies, often culturally dominant.

This chapter is concerned with the cultural effects of this sudden –
and possibly unsolicited – promotion of Bollywood cinema into the

British cultural mainstream. On one hand, this impromptu interest in popular Indian culture looks suspiciously faddish and fetishistic, ostensibly flattering but suspiciously patronising, and reminiscent of both Edward Said's description of Orientalism as 'a Western style for dominating, restructuring, and having authority over the Orient' and Peter Brook's infamous appropriation of *The Mahabharata* (1985).[4] It appears opportunistic, symptomatic of a superficial multiculturalism that feigns a liberal interest in 'other' cultures while so limiting their representation that it functions, instead, as racist. In this view, mainstream British culture produces, commodifies, and appropriates Indian chic as a badge of multicultural liberalism while making no significant attempt either to allow Asian cultures to represent themselves or properly to understand what is distinctive about those cultures. On the other hand, perhaps this mainstream British interest in Asian cultures bodes well for them as well as for British culture more broadly, giving Asian cultures in Britain an opportunity to escape their former ghettoisation, to articulate their identities and concerns in a broader context, and to claim and attain greater cultural authority. Beyond this, perhaps it provides important opportunities: for British Asians to produce not self-stereotyping and self-denigrating cultural tourism but cultural affirmation and provocation;[5] to articulate and even create the specificity of British Asian hybrid, diasporic cultures; and significantly to destabilise, redefine, and hybridise what it means to be 'British'.[6]

To ground my analysis of Bollywood in Britain, this chapter focuses on two recent stage versions of Bollywood film, one by the British Asian touring theatre company Tamasha, *Fourteen Songs, Two Weddings and a Funeral* (first produced in 1998 and revived in 2001), and the other initiated and produced by the British megamusical magnate Andrew Lloyd Webber for production at London's Apollo Victoria Theatre, *Bombay Dreams* (first produced in 2002). This selection sets up a number of points of blatant contrast, to do most obviously with the status and cultures of the producing companies as well as the scales of production. In so doing, it does not aim bluntly to demonise Lloyd Webber as an imperialist tyrant and to sanctify Tamasha as the noble resistance. Instead, it aims to evaluate more carefully what the dynamic cultural effects of both productions were and are, a remit that demands attention also to the two productions' points of comparison: most importantly, their adaptation of Bollywood film conventions.

Before examining the cultural effects of these particular adaptations of Bollywood cinema, therefore, this chapter considers first the

cultural effects of Bollywood cinema itself. For Bollywood's many detractors, any attempt to produce progressive social effects by making or
adapting this cinema is doomed to fail because they see it as an inherently conservative and derivative hybrid colonial form, capable of articulating nothing that is either progressive or authentically Indian. There
is an increasing body of criticism, though, that sees a radical potential
in both Bollywood and its American cognate, the classic Hollywood
musical of the 1930s–50s, and that pays closer attention to the cultural
and political contexts that generate these film forms' apparently conservative cultural expression. Finally, some criticism sees Bollywood's
inherent hybridity as not a failure but an accurate representation of
Indian identities that cannot be essentialised, a symptom of Indian
hybridity in a postcolonial, globalised age. To contextualise how British
Bollywood stage adaptations might function, this chapter begins by
examining some of these arguments to unpack Bollywood cinema's
potential as a model and vehicle of cultural articulation and intervention, both within India and throughout the Asian diaspora.

I argue that these British adaptations certainly engage with
Bollywood cinema's risks of cultural appropriation and trivialisation as
well as conservative retrenchment. And I argue that it is necessary to
be wary of these risks, as it is to heed the salutary reminder that British
Asian communities might have good reason to take refuge in conservative utopian fantasies in response to lived experiences of ongoing oppression and/or marginalisation. However, I also argue that these
productions variably affirm a distinctive British Asian hybrid cultural
identity, raising the profile of British Asians, articulating their cultural
differences and fundamentally revising both what it means to be British
and how to be British. As Mary-Karen Dahl has argued in a related
context,

> As long as cultural difference is seen as deeply threatening to the
> English way of life, cultural praxis must be one field where the fate of
> the nation is contested. Certainly a new generation of black British
> theatre workers are already on the field of play. Their tactical command
> of theatre's disciplines, and their diverse strategies are … producing
> visions of culture and of the new Britain that – like their histories – will
> not be contained, repressed, or denied. [7]

Finally, I suggest that the analysis of this chapter is urgent because of the
general conditions Dahl suggests and because of the particular attention
currently being paid to Bollywood. In Britain, this attention is manifest not

only in recent theatre but pervasively, in cinemas, galleries and high-street shops, and on television in the BBC's Bollywood dance link between programmes (2003), the Walkers Crisps 'Great British Takeaway' and 'Free Meals' advertisements (2003), and the pop video featuring *Bombay Dreams* dancers for 'Spirit in the Sky' (2003), covered by Gareth Gates and the Kumars, a fictional British Asian family from the spoof celebrity interview television show, *The Kumars at No. 42* on BBC2.[8] Elsewhere in the West, it is demonstrated in the increasing 'Bollywoodisation' of Hollywood cinema,[9] and in *Bombay Dreams'* opening on Broadway in spring 2004.

## The Bollywood cinema industry

Putting debates about its cultural effects momentarily aside, one thing is undisputable about popular Indian cinema: it is an enormous industry. With major production centres in Mumbai, Madras, Calcutta, Bangalore, and Hyderabad, it is 'well known collectively as the world's largest national film industry'.[10] In his informative and critically astute book, *Bollywood Cinema: Temples of Desire* (2002), Vijay Mishra noted that, since 1981, almost fifteen thousand films had been produced in India. By 1983, 'it was India's sixth-largest industry, grossing around $600 million annually and employing some three hundred thousand workers'.[11] In 1985, India produced 905 feature films in at least eighteen different languages; 185 of these films were in Hindi, the dominant language of the Mumbai – or Bollywood – film industry. In 1991, India produced 215 Hindi films.[12] The scale of production of Indian film is mirrored in its scale of distribution, and it is increasingly coming to be recognised as not only a national cinema but also a global cinema. According to Mishra, in India alone 'eight hundred films a year [are] shown in more than thirteen thousand predominantly urban cinemas, viewed by an average of 11 million people each day'; they are also 'exported to about a hundred countries'.[13] Foreign markets – especially those made up of non-resident Indian populations – contribute increasingly to Indian films' financial success. In the early 1990s, overseas sales reportedly made up 10 to 15 per cent of a Bollywood film's earnings; in 2001, Bollywood films earned about 65 per cent of their takings outside of India, largely because of the value of Western currencies.[14] In 1994, the UK reportedly constituted over 50 per cent of the global financial market for Indian films.[15] Bollywood's widespread distribution and influence is unquestionable, but what is Bollywood cinema, and what are its cultural effects for its enormous global audiences?

## Bollywood as conservative derivative

Certainly some of these hundreds of films produced in India could be classified as 'third cinema' – non-Western arthouse cinema – but a vast majority of them are popular. And the enormous scale and rapid rate of production of this popular Indian film means inevitably that it is both commercially driven and relentlessly formulaic, consistently composed of numerous song and dance numbers incorporating several glamorous costume changes, a simple plot habitually concerned with a conflict between tradition and change, and variable amounts of *masala* (literally spice), often provided through violence and/or extreme sensuality (but not explicit sex).[16] For many of its critics, the formula of Bollywood cinema is most manifest in a variety of derisory features. In an early influential UK article on Bollywood cinema, Rosie Thomas observes, 'Compared with the conventions of much Western cinema, Hindi films appear to have patently preposterous narratives, overblown dialogue (frequently evaluated by filmmakers on whether or not it is "clapworthy"), exaggeratedly stylized acting, and to show a disregard for psychological characterization, history, geography, and even, sometimes, camera placement rules.'[17] For Bollywood's many detractors, this commercially driven generic standardisation utterly hijacks popular Indian films' potential to be culturally progressive. Thus it is accused of 'parasitism, low cultural form, [and an] absence of political awareness',[18] it is dismissed as inane cultural drivel, and it is defamed as illogical, shoddy, and embarrassing.

Alongside some of the rather unconsidered dismissals of Bollywood cinema, writes Thomas,

> There are also, of course, more serious and considered critical positions within India, notably of the politically conscious who argue, quite cogently, that Hindi cinema is capitalist, sexist, exploitative, 'escapist' mystification, politically and aesthetically reactionary, and moreover that its control of distribution networks blocks opportunities for more radical practitioners.[19]

It is capitalist as an industry because it buys into and reproduces a capitalist free market economy; as a visual and narrative discourse, it is capitalist because it fetishises objects such as ornate costumes and food and focuses on middle-class wealth rather than (widespread) Indian poverty. It is sexist in its representations of women, both visually, in imagery replete with bare bellies and deep cleavages, and in narrative, where women are often the objects of exchange between men. It is 'escapist' mystification because it sells lifestyle fantasies that are simply unachievable for the vast – impoverished – majority of its audiences. And it is conservative both formally – because it constantly reproduces itself in only slightly modified forms – and politically – because it leads inevitably to narrative resolutions that reassert the status quo. Since at least the mid-1990s, in a trend fuelled by the huge success of *Hum Aapke Hain Koun ...!* (1994) which I discuss in more detail below, this resolution has featured the discovery that a perceived conflict between tradition and 'true love' is not a conflict after all, and the resulting celebratory wedding.[20] Furthermore, Bollywood cinema is accused of falsely homogenising Indian cultures. Despite India's enormous diversity – of languages, religions, classes, geographies, and so on – the Hindu, North Indian, patriarchal, middle-class perspective favoured by the Hindi cinema of Mumbai predominates, both because it is widely distributed and because it has been adopted as a model for many other regional cinemas, bringing it 'closer to being an all-India cinema', in Mishra's opinion.[21] Thus, Indian popular cinema risks smoothing over and standardising Indian cultural differences, rather than helping to articulate and even foster their distinctiveness.

Alongside all of these criticisms is another one that is especially important when evaluating Indian popular cinema's 'Indian-ness', or its potential to articulate Indian cultural specificity, especially when imported into the context of the UK, where Asian cultures are often marginalised and subject to neo-imperialism. This is the argument that Bollywood cinema in particular is intrinsically westernised, that it is a derivative colonial form. There are two possible sources of this perceived imperial influence: the more deeply historically embedded source is British theatre practice, long imported to India and embraced most strongly by the minority Parsi community in its theatre; and the more recent source is Hollywood cinema. Tracing the roots of Bollywood cinema, Mishra acknowledges the influences of traditional Indian folk plays and myths, especially of the *Ramayana* and the *Mahabharata*; but he also points to the influence of the Parsi theatre. This, he argues, was in turn especially strongly shaped by imported British theatre traditions, particularly the use of the proscenium arch stage which was radically different from the open staging of precolonial and early colonial India and produced an emphasis on frontality in theatre production that is now deeply structured into Bollywood films, most notably in their smile-at-the-camera song-and-dance sequences.[22] The potential problem with this imperial influence is that it attributed greater value to the imperial model and consequently displaced and devalued preceding Indian traditions. This is certainly Mishra's opinion, at least in part, implicit in his analysis of the Parsis: 'The Parsis of India, it must be said, were a thoroughly colonial lot and perhaps colonialism's best hybrid Other and mimics. Given their numerically marginalized status in India, they were more likely to be *complicit in the project of imperialism*.'[23] The influence of classic Hollywood (and Broadway) musicals is referenced in Bollywood's mimicking name, as well as in many of its generic features. The danger of this influence is that Indian cultural practice is again devalued and displaced, this time by American cultural neo-imperialism. Further, Bollywood cinema risks reproducing many of the Hollywood musical's potential political problems. While acknowledging that the classic Hollywood musical is 'Formally bold', the influential historian of the form Jane Feuer argues that it is nevertheless 'culturally the most conservative of genres'.[24]

## Bollywood as mimicry and fantasy

Criticisms are certainly stacked high against Bollywood cinema and its roots, but there are also those who see it as having considerable politically progressive potential. For brevity, I will concentrate on responses to two areas of criticism here: first, accusations of colonial mimicry; and second, accusations of political conservatism.

Where Bollywood's critics read its colonial hybridity as a detraction, its supporters read this instead as both a source of creative invention and, integrally, a means of undermining – rather than, or as well as, promoting – the imperial model. While Mishra acknowledges the Parsis' motivations for mimicking the imperial power's theatre practices – to protect themselves, as a minority – he nevertheless implicitly criticises them for doing so. He also, however, points out that 'in matters of creative hybridity [the Parsis'] contribution to Bombay culture was enormous', suggesting they brought something distinctive to Bombay culture that other domestic and imperial models did not, specifically, a hybridised Indian/British theatre practice. He makes a similar argument for the imperial roots of Bollywood cinema, writing, 'in Bombay Cinema (which began as a colonial form) one of the great borrowed literary forms has been melodrama. The expressive possibilities of this mode, I argue, are taken up in a *highly localized* manner by Bombay Cinema.' In an extension of this argument, he writes, 'Like its literary antecedent – the gothic novel – the Indian gothic [of Bollywood cinema] draws upon the discourses of melodrama and sentimentality. To these we need to add Indian aesthetic theories of the wonderful, the horrific, and so on, and the very Indian narrative of reincarnation, or rebirth.'[25]

In each of these examples, the colonial form is similar to, but significantly differs from, the imperial model. As postcolonial theorist Homi K. Bhabha has famously put it, colonial mimicry is *'almost the same, but not quite'*, *'Almost the same but not white'*.[26] The colonial subject does not simply adopt the imperial model wholesale, but adapts and modifies it: 'to be Anglicized', observes Bhabha, 'is *emphatically* not to be English'.[27] Thus, colonial discourse produces new expressive possibilities for the colonial subject, and it potentially undermines the putative superiority of the imperial model by demonstrating that its features are neither permanent nor universally desirable. Instead of flattering and reinforcing the superiority of the imperial model, colonial mimicry menaces, destabilises, and challenges that assumed authority; instead of being imitative and self-effacing, the colonial hybrid is innovative and at least partly self-expressive.

Bollywood cinema has many distinctive features that reinforce these claims that it is both different from imperial models and expressive of Indian cultural experiences. Thomas points out that 'Bombay filmmakers repeatedly stress that they are aiming to make films which differ in both format and content from Western films, that there is a definite skill to making films for the Indian audience, that this audience has specific needs and expectations, and that to compare Hindi films to those of the West, or of the Indian "art" cinema, is irrelevant'.[28] In popular Hindi cinema: storylines are seldom linear and are often interrupted by spectacle; heightened emotion is crucial and contrasts explicitly with the perception of Western films as 'cold'; 'entertainment values' such as songs, dances, and fights are skilfully integrated into the film; familiarity and repetition are emphasised over novelty; and myths and values – especially those related to religion and patriotism – are distinctly 'Indianised'.[29] Instead of seeing popular Hindi films as illogical or preposterous, it is more appropriate to see them as being organised according to fundamentally *different* logics from those that dominate Western film cultures.

Rather than being apolitical, these distinctive features hold politically progressive potential. Ravi S. Vasudevan argues, for example, that Bollywood makes much more extensive use of direct address and frontality in performance than does classic Hollywood cinema. This frontality is adopted in both *Fourteen Songs, Two Weddings and a Funeral* and *Bombay*

*Dreams*, as illustrated in the song sequences pictured in figures 20, 21, and 23, below. 'At one level', Vasudevan suggests, 'this form of spectatorial subjectivity can deny the atomising modernity associated with the construction of individuation and a privatised sphere for the couple.'[30] Consequently, he proposes, Bollywood audiences and characters are drawn into *communitas* – into an incipient political community – rather than being singled or coupled off in the hermetic isolation that he sees as the outcome of many classic Hollywood film musicals. Bollywood's direct-to-camera address acknowledges and prioritises its audience as the privileged object of address, the intended audience of its spectacle. By contrast, the fourth-wall-observing 'internalised' address of many classic Hollywood films excludes and implicitly devalues its audience. Bollywood cinema is not as irreducibly conservative as some of its critics might claim; its central narratives may be conservative, but its structuring of identification and its production of group identity is not.

Furthermore, Bollywood may adopt and adapt elements from imperial and Hollywood models, but it also significantly and literally *displaces* Hollywood cinema, in particular by directly usurping its market share and so undermining the global cultural centrality it seeks. Vasudevan notes, 'in certain countries such as India the commercial film has, since the dawn of the "talkies", successfully marginalized Hollywood's weight in the domestic market. [I]t constitutes something like a "nation-space" against the dominant norms of Hollywood, and so ironically fulfils aspects of the role which the avant garde third cinema proclaims as its own.'[31]

Bollywood cinema may not be, like third cinema, *radically* different from Hollywood cinema, but it is significantly different. And it is sufficiently popular for the cultural effects of this difference to be – if not profound in the ways that third cinema might aim to be – at least pervasive.

The second major criticism of Bollywood cinema I want to address is the claim that it is politically reactionary. Two central critical responses to this claim are: first, that Bollywood cinema is not as conservative as at first it might appear; and, second, that overt radicalism may be a luxury most of Bollywood's filmmakers and audiences cannot afford, and that Bollywood's apparent conservatism actually fulfils important cultural needs. The first argument has been made about many ostensibly conservative cultural forms, from Shakespearean comedy to melodrama, to popular fiction, to 'women's pictures' of the 1930s and 1940s, to soap opera, to other popular Hollywood cinema.[32] And it proposes that, although many of these forms may end with restorative, even status-quo-affirming conclusions, these are less powerful than the transgressions that have made up the bulk of the narrative, so that the transgressions are never fully contained. Thus, for example, although many Bollywood films may be organised around the exchange of a woman from her father's household to her husband's, for most of the film she is in transition, challenging both of those containing patriarchal structures, often explicitly. A film's concluding conservatism may shift its predominant exploration of transgression, but it need not erase or overwhelm it.

Despite these points, it would be difficult to claim that Bollywood cinema is radically oppositional. Significantly, though, this feature holds some politically progressive potential, or must at least be considered in cultural context. One way to account for the films' enormous appeal to underprivileged audiences who will never attain the fantasy lives depicted is to say that those audiences are foolishly duped into believing in this unattainable fantasy. Another way is to say that those audiences willingly take comfort in the fantasy of utopia that the films provide even as they recognise that it is a fantasy or a consoling fiction. This is the argument Richard Dyer poses for classic Hollywood musicals, suggesting that in the face of underprivileged audiences' lived experiences of scarcity, exhaustion, dreariness, manipulation, and fragmentation, musicals offer filmic experiences of abundance, energy, intensity, transparency, and community.[33] For Kenneth MacKinnon, classic Hollywood musicals suggest 'that there is space beyond humdrum, burdensome everyday reality, and that that space belongs to the underprivileged, those who experience discrimination in the "real world", a world which becomes markedly less real in the musical'.[34] Musicals, their proponents argue, offer utopias beyond oppression.[35]

The argument is directly transferable to extravagant, exuberant, spectacular, playful, utopian Bollywood cinema and its audiences. Vasudevan speculates that Bollywood cinema has a special – perhaps reassuring – resonance in what he calls 'transitional' societies, for example, societies coming out of colonialism. Mishra proposes that Bollywood films and videos serve precisely this function – as well as others – in the UK: '"racist" Britain degrades the Indian diaspora to such an extent that it retreats into the secure spectacle of Bombay Cinema'.[36] And Geeta Kapur and Ashish Rajadhyaksha argue that the Bombay Hindi film industry 'provided a language of exchange for the rest of India [and Indian expatriates] – images, prose, songs and sheer *rhetoric* that is about arriving, about survival'.[37] Thus, to indulge in the multiple conservative pleasures of Bollywood cinema – its song and dance, action, colour, music, emotions, reassuring plots, spectacular scenography and costumes – is not to be duped but rather to be politically expedient. It is to choose to dream.

## Adapting Bollywood in British theatre

Bollywood cinema has at least dual potential: first, to be conservative, and second, to be more progressive by expressing and developing hybrid Indian identities and providing socially constructive consoling fictions. This dual potential means, however, that the effects of Bollywood cinema are multiple, unstable, even volatile. Thus, the cultural effects of adapting the form for live performance in the UK cannot be presumed to be the same from production to production. In the following sections, I examine Tamasha Theatre Company's *Fourteen Songs, Two Weddings and a Funeral* and Andrew Lloyd Webber's *Bombay Dreams*. Exploring how these productions adapt Bollywood cinema, I concentrate on each production's relationship to and attitude towards Bollywood sources and Asian cultures more broadly, focusing especially on whether these productions embrace, query, mock, or disregard Bollywood's conventions. I consider, for example, the implications of *Fourteen Songs'* apparently quite straightforward adaptation of the enormously successful Bollywood film *Hum Aapke Hain Koun ...! (HAHK,* 1994) as an effective endorsement of Bollywood's dominant codes, despite the fact that those codes have been extensively criticised by Bollywood's detractors – and *HAHK's* detractors in particular. And I consider *Bombay Dreams'* apparently more ironic attitude towards its Bollywood sources, as well as the implications of what can thus be seen, at least in part, as a disavowal of the production's Indian source material and source cultures. I am centrally concerned with how these productions either contributed to constraining and oppressing British Asian cultures or facilitated the dynamic expression and development of those cultures. I argue that *Fourteen Songs'* overt and deep commitment to Bollywood cinema allowed it to function centrally as a vehicle of cultural affirmation for British Asian identities while also suggesting a modest critique of whitewashed representations of British identity. And I argue that while *Bombay Dreams* also went some considerable way towards affirming British Asian identities, its much more ambivalent relationship to Bollywood conventions ultimately compromised that affirmation and put it at risk of being what one reviewer called 'a Eurocentric Bombay mix for cultural tourists'.[38]

## Tamasha's record

Whatever the specific cultural effects of *Fourteen Songs* may be, Tamasha's aim to produce work that speaks to and for British Asian audiences cannot be faulted. Founded by Sudha Bhuchar and Kristine Landon-Smith in London in 1989, Tamasha 'aims to reflect through theatre the Asian experience – from British Asian life to authentic accounts of life in the Indian sub-continent, adapting works of literature and classics to commissioning new work from a range of writers'.[39] To 2003, they have produced eleven major shows, all of which have explored cultural experiences in both the Indian subcontinent and, especially latterly, British Asian communities. The first two productions, *Untouchable* (1989) and *House of the Sun* (1991), were both set in India, were adaptations of Indian novels and explored caste and the effects of post-partition migration, respectively. *Women of the Dust* (1992) was commissioned by Oxfam to mark its fiftieth anniversary and focused on 'an itinerant, all-female workforce gathering on a dusty Delhi construction site'.[40] It toured India in 1993 and its radio version won a Commission for Racial Equality (CRE) Media Award.[41] *A Shaft of Sunlight* (1994) was also set in India and explored a Muslim–Hindu mixed marriage. *A Tainted Dawn* (1997) was based on the company's improvisations inspired by short stories on the partition of India and Pakistan. *Ghostdancing* (2001), by Deepak Verma, adapted *Thérèse Raquin* to a town in the Punjab, while *A Yearning* (1995) transposed Lorca's *Yerma* to a Punjabi community in contemporary Birmingham and won Tamasha another CRE Race in the Media Award for its radio version. *East Is East* (1996) explored the cultural conflicts experienced by a mixed white English/Asian family living in Northern England in the 1970s, often to great comic effect. *Balti Kings* (1999) was set in Balti restaurants in the English Midlands and explored the interaction of Asian and English cultures and values, and *Strictly Dandia* (2003) was set in British Asian leisure centres in North London and again explored conflicts between different generations of British Asians.

As all of these examples demonstrate, Tamasha consistently makes work that aims to address the concerns of its British Asian audiences, whether those concerns relate to experiences in South Asia or Britain. Along with other black and Asian British playwrights and theatre companies, Tamasha has been credited with productively shifting the concerns of British political theatre. May Joseph, for example, argues that black and Asian British theatre has challenge[d] not only mainstream theatrical conventions, but the orthodoxies of British left theater as well. Immigrant producers compli- cated the preoccupations of left playwrights – class, labor, left politics, the welfare state – with the diasporic history of immigration, assimila- tion, race, colonialism, and the transnational memories of arrival.

Thus, she argues, it has altered the landscape of British political theatre and helped to forge 'a diasporic identity of Britishness'. [42]

Tamasha also aims literally to address a widespread British Asian audience by touring its productions – usually to the Birmingham Repertory Theatre and London's Lyric Hammersmith as well as theatres in other cities including Bristol and Edinburgh – and by adapting at least five of its productions for BBC radio.[43] Although Tamasha's shows are set in both the 'old' world and the 'new', unlike fellow British Asian theatre company Tara Arts[44] it does not use 'old' performance discourses such as folk drama from Delhi, the martial art Kalari, and the Gujerati folk drama Bhavai.[45] Thus, its strategy is to use popular performance discourses that do not require specialist knowledge to be understood and that will be familiar to broad audiences across generations in Britain's Asian diaspora. *Fourteen Songs*, for example, explicitly uses familiar conven- tions from Bollywood cinema, and *East Is East* employs conventions of television situation comedy. Maybe partly because of this use of mass media performance discourses, Tamasha has enjoyed crossover success into radio and film: *East Is East* was released as a feature film directed by Damian O'Donnell in 1999 and won numerous awards.[46] All of this indi- cates Tamasha's aim to produce theatre that has constructive social and political effects for British Asian audiences: the company makes work about issues of cultural relevance to British Asian audiences, does so in accessible performance discourses, and actively seeks out its audiences around Britain by touring and working across a variety of media.

*Fourteen Songs, Two Weddings and a Funeral* indicates some of the possi- ble advantages of this approach as well as, however, some of the possible problems. Most crucially, it suggests the conflicting dynamics of adopting the popular Bollywood form.

### The ambivalent potential of *Hum Aapke Hain Koun ...!*

Tamasha's *Fourteen Songs, Two Weddings and a Funeral* was a direct adapta- tion of the 1994 enormous Bollywood hit directed by Sooraj Barjatya, *Hum Aapke Hain Koun ...!*, the title of which translates as *Who Am I to You?*

and is popularly abbreviated to *HAHK*.[47] Both film and play follow the fortunes of a pair of brothers and a pair of sisters. After initial courting and negotiations, elder brother Rajesh marries elder sister Pooja. When Pooja tragically dies in an accident, tradition dictates that the younger sister Nisha must marry the widower, her brother-in-law Rajesh; however, her heart is set on the other brother, Prem. Preparations for Nisha's and Rajesh's wedding are dutifully being played through when, at the last minute, the love between Nisha and Prem is discovered and the widowed brother Rajesh happily encourages Nisha to marry his brother instead of himself. Thus, both film and play stage a conflict between marriage as a function of family duty and marriage as the outcome of love and choice, and they both neatly have their cake and eat it too by conflating duty and love when the elder brother as patriarch endorses the love match, conveniently producing an 'arranged love match'.[48]

As the political potential of Bollywood cinema broadly conceived is widely disputed, the political potential of this particular film has been contentious: probably more pervasively, it has been damningly identified as egregiously conservative, most forcefully by Indian cultural and theatre critic Rustom Bharucha; but it has also been recognised as culturally productive, in most detail by Patricia Uberoi. The cultural potentials at stake in the case of this film are especially high because, at the time of its release, *HAHK* was believed to be the most popular Bollywood film to date. Dismissed in a pre-release assessment as an overlong wedding home video, *HAHK* went on to become one of the most popular Hindi films of all time, garnering 'the apocryphal status of films that are shown somewhere in India every day of the year',[49] and making around £20.8 million, or over '100 crores of rupees'.[50] As Uberoi notes, '*HAHK* is similarly said to have broken all records for the sale of Hindi film music ... the plagiarization of the music cassette generating also a notable court case'.[51] If so many Indians were seeing this film so many times, and were voraciously listening to its music, how was it affecting them culturally?

Badly, in the opinions of Nikhat Kazmi and Rustom Bharucha. For Kazmi, the film represented 'an unbridled westernisation of value systems and world-views' and was 'regressive and archaic', upholding 'a moral order that sanctifies tradition as opposed to the modern and re-entrenches a social system that is feudalistic, patriarchal and rigidly hierarchical'. 'Tradition', he writes, 'then becomes the keyword in [director] Barjatya's credo of cinema.'[52] Kazmi defines westernisation – rather idiosyncratically – by the absence of real conflict,[53] and he also has his cake and eats it too by accusing the film of being both westernised and traditional. Nevertheless, his suggestions that the film lacked *masala* and endorsed an arch conservatism are shared and expanded on by Bharucha. For Bharucha, the film was 'vacuous', 'one of the most banal superhits in the history of Indian cinema', and 'totally dispense[d] with a plot and all the "masala" associated with sex and violence'. An 'emphatically clean film', it was consistently fun, lacking any variety, and especially any cynicism, criticism or the sustained disruptive perspectives of a malcontent.[54] As Bharucha notes, Richard Dyer has argued that musicals not only invoke utopia, they also interrupt it – for example, in the disjunction between narrative continuity and disruptive songs. It is in this interruption, Dyer argues, that musicals and their audiences are able to be self-reflexive about the utopias the musicals create.[55] For Bharucha, *HAHK* lacked this critical self-reflexivity because it was 'almost frighteningly hermetic in construction', relentlessly portraying an 'affirmatively harmonious world' without parody. Further, by eschewing cultural contextualisation, the film produced a monocultural – upper-class Hindu–Indian identity, as it 'dealt' with the problems of Indian poverty simply by omitting them. Finally, it fetishised desire by presenting the stars in close-up – not unusually, of course, for a popular romantic film – and, more unusually, by producing a constant parade of consumer goods, especially food and drinks.[56]

These criticisms have strength as well as the benefit of Bharucha's familiar impressive rhetorical style, but it is worthwhile to consider some rejoinders to them. While the film's ending certainly fulfilled (patriarchal) tradition, it also fulfilled the characters' individual love/desire, so its capitulation to tradition cannot be seen as absolute. Further, the film's narrative may have been conventionally patriarchal, following the rites of exchange of two women between two patriarchal families, but women in the film were not entirely subordinated. Female lead Madhuri Dixit as Nisha is credited with having films written just for her, got top billing in *HAHK*, above her male counterpart, and is recognised as having ambivalent signification as both (traditional) mother figure and femme fatale.[57] While the female leads of Tamasha's production – Parminder Nagra in 1998 and Mala Ghedia in 2001[58] – did not have Dixit's level of celebrity and power, Tamasha's production was nevertheless female-led because it was adapted and directed by Tamasha's women directors, Bhuchar and Landon-Smith. Finally, Nisha spends much more of the narrative operating as a joker than as an acquiescent daughter or wife.

Both Kazmi and Bharucha deride *HAHK* for lacking the kind of conflict that facilitates resistant readings, but they nevertheless present resistant readings themselves; so it is not outrageous to imagine that other audiences might too. Nor is it outrageous to imagine, as Uberoi suggests, that audiences might both enjoy the utopian fiction and simultaneously, critically, recognise it as a fiction, not least because the film presents itself precisely as so hermetically complete and contained – within two extended families, within two homes, with very little reference to broader cultural or historical contexts.[59] It is incontestable that the film was monocultural and that it indulged in commodity fetishism. But it might also be the case that these criticisms are less significant for British Asian cinema, video, and cable television audiences for the film than for resident Indian audiences, because the articulation of Indian difference per se – as well as various Indian differences – serves a useful cultural function in this context of diaspora; what Madhu Jain identifies as the film's pan-Indian identity actually allows *HAHK* to travel globally and to help build alliances and identifications for a diasporic community.[60] Further, not including extensive references to Indian poverty avoids the risk of romanticising it – as *Bombay Dreams* risks in what *Independent on Sunday* reviewer Robert Butler identifies as that musical's 'sanitised' portrayal of the slum where the romantic lead character Akaash is supposed to have grown up (see figures 21 and 22, below).[61] Finally, Uberoi argues that the film definitely idealises the (traditional) family, but she proposes that it does so in order to act as an icon of the nation, thereby producing a consoling fiction about the nation 'in a time of change, uncertainty and crisis'.[62] This argument is relevant for both resident Indian audiences and diasporic British Asian audiences. Thus, while the potential of *HAHK* as a vehicle for cultural criticism must certainly be qualified, it cannot be entirely repudiated.

## Tamasha's Bollywood or bust *Fourteen Songs, Two Weddings and a Funeral*

Given the relative conservativism of HAHK, I do not attempt to argue here that Tamasha's stage adaptation by company co-directors Bhuchar and Landon-Smith was somehow miraculously radical. However, I do argue that the production was robustly culturally affirmative for Indian diasporic communities, realigning and potentially improving their position in British culture and revising British identities more broadly. Second, I argue that the production avoided the risks of Orientalism and appropriation delineated at the beginning of this chapter by invoking a subtle postcolonial mimicry that destabilised any assumed English purity or superiority.

The production was culturally affirmative, first, because it acknowledged and promoted the pleasures and popularity of the film for Indian audiences, both within India and beyond, heartily endorsing the sensibilities that make this form of film popular rather than rejecting or reviling them. While I do not have precise information on the film's popularity in the UK, statistics point to its success amongst other non-resident Indian populations ... for example, the film ran 'in Fiji for three months and for nine weeks in the New York–New Jersey area'.[63] Appropriately for a company whose name translates as 'spectacle', Tamasha did not try to play down what some see as the embarrassing conventions of Bollywood but, instead, it celebrated them. As the back cover blurb on the published text proudly states, '*Fourteen Songs, Two Weddings and a Funeral* is a spirit-lifting and enchanting love story lavishly told in true Bollywood style' and features 'the classic Bollywood film ingredients of romance, drama and comedy'.[64] All present and correct were the then-trendy Bollywood long title, conventional Bollywood romantic narrative (see figure 19), performance styles (including the use of extreme frontality, as shown in figure 20), Indian settings, references to religion and familial duty, and emphases on emotion, spectacle, and (familial) community rather than – or as well as – individual interest. Anne Fuchs notes that the 'impression of watching and physically participating in a Bollywood movie was further enhanced' through aspects of staging, such as the 'sharply-raked seating and the flat performance space at the level of the first row', at least in production at the Birmingham Repertory Theatre if not consistently elsewhere.[65] This impression was further enhanced through casting that was British Asian, wholly in the 1998 production and almost entirely in 2001. Richard Dyer has identified a latent racism in classic American film musicals, whose celebration of expressivity and freedom, he argues, extends primarily to their (predominantly) white characters and less to their (infrequent) black ones.[66] One of Bollywood's – and *Fourteen Songs*' – innovations in this context is to revise the white colonisation of musicals – and, consequently, of their narratives of freedom – by populating them with Asians. Most crucially, though, the production's primary achievement was not to colonise a dominant Western form by populating it with Asians, but rather unabashedly to celebrate an Eastern form. 'I think [the show is] popular', said Bhuchar, 'because it is not a send-up of Bollywood but played within the spirit of it.'[67]

The production was culturally affirmative also because it specifically and unapologetically addressed British Asian audiences as a matter of primary importance, and it did so in at least three ways. First, it used the

19 Prem (left, Pushpinder Chani) and Nisha (Mala Ghedia) embrace in Tamasha Theatre Company's 2001 production of *Fourteen Songs, Two Weddings and a Funeral*

20 The cast face front in Tamasha Theatre Company's 2001 production of *Fourteen Songs, Two Weddings and a Funeral*

popular Indian form of Bollywood film. Tamasha's overt and extensive engagement with popular, mass, and contemporary Asian cultural forms indicates its ambition to attract not only a British Asian audience that is traditionally theatregoing but also a much larger one that is not. Barnaby King and Anne Fuchs have both identified Tamasha's performance discourses as westernised.[68] This may be more true (if debatable) of shows such as *East Is East* and *Balti Kings* that adopt generic features which are more obviously televisual, especially features of situation comedy. In the case of *Fourteen Songs*, however, the references are clearly to the Indian popular cultural form of Bollywood cinema, although, as I have suggested above, it is important to see this form as already significantly culturally hybrid.

Second, Tamasha took this show specifically to theatres that were local for many British Asian audiences. In the 2001 tour, for example, *Fourteen Songs* played in West London and the Midlands as well as in Manchester, Bristol, and Guildford.[69] Fuchs reports that at the Birmingham Rep, for example, 'the house was packed nightly with a 95 per cent Asian Black audience'.[70] Referring to a subsequent Tamasha production, *Balti Kings*, Bhuchar commented, 'Tamasha has a loyal audience in Birmingham, and we wanted to given them something local'.[71]

Third, while performed predominantly in English, *Fourteen Songs* employed language, phrases, speech patterns, and cultural references that would have been familiar to a British Indian audience. Characters used familiar sayings, such as 'Don't be a bone in the kebab', and referred to such Indian icons as Indra, God of wind, and Kapil Dev, cricketer.[72] Hindi language was used throughout, especially in greetings such as 'Namaskar' and conventions of respectful address such as 'Bhai Sahib', and by the older characters.[73] This may partly reflect the use of a mother tongue for many immigrant communities, where younger people who may be second-generation immigrants might be more familiar with exclamations and sayings, and older people, who actually immigrated to Britain, are more fluent. This might also indicate the way the play's productions could have served multiple purposes for different age communities of audience, as Mishra suggests Bollywood videos might do for diasporic audiences, fulfilling a nostalgic desire (for example, to hear the mother tongue) for an older audience, and legitimising a sense of cultural difference for a younger audience.[74] Finally, the play's use of Hindi and other Indian references might simply have contributed to disturbing the – theatrical and cultural – dominance of English. In this sense, the production practised what Tara Arts director Jatinder Verma has called 'Binglishing' the stage. He glosses 'Binglish' as '"black English", "being English", "beastly English", "bastardly English", "be English"', and argues, 'all these nuances are implicit in this term for that particular negotiation between English and Indian languages and sensibilities that is under way in contemporary England'.[75] For Verma, this use of hybrid language in British Asian performance precisely articulates the hybridity not only of British Asian cultures but also of British culture more broadly. Binglish, he suggests,

> comes really from a recognition of what's happened in England in the time that I've been here – now close on thirty years – which is that all purities or all notions of the authentic have been blown sky high. What is an authentic British diet, what is authentic British music, what is it to be the authentic English man? Who can with any truth, with any honesty, say what that is? All one can say is that there are fractures, there are fragments, there are Binglishes, really, in the very texture of our language.[76]

By using and endorsing a popular Indian performance form and explicitly addressing a British Asian audience, *Fourteen Songs* repeatedly affirmed the distinctiveness and value of British Asians' cultural differences.

As Verma's analysis begins to suggest though, *Fourteen Songs* was not only culturally affirmative for British Asian communities; it was also culturally interrogative and even critical towards a putatively dominant and authentic English culture in particular. This was initiated in the production's 'Binglish' language, which we might also understand through Bhabha's term mimicry as a language that was '*almost the same, but not quite*', '*Almost the same but not white*', anglicised but '*emphatically* not …. English'. But this mimicry was enhanced through reference to the production's second unavoidable film intertext: the English romantic comedy regarded in its time, like *HAHK* in its Indian context, as 'the most successful British film of all time', Mike Newell's 1994 hit *Four Weddings and a Funeral*.[77] With *Hum Aapke Hain Koun…!* translatable as *Who Am I to You?*, Tamasha clearly chose to name their production in a way that not only was descriptive but would also inevitably invoke *Four Weddings*. *Fourteen Songs* was 'almost the same' as *Four Weddings* in its title, its narrative organisation around weddings and a death, and numerous features arising from the fact that it was a romantic comedy. But its sameness was 'not quite', first, because it told its Indian source text's story in Bollywood style and made no other explicit reference to *Four Weddings*, and second because it was totally peopled with Indian characters where *Four Weddings*

had none. There is more to this than a statement of the obvious: it is especially significant that *Four Weddings* included no visibly non-white Britons
because it was otherwise clearly at pains to show 'difference' in British
culture by including characters who were Scottish, gay, (moderately)
punk, and deaf. Critics have suggested that financial motivations inspired
*Four Weddings*' filmmakers both to construct 'a tourist's-eye view of Britain
… a view of British life which is much more like the rest of the world *wants*
it to be than it actually is'[78] and also unashamedly to flatter an American
audience by portraying American openness as the essential antidote to the
'starched, emotionally constipated' English repression manifested in lead
character Charles, played by Hugh Grant.[79] However much the filmmakers and their critics might try to disavow the accuracy of the film's
vision of Britishness, though, *Four Weddings*' unabashedly whitewashed,
racially exclusive British identity was latently racist, a point that was subtly
but comprehensively challenged by *Fourteen Song*'s '*not white*' mimicry –
and, indeed, by its reverse imperialist piggy-backing exploitation of *Four
Weddings*' title in *Fourteen Songs*' own bid to achieve widespread popularity.

   *Fourteen Songs, Two Weddings and a Funeral* made two ideologically
complementary manoeuvres. First, by flagrantly indulging Bollywood
film conventions – by going for Bollywood or bust – *Fourteen Songs* affirmed
the particular Indian sensibilities that Bollywood both responds to and
creates. In the diasporic context of the UK, this privileging of British
Asian audiences and Bollywood forms of address challenged dominant
hierarchies of cultural power that normally disadvantage minority immigrant communities. Second, the production performed a subtle mimicry
of dominant British culture, implicitly questioning the myth of British
racial and ethnic purity naturalised in the enormously popular *Four
Weddings and a Funeral*. The production affirmed British Asian cultural
difference and implicitly posited intrinsic *British* cultural difference.

### Andrew Lloyd Webber's *Bombay Dreams*: dancing a Bollywood two-step

*Bombay Dreams* shares with *Fourteen Songs* at least a degree of positive
British Asian cultural affirmation because it adopts and embraces many
Bollywood conventions. It opened in a Really Useful Company production at the Apollo Victoria Theatre in London in June 2002, and
one of the central Bollywood conventions it reproduced was plot. The
musical traces the rising fortunes of the impoverished hero, Akaash
(figure 21), and his evolving, initially impossible romance with Priya,

who is both a social realist filmmaker herself and the privileged daughter of a corrupt Bollywood filmmaker. Raised in a Mumbai slum (figure 22), Akaash's ambition is to become a Bollywood star. Having managed to insinuate his way on-stage during a televised beauty contest, he sings and is talent-spotted by Priya's father. The musical follows his indoctrination into Bollywood performance conventions, his rising stardom, his denial of his slum 'family', and his troubled relationship with Priya, who is both engaged to someone else and contemptuous of Bollywood cinema, with its hack fantasies, refusal to address social realities, and happy-ever-after endings. Eventually, Priya's fiancé is found to be corrupt, Priya and Akaash somehow resolve their anti- and pro-Bollywood ideological differences, and they are united in a bittersweet ending which at once adopts Bollywood conventions (by ending happily ever after) and sidesteps them (by being bittersweet). (Numerous rousing encores, however, suggest that the production could not resist the temptation to end finally happily ever after, a point I will return to below.) Typically, for a Bollywood narrative, *Bombay Dreams* explores conflicts between duty and love and tradition and modernisation and, like *Fourteen Songs*, resolves these conflicts as the characters accept their familial duties even as they indulge their love. Other typical Bollywood conventions include nineteen songs, one wedding, two murders, numerous dances, and elaborate

21 Akaash (Stephen Rahman-Hughes) in the slum in *Bombay Dreams*

**22** Shanti (Adlyn Ross) in the slum in *Bombay Dreams*

**23** Rani (Sophiya Haque) singing 'Shakalaka Baby' in a fountain in *Bombay Dreams*

scenographies, including a large Diwali holiday procession featuring numerous elephant placards and colourful umbrellas, a rain scene, and an on-stage fountain (figure 23).[80]

The production's Bollywood credentials were also endorsed by the composition of its artistic team, which included many Bollywood stars, the likes of which were presumably beyond the budget of a company like Tamasha and contributed to *Bombay Dreams*' production cost of £4.5 million that took over a year to recoup.[81] *Bombay Dreams* composer A. R. Rahman is perhaps the single most celebrated Bollywood composer and has sold over a hundred million soundtrack albums worldwide, a number in excess of Madonna's and Britney's sales combined (as numerous critics gleefully hastened to note).[82] Co-authors of the original concept were Andrew Lloyd Webber and Shekhar Kapur, who has directed 'numerous successful Bollywood films including *The Bandit Queen*, *Mr. India*, and *Masoon*'.[83] Choreographers were Anthony Van Laast and Farah Khan who has worked on many Bollywood films, including Aditya Chopra's blockbuster *Dilwale Dulhaniya Le Jayenge* (1995).[84] And some performers had performed in Bollywood films; for example Sophiya Haque, who played the role of Bollywood femme fatale Rani in autumn 2003.

The production was also replete with British Asian performers. Auditions were held around the UK, including in Bradford and Leeds where there are large Asian communities,[85] and reviewer Barbara Newman noted that the opening cast was 'entirely Anglo-Indian'[86] (although subsequent casts apparently were not). The book was written by Meera Syal, the British Indian actress and writer perhaps most popularly known for her television portrayal of 'naughty granny Ummi' in *The Kumars at No. 42*, and her collaboration on the sketch-based comedy show *Goodness Gracious Me*, for both BBC radio and television.[87] The production used Asian speech cadences and Hindi language, as in the Act Two opening song 'Chaiyya Chaiyya', although it did so perhaps moderately less than did *Fourteen Songs*. Finally, the website provided a community service by advertising dates and locations for Melas (cultural festivals) throughout England.[88] Overall, the production engaged extensively with Bollywood cinema and its conventions, went a considerable way in endorsing those conventions and their appreciation, provided a community service, and employed and promoted Asian and British Asian artists on a scale never before even remotely approached by any other British megamusical.

These achievements noted, there nevertheless remain several reasons to exercise caution over assessing the cultural value of *Bombay Dreams* for

British Asian cultures and communities. The most important of these is that, although the musical had numerous Asian contributing artists, it also had many non-Asian ones. Thus, while it was certainly partly a (British) Asian production, it was also significantly a non-Asian production as well. This is not to argue that only artists with Asian blood can authentically represent Asian experience – such an argument would go against the informing logic of this entire book. But I do mean to argue that this participation of numerous artists with less *cultural* access to Indian cultures – as differentiated from some putative genetic access to them – put *Bombay Dreams* especially at risk of reproducing what Edward Said famously identified as Orientalist versions of non-Western cultures which portray the Occident as superior through implicit contrast with a patronised Orient. Further, there is the risk that *Bombay Dreams'* market dominance potentially displaced other (possibly less Orientalist) British-Asian theatre work. Krishnendu Majumdar argued in *The Guardian*, for example, that such a high-profile, widely marketed, long-running representation of Asian culture as *Bombay Dreams* risked overshadowing the work of Asian or British-Asian playwrights such as Tanika Gupta and Ayub Khan-Din, author of Tamasha's successful *East Is East*.[89] Non-Asian contributing artists to *Bombay Dreams* included theatre and opera director Steven Pimlott, and lyricist Don Black who had collaborated with Lloyd Webber before on *Sunset Boulevard* (1993), *Song and Dance* (1982), and *Aspects of Love* (1989).[90] Black's lyrics for *Bombay Dreams* were roundly criticised for being touristy and westernised and for 'dragging the show down into West End clichéd bathos'.[91] Certainly, they were familiarly Western (or typically Lloyd Webber and/or Don Black) in their sometimes predictable phrasing.

Given the absolute centrality to Bollywood cinema of a highly distinctive style of formal construction, performance, aesthetic organisation, dance, and song, the Really Useful Group's decision not to hire an Indian or British Indian director and lyricist deeply culturally familiar with both Bollywood cinema and – importantly – its informing sensibilities is extremely problematic. It betrays, first, the production's ambivalent commitment to actually celebrating and making a Bollywood adaptation; second, its reservation of the role of at least one of the writers for a white Englishman in a gesture of 'textual patriotism' familiar from the discussion in the last chapter; and third, its failure to protect itself more fully against descending into Orientalism.

Of course, the most infamous non-Asian collaborator on – and instigator of – *Bombay Dreams* was, as producer and co-conceiver, Andrew Lloyd Webber, the consummate and phenomenally popular composer of

English megamusicals who had twenty-seven productions of his work playing around the world in July 2000.[92] There are at least three reasons to be sceptical about Lloyd Webber's commitment and ability to produce a culturally respectful and non-Orientalising Bollywood stage musical. One: his musicals are less likely to address wide social issues than those of, for example, Claude-Michel Schoenberg and Alain Boublil who created *Les Misérables*. More likely to focus instead on 'personal healing or catharsis',[93] Lloyd Webber's musicals resist portraying the sense of community that Vasudevan sees as intrinsic to Bollywood cinema, with its frontality and direct address.[94] Two: if, as Michael Coveney argues, Lloyd Webber's 'constant quest [is] to write musical theatre that speaks to as wide an audience as possible',[95] his shows risk being culturally vague, 'sanitised and packaged', giving a flavour (or using a cliché) of the culture referred to, but not portraying – or respecting – that culture with any complexity. 'This is where crosscultural becomes almost cultureless', argued John Peter in his *Sunday Times* review.[96] Third: if another of Lloyd Webber's 'constant quests' is to produce musicals that are financially successful, then it is fair to speculate that his interest in Bollywood is opportunistic. In related ways, his role as producer, along with his enormous success as a megamusical magnate, may mean his decisions were given preferential (financial) weight. Notable in this context is the colossal scale of Lloyd Webber's financial success: in December 1999, for example, it was announced that *The Phantom of the Opera* 'had taken in more money than any other production on stage or screen (£1.88 billion/approximately $2.8 billion), surpassing huge money-making films such as *Star Wars* and *Titanic*.[97] In *Bombay Dreams*' market context, other collaborators' suggestions would have been hard pressed to stand up to the persuasiveness of Lloyd Webber's astronomical revenue figures.

A potential benefit of Lloyd Webber's huge popularity is that while his *Bombay Dreams* may present a diluted version of Bollywood cinema, it is nevertheless introducing Bollywood to vast audiences who may not otherwise know it, either through its films or through the work of fringe companies such as Tamasha. Further, this introduction may be less problematic than Majumdar suspects: perhaps Lloyd Webber's enormous fantasy-loving audience will become a whole new audience for Bollywood films and will develop a respectful knowledge of Asian cultures beyond what *Bombay Dreams* superficially provides.

But there are two final caveats I would like to explore about the cultural value of *Bombay Dreams* for British Asians as well as for other audiences. First, there is the problem of the musical's ambivalent engagement

with Bollywood form. Second, there is the problem of its explicit use of
the Hijra or eunuch character, Sweetie, as a vehicle of local and sexual
colour and an expendable plot device. The musical's exploitation of
Sweetie's sexual and cultural difference is, I suggest, symptomatic of its
exploitation of cultural difference more broadly.

Ultimately, *Bombay Dreams* is just a little too ironic and dismissive in
its handling of Bollywood cinema to be properly respectful of
Bollywood's difference – the kind of wholesale cultural difference that
*Fourteen Songs* observed and that Thomas and Mishra identify as foundational both to this film form and for its audiences. *Bombay Dreams* exploits
Bollywood's – playful, spectacular, moving – conventions and simultaneously holds itself aloof from them, as though they are embarrassing. Most
importantly, it does this by being not precisely Bollywood itself, but by
being meta-Bollywood, or *about* Bollywood. Thus it is able to include the
classic Bollywood cinema features of lip-synched songs, the almost oblig-
atory wet sari scene, extraordinary scenographies, romantic leads of film-
star attractiveness, and extravagant non-naturalistically incorporated
song and dance sequences such as the 'Shakalaka Baby' song scene
performed by Rani in a working fountain (figure 20). But the production
is simultaneously able to distance itself from Bollywood's extraordinary
conventions by containing them within its film-within-the-musical narrative. In its own narrative logic, it is not *Bombay Dreams* that shows these
things; rather, it is the Bollywood films being made by characters within
the musical who show these things. Further, the *Bombay Dreams* narrative
that surrounds the Bollywood films-within-the-musical clearly indicates
its disdain for the form. Advocates of Bollywood are corrupt: underprivileged Akaash abandons his adopted slum family when he ascends to
Bollywood stardom, and Priya's father, the Bollywood director, is a senior
member of a Bollywood mafia and begins the production in gaol for his
crimes. Bollywood's most outspoken detractor in the show is the articulate, ethically committed social realist filmmaker Priya. Ultimately, she
recognises Bollywood's pleasures and emotional honesty, but only after
having spent the whole of the musical deriding them.

Susanna Clapp in the *Observer* criticised *Bombay Dreams* for wanting it
both ways: to ridicule Bollywood for its corruption and naivety while still
enjoying it for its spectacle and fun. Michael Billington reiterated this in
the *Guardian*, while Roger Foss in *What's On* thought the show achieved a
balance between the two positions.[98] As the bittersweet ending combined
with rousing encores suggest, the production is deeply ambivalent about
its relationship to Bollywood's conventions in a way that compromises its

respect for the form. Its narrative logic concludes by rejecting Bollywood's utopianism, but its staging concludes by embracing that utopianism through joyous encores. The production dances a Bollywood two-step: it positions itself as intellectually superior to Bollywood, but it nevertheless exploits Bollywood's sense of carnival to send its audience out singing (to buy the CD). This knowing attitude towards Bollywood – taking what it wants but indicating its shrewd disavowal of the form – suggests a classic Orientalist practice: *Bombay Dreams* indulges the Eastern form as a means of portraying its own superiority to that form.

The production's exploitative relationship to the 'local colour' of Bollywood is epitomised in its treatment of the character Sweetie, a Hijra or eunuch. Meera Syal describes India's 'large eunuch population' as 'regarding themselves as the Third Sex with a special place within society', being 'supreme entertainers', and holding 'a mythic, almost magical status'. [99] *Bombay Dreams* invokes all three of these aspects of Hijra signification. Sweetie is Akaash's close friend from the slum, secretly fancies him, and features strongly in the musical, both in the narrative and in its performance. In performance, Sweetie is an entertainer, providing visual pleasure in her/his elegant traditional women's attire, musical pleasure through singing in a high register, and the pleasure of intrigue in sexual difference. Sweetie contributes to the narrative by: helping Akaash to gatecrash the beauty contest where he has his big break; articulating the loss Akaash's slum family feels when he has abandoned them; and being murdered by the Bollywood mafia, an occurrence which perhaps magically – restores the moral register that Akaash had lost on his dizzying rise to stardom and that compels him to reclaim his slum family and roots.

Despite occupying a position of narrative centrality, Sweetie functions largely as a spectacle and a plot device, providing visual and musical diversion, and facilitating, ultimately, not her/his own romantic narrative of stardom and romance with Akaash but rather the dominant narratives of (heterosexual male) Akaash's success and Akaash and Priya's (heterosexual) romance. Sweetie's access to the beauty contest propels not Sweetie to stardom but Akaash. And Sweetie's romantic interest in Akaash provides the diversion of a second romantic sub-plot (somewhat parallel to Priya's with her fiancé), but it leads ultimately and directly to the union of Akaash and Priya. In the solo 'Closer than Ever', Sweetie sings about what she/he really wants – but instead of this desire involving Sweetie winning Akaash, it involves Akaash winning Priya. The eunuch sacrifices her/his 'different' desire for the heterosexual couple, and the production literally sacrifices the eunuch for the dominant narrative by killing Sweetie off to bring about

Akaash's moral redemption. Sweetie's distinctive differences are mobilised to add local and sexual colour and to attract audiences of and to ethnic and sexual difference, but those differences are not ultimately permitted either to persist or to triumph; indeed, they are violently extinguished. Again the musical has it both ways, incorporating Sweetie as a singing, dancing epitome of cultural and sexual difference, but simultaneously denying that difference by refusing to see it through to a narrative conclusion where Sweetie attains either stardom or the man of her/his dreams. The production invokes difference, but works also to disavow it.

Bombay Dreams made two ideologically contradictory manoeuvres. First, by indulging Bollywood conventions and employing numerous British Asian and Asian artists, the production endorsed British Asian cultural differences and, like Fourteen Songs, challenged dominant cultural hierarchies that normally disadvantage minority communities. However, the production radically compromised these effects by simultaneously undermining its commitment to Bollywood and Indian cultural difference through a variety of means: coupling the work of its Asian and British Asian artists with the work of artists with notably less cultural access to Bollywood and its sensibilities; disavowing its endorsement of Bollywood's conventions by placing those that are most extremely different from Western conventions inside its films-within-the-musical; and exploiting the character with the greatest signification of cultural difference, Sweetie, by employing her/him for visual and musical pleasure and narrative progression but ultimately, violently, containing her/his difference. Bombay Dreams' Bollywood two-step went some way towards affirming Indian and British Asian cultural differences, but in a gesture that appears finally opportunistic.

### Bollywood in Britain and beyond: affirmation, hybridity, mimicry, and risk

These two productions illustrate some of the opportunities and hazards of adapting the already contested cultural form of Bollywood cinema for the stage in contemporary Britain. First and foremost, to adapt Bollywood cinema in Britain is to acknowledge and pay respect to both Bollywood's phenomenal cultural importance in India and throughout the Asian diaspora, and the distinctive cultural attitudes, values, and ideologies that Bollywood articulates. It is to endorse the value of Asian cultural differences and to do so in a way that challenges the long-standing oppression of those differences within Britain. It is also to acknowledge the popularity of

Bollywood's often conservative, utopian fictions for its audiences, and perhaps to go some way towards addressing why these utopian fictions are particularly attractive to (or needed by) British Asian audiences and why these audiences seek 'images, prose, songs and sheer *rhetoric* that is about arriving, about survival'.[100] Second, to adapt Bollywood in Britain is to explore the fundamental hybridity of both Asian cultures and British cultures. Bollywood is a distinctive cultural form but it is not a pure form. It articulates the hybridity of India's postcolonial identities and, when imported to the UK, it indicates British identities' hybridity, or 'Binglishing'. When explicitly linked with dominant British forms (such as *Four Weddings and a Funeral*), Bollywood in Britain also presents the opportunity for some productive mimicry, challenging the dominance of those British forms and potentially revealing their racial prejudices by playing them '*almost the same, but not quite*', '*Almost the same but not white*'.[101]

At its most productive, Bollywood in Britain has the potential to change British Asian identities, British identities, and British cultural practices. It can improve Asian cultural experience in the UK by promoting Asian cultural difference. It can shift the meanings of 'British' away from culturally purist and exclusive definitions to more diverse ones. And it can diversify and hybridise British cultural practice by fundamentally altering – even 'Bollywoodising' – the 'English' musical. Evidence of this 'Bollywoodising' is the coming full circle of the proscenium-arch-induced frontal performance that travelled from England, was adopted by the Parsis in India and influenced their theatre, influenced Bollywood film, and has now come back – hybridised – to Britain. Further evidence is A. R. Rahman's crossover success in the British musical industry: he is reported to be doing the music for a musical adaptation of the English epic *The Lord of the Rings* in 2005.[102] Finally, these examples of British stage Bollywood demonstrate the particular strength of theatre as a vehicle for adapting Bollywood and for realising its politically progressive effects. Theatre accommodates Bollywood's frontality and spectacle and it nurtures its sense of *communitas*, extending it beyond the British Asian homes where Bollywood films have long been viewed, and into theatres that are likely to attract a more mixed audience, including British Asians and non-Asian Britons.

Lest all of these potential benefits make us complacent about the cultural effects of Bollywood in Britain, however, it is worth remembering the risks of cultural appropriation that Lloyd Webber's *Bombay Dreams* demonstrates, at least in part. And it is particularly worth remembering these risks as *Bombay Dreams* opens in a revised form at one of New York's largest and most prominent venues, the 1600-seat Broadway Theatre.[103] On a positive note, as in Britain, *Bombay Dreams'* production in the USA may help to affirm a sense of cultural difference for a large non-resident Indian population and to hybridise American cultural identities as well as the Broadway musical. However, given Lloyd Webber's plans to have *Bombay Dreams'* book rewritten by Thomas Meehan – who wrote the book for such an iconic American (dream) musical as *Annie* – and possibly to incorporate new American characters, the risk that *Bombay Dreams* will serve a dominant American, Orientalising cultural agenda more than an American Asian cultural agenda seems ominously possible.[104]

## Notes

1  James Collard, 'Bollywood', *The Times* (6 April 2002), p. 22.
2  The appropriateness of the term 'Bollywood' is disputed: some see it as patronising, derivative, homogenising, and inaccurate; others see it as affectionate and a fair reflection of popular Hindi cinema's unabashed populism and commercialism; many see it as both. While acknowledging its problematics, I adopt the term here because of its common and continuing usage in popular discourse and in the critical discourse of many Asian and non-Asian scholars alike.
3  Heather Tyrrell, 'Bollywood in Britain', *Sight and Sound* 8:8 (1998), 20–2, pp. 20–1.
4  Edward W. Said, *Orientalism* (Harmondsworth: Penguin, [1978] 1985), p. 3. As mentioned in Chapter 5, Rustom Bharucha led the critique of Brook's production of *The Mahabharata* in his collection of essays *Theatre and the World: Performance and the Politics of Culture* (London: Routledge, revised edn, 1993).
5  Prominent British Asian immigrant theatre director Jatinder Verma makes this distinction between providing cultural tourism and cultural provocation, arguing that his theatre company, Tara Arts, does the latter. Verma in Graham Ley, 'Theatre of migration and the search for a multicultural aesthetic: twenty years of Tara Arts', *NTQ: New Theatre Quarterly* 13 (52, 1997), 349–71, p. 356.
6  This chapter considers these issues of cultural appropriation and articulation through a focus on British Asian cultures, but they are also pertinent to other minority cultures in the UK and elsewhere. For a complementary analysis of, for example, the Notting Hill Carnival in London and its gradual appropriation as black exotica by dominant capitalist market forces see Gavin Carver, 'The effervescent carnival: performance, context, and mediation at Notting Hill', *NTQ: New Theatre Quarterly* 16:1 (61, 2000), 34–49.
7  Mary-Karen Dahl, 'Postcolonial British theatre: black voices at the center', in J. Ellen Gainor (ed.), *Imperialism and Theatre: Essays on World Theatre, Drama and Performance* (London: Routledge, 1995), pp. 38–55, p. 53, ellipsis added.
8  Lynn Barber, 'Loser takes all', *Observer* (2 March 2003).
9  I adapt the term from Vinayak Chakravorty who refers to the ways Bollywood cinema has obviously influenced such Western-produced films as *The Guru* (d. Daisy von Scherler Mayer, 2001) and Baz Luhrmann's *Moulin Rouge* (2001). Luhrmann has acknowledged Bollywood cinema as a key inspiration in making

*Moulin Rouge*. Vinayak Chakravorty, 'Dancing to Bollywood's tune', *Hindustan Times.com* (n.d.), www.hindustantimes.com/2002/Nov/29/674_105475,00310006.htm (accessed January 2004).

10 Ashish Rajadhyaksha, Introduction, in Rajadhyaksha and Paul Willeman (eds), *Encyclopaedia of Indian Cinema* (London/New Delhi: British Film Institute/Oxford University Press, revised edn, 1997), pp. 10–12, p. 10.

11 Vijay Mishra, *Bollywood Cinema: Temples of Desire* (London: Routledge, 2002), p. 1.

12 Rajadhyaksha and Willeman (eds), *Encyclopaedia of Indian Cinema*, p. 33.

13 Mishra, *Bollywood Cinema*, p. 1.

14 Ashok Banker, *The Pocket Essential Bollywood* (Harpenden: Pocket Essentials, 2001), p. 8.

15 Manjunath Pendakur and Radha Subramanyam point out that this is due partly to the size of the diasporic Indian population in the UK (an estimated one million families in 1994) and partly to the strength of UK currency and the relatively high security provided by strictly enforced anti-piracy laws. Pendakur and Subramanyam, 'India. Part 1: Indian cinema beyond national boundaries', in John Sinclair, Elizabeth Jacka, and Stuart Cunningham (eds), *New Patterns in Global Television: Peripheral Vision* (Oxford: Oxford University Press, 1996), pp. 67–82, p. 78.

16 Rosie Thomas, 'Indian cinema: pleasures and popularity' *Screen* 26:3/4 (1985), 116–31, p. 124, partially rpt as Rosie Thomas, 'Popular Hindi cinema', in John Hill and Pamela Church Gibson (eds), *World Cinema: Critical Approaches* (Oxford: Oxford University Press, 2000), pp. 157–8. I acknowledge that Bollywood's enormous and diverse cinematic output means that not all of the generalisations I make here hold true for all Bollywood films.

17 *Ibid.*, p. 127.

18 Mishra, *Bollywood Cinema*, p. xix.

19 Thomas, 'Indian cinema', p. 119.

20 Other recent films which produce this or a similar narrative include, for example: director Aditya Chopra's *Dilwale Dulhania Le Jayenge* (1995) and *Mohabbatein* (2000), *Kuch Kuch Hota Hai* (d. Karan Johar, 1998), and *Kaho Na Pyar Hai* (d. Rakesh Roshan, 2000).

21 Mishra, *Bollywood Cinema*, p. 3.

22 *Ibid.*, pp. 8–9. See also Thomas, 'Indian cinema', p. 130.

23 Mishra, *Bollywood Cinema*, p. 8, emphasis added.

24 Jane Feuer, *The Hollywood Musical* (London: Macmillan, [1982] 2nd edn, 1993), p. x.

25 Mishra, *Bollywood Cinema*, pp. 8, 35 (emphasis added) and 38.

26 Homi K. Bhabha, 'Of mimicry and man: the ambivalence of colonial discourse', in Bhabha, *The Location of Culture* (London: Routledge, 1994), pp. 85–92, pp. 86 and 89, all emphases original; originally published in *October: Anthology* (Boston: MIT Press, 1987).

27 *Ibid.*, p. 87, emphasis original.

28 Thomas, 'Indian cinema', p. 121.

29 *Ibid.*, pp. 121 and 131.

30 Ravi S. Vasudevan, 'The politics of cultural address in "transitional" cinema: a case study of Indian popular cinema', in Christine Gledhill and Linda Williams (eds), *Reinventing Film Studies* (London: Arnold, 2000), pp. 130–64, pp. 151–2.

31  *Ibid.*, p. 130.

32  See, for example: Alexander Leggatt (ed.), *The Cambridge Companion to Shakespearean Comedy* (Cambridge: Cambridge University Press, 2002); Molly Haskell, *From Reverence to Rape: The Treatment of Women in the Movies* (Chicago: University of Chicago Press, 2nd edn, 1987); Christine Geraghty, *Women and Soap Opera: A Study of Prime Time Soaps* (Cambridge: Polity, 1991); Richard Dyer, *Only Entertainment* (London: Routledge, 2nd edn, 2002); and Stacey Wolf, *A Problem Like Maria: Gender and Sexuality in the American Musical* (Ann Arbor: University of Michigan Press, 2002).

33  Richard Dyer, 'Entertainment and utopia', in Dyer, *Only Entertainment*, pp. 19–35, p. 26; originally published in *Movie* 24 (1977).

34  Kenneth MacKinnon, '"I keep wishing I were somewhere else": space and fantasies of freedom in the Hollywood musical', in Bill Marshall and Robynn Stilwell (eds), *Musicals: Hollywood and Beyond* (Exeter: Intellect Books, 2000), pp. 40–6, p. 44.

35  For a neat summary of the argument see Bill Marshall and Robynn Stilwell, Introduction, Marshall and Stilwell (eds), *Musicals*, pp. 1–4, p. 2.

36  Mishra, *Bollywood Cinema*, p. 246. Mishra develops his analysis of the compensatory function of the 'imaginary homeland' for diasporic communities in Vijay Mishra, 'The diasporic imaginary: theorizing the Indian diaspora', *Textual Practice* 10:3 (1996), 421–47, pp.423–4.

37  Geeta Kapur and Ashish Rajadhyaksha, 'Bombay/Mumbai, 1992–2001', in Iwona Blazwick (ed.), *Century City: Art and Culture in the Modern Metropolis* (London: Tate Publishing, 2001), pp. 16–41, p. 18, emphasis original.

38  Roger Foss, review of *Bombay Dreams*, Apollo Victoria, London, *What's On* (26 June 2002), rpt in *Theatre Record* 22:13 (16 July 2002), 847. Numerous reviews of the original production of *Bombay Dreams* are reprinted in *Theatre Record* 22:13 (16 July 2003), 841–8.

39  This is part of the company's mission statement, included near the front of their published plays; for example, Sudha Bhuchar and Kristine Landon-Smith, *House of the Sun* (London: Nick Hern Books, 1999), n. p. Other published plays include: Sudha Bhuchar and Kristine Landon-Smith, *Untouchable*, adapted from the novel by Mulk Raj Anand (London: Nick Hern Books, 1999); Ruth Carter, *Women of the Dust* (London: Nick Hern Books, 1999); Abhijat Joshi, *A Shaft of Sunlight* (London: Nick Hern Books, 1999); Sudha Bhuchar and Kristine Landon-Smith, *A Tainted Dawn* (London: Nick Hern Books, 1999); Ruth Carter, *A Yearning* (London: Nick Hern Books, 1999); and Ayub Khan-Din, *East Is East* (London: Nick Hern Books, 1997).

40  Carter, *Women of the Dust*, back cover.

41  *Tamasha Theatre Company*, www.tamasha.org.uk; path: Artistic Directors (accessed August 2003).

42  May Joseph, *Nomadic Identities: The Performance of Citizenship* (Minneapolis: University of Minnesota Press, 1999), p. 96.

43  *Tamasha Theatre Company*, www.tamasha.org.uk/About_Us/about_us.html (accessed August 2003).

44  Although Tara Arts (founded by Jatinder Verma in 1977) provides a much more longstanding example of British Asian theatre practice, I do not concentrate on it

here because it has already received much more extensive critical analysis. For more on Tara Arts and Verma's theories in particular see: Jatinder Verma, 'Binglish: a *jungli* approach to multi-cultural theatre', *Studies in Theatre Production* 13 (1996), 92–8; Jatinder Verma, '"Binglishing" the stage: a generation of Asian theatre in England', in Richard Boon and Jane Plastow (eds), *Theatre Matters: Performance and Culture on the World Stage* (Cambridge: Cambridge University Press, 1998), pp. 126–34; Jatinder Verma, 'The challenge of Binglish: analysing multi-cultural productions', in Patrick Campbell (ed.), *Analysing Performance* (Manchester: Manchester University Press, 1996), pp. 193–202; Jatinder Verma, 'Cultural transformations', in Theodore Shank (ed.), *Contemporary British Theatre* (London: Macmillan, revised edn, 1996), pp. 55–61; and Jatinder Verma, interview, in Maria M. Delgado and Paul Heritage (eds), *In Contact with the Gods?: Directors Talk Theatre* (Manchester: Manchester University Press, 1996), pp. 277–98.

45 Verma discusses the influences of these forms on his company's work in his interview with Ley, 'Theatre of migration', pp. 352–4.

46 These include: Best Screenplay in the 1999 British Independent Film Awards as well as Best British Film, Best British Screenwriter (for Ayub Khan-Din), and Best British Producer (for Leslee Udwin) at the 1999 awards of the London Film Critics Circle. *British Independent Film Awards*, www.bifa.org.uk/person.php? person=145 (accessed November 2003); and 'Beauty outshines the Bard', *BBC News Entertainment* (3 March 2000), news.bbc.co.uk/1/hi/entertainment/ 664688.stm (accessed November 2003).

47 Mishra, *Bollywood Cinema*, p. 273.

48 I borrow the term from Patricia Uberoi, 'The diaspora comes home: disciplining desire in *DDLJ*', *Contributions to Indian Sociology* 32:2 (1998), 305–36, p. 306.

49 Mishra, *Bollywood Cinema*, p. 66.

50 Pratik Joshi, 'The classics and blockbusters', in Joshi (ed.), *Bollywood* (London: Dakini, 2001), pp. 89–135, p. 131; Patricia Uberoi, 'Imagining the family: an ethnography of viewing *Hum aapke hain koun ...!*', in Rachel Dwyer and Christopher Pinney (eds), *Pleasure and the Nation: The History, Politics and Consumption of Popular Culture in India* (New Delhi: Oxford University Press, 2001), pp. 309–51, p. 341.

51 Uberoi, 'Imagining the family', p. 341. Uberoi cites S. Zaveri, 'Heart busters', *E-times* (30 December–5 January 1994), 4–7.

52 Nikhat Kazmi, *The Dream Merchants of Bollywood* (New Delhi: UBS Publishers' Distributors, 1998), pp. 186 and 189.

53 *Ibid.*, p. 186.

54 Rustom Bharucha, 'Utopia in Bollywood: *Hum Aapke Hain Koun ...!*', *Economic and Political Weekly* 30:15 (15 April 1995), 801–4, pp. 801–2.

55 Dyer, 'Entertainment and utopia', cited in Bharucha, 'Utopia in Bollywood', p. 801.

56 Bharucha, 'Utopia in Bollywood', pp. 802–4.

57 Kazmi, *The Dream Merchants*, pp. 53–4; Banker, *The Pocket Essential Bollywood*, p. 75.

58 Sudha Bhuchar and Kristine Landon-Smith, *Fourteen Songs, Two Weddings and a Funeral*, based on Rajshri Productions' film *Hum Aapke Hain Koun* (London: Methuen, 2001), n.p.

59  Uberoi, 'Imagining the family', p. 311.
60  Madhu Jain, 'Bollywood: next generation', in Joshi (ed.), *Bollywood*, pp. 299–343, p. 332.
61  Robert Butler, review of *Bombay Dreams*, *Independent on Sunday* (23 June 2002), rpt in *Theatre Record* 22:13, p. 844.
62  Uberoi, 'Imagining the family', p. 340.
63  Mishra, *Bollywood Cinema*, p. 240.
64  Bhuchar and Landon-Smith, *Fourteen Songs*, back cover.
65  Anne Fuchs, 'From Lorca to Bollywood: cultural adaptation in the plays of the British Asian Tamasha Theatre Company', *Cycnos* 18:1 (2001), 163–72, p. 171.
66  Richard Dyer, 'The colour of entertainment', in Dyer, *Only Entertainment*, pp. 36–45; originally published in *Sight and Sound* 5:11 (1995).
67  Sudha Bhuchar, 'Arts etc.; answer the questions!', *Independent* (30 September 2001), p. 8.
68  Barnaby King, 'Landscapes of fact and fiction: Asian theatre arts in Britain', *NTQ: New Theatre Quarterly*, 16:1 (61, 2000), 26–33, p. 29; Fuchs, 'From Lorca to Bollywood', pp. 165–6.
69  Venues played were the Lyric Hammersmith (London), the Nottingham Playhouse, the Lawrence Batley Theatre (Huddersfield), The Lowry (Manchester), the Bristol Old Vic, the Yvonne Arnaud Theatre (Guildford), and the Birmingham Repertory Theatre. Bhuchar and Landon-Smith, *Fourteen Songs*, n.p.
70  Fuchs, 'From Lorca to Bollywood', p. 171.
71  Sudha Bhuchar quoted in Chris Arnot, 'Arts: theatre: stand by your nan', *Guardian* (5 January 2000), section 2, p. 14.
72  Bhuchar and Landon-Smith, *Fourteen Songs*, pp. 2, 3, and 14.
73  Bhuchar and Landon-Smith, *Fourteen Songs*, pp. 2, 5, 10 and *passim*.
74  Mishra, *Bollywood Cinema*, p. 247.
75  Verma, '"Binglishing" the stage', p. 126.
76  Verma quoted in Ley, 'Theatre of migration', p. 365.
77  Nick Roddick was writing in late 1994 when *Four Weddings* was still showing in cinemas worldwide, but he reported that it was then predicted to earn £250 million. Nick Roddick, '*Four Weddings* and a final reckoning', *Sight and Sound* 5:1 (1995), 12–15, pp. 13–14.
78  *Ibid.*, p. 15, ellipsis added, emphasis original.
79  Peter Matthews, 'True confetti', *Modern Review* 1:15 (1994), 20.
80  A sense of this spectacle also comes across on the show's flashy, colourful, image-oriented website, *Bombay Dreams*, www.bombaydreamsthemusical.com (accessed November 2003).
81  '*Bombay Dreams* week', *BBCi Asian Life Film* (20 June 2003), www.bbc.co.uk/asian-life/film/indiansummer/bombaydreams/index.shtml (accessed November 2003); Arthur J. Pais, '*Bombay Dreams* to come true in New York', *rediff.com* (8 September 2003), in.rediff.com/movies/2003/sep/08bd.htm (accessed November 2003).
82  See, for example, the reviews by Alastair Macaulay, *Financial Times* (21 June 2002), Michael Coveney, *Daily Mail* (21 June 2002), Robert Gore-Langton,

*Express* (21 June 2002), and Georgina Brown, *Mail on Sunday* (23 June 2002), all rpt in *Theatre Record* 22:13.

83 *Bombay Dreams* Programme (London: Apollo Victoria Theatre, n.d. [2003]), n.p..

84 *Bombay Dreams* Programme, n.p. *Dilwale Dulhaniya Le Jayenge*, or *DDLJ*, translatable as 'The Brave Heart Will Take the Bride', explores Asian diasporic courtship and marriage. For analysis see Uberoi, 'The diaspora comes home'.

85 Vanessa Thorpe, 'West End looks to East for next hit: Royal Opera House follows Lloyd Webber in bringing romance of Bollywood to Britain's stage and screen', *Observer* (5 November 2000), p. 9.

86 Barbara Newman, '*Bombay Dreams* and *The Fairy Queen*: another opening, another show', *The Dancing Times* 92 (1004, 2002), 29–31, p. 29.

87 *Bombay Dreams* Programme, n.p.

88 Mela sites advertised included Bradford, Birmingham, Croydon, Walthamstow, Slough, Middlesborough, Manchester, Leicester, East London, and Leeds. 'The Show', *Bombay Dreams*, www.bombaydreamsthemusical.com/Frameset.html (accessed February 2004).

89 Krishnendu Majumdar, 'Theatre: Salaam Bombay', *Guardian* (21 February 2001), p. 16.

90 *Bombay Dreams* Programme, n.p., and Paul Prece and William A. Everett, 'The megamusical and beyond: the creation, internationalisation, and impact of a genre', in Everett and Paul R. Laird (eds), *The Cambridge Companion to the Musical* (Cambridge: Cambridge University Press, 2002), pp. 246–65, p. 252.

91 Alastair Macaulay, *Financial Times* (21 June 2002); see also reviews by Sheridan Morley, *International Herald Tribune* (26 June 2002), and John Nathan, *Jewish Chronicle* (5 July 2002); all rpt in *Theatre Record* 22:13.

92 Prece and Everett, 'The megamusical and beyond', p. 250.

93 *Ibid.*, p. 250.

94 Vasudevan, 'The politics of cultural address', pp. 151–2.

95 Michael Coveney, *The Andrew Lloyd Webber Story* (London: Arrow Books, 2000), p. 4.

96 John Peter, *Sunday Times* (23 June 2002), rpt in *Theatre Record* 22:13.

97 Prece and Everett, 'The megamusical and beyond', p. 250.

98 See reviews by Susanna Clapp, *Observer* (23 June 2002), Michael Billington, *Guardian* (20 June 2002), and Foss, *What's On* (26 June 2002), all rpt in *Theatre Record* 22:13.

99 Meera Syal, 'Bombay-Mumbai', in *Bombay Dreams* Programme, n.p.

100 Kapur and Rajadhyaksha, 'Bombay/Mumbai, 1992–2001', p. 18, emphasis original.

101 Bhabha, 'Of mimicry and man', pp. 86 and 89, all emphasis original.

102 *Theatre Record* 23:21 (11 November 2003), future London schedule insert, n.p.

103 Pais, '*Bombay Dreams* to come true in NY'.

104 *Ibid.*, and '*Bombay Dreams* publicity', *Bollywood Blitz*, www.bollywoodblitz.com/news/bollywoodnews.php?newsarticle=11 (accessed November 2003).

# 7

## Re-imagining the imperial metropolis

Cities are the focus of much of our national life. They are … cradles of creativity – economically, culturally, socially and politically. They are also, of course, the locus of many of our most well-rehearsed national problems. And … they also pose some of the toughest challenges to (and perhaps best hopes for) democracy. (Ash Amin, Doreen Massey, and Nigel Thrift, *Cities for the Many Not the Few*, Bristol: Policy Press, 2000)

Because this book aims in part to challenge the metropolitan dominance of British cultural practices and British theatre and performance studies in particular, it seems fitting to conclude by interrogating the cultural practices of the metropolis itself. Thus, the underlying questions of this chapter are: what does and can the metropolis do for culture and for cultural identities?, and, to echo Amin, Massey, and Thrift, what challenges to and hopes for cultural democracy does the metropolis present?[1]

For many, the answers to these questions are overwhelmingly positive: the metropolis accommodates and stimulates the wandering, reflecting, and pondering flâneur; it generates new, hybrid identities, cultural practices, and meanings; and most importantly it tolerates and promotes cultural differences, of race, ethnicity, nationality, sexuality, gender, ability, age, and so on, facilitating genuinely democratic participation and expression. For others, however, this is a naively utopian vision of the metropolis, confounded by observations that the metropolis produces not wide social inclusion but social exclusions and oppressions. These critics point out that, while the metropolis may accommodate flâneurs, it does not allow everyone to adopt the flâneur's apparently easy mobility which is actually a function of privilege, especially race, class and gender privilege. Worse, they argue, instead of generating hybrid identities and meanings and promoting cultural difference and democratic expression, the metropolis can dominate, assimilate and homogenise differences, repressing them instead of supporting them. As Chapter 4 on the Edinburgh festivals suggested, the potential globalisation of the city risks limiting the opportunities and choices for cultural expression that are available there:

apparently infinite consumer choice may in fact be infinitely self-replicating, near-identical consumer choice. Similarly, the metropolis's apparent openness to cultural difference and new identities can be seen, less positively, as imperialist. Instead of protecting cultural differences, the metropolis assimilates them to serve its own imperial purposes, such as the cultivation of a self-promoting and self-interested narrative of the metropolis as benignly tolerant of difference.

To investigate some of the metropolis's cultural risks and potentials, this chapter focuses on London as a potentially imperial space and considers how that imperialism might be challenged through the cultural practices of installation art. To set up what is at risk in an imperial metropolis, it examines, first, some of the ways that imperial authority is spatially and culturally inscribed and enacted in London. Arguing that this inscription is, however, intrinsically unstable, it then examines black British artist Steve McQueen's 2002 film installation in the disused Lumière Cinema on St Martin's Lane in London's West End, *Caribs' Leap/Western Deep*. It considers how that work proposed a radical critique of imperialism generally and, particularly, of a historical but persistent imperialism in London. It argues that this work, like many others commissioned by the London-based art commissioning company Artangel, spatially, visually, and performatively reoriented its audiences within the metropolis, proposing and provoking a postcolonial critique of the metropolis's imperialism.[2] By positing an alternative spatial logic to the city, the installation challenged London's dominant imperialist spatial logics and the imperialist social relations they can produce. In contrast to dominant imperialist spatial discourses that privilege monumentality and ostentation, it explored an alternative subterranean perspective. In contrast to dominant visual discourses that privilege light and visibility, it proposed alternatives that explored the poetics of darkness and obscurity. And instead of encouraging and rewarding passive acceptance, it provoked audiences actively to participate and, so, performatively to change their relationships to the city. The Lumière Cinema installation of *Caribs' Leap/Western Deep* challenged the metropolis's latent imperialism, helping to realise its potential to be a space of more democratic expression and participation.

This chapter focuses on this single installation in order to examine it and its references in detail, but I have selected it both because it demonstrates effective strategies for challenging the metropolis's imperialism in particular, and because it is indicative of the kinds of creative, embodied political interventions that recent installation art – and Artangel's commissions in particular – have made in relation to a growing number of the metropolis's potential discriminations, including discriminations related to gender,[3] nationality and class,[4] 'race' and religion,[5] nominations of sites as (benign) neighbourhoods or (malignant) wastelands,[6] and consumerism.[7] It also indicates the kinds of political interventions that recent black British filmmakers and filmmaking collectives have achieved.[8]

## Building an imperial metropolis

In the analyses of historians and geographers alike, London has literally been built to enhance its imperial identity as the capital of a nation with a once-strong sense of a manifest destiny to colonise, control, and 'improve' other parts of the globe. London's imperial identity has been enhanced through material constructions which celebrate and memorialise that identity, and which assume positions and perspectives of dominance and control that mimic London's perceived global dominance. Notable in this built environment are various imperial memorials that both occupy and metaphorically observe the city in ways that grant them and the state figures and bodies they represent – especially the monarchy, army, navy, and government – persistent authority and privilege.

Three famous examples are the Victoria Memorial, the Albert Memorial, and Trafalgar Square. A large part of the centre of London is organised around the dominating imperial gaze of Queen Victoria in the Victoria Memorial unveiled in 1911 outside of Buckingham Palace and gazing down the Mall towards Admiralty Arch and Trafalgar Square. At the same time that the Memorial was erected, the Mall was widened and the connection to Trafalgar Square opened up, simultaneously extending Victoria's panoptical gaze and expanding the ground for displays of imperial power, such as processions and parades.[9]

Similarly, the memorial that Victoria erected for her husband, Hyde Park's Albert Memorial (completed in 1875), gazes out over – and metaphorically controls – South Kensington. Expensive shops including Harrods, expensive domestic real estate, and cultural institutions including the Victoria and Albert Museum and the Albert Hall now dominate this part of London. However, this location's association with class privilege is long-standing and reinforces its once-strong association with imperial power. In the nineteenth century, South Kensington was reportedly known 'to colonial ex-patriates as "Asia Minor" on account of the large number of colonial-returned living there'.[10] Many 'colonial-returned' would have been actual agents of empire, its administrators and governors, merchants and soldiers.

Perhaps most famously, there is Trafalgar Square, named after Britain's victorious 1805 sea Battle of Trafalgar with France (with whom it was then competing for colonies and colonial trade) and in which Lord Nelson died. The Square is loaded with imperial signifiers, from its commanding column erected in 1843 and topped with a statue of Nelson, to its bas-reliefs of Nelson's most famous battles, its inset bronze replicas of Britain's Standard Imperial Measures, and its various statues of, amongst other figures, King George IV (reigned 1820–30) and Sir Henry Havelock, a General in the Indian Army credited with helping to suppress the 'Indian Mutiny' of 1857.[11] As Ronald Mace notes in his book *Trafalgar Square: Emblem of Empire*, 'Trafalgar Square and its several monuments, of course, speak the language of the ruling class. To the mass of ordinary people whose exploitation and death through nearly three centuries had enabled the ideal of Empire to be realised, the Square offers no bronze or granite memorial.'[12]

The imperialism materially inscribed in the city is not only dominating, it is also assimilating, as when the metropolis casts itself as the benevolent imperial patron of a variety of colonial places and cultures, all sited conveniently within the metropolis. As commonwealth offices proliferated in London in the early twentieth century – Australia House in 1914, India House in 1924, Canada House in 1925, and Africa House in 1928, for example[13] – a pair of London Underground posters displayed in 1933 (figure 24) invited riders to 'Visit the Empire'. They located Western Australia on the Strand and India at Aldwych and they encompassed Burma, Malaya, Nigeria, South Africa, and the East Indies (in one poster), and Newfoundland, British Guiana, and Jamaica (in the other), all within 'the familiar logo of the London Underground ... transformed into a belt around the world'.[14] The posters posed those nations' colonial offices in London – as well as the Imperial Institute, Madame Tussauds, 'the Museums' of South Kensington, and 'the Zoo' of Camden Town – as standing metonymically for the nations themselves, and it thereby cast London metonymically as the (imperial) globe. The Commonwealth, with all of its real cultural differences, was diminished and domesticated, both in the sense that it was brought 'home' to London and because its populations were largely represented by benign, storybook-suited illustrations of animals, buildings, fruits, foliage, and people attired in clichéd ethnic costumes. While such imagery may seem somewhat preposterous today, geographers Felix Driver and David Gilbert note that it was 'neither novel nor exceptional' at the time.[15]

Even so, these examples of the inscription of British imperialism in London obviously originated in earlier ages, closer to the 'great' age of

British Empire, so it might seem fair to argue that such imperial meanings are no longer being inscribed in the metropolis. However, as the
examples of the Victoria and Albert Memorials and Trafalgar Square
make clear, these imperial monuments remain; they persist materially and
so, importantly, do some of their imperial ideological effects, a point
supported by their ongoing public subvention. The Albert Memorial was
reopened in 1998 after a decade-long restoration costing the state over
£11 million.[16] And London Mayor Ken Livingstone pedestrianised the
north end of Trafalgar Square in 2003. This reinforced the Square's links
to state monuments such as the National Gallery, which it now leads to
directly, but it also revised some of the city's in-built imperial elitism by
expanding access to the city centre for pedestrians and public transport,
especially buses – formerly known as omnibuses, or buses for all.

Other state monuments, such as the Victoria and Albert Museum,
the British Museum, and the British Library (which houses the Oriental
and India Office collection), persist in practising what might be seen as
imperial performatives – repeated presumptions that they know different

24 London Underground *Visit the Empire* posters by Ernest Michael Dinkel, 1933

cultures better than those cultures know themselves. Such presumptions are perhaps tempting when these monumental institutions own or control so many material resources – such as artworks and archives – that convey important parts of other nations' histories and cultures. But these presumptions are especially problematic when the resources are literal or metaphorical spoils of empire. Such imperial performativity is at the centre of debates over the Greek Elgin Marbles owned by the British Museum. Lord Elgin, a British ambassador to the Sultan of Turkey who ruled Greece at that time, acquired these sculptures from Athens', Acropolis in 1801–3, and they were identified by Lord Byron in 1812 as 'poor plunder from a bleeding land'.[17] Debate continues over Britain's moral and/or legal right to the Marbles, considering they were removed from Greece when it was under the rule of a foreign power. Other exhibitions may benefit less from such explicit acts of imperial exploitation, but they may nevertheless profit from the UK's long-standing disproportionate global power. Exhibitions that might be examined in more detail in this context are, for example, 'Trading Places', on the East India Company from 1600 to 1834, at the British Library in 2002, and, also in 2002, the Victoria and Albert Museum's 'Cinema India: The Art of Bollywood', cited at the beginning of the last chapter.[18]

Furthermore, London Underground posters continue to portray the metropolis as 'home' to the world although not through quite the same language or visual discourses as were deployed in 1933, and with an explicit sense of irony. A series of posters for a 2003 London Underground campaign, for example, showed people manifesting a variety of visible cultural differences – a punk, an elderly woman, an Asian family – looking 'at home' in a variety of sites around London (figure 25). The campaign's slogan claimed, 'You ♥' a part of London and 'We ⊖' the same place. All the cultural differences represented in the campaign were conflated within the rhetorically equated subject positions 'you' and 'we'. And, again, those differences were domesticated in a visual discourse emphasising homeliness (with characters looking 'at home') as well as in the implicit claim – evoked through the rhetorical equation of the heart symbol with the Tube symbol – that everyone 'loves' London and its Tube. What makes these images less assimilating than their 1930s counterparts, however, is their inbuilt irony. With at least seventeen chickens (familiar from the windows of Chinatown's restaurants) hanging in the white man's suburban picture window, and the black female café worker proudly sporting at least four cricket jumpers, the images were self-consciously hyperbolic. Similarly, the heart symbol evoked a rhetoric

**25** Two posters in Transport for London's 'You ♥ London' campaign (2003)

that was self-consciously nostalgic – for a hippy era of peace and love, and for a fantasy of youthful love simply expressed in $x$ ♥ $y$ equations that can be easily etched on to school desks and toilet cubicle walls.

Despite this irony, what persists is an attitude that London benignly incorporates a vast range of cultural differences. As social historian John Eade points out, this attitude is pervasively reiterated in the discourse of contemporary London tourist guidebooks, especially in their oft-repeated claim that, in the metropolis of London, virtually every type of international cuisine imaginable can be had.[19] Perhaps most tellingly, while London persists in memorialising imperialism, as Rodney Mace suggested above, it does not memorialise those sacrificed by empire; nor, as Bill Schwarz points out, has it even begun to commemorate the end of empire.

> There are in the capital no statues or monuments marking or celebrating the end of empire. There is no statue of Nehru or Nkrumah in Parliament Square, nor even a relief of Harold Macmillan in Cape Town declaring – poised, steely, but ultimately bewildered – that the winds of change were about to blow. In design and organisation London, Birmingham, Glasgow all still signify the imperial past, a past memorialised in the built environment.[20]

## The unstable apparatus of metropolitan imperialism

This is not to say, however, that these imperial articulations of the nation manifested in the metropolis must necessarily and indefinitely predominate. In any space, meanings are produced socially; the built environment, its histories, and its signs affect this process, but they do not predetermine it. As Amin, Massey, and Thrift suggest, 'cities are essentially hybrid and inevitably conflictual. This is part of their creative character and their dynamism.'[21] Thus, historians have noted that, while the metropolis of London certainly administered the colonisation of large parts of Africa and elsewhere, it also more recently – if inadvertently – at least contributed to the dismantling of Africa's colonial regimes by providing a site for the development of 'the emerging discourse of pan-Africanism':[22] 'the capital itself worked as an intellectual organiser, allowing West Africans to talk with West Indians, North Americans from Harlem with black British'.[23] As Jonathan Schneer notes, 'an imperial city is cosmopolitan, and a cosmopolitan city contains anti-imperialists'.[24]

Even those metropolitan sites specifically dedicated to signifying empire have been mobilised to challenge imperialism. Trafalgar Square was designed as an imperial space, but – indeed, precisely because of its state-sanctioned design and signification – it has long and repeatedly been co-opted 'as a site of political demonstration and protest',[25] a site

where state power has been challenged, rejected, mocked, and disre-
garded. Since 1998, the Square's many imperial monuments have been
quietly joined by a series of temporary artworks on the otherwise vacant
fourth plinth that have repeatedly refused to celebrate war heroes and
have rejected discourses of monumentality.[26] Louder protest in Trafalgar
Square has campaigned for women's suffrage, work and fair wages, the
right to freedom of assembly and speech, withdrawal from the Suez in
1956, and nuclear disarmament, among many other things.[27]
Importantly, in the context of this chapter, the Square has also been the
site of various anti colonial protests for such things as the release of
Irish prisoners in the 1920s, Indian independence in the 1940s, and,
more recently, the abolition of apartheid in South Africa.[28] It has also
been the site of protests against neo-imperialism, most notably as the
destination of the 20 November 2003 anti-war march that specifically
protested against George W. Bush's state visit to the UK and concluded
with the toppling of a five-metre effigy of the President, in ironic reference to the toppling of Saddam Hussein's statue in Baghdad on 9
April 2003.[29]

As the toppling of Saddam's statue and the anti-state occupations
of Trafalgar Square illustrate, monuments to state power and imperial
control may themselves be read as nostalgic, anxious, overblown
attempts to render permanent and secure what is inevitably and already
transient. They exemplify what Edward Said has described as 'the tension between the synchronic panoptical vision of domination – the
demand for identity, stasis – and the counter-pressure of the diachrony
of history – change, difference'.[30] The point is illustrated in P. B.
Shelley's famous poem 'Ozymandias' (1817). The words on
Ozymandias's pedestal command its beholders to 'Look on my works,
ye Mighty, and despair!' But the pedestal is now topped only with 'trun-
kless legs of stone', 'Near them, on the sand, / Half sunk, a shattered
visage lies', and 'Nothing beside remains'. What must once have been
an impressive monument to a powerful empire has been reduced to a
'colossal wreck'.[31] The sheer number and scale of London's many mas-
sive ornate monuments to British empire bespeak a desire, like
Ozymandias's, to render permanent and static what was instead
changing, temporary and declining, particularly by the end of Victoria's
reign. That said, markers of the end of empire – for example, the televised toppling of Saddam's statue or Bush's effigy – can themselves
take on memorial status, and be seen equally as anxious attempts to
render permanent what are also transient events.

Although the metropolis may display no monuments to the end of empire, as Schwarz notes, within the 'larger public *mise-en-scène* authentically post-colonial cultures thrive in even the most unexpected locales'; they 'operate deep inside the culture of the metropolis'.[32] They may not be as insistently visible as state-funded monuments, but they are present and active. In this analysis, as observers from Sigmund Freud to Peter Ackroyd have noted, a metropolis is more like a palimpsest – with often-conflicting histories overlapping in space and time – than it is like a linear narrative – with one dominant story.[33] Jane M. Jacobs notes that 'the grand ideas of empire [are] unstable technologies of power which reach across time and space'.[34] These ideas may reach powerfully across time and space but they are intrinsically unstable, contested by different and sometimes contradictory coincidental ideas and practices. Thus, metropolitan manifestations of empire may be pervasive, powerful, and oppressive, but they can nevertheless be engaged with, challenged, undermined, and revised – and this is partly what Steve McQueen's *Caribs' Leap / Western Deep* installation did.

## Steve McQueen's *Caribs' Leap/Western Deep* at the Lumière Cinema

Artangel exhibited McQueen's films *Caribs' Leap* and *Western Deep* at the disused Lumière Cinema on St Martin's Lane in London from 3 October to 10 November 2002.[35] Admission was free. The films had been shown previously – at the art festival Documenta in Kassel, Germany – and would be shown subsequently, for example in France, but their London exhibition was the only one that showed them in a found site as opposed to a gallery. The Lumière had been a fairly upmarket arthouse repertory cinema until the mid-1990s, but it was closed when the 1960s office block it was under was transformed in 1999 to the elite St Martin's Lane Hotel, run by Ian Schrager (former impresario of New York's Studio 54) and designed by Philippe Starck. To enter the Lumière for McQueen's installation was to enter a different building. Where there had once been a coffee bar, a foreign film video sale stand, wall-to-wall carpets, and soft lighting, there were now exposed concrete floors, wires and pipes, electricians' notes scribbled on the walls, and bald fluorescent lighting. But if the entryway was cold and bleak, the cinema was colder and bleaker. All the seating had been removed, leaving a tiered concrete auditorium with a pockmarked floor where bolts securing the chairs had been ripped out. Into this vast, empty, unheated space, Artangel and McQueen had inserted a curved part-wall about half-way down the auditorium and roughly parallel to the main screening wall.

For *Caribs' Leap*, the audience was first ushered into the upper half of the auditorium space, between the back wall and the inserted wall. On the audience's entry, *Caribs' Leap*'s two films were already playing, one on the back wall of the auditorium, and one on the inserted wall. The projection on the inserted wall was bigger and normally showed only a pale blue space, eventually recognisable as a sky. The light reflecting from this sky into the auditorium was diffuse and soft. Occasionally, a human figure – who looked dark-skinned and male but was indistinct – fell through the space in slow motion (figure 26). Sometimes he appeared nearer, and sometimes he appeared farther away. We never saw where he came from – or whether he fell, jumped, or was pushed – and we never saw him land. The projection on the back wall was smaller and showed a variety of scenes of apparently 'everyday life' on the Caribbean island of Grenada: the sea moving, a dog scurrying around on the beach, children on the beach, the dead in coffins at an undertaker's, a shed burning, trees, buildings, and a man making little boats out of coconut shells and transparent paper. The aesthetic was observational, documentary in style, and, although the place looked beautiful, it was neither overtly exoticised – the sky was sometimes overcast, and figures were not sexualised – nor domesticated, as in the storybook illustrations of the Tube's 'Visit the Empire' posters. It was a Caribbean island, but not as a promotional tourist video might show it. The only sound during the screening of these films was similar to a gentle wind but, like the falling figure, it too was indistinct.

Leaflet information about these films was provided on entry to the space and explained the history McQueen alluded to in the 'falling' film. These films take their name from a place in Grenada – his parents' birthplace – called Le Morne des Sauteurs, or Leapers' Hill. When the French 'bought' and colonised Grenada in the mid seventeenth century, they reportedly drove the native islanders off their land and persecuted them. Some islanders who refused to accept French rule fled to the north and eventually leapt into the sea, rather than give themselves up. Ceded to the British in 1783, Grenada gained independence only in 1974.[36] Thus, the two parts of *Caribs' Leap* juxtaposed a film evoking the moment of Grenada's colonial conquest (and its resistance) with a film evoking its postcolonial present. The luminosity of the past 'falling' film bathed, infused, and slightly washed out the film of the present.[37]

After these films had played for about half an hour, the audience was ushered into the lower screening space for *Western Deep*. Once the

**26** Still from Steve McQueen, *Caribs' Leap* (2002)

audience was seated on the cold floor, the auditorium was plunged into profound, almost palpably thick darkness before the film began. This single film was played against the usual screening wall of the auditorium, covering an enormous part of this space. The film showed miners – all black – working in 'the deepest working (gold) mine in the world, at Western Deep, Tau Tona in South Africa'.[38] As *Guardian* reviewer Adrian Searle noted, this is a mine 'still owned and operated, according to the exhibition guide, by the company that ran it during apartheid, and nothing much here has changed'.[39] Again using a documentary style, the film followed the miners going down to the mine in a lift (a two-mile descent). It showed them working the mine, performing regimented exercises above ground, and being subjected to medical tests. Using only ambient lighting, the film was often almost completely black; the parts in the mine, for example, were only fleetingly illuminated by the lights from the miners' helmets and the light reflecting off the mine walls and glancing off their sweating skin (figure 27). The sound in this film was also ambient and combined sections of near silence with sections that were profoundly loud – for example, the clanging of the lift's mechanics and the roar of drilling echoing in the underground chambers. As was *Caribs' Leap*, *Western Deep* was filmed on Super-8, achieving a grainy, 'sticky' effect.[40]

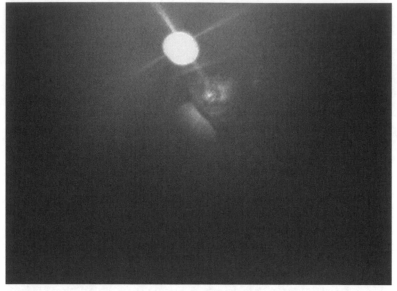

27 Still from Steve McQueen's *Western Deep* (2002)

### Reconfiguring the spatial logics of the imperial metropolis

Primarily by reconfiguring its audiences' perspectives, McQueen's installation proposed alternative spatial and visual logics for the metropolis. By
challenging dominant – imperialist – patterns of spatial and visual organisation, it challenged dominant imperialist social patterns and asserted the
relevance of McQueen's own black perspective without allowing it to be
either dominated by or assimilated to an imperialist logic. These effects
were achieved through a variety of means, mostly spatial and visual, and
I consider these here in four categories: the geographical location of the
installation and the history of that location; the spatial arrangement of
the installation; the audience's physical experiences of viewing the installation; and the form and content of the films themselves.

### Occupying the centre, gently

By choosing to locate their installation in the centre of London, just up
from Trafalgar Square on St Martin's Lane (which actually predates
Trafalgar Square),[41] McQueen and Artangel literally and figuratively –
but unobtrusively – penetrated the imperial city. The Lumière was a suitable site from which to critique imperialism because it was distinctly a

site of cultural privilege and was proximate to London's imperial centre as well as such national institutions as the National Gallery, the National Portrait Gallery, the Royal Opera House, and the home of the English National Opera, the London Coliseum. By showing the exploitation of black workers in South Africa and the colonial persecution of Grenada's islanders, McQueen literally transposed to central London the barbaric 'heart of darkness' behaviour that Western myth and literature have long fantasised is located in some remote, anonymous backwater deep in central Africa – but that might be located more accurately, as Joseph Conrad suggested in his famous story 'Heart of Darkness' (1899), in the heart of the imperial fantasist/coloniser and at the administrative heart of the empire, namely the imperial city. By showing his films where he did, McQueen challenged the imperial centre to account for its responsibility for this barbaric colonial exploitation and to acknowledge that this exploitation is an underlying foundation on which the metropolis, its wealth and its empire have been built.

At the same time, however, the Lumière Cinema was not an imperial monument, which would have made McQueen's postcolonial 'occupation' more literal but would also have required him to adopt imperialism's monumental, triumphant practices and sites in a way he avoided. Where imperialism's monuments are often static and elevated in a (failed) bid to enact their own permanence and omniscience, McQueen's installation was by contrast – and in direct riposte – moving and subterranean in recognition of its temporary and partial perspective. Thus, it opposed the omnipotent vision claimed by imperial monuments such as Nelson's Column, the Albert Memorial and the Victoria Memorial, as well as by a class 'elevated' by privilege. It replaced this vision with a dark, restricted, underground vision, thereby acknowledging and endorsing an alternative, literally underground perspective. On a personal and professional level, the screening of McQueen's film in the Lumière Cinema was about occupying a site and position of acknowledged achievement and privilege he had never imagined he would gain access to as a filmmaker. 'This was my favourite theatre', he told *Sight and Sound* reporter Gareth Evans. 'I can't believe I'm back here showing my films.'[42]

## Revising the centre

As well as occupying central London, the installation presented an alternative version of that centre, a version that contested the centre's assumption of privilege and its domination by an imperial panoptical

gaze. The installation's challenge to privilege relied partly on its audience's familiarity with the Lumière Cinema in its former, relatively opu-
lent incarnation. A site that was clearly once luxurious and comfortable
became derelict, emptied, cold, stark, dusty, literally distressed, and
potentially distressing, an apparently casually discarded residue of the
luxurious hotel development above. The site's relative poverty as man-
ifestly experienced in McQueen's installation contrasted sharply with its
former opulence as well as with the current lavishness of the upstairs
St Martin's Lane Hotel which bills itself as an 'urban resort' and is so
'cleanly' designed – and assumes it is so well known to its jet-set clientele – that it does not deign to despoil its all-glass surface by advertising
its name outside.[43] Further, the films' postcolonial awareness contrasted
with hotel designer Philippe Starck's apparently unreconstructed attitudes towards the 'glamour' of empire: he claimed that for his design
of the Hotel's Asia de Cuba restaurant he had 'drawn inspiration from
the Belgian Congo of the 1950s'.[44] By the 1950s, the outright brutality
of Belgian King Leopold's rule of the Congo (1885–1908) – the inspiration for Conrad's 'Heart of Darkness' – had been replaced by a less
violent Belgian state rule. But although 'the Belgian Congo of the 1950s'
might have been glamorous for its Belgian colonisers, for the Congo's
indigenous peoples it was still marked by endemic paternalistic rule that
maintained their subservience, limited their access to education, prevented them from developing an educated, domestic class of leaders,
and contributed directly, after independence in 1960, to domestic chaos
and civil war.[45] McQueen's temporal and spatial juxtaposition of poverty
and affluence, and postcolonial awareness and imperial arrogance, again
indicated the economic and colonial exploitation on which the stability
of the imperial centre's wealth rests – quite literally in the case of the
St Martin's Lane Hotel.

Another related important point made by McQueen's installation
was that opportunities for non-commercial art practice were being sacrificed through the metropolis's continuing colonisation by global financial
capital. While the Lumière Cinema was elite, its repertory had not generally been highly commercial. The site's 'colonisation' by Schrager's chain
of hotels meant the demise of an important one of London's relatively
few remaining repertory cinemas and the consequent loss of opportunities for independent filmmakers to exhibit their work.

The subterranean site chosen by McQueen and Artangel was
further significant because it resonated with – while clearly not imagining
it could reproduce – the miners' experience depicted in *Western Deep*,

again evoking the difficult work that is performed in horrible conditions out of economic necessity in the South and that serves to maintain the economic advantages – and leisure – of the North. By showing people in Grenada seemingly just 'hanging out' and falling, the installation did not posit a North/South, leisure/work set of binary oppositions, but it did bring to bear a focus on work and its politics – who does it, how it is done, who has none, who benefits from it, and so on. McQueen implicitly explores this kind of articulation of the varieties of work and non-work throughout his own art practices, by making them appear 'artless' when in fact they are not.

## Reorienting perspectives

The physical sense of resonance for the audience with the experiences of those depicted in McQueen's films was further reinforced in several other ways. *Western Deep* could not remotely expect actually to produce for its audiences its miners' experiences – an objective that would have been, in any case, presumptuous. However, it could and clearly did aim to create resonances with the miners' experiences, especially to intimate the profound discomfort of their conditions of labour by, in McQueen's words, 'bring[ing] the smell back, not just the images'.[46] Central to this effect was the audience's gradual descent, deeper and deeper into the cinema, down first into the viewing area for *Caribs' Leap* and second into that for *Western Deep*. Even more important was the descent into increasing, 'disorienting and claustrophobic'[47] darkness, the impression of which was enhanced in *Western Deep* by contrast with the relative luminosity of the preceding *Caribs' Leap*. For reviewer Sarah Whitfield, 'When the lights went down [for *Western Deep*], the blackness was unrelieved and almost intolerable. This was the moment when the audience might have felt, with reason, that it had been sealed two miles underground.'[48]

Other conditions were important too: the cold, dank space; the rock-hard floor; the thunderous noise; the evacuating silence; and the radical shifts from *Caribs' Leap*, with its wide horizontal planes of sky and sea and its sense of physical and narrative openness, to *Western Deep*, with its vertical plane of mine shaft, its physical sense of oppression, and its narrative containment.[49] All of these sensorially both deprived and overwhelmed *Western Deep*'s audience and physically addressed them in ways typical in McQueen's work. As reviewer Bénédicte Ramade observes, 'Almost all his works disorient, make uneasy and accentuate the sensation of being there, of looking and sensing, they are disturbing because of their presence.'[50]

Mark Durden notes McQueen's consistent interest in 'mak[ing] films which impact on the viewer, to forcibly make us feel involved, active rather than passive'.[51] And McQueen himself acknowledges his aim to engage his audience physically – both literally and metaphorically. 'You are very much involved with what is going on,' he says. 'You are a participant, not a passive viewer ... I want to put people into a situation where they're sensitive to themselves watching the piece.'[52] He elaborates:

> I like to make films in which people can almost pick up gravel in their hands and rub it but at the same time, I like the film to be like a wet piece of soap – it slips out of your grasp; you have to physically move around, you have to readjust your position in relation to it, so that *it* dictates to you rather than you to *it*.[53]

In a problematising engagement with the politics of agency, McQueen's work *compels* its audience to *be active*.

While perhaps less radically than *Western Deep*, *Caribs' Leap* also compelled its audiences performatively to approach the physical experiences of its filmic subjects, especially the falling body/bodies (the film was ambiguous about whether it showed or meant to suggest the same or different bodies). While the audience of *Caribs' Leap* was not compelled actually to fall, we were compelled to look down into the open sky space of the 'falling' film, potentially inducing a sense of vertigo. Further, like the bodies in this film, we were compelled repeatedly to twist, a movement that not only mimicked that of the falling figure but also emphasised a gaze that neither had nor claimed the (imperial) privilege of being all-seeing. Because of the downward rake of the auditorium, most audience members I observed stood or sat facing down towards the 'falling' film. However, because we were given two films to watch simultaneously, one in front and one behind us, the latter involving a lot more apparent action, many members of the audience looked back and forth between the two films, twisting to try to 'catch', alternately, the falling man and the shifts in action and locale in the 'upper' film. For Whitfield, the films' compulsion of their audience to choose where to look was uncomfortable not only physically but also ethically, provoking her to ask

> Which screen to look at? And for how long? The temptation to ignore the busy, banal scenes of village life shot in a documentary style and to linger instead on the empty sky, waiting for the next body to fall, left this viewer with a sense of voyeurism and guilty unease: manipulating the audience is part of the work.[54]

For my part, I found myself captivated by the activity in the scenes of village life, eager to identify a narrative or a set of links in them, and self-conscious that I was neglecting what felt like a challenge literally to notice and metaphorically to catch the apparently randomly falling bodies of the other film.

## Navigating the black Atlantic

Finally, the films themselves, in form and content, contributed to challenging the metropolis's dominant imperialist perspective in a variety of different ways. First, as in many of McQueen's other works, *Western Deep* in particular made extensive and often subtle use of a formal visual discourse emphasising and prioritising blackness. Here and elsewhere in his work, this emphasis appears to be posed as a strategic challenge to the preferential cultural treatment usually accorded to things light and white, as well as to the ideological import of this partiality. The catalogue for his *Speaking in Tongues* exhibition at the Musée d'Art Moderne de la Ville de Paris in early 2003, for example, inverts conventional typographic form by being made up of white text on a black ground; blank pages and spaces are black, not white.[55] Many of his films, too, are literally films noir, featuring black figures (often himself) and black spaces. The effect of this inversion of dominant filmic discourses is to compel thinking about the ideological implications of the film noir where, as Jane M. Jacobs and others have observed, blacks and other non-whites rarely appear but where the ideological implications of the good/bad and white/black binaries are foundational.[56] McQueen's 2001 digitally recorded film *Illuminer*, for example, showed him lying on a hotel bed watching television. Because the camera was set on top of the television, what was being broadcast was not visible, and McQueen himself, illuminated by the variable light cast by the television, was only inconsistently visible. His description of planning the film suggests he intended directly to point up and engage with the digital camera's inbuilt 'discriminations' (to use an obviously loaded term): 'The fact of the matter was that as soon as I picked up the digital camera I knew that it would fight the blackness to try to make sense of it all. That's what they do.'[57] *Western Deep* seems in some ways to have relished its darkness, at the same time as it acknowledged the torment for the miners of working in such abject conditions.

Formally, the films also adopted a predominantly anthropological, documentary style but provided no verbal or educational narrative,

resisting the assimilating effects of imperialist discourses, however well
intentioned they may be. Further, the films combined documentary and
fictional styles (the latter especially in the 'falling' film),[58] according
neither one higher status. And they overlapped and inverted histories,
moving from the past/present in Grenada to the present in South Africa,
emphasising the correlation of these histories and geographies instead of
separating them in time and space as conventional histories might do.

Through their content, the films inserted into – and asserted in – the
metropolitan centre a personal history. Typically, for McQueen, this
personal, subjective perspective was not explicitly narrated, but it clearly
informed the films, as does his presence in many of his earlier films such
as *Bear* (1995) and *Deadpan* (1997). *Caribs' Leap*, in particular, was partly an
exploration of his family's recent past in Grenada, as his parents' birthplace and the site of his grandmother's funeral, the occasion of which
brought him to Grenada and inspired him to make the film.[59] The films
made no explicit reference to his grandmother's death, but the 'everyday'
film did visit the undertaker's, and *Caribs' Leap*'s other film, of course,
invoked the deaths of her – and McQueen's own – Caribbean predecessors. For the films to intervene in the metropolis's imperial dominance, it
is enough that they simply suggested a postcolonial personal history and
story.

The films also inserted into the metropolitan centre a postcolonial
cultural history – and a postcolonial cultural present. While McQueen
insists he does not aim directly to make black activist work, he acknowledges that it inevitably informs what he does: 'I'm not saying I avoid it. I
can't literally, so I don't try.'[60] He also acknowledges that he has been
affected by institutional racism, for example during his schooling in
London.[61] Clearly, these films were interested in exploring colonialism's
cultural effects. Gareth Evans observes that 'Both films are potent studies
of colonialism's afterburns, developing McQueen's trademark concerns
with freedom and restraint, resistance and repression'.[62] *Caribs' Leap*
invoked a history of lethal imperial invasion, and both films alluded to
economic exploitation, the gold mine of *Western Deep* more directly, but
the quasi-touristic visual discourse of *Caribs' Leap*, nevertheless, obliquely.
Formally, as in many of McQueen's other works, both films simultaneously explored the freedom of movement and the restraint of stasis: they
were compelled to be repeated, the falling man almost floated, the miners
were trapped in the darkness and within the frame. As Evans suggests, the
postcolonial subject may live in freedom (or movement) but nevertheless
carry his or her history of subjugation (or restraint).

By bringing these two postcolonial places and narratives, from Africa and the Caribbean, to London, McQueen connected the three. Rhyming their names and literally showing them opposite each other, the installation asked what Western Deep, South Africa, and Caribs' Leap, Grenada, have in common. But by situating them both in London, it also implicitly asked what they have in common with London, England. One inevitable answer is an imperial history of slavery, wherein Europeans transported African slaves via the so-called 'middle passage' to the Caribbean to cultivate crops that were in turn exported to Europe where wealth accumulated grossly disproportionately. McQueen joined up these nodal points on the triangular Atlantic traffic route of slavery and its legacies and, in so doing, explicitly linked the economic and social exploitations portrayed in his films with the economic prosperity of London; implicitly, he called the imperial metropolis to account for its colonial exploitations. He contributed to the kind of revised historical analysis that black British cultural theorist Paul Gilroy has called for, an analysis that comprehensively rethinks 'the impact of the brutal market activity in human beings which culminated in coffee, sugar, chocolate and tea, not to mention new forms of banking, insurance and governmental administration, becoming familiar – even essential – elements in the common European habitus'.[63] Significantly, though, by not naming London, McQueen inverted the usual colonial power hierarchy by refusing the metropolis the centrality and superiority it normally assumes in relation to its colonial others.

Of course, a second thing the three sites invoked by McQueen's installation have in common is precisely the people who have travelled slavery's triangular trade route, who have travelled – whether historically, literally, or metaphorically – what Gilroy has influentially called the black Atlantic.[64] McQueen's invocation of the black Atlantic had at least three potentially transforming effects for the imperial metropolis. First, it again challenged the metropolis to account for its involvement in the slave trade by providing another reference for the falling figure in *Caribs' Leap*: the many slaves who were thrown – or who leapt – overboard during the notoriously treacherous middle passage. Although historians debate just how high slave mortality was during the middle passage, they generally agree that it was relatively high owing to a great number of causes, including disease, accident, rebellion, suicide, natural disaster,[65] and murder, especially by drowning.[66] In this context, McQueen's invocation of the black Atlantic also invited its audiences to reconsider the falling figure as a flying figure who escapes – and defeats – enslavement by rejecting the white

European ideology that sees it as preferable to death.[67] And it invited its
audiences to engage in the continual movement that articulates the experience of (black) diaspora – that describes black identities' formation as a
product more of their routes than of their roots.[68]

Second, Gilroy argues that the black Atlantic invokes an alternative
post-Enlightenment history to the dominant European one of progress,
pointing out that that history is tenable only if the (black) history of slavery is repressed. Third, he argues, it invokes a transatlantic, shared black
identity that might work powerfully as a co-operative bloc to contest
empire's residual effects. For Gilroy, the usual nation-based study of black
cultures (e.g. black British, African-American) is inadequate because it is
important to see black cultures in relation not only to the other cultures in
their immediate geo-political contexts but also to other black cultures,
however distantly geographically removed they may be. McQueen's films
by no means equated the three black identities he presented; indeed, the
contrasts between *Caribs' Leap* and *Western Deep* were some of the films'
most notable features. However, they did allow connections to be made
across the diaspora of Gilroy's black Atlantic, especially in relation to the
otherwise repressed black history of colonialism and its 'afterburns', or
persistent structures of exploitation. Further, they allowed practical
connections to be made across the diaspora, through both making and
showing the work. McQueen has commented that part of what initially
attracted him to filmmaking as an art practice was 'the whole idea of
working with people': 'You're living with people for a week, a month, or
six months – sometimes even a year, to make a film. So it's a relationship-
building thing.'[69] And he has also expressed his commitment to showing
*Western Deep* to its filmic subjects: 'we're going to show the film in the mine.
We need to take it back to them.'[70]

Coming after 11 September 2001, the images of falling bodies in
*Caribs' Leap* also evoked the specific event of the attacks on New York's
World Trade Center towers.[71] The potential effects of this evocation
were multiple and take resonance from Gilroy's idea of the effective
continuum of the black Atlantic as well as from what Doreen Massey has
called 'a global sense of place' – 'a sense of place which is extroverted,
which includes a consciousness of its links with the wider world, which
integrates in a positive way the global and the local'.[72] For example, this
evocation placed the World Trade Center attacks in a deeper historical
context of (colonial and transatlantic slave trade) terrorism, it potentially
spoke to Londoners' anxieties – especially soon after 11 September 2001
– of experiencing similar attacks, and, by showing a non-white man

falling, it perhaps focused on the many non-white World Trade Center workers who died in the attacks.

The other potentially transforming effect this invocation of the black Atlantic had for the imperial metropolis was to point up its postcolonial hybridity, to challenge whatever residual fantasies of English purity it might have. For it is not just Caribbean sugar that has long been in the metropolis. In a 1989 lecture in the United States, eminent black British cultural theorist Stuart Hall claimed:

> People like me who came to England in the 1950s have been there for centuries; symbolically, we have been there for centuries. I am the sugar at the bottom of the English cup of tea. ... There are thousands of others beside me that are ... the cup of tea itself. Because they don't grow it in Lancashire, you know. ...
>
> Where does it come from? Ceylon – Sri Lanka, India. That is the outside history that is inside the history of the English. There is no English history without that other history. The notion that identity has to do with people that look the same, feel the same, call themselves the same, is nonsense.[73]

'Arguably', as Bill Schwarz puts it, 'the culture of insular England was formed as much by its overseas possessions as by the island territory; and in its own – often resoundingly reactionary – way white English ethnicity is, despite all protestations to the contrary, a hybrid'.[74] As McQueen's installation subtly reminded its audience, the metropolis is a hybrid, perhaps lacking built memorials to the end of empire, but providing a home for millions of people who are, in some ways, living memorials to the end of empire. McQueen's installation was not a triumphant, enormous, concrete memorial celebrating empire's demise; rather, it was an ephemeral but persistently memorable intervention in the metropolis's enduring imperial fantasy.

## Caribs' Leap/Western Deep/~~London~~

Temporarily, provisionally, and for a limited audience – but powerfully – Steve McQueen's 2002 installation *Caribs' Leap/Western Deep* at the Lumière Cinema conjured the potential of the imperial metropolis to be a more democratic space, to be a space where the metropolis's cultural differences could be articulated without being assimilated, and where the metropolis's past and living histories of imperial exploitation could be called to account. It suggested alternative, non-dominant ways of seeing, occupying, understanding, and bodily experiencing the city. It emphasised the cultural importance of ways of seeing and occupying to our systems of values, and it began to reorient those values. It depicted in narrative and form, as well as – modestly – in embodied practice, alternative experiences of being, including specifically postcolonial experiences of exploitation. It expressed a black filmmaker's perspectives without allowing those to be dominated or assimilated by the imperial metropolis's self-serving narratives of benign multiculturalism. And it invoked Massey's concept of a 'global sense of place', a sense that we share interests with and responsibilities for the fellow members of our communities, which includes not just those in our immediate environments but everyone who is interconnected everywhere – as well as across time – in the world. McQueen has commented, 'We're all trapped, but what I want from film is to capture those brief moments of escape'.[75] However briefly, this installation captured the metropolis's democratic promise and, more broadly, demonstrated the potential of cultural practices or imaginings to enable the open, democratic expression of diverse but mutually dependent communities.

## Notes

1  Ash Amin, Doreen Massey, and Nigel Thrift, *Cities for the Many Not the Few* (Bristol: Policy Press, 2000), p. v.

2  The London-based art commissioning company Artangel has no home gallery but seeks suitable sites for each of its commissions and focuses especially on commissioning artists to engage with London's architecture and social environments. Commissioned work is predominantly installation art, film, video, audio recording, and performance, and often combines two or more of these forms. For more information on the company and its commissions see the Artangel website, www.artangel.org.uk (accessed January 2004), and the company's book, Gerrie van Noord (ed.), *Off Limits: 40 Artangel Projects* (London: Merrell, 2002).

3  See, for example, the Artangel-commissioned East London and City audio-recorded walk by Canadian artist Janet Cardiff, *The Missing Voice (Case Study B)*, available to borrow from the Whitechapel Library and published as Janet Cardiff, *The Missing Voice (Case Study B)*, James Lingwood and Gerrie van Noord (eds) (London: Artangel Afterlives, 1999). Amongst other things, the walk invites its listener/walker to focus on a woman's experience of the environment traversed in the walk. For an analysis of the work's feminist potential see Jen Harvie, 'Being her: presence, absence and performance in the art of Janet Cardiff and Tracey Emin', in Maggie B. Gale and Viv Gardner (eds), *Auto/Biography and Identity: Women, Theatre and Performance* (Manchester: Manchester University Press, 2004).

4  For example, the 1996 Artangel-commissioned *Empty Club* by Mexican artist Gabriel Orozco in the former Devonshire Club in Piccadilly, central London, which partly explored issues of English class and gender privilege and their relation to leisure and access. Gabriel Orozco, *Empty Club* (London: Artangel, 1998).

5  For example, the 1999 Artangel-commissioned Whitechapel walk by Rachel Lichtenstein that retrieved and recorded information and impressions about 'the almost vanished work of Jewish Whitechapel' in London's East End. Rachel Lichtenstein, *Rodinsky's Whitechapel* (London: Artangel, 1999), p. 4.

6  For example, the 2002 Artangel-commissioned installation near King's Cross station in North London by Richard Wentworth, *An Area of Outstanding Unnatural Beauty*, which invited its participants to re-examine and re-evaluate what might conventionally be seen largely as derelict wasteland.

7  For example, Michael Landy's *Break Down*, a 2001 Artangel-commissioned installation in the former C&A department store on London's main commercial thoroughfare, Oxford Street. During the course of the installation, Landy destroyed all of his material goods, from his car to his clothes, in a direct inversion of Oxford Street's usual commercial function of selling goods – or perhaps in an acceleration and extension of the built-in obsolescence of contemporary commodities. Michael Landy, *Break Down* (London: Artangel, n.d. [2001]).

8  See, for example, the films of Isaac Julien, Pratibha Parmar, and the Sankofa Film Collective. See also: Kobena Mercer, 'Diaspora culture and the dialogic imagination: the aesthetics of black independent film in Britain', in Mbye B. Cham and Claire Andrade-Watkins (eds), *Blackframes: Critical Perspectives on Black Independent Cinema* (Cambridge, MA: MIT Press, 1988), pp. 50–61; Karen Alexander, 'Black British cinema in the 90s: going going gone', in Robert Murphy (ed.), *British Cinema of the 90s* (London: BFI Publishing, 2000), pp. 109–14; and Satinder Chohan, 'Film and cinema', in Alison Donnell (ed.), *Companion to Contemporary Black British Culture* (London: Routledge, 2002), pp. 114–17.

9  Tori Smith, '"A grand work of noble conception": the Victoria Memorial and imperial London', in Felix Driver and David Gilbert (eds), *Imperial Cities: Landscape, Display and Identity* (Manchester: Manchester University Press, 1999), pp. 21–39, p. 28.

10  A. D. King, *Global Cities: Post-Imperialism and the Internationalisation of London* (London: Routledge, 1990), p. 65.

11  Rodney Mace, *Trafalgar Square: Emblem of Empire* (London: Lawrence and Wishart, 1976), pp. 50, 90, 101, 17, 111, and 117.

12  *Ibid.*, p. 19.

13  King, *Global Cities*, p. 80.

14  Felix Driver and David Gilbert 'Imperial cities: overlapping territories, intertwined histories', in Driver and Gilbert (eds), *Imperial Cities*, pp. 1–17, pp. 1–2.

15  Driver and Gilbert, 'Imperial cities', p. 1.

16  'Transforming Trafalgar Square', *London*, www.london.gov.uk/mayor/trafalgar_square/index.jsp (accessed November 2003); 'Entertainment: memorial to Queen's lost love comes clean', *BBC News Online Network* (21 October 1998), www.bbc.co.uk/1/hi/uk/198016.stm (accessed November 2003); Chris Brooks (ed.), *The Albert Memorial: The Prince Consort National Memorial: Its History, Contexts, and Conservation* (New Haven and London: Yale University Press, 2000).

17  Lord Byron, *Childe Harold's Pilgrimage*, canto ii (1812), cited in 'Elgin Marbles', in Ian Chivers (ed.), *The Concise Oxford Dictionary of Art and Artists* (Oxford: Oxford University Press, 1996), *Oxford Reference Online*, www.oxfordreference.com/views/ENTRY.html?subview=Main&entry=t3.e798 (accessed February 2004).

18  'Exhibitions', *British Library*, www.bl.uk/whatson/exhibitions/trading home.html (accessed October 2003).

19  John Eade, *Placing London: From Imperial Capital to Global City* (New York: Berghahn Books, 2000).

20  Bill Schwarz, 'Afterword: postcolonial times: the visible and the invisible', in Driver and Gilbert (eds), *Imperial Cities*, pp. 268–72, p. 272. As Alan Rice notes, the case is the same with London's failure to memorialise its participation in the Atlantic slave trade. Alan Rice, *Radical Narratives of the Black Atlantic* (London: Continuum, 2003), p. 204.

21  Amin *et al.*, *Cities for the Many*, p. vi.

22  Driver and Gilbert, 'Imperial cities', p. 13.

23  Bill Schwarz, 'Black metropolis, white England', in Mica Nava and Alan O'Shea (eds), *Modern Times: Reflections on a Century of English Modernity* (London: Routledge, 1996), pp. 176–207, p. 178.

24  Jonathan Schneer, 'Anti-imperial London: the Pan-African Conference of 1900', in Driver and Gilbert, *Imperial Cities*, pp. 254–67, p. 265.

25  Driver and Gilbert, 'Imperial cities', p. 13.

26  In 1998, the Royal Society for the encouragement of Arts, Manufactures and Commerce (RSA) commissioned three works to be displayed temporarily on the fourth plinth, including Mark Wallinger's life-size Christ, *Ecce Homo* (1999), and Rachel Whiteread's translucent inverted resin plinth, *Monument* (2001). The Fourth Plinth project has since been taken up and continued by London's Mayor Ken Livingstone. 'Trafalgar Square', *Fourthplinth*, www.fourthplinth.co.uk/trafalgar.htm (accessed January 2004).

27  Mace, *Trafalgar Square*, pp. 299–322 and *passim*.

28  *Ibid.*, plate 43, n.p., and pp. 299–322, and Driver and Gilbert, 'Imperial cities', p. 13.

29  Jamie Wilson and Matthew Taylor, 'And down comes the statue ... but this time it's Trafalgar Square', *Guardian* (21 November 2003).

30  Edward Said, *Orientalism* (New York: Pantheon, 1978), p. 240, cited in Homi K. Bhabha, 'Of mimicry and man: the ambivalence of colonial discourse', in Homi K. Bhabha, *The Location of Culture* (London: Routledge, 1994), pp. 85–92, p. 86, originally published in *October: Anthology* (Boston: MIT Press, 1987).

31  P. B. Shelley, 'Ozymandias' (1817), in P. B. Shelley, *The Complete Poetical Works of Percy Bysshe Shelley*, Thomas Hutchinson (ed.) (London: Oxford University Press, [1905] 1952), p. 550.

32  Schwarz, 'Afterword', p. 272.

33  Sigmund Freud, 'Civilization and its discontents', in Freud, *Civilization, Society and Religion* (London: Penguin, 1985), pp. 251–340, pp. 256–9; Peter Ackroyd, *London: The Biography* (London: Chatto and Windus, 2000).

34  Jane M. Jacobs, *Edge of Empire: Postcolonialism and the City* (London: Routledge, 1996), p. 158.

35 McQueen was born in West London in 1969 and raised there. He won the Turner Prize in 1999. See Laurence Bossé, Foreword, trans. John Tittensor, in Steve McQueen, *Speaking in Tongues* (Paris: Paris-Musées, 2003), pp. 10–13, p. 12.

36 'History and Culture', *Grenada*, www.grenada.org/gdhis01.htm (accessed October 2003).

37 Charles-Arthur Boyer, 'Steve McQueen: rêver dans le bruit du monde', trans. C. Penwarden, *Art Press* 287 (2003), 30–4, p. 33.

38 Gareth Evans, 'Journey to the deep', *Sight and Sound* 12:12 (2002), 12.

39 Adrian Searle, 'Into the unknown', *Guardian* (8 October 2002).

40 Evans, 'Journey to the deep'.

41 See, for example, the 1796 survey drawing of the Royal Mews reprinted in Mace, *Trafalgar Square*, p. 27.

42 Steve McQueen quoted in Evans, 'Journey to the deep'.

43 'St Martin's Lane', *Ian Schrager Hotels*, www.ianschrragerhotels.com/home_search.html?stmartinslane (accessed November 2003).

44 'London Calling', *Vanity Fair* (October 1999), rpt at 'St Martins' Lane, Press and Media', *Ian Schrager Hotels*, www.ianschrragerhotels.com/press/articles/sml/vanity_fair_oct_1999.pdf (accessed November 2003).

45 Dawn Bastian Williams, Robert W. Lesh, and Andrea L. Stamm, *Zaïre* (Oxford: Oxford University Press, 1995), p. xxiv; Jan Palmowski, 'Democratic Republic of Congo (Zaïre)', *A Dictionary of Contemporary World History* (Oxford: Oxford University Press, 2003), *Oxford Reference Online*, www.oxfordreference.com/views/ENTRY.html?subview=Main&entry=t46.e543 (accessed February 2004).

46 McQueen quoted in Evans, 'Journey to the deep'.

47 Evans, 'Journey to the deep'.

48 Sarah Whitfield, 'London: Douglas Gordon/Steve McQueen', *The Burlington Magazine* 145:1198 (2003), 46–7, p. 46.

49 Boyer, 'Steve McQueen', p. 34.

50 Bénédicte Ramade, 'Steve McQueen, in focus', *L'Oeil* 544 (2003), 32–3, p. 32 (my trans.).

51 Mark Durden, 'Viewing positions: Steve McQueen', *Parachute* 98 (2000), 18–25, p. 25.

52 Steve McQueen quoted in Patricia Bickers, 'Let's get physical: Steve McQueen interviewed by Patricia Bickers', *Art Monthly* 202 (1996–97), 1–5, p. 2, ellipsis added.

53 McQueen in Bickers, 'Let's get physical', p. 5, emphasis original.

54 Whitfield, 'London', p. 46.

55 McQueen, *Speaking in Tongues*.

56 Jane M. Jacobs, 'Noir', in Steve Pile and Nigel Thrift (eds), *City A–Z* (London: Routledge, 2000), pp. 165–8, p. 165.

57 Steve McQueen, Interview with Hans Ulrich Obrist and Angeline Scherf, in McQueen, *Speaking in Tongues*, pp. 14–29, p. 26.

58 As illustrated in Artangel's photographic archive for this piece, the 'falling' film was composed in a studio against a neutral background. Models lay down on – and dangled over the edges of – a small platform raised over a powerful fan that lifted their hair and clothes as though they were falling. Images of these 'falling' people were then superimposed on images of sky.

59  Steve McQueen, '*Caribs' Leap/Western Deep*', in van Noord (ed.), *Off Limits*, pp. 52–5, p. 55.

60  Steve McQueen quoted in Iwona Blazwick, 'Oh my god! Some notes from a conversation with Iwona Blazwick, Jaki Irvine and Steve McQueen', *Make* 75 (1997), 5–7, p. 7.

61  In a *Guardian* interview with McQueen, Libby Brooks recounts the following: 'Not so long ago, he was invited back to his old school to give out awards. "You know Stephen Lawrence didn't die in vain, because the headmaster said to me, 'Yes, it was a racist school, wasn't it?'" He shrieks: "Now you can tell me? I'm 32, mate! You nearly ruined my fucking life."' (Libby Brooks, '"It's good to keep a clean head"', *Guardian* (30 September 2002).) Poor police handling of the murder investigation of black teenager Stephen Lawrence in South London in April 1993 led to an official enquiry that ultimately found the investigation to have been marred by 'institutional racism'.

62  Evans, 'Journey to the deep'.

63  Paul Gilroy, 'The sugar you stir … ', in Paul Gilroy, Lawrence Grossberg, and Angela McRobbie (eds), *Without Guarantees: In Honour of Stuart Hall* (London: Verso, 2000), pp. 126–33, p. 127. For more detail on how luxury products of slave labour such as tea, sugar, and tobacco created a huge British market and fashioned British cultural practices and, in some respects, British cultural identities, see for example James Walvin, *Britain's Slave Empire* (Stroud: Tempus, 2000), pp. 23ff.

64  Paul Gilroy, *The Black Atlantic: Modernity and Double Consciousness* (London: Verso, 1993).

65  Herbert S. Klein, *The Atlantic Slave Trade* (Cambridge: Cambridge University Press, 1999), p. 159.

66  Rice, *Radical Narratives of the Black Atlantic*, p. 69.

67  *Ibid.*, pp. 82–119; Gilroy, *The Black Atlantic*, pp. 63–8.

68  Gilroy, *The Black Atlantic*, pp. 13–19.

69  McQueen quoted in Bickers, 'Let's get physical', p. 2.

70  McQueen quoted in Evans, 'Journey to the deep'.

71  This was noted in, for example, Evans, 'Journey to the deep', Searle, 'Into the unknown', and Whitfield, 'London', p. 46.

72  Doreen Massey, 'A global sense of place', *Marxism Today* (June 1991), 24–9; rpt in Doreen Massey, *Space, Place and Gender* (Cambridge: Polity Press, 1994), pp. 146–56, p. 155.

73  Stuart Hall, 'Old and new identities, old and new ethnicities', in Anthony D. King (ed.), *Culture, Globalization and the World-system: Contemporary Conditions for the Representation of Identity* (London: Macmillan, 1991), pp. 41–68, pp. 48–9; ellipses added. Jatinder Verma's term 'Binglish', discussed in Chapter 6, articulates a similar theorisation of cultural hybridity.

74  Schwarz, 'Black metropolis', p. 190.

75  McQueen in Evans, 'Journey to the deep'.

# References

## Books and articles

Ackroyd, Peter, *London: The Biography*, London: Chatto and Windus, 2000.

Adams, David, *Stage Welsh: Nation, Nationalism and Theatre: The Search for Cultural Identity*, Llandysul: Gomer, 1996.

Agnew, Denis, 'The Scottish National Theatre dream: the Royal Lyceum in the 1970s; the Scottish Theatre Company in the 1980s', *International Journal of Scottish Theatre* 2:1 (2001).

Alexander, Karen, 'Black British cinema in the 90s: going going gone', in Robert Murphy (ed.), *British Cinema of the 90s*, London: BFI Publishing, 2000.

Alfino, Mark, John S. Caputo, and Robin Wynyard (eds), *McDonaldization Revisited: Critical Essays on Consumer Culture*, Westport, CT, and London: Praeger, 1998.

Allain, Paul, and Jen Harvie, *The Routledge Companion to Theatre and Performance*, London: Routledge, forthcoming.

Althusser, Louis, *For Marx*, trans. Ben Brewster, New York: Pantheon Books, 1969.

Amin, Ash, Doreen Massey, and Nigel Thrift, *Cities for the Many Not the Few*, Bristol: Policy Press, 2000.

Anderson, Benedict, *Imagined Communities: Reflections on the Origin and Spread of Nationalism*, London: Verso, 1983; 2nd edn 1991.

——, *The Spectre of Comparisons: Nationalism, Southeast Asia, and the World*, London: Verso, 1998.

Armitstead, Claire, 'LIFTing the theatre: the London International Festival of Theatre', in Shank (ed.), *Contemporary British Theatre*.

Arnold, Nell, 'Festival tourism: recognizing the challenges; linking multiple pathways between global villages of the new century', in Bill Faulkner, Gianna Moscardo, and Eric Laws (eds), *Tourism in the 21st Century: Lessons from Experience*, London: Continuum, 2000.

Artaud, Antonin, *The Theatre and Its Double*, trans. John Calder, London: John Calder, 1977.

*Arts Council Annual Report 1950/51*, London: Arts Council of Great Britain, 1951.

Aston, Elaine, and Janelle Reinelt (eds), *The Cambridge Companion to Modern British Women Playwrights*, Cambridge: Cambridge University Press, 2000.

Bain, Alice, *The Fringe: 50 Years of the Greatest Show on Earth*, Edinburgh: Scotsman Publications, 1996.

Bakhtin, Mikhail M., *The Dialogic Imagination*, trans. Caryl Emerson and Michael Holquist, Holquist (ed.), Austin: University of Texas Press, 1981.

——, *Problems of Dostoevsky's Poetics*, ed. and trans. Caryl Emerson, Minneapolis: University of Minnesota Press, 1984.

——, *Rabelais and His World*, trans. Hélène Iswolsky, Bloomington: Indiana University Press, 1984.

Balakrishnan, Gopal (ed.), *Mapping the Nation*, London: Verso, 1996.

Banker, Ashok, *The Pocket Essential Bollywood*, Harpenden: Pocket Essentials, 2001.

Barish, Jonas, *The Antitheatrical Prejudice*, Los Angeles: University of California Press, 1981.

Barker, Clive, 'The possibilities and politics of intercultural penetration and exchange', in Patrice Pavis (ed.), *The Intercultural Performance Reader*, London: Routledge, 1996.

Baudrillard, Jean, *The Illusion of the End*, trans. Chris Turner, Cambridge: Polity Press, 1994.

Bayley, Stephen, *Labour Camp: The Failure of Style over Substance*, London: B. T. Batsford, 1998.

Bennett, David (ed.), *Multicultural States: Rethinking Difference and Identity*, London: Routledge, 1998.

Bewes, Timothy, and Jeremy Gilbert (eds), *Cultural Capitalism: Politics After New Labour*, London: Lawrence and Wishart, 2000.

Beynon, John, and David Dunkerley (eds), *Globalization: The Reader*, London: Athlone Press, 2000.

Bhabha, Homi K., *The Location of Culture*, London: Routledge, 1994.

——, 'Of mimicry and man: the ambivalence of colonial discourse', in Bhabha, *The Location of Culture*.

Bhabha, Homi K. (ed.), *Nation and Narration*, London: Routledge, 1990.

Bharucha, Rustom, *The Politics of Cultural Practice: Thinking Through Theatre in an Age of Globalization*, London: Athlone Press, 2000.

——, *Theatre and the World: Performance and the Politics of Culture*, London: Routledge, revised edn, 1993.

——, 'Utopia in Bollywood: *Hum Aapke Hain Koun …!*', *Economic and Political Weekly* 30:15 (15 April 1995).

Bhuchar, Sudha, and Kristine Landon-Smith, *Fourteen Songs, Two Weddings and a Funeral*, based on Rajshri Productions' film *Hum Aapke Hain Koun*, London: Methuen, 2001.

——, *House of the Sun*, London: Nick Hern Books, 1999.

——, *A Tainted Dawn*, London: Nick Hern Books, 1999.

——, *Untouchable*, adapted from the novel by Mulk Raj Anand, London: Nick Hern Books, 1999.

Bickers, Patricia, 'Let's get physical: Steve McQueen interviewed by Patricia Bickers', *Art Monthly* 202 (1996–97).

Billig, Michael, *Banal Nationalism*, London: Sage, 1995.

Billington, Michael, *One Night Stands: A Critic's View of Modern British Theatre*, London: Nick Hern Books, 1994.

Blair, Tony, *New Britain: My Vision of a Young Country*, London: Fourth Estate, 1996.

Blazwick, Iwona, 'Oh my god! Some notes from a conversation with Iwona Blazwick, Jaki Irvine and Steve McQueen', *Make* 75 (1997).

*Bombay Dreams* Programme, London: Apollo Victoria Theatre, n.d. [2003].

Boniface, Priscilla, 'Theme park Britain: who benefits and who loses?', in J. M. Fladmark (ed.), *Cultural Tourism*, London: Donhead Publishing, 1994.

Bossé, Laurence, Foreword, trans. John Tittensor, in McQueen, *Speaking in Tongues*.

Bourdieu, Pierre, *Distinction: A Social Critique of the Judgement of Taste*, trans. Richard Nice, London: Routledge and Kegan Paul, 1984.

Boyer, Charles-Arthur, 'Steve McQueen: rêver dans le bruit du monde', trans. C. Penwarden, *Art Press* 287 (2003).

*The British Council: Speeches Delivered on the Occasion of the Inaugural Meeting at St. James's Palace on 2nd July, 1935*, privately printed by the British Council: London, 1935.

*British Drama in Profile 2002*, London: The British Council, 2001.

Brook, Peter, *The Empty Space*, Harmondsworth: Penguin Books, 1972.

Brooks, Chris (ed.), *The Albert Memorial: The Prince Consort National Memorial: Its History, Contexts, and Conservation*, New Haven and London: Yale University Press, 2000.

Bruce, George, *Festival in the North: The Story of the Edinburgh Festival*, London: Robert Hale and Company, 1975.

Bryden, Ronald, Afterword, in Daubeny, *My World of Theatre*.

Bryman, Alan, *Disney and His Worlds*, London: Routledge, 1995.

Bryne, Eleanor, and Martin McQuillan (eds), *Deconstructing Disney*, London: Pluto Press, 1999.

Buckland, Fiona, 'Towards a language of the stage: the work of DV8 Physical Theatre', *NTQ: New Theatre Quarterly* 11:44 (1995).

Bull, John, *Stage Right: Crisis and Recovery in British Contemporary Mainstream Theatre*, London: Macmillan, 1994.

Butler, Judith, *Gender Trouble*, London: Routledge, tenth anniversary edn, 1999.

Byrne, Ophelia, *The Stage in Ulster from the Eighteenth Century*, Belfast: Linen Hall Library, 1997.

Byrne, Ophelia (ed.), *convictions*, Belfast: Tinderbox Theatre Company, 2000.

——, *State of Play? The Theatre and Cultural Identity in 20th Century Ulster*, Belfast: The Linen Hall Library, 2001.

Callery, Dymphna, *Through the Body: A Practical Guide to Physical Theatre*, London/New York: Nick Hern Books/Routledge, 2001.

Cameron, Alasdair, 'Glasgow's Tramway: little Diagilevs and large ambitions', *Theatre Research International* 17:2 (1992).

——, 'Experimental theatre in Scotland', in Shank (ed.), *Contemporary British Theatre*.

Cardiff, Janet, *The Missing Voice (Case Study B)*, James Lingwood and Gerrie van Noord (eds), London: Artangel Afterlives, 1999.

Carlson, Marvin, *The Haunted Stage: The Theatre as Memory Machine*, Ann Arbor: University of Michigan Press, 2001.

Carter, Gary, 'In the plush hush of the mainstream: Gary Carter talks to DV8's Lloyd Newson', *Dance Theatre Journal* 10:4 (1993).

Carter, Ruth, *Women of the Dust*, London: Nick Hern Books, 1999.

——, *A Yearning*, London: Nick Hern Books, 1999.

Carver, Gavin, 'The effervescent carnival: performance, context, and mediation at Notting Hill', *NTQ: New Theatre Quarterly* 16:1 (61, 2000).

Carville, Daragh, 'Male Toilets', in Byrne (ed.), *convictions*.

Caughie, John, 'Becoming European: art cinema, irony and identity', in Petrie (ed.), *Screening Europe*.

Chamberlain, Franc, and Ralph Yarrow (eds), *Jacques Lecoq and the British Theatre*, London: Routledge, 2002.

Chaudhuri, Una, 'Beyond a "taxonomic theater": interculturalism after postcolonialism and globalization', *Theater* 32:1 (2002).

Cheah, Pheng, and Bruce Robbins (eds), *Cosmopolitics: Thinking and Feeling Beyond the Nation*, Minneapolis: University of Minnesota Press, 1998.

Chivers, Ian (ed.), *The Concise Oxford Dictionary of Art and Artists*, Oxford: Oxford University Press, 1996.

Chohan, Satinder, 'Film and cinema', in Alison Donnell (ed.), *Companion to Contemporary Black British Culture*, London: Routledge, 2002.

CIEPAG, *Creative Industries: Exports: Our Hidden Potential*, London: DCMS, 1999.

Combrink, Annette I., '"The arts festival as healing force" (Athol Fugard): the role of the two major arts festivals and possible resurgences in South African drama', in Marcia Blumberg and Dennis Walder (eds), *South African Theatre as/and Intervention*, Amsterdam: Rodopi, 1999.

Complicite, *Mnemonic*, London: Methuen, revised edn, 2001.

——, *Complicite Plays 1*, London: Methuen, 2003.

Cousin, Geraldine, 'An interview with Mike Pearson of Brith Gof', *Contemporary Theatre Review* 2:2 (1994).

Coveney, Michael, *The Andrew Lloyd Webber Story*, London: Arrow Books, 2000.

——, *The Citz: 21 Years of the Glasgow Citizens Theatre*, London: Nick Hern Books, 1990.

Crawford, Iain, *Banquo on Thursdays: The Inside Story of 50 Years of the Edinburgh Festival*, Edinburgh: Goblinshead, 1997.

Crawford, Mairtín, 'Convicted in the Crum', *Fortnight* (December 2000).

*Creative Industries Mapping Document*, London: DCMS, 1998.

*Creative Industries Mapping Document*, London: DCMS, 2nd edn, 2001.

Culler, Jonathan, 'Anderson and the novel', *diacritics* 29:4 (1999).

Dahl, Mary-Karen, 'Postcolonial British theatre: black voices at the center', in J. Ellen Gainor (ed.), *Imperialism and Theatre: Essays on World Theatre, Drama and Performance*, London: Routledge, 1995.

Dale, Michael, *Sore Throats and Overdrafts: An Illustrated Story of the Edinburgh Festival Fringe*, Edinburgh: Precedent Publications Ltd, 1988.

Daubeny, Peter, *My World of Theatre*, London: Jonathan Cape, 1971.

Davies, Andrew, *Other Theatres: The Development of Alternative and Experimental Theatre in Britain*, London: Methuen, 1987.

Davis, Colin, *British Pavilion, Seville Exposition 1992. Nicholas Grimshaw and Partners*, London: Phaidon, 1992.

De Jongh, Nicholas, *Not in Front of the Audience: Homosexuality on Stage*, London: Routledge, 1992.

Derrida, Jacques, *The Other Heading: Reflections on Today's Europe*, trans. Pascale-Anne Brault and Michael B. Naas, Bloomington and Indianapolis: Indiana University Press, 1992.

Dodgson, Elyse, 'International playwrights at the Royal Court Theatre', *On Tour* 16 (July 2000).

Donaldson, Frances, *The British Council: The First Fifty Years*, London: Jonathan Cape, 1984.

Dorfman, Ariel, and Armand Mattelart, *How to Read Donald Duck: Imperialist Ideology in the Disney Comic*, trans. David Kunzle, New York: International General, 1984.

Driver, Felix, and David Gilbert, 'Imperial cities: overlapping territories, intertwined histories', in Driver and Gilbert (eds), *Imperial Cities*.

Driver, Felix, and David Gilbert (eds), *Imperial Cities: Landscape, Display and Identity*, Manchester: Manchester University Press, 1999.

Dromgoole, Dominic, Introduction, *Bush Theatre Plays*, London: Faber and Faber, 1996.

Dugdale, Sasha, 'Revolutions and revelations', *On Tour* 16 (2000).

Dunn, Tony, 'Sated, starved or satisfied: the languages of theatre in Britain today', in Shank (ed.), *Contemporary British Theatre*.

Durden, Mark, 'Viewing positions: Steve McQueen', *Parachute* 98 (2000).

Dyer, Richard, 'The colour of entertainment', in Dyer, *Only Entertainment*.

——, 'Entertainment and utopia', in Dyer, *Only Entertainment*.

——, *Only Entertainment*, London: Routledge, 2nd edn, 2002.

Eade, John, *Placing London: From Imperial Capital to Global City*, New York: Berghahn Books, 2000.

Eagleton, Terry, *Literary Theory: An Introduction*, Oxford: Basil Blackwell, 1983.

Edgar, David (ed.), *State of Play: Playwrights on Playwriting*, London: Faber and Faber, 1999.

*Edinburgh Festival Fringe Annual Report 2001*, Edinburgh: Edinburgh Festival Fringe, 2002.

'Edinburgh Showcase 2001', *On Tour* 17 (2001).

'Edinburgh Showcase 2001', *On Tour* 18 (2001).

Edwardes, Jane, 'Directors: the new generation', in Shank (ed.), *Contemporary British Theatre*.

Edwards, Owen Dudley, 'Cradle on the tree-top: the Edinburgh Festival and Scottish theatre', in Stevenson and Wallace (eds), *Scottish Theatre Since the Seventies*.

Eley, Geoff, and Ronald Grigor Suny (eds), *Becoming National: A Reader*, Oxford: Oxford University Press, 1996.

Elsom, John, *Post War British Theatre*, London: Routledge and Kegan Paul, 1979.

——, 'United Kingdom', in Don Rubin (ed.), *The World Encyclopedia of Contemporary Theatre*, Vol. 1, *Europe*, London: Routledge, 1994.

Evans, Gareth, 'Journey to the deep', *Sight and Sound* 12:12 (2002).

Fairclough, Norman, *New Labour, New Language?*, London: Routledge, 2000.

Featherstone, Mike, *Undoing Culture: Globalization, Postmodernism and Identity*, London: Sage, 1995.

Festival Fringe Society, The, *How to Do a Show on the Fringe*, Edinburgh: The Festival Fringe Society, 2000.

Feuer, Jane, *The Hollywood Musical*, London: Macmillan, [1982] 2nd edn, 1993.

Filewod, Alan, *Performing Canada: The Nation Enacted in the Imagined Theatre* (*Textual Studies in Canada* 15), Kamloops, BC: University College of the Cariboo, 2002.

Findlay, Bill (ed.), *A History of Scottish Theatre*, Edinburgh: Polygon, 1998.

*First Ten Years: Eleventh Annual Report, The*, London: Arts Council of Great Britain, 1956.

Fjellman, Stephen M., *Vinyl Leaves: Walt Disney World and America*, Boulder: Westview Press, 1992.

Foucault, Michel, 'Nietzsche, genealogy, history', in Foucault, *Language, Counter-memory, Practice: Selected Essays and Interviews*, Donald F. Bouchard (ed.), trans. Bouchard and Sherry Simon, Oxford: Basil Blackwell, 1977.

Fowler, John, ' Theatre and nation', *In Scotland* 3 (2000).

Freshwater, Helen, 'The ethics of indeterminacy: Theatre de Complicite's *Mnemonic*', *NTQ: New Theatre Quarterly* 17:3 (67, 2001).

Freud, Sigmund, 'Civilization and its discontents', in Freud, *Civilization, Society and Religion*, London: Penguin, 1985.

Fricker, Karen, review of *convictions*, *Irish Theatre Magazine* 2:8 (2001).

——, 'Tourism, the festival marketplace and Robert Lepage's *The Seven Streams of the River Ota*', *Contemporary Theatre Review* 13:4 (2003).

Fuchs, Anne, 'From Lorca to Bollywood: cultural adaptation in the plays of the British Asian Tamasha Theatre Company', *Cycnos* 18:1 (2001).

Garattoni, Marina, 'Scottish drama at the Edinburgh Fringe until the seventies', in Valentina Poggi and Margaret Rose (eds), *A Theatre that Matters: Twentieth-century Scottish Drama and Theatre: A Collection of Critical Essays and Interviews*, Milan: Edizioni Unicopli, 2000.

*Gate Biennale*, London: Methuen, 1996.

Gellner, Ernest, *Nations and Nationalism*, Oxford: Basil Blackwell, 1983.

Geraghty, Christine, *Women and Soap Opera: A Study of Prime Time Soaps*, Cambridge: Polity, 1991.

Giannachi, Gabriella, and Mary Luckhurst, *On Directing: Interviews with Directors*, London: Faber and Faber, 1999.

Gilbert, Helen, *Sightlines: Race, Gender, and Nation in Contemporary Australian Theatre*, Ann Arbor: University of Michigan Press, 1998.

Gillis, John R., 'Introduction: memory and identity: the history of a relationship', in Gillis (ed.), *Commemorations: The Politics of National Identity*, Princeton: Princeton University Press, 1994.

Gilroy, Paul, *The Black Atlantic: Modernity and Double Consciousness*, London: Verso, 1993.

——, 'The sugar you stir …', in Paul Gilroy *et al.* (eds), *Without Guarantees*.

Gilroy, Paul, Lawrence Grossberg, and Angela McRobbie (eds), *Without Guarantees: In Honour of Stuart Hall*, London: Verso, 2000.

Giroux, Henry, *The Mouse that Roared: Disney and the End of Innocence*, Lanham, MD: Rowman and Littlefield, 1999.

Gómez-Peña, Guillermo, *Dangerous Border Crossers: The Artist Talks Back*, London: Routledge, 2000.

Goorney, Howard, *The Theatre Workshop Story*, London: Methuen, 1981.

Gorman, Damian, 'Judge's Room', in Byrne (ed.), *convictions*.

Gottlieb, Vera, and Colin Chambers (eds), *Theatre in a Cool Climate*, Oxford: Amber Lane Press, 1999.

Gradinger, Malve, 'Pina Bausch', in Martha Bremser, *Fifty Contemporary Choreographers*, London: Routledge, 1999.

Grant, David, 'Tim Loane in conversation with David Grant', in Lilian Chambers, Ger FitzGibbon, and Eamonn Jordan (eds), *Theatre Talk: Voices of Irish Theatre Practitioners*, Dublin: Carysfort Press, 2001.

Gratton, C., and G. Richards, 'The economic context of cultural tourism', in Greg Richards (ed.), *Cultural Tourism in Europe*, Wallingford: CAB International, 1996.

Graver, David, and Loren Kruger, 'Locating theatre: regionalism and interculturalism at Edinburgh', *Performing Arts Journal* 15:2 (44, 1993).

Gray, Clive, *The Politics of the Arts in Britain*, London: Macmillan, 2000.

Griffin, Gabriele, *Contemporary Black and Asian Women Playwrights in Britain*, Cambridge: Cambridge University Press, 2003.

Hall, Peter, *The Necessary Theatre*, London: Nick Hern Books, 1999.

Hall, Stuart, 'European cinema on the verge of a nervous breakdown', in Petrie (ed.), *Screening Europe*.

——, 'Old and new identities, old and new ethnicities', in Anthony D. King (ed.), *Culture, Globalization and the World-system: Contemporary Conditions for the Representation of Identity*, London: Macmillan, 1991.

Hardt, Michael, and Antonio Negri, *Empire*, Cambridge, MA: Harvard University Press, 2000.

Harewood, Lord (George Lascelles, 7th Earl of Harewood), *The Tongs and the Bones: The Memoirs of Lord Harewood*, London: Weidenfeld and Nicolson, 1981.

Harrington, John P., and Elizabeth J. Mitchell, Introduction, in Harrington and Mitchell (eds), *Politics and Performance in Contemporary Northern Ireland*.

Harrington, John P., and Elizabeth J. Mitchell (eds), *Politics and Performance in Contemporary Northern Ireland*, Amherst: University of Massachusetts Press, 1999.

Harvie, Jen, 'Being her: presence, absence, and performance in the art of Janet Cardiff and Tracey Emin', in Maggie B. Gale and Viv Gardner (eds), *Auto/Biography and Identity: Women, Theatre and Performance*, Manchester: Manchester University Press, 2004.

——, 'Cultural effects of the Edinburgh International Festival: elitism, identities, industries', *Contemporary Theatre Review* 13:4 (2003).

——, 'DV8's *Can We Afford This*: the cost of devising on site for global markets', *Theatre Research International* 27:1 (2002).

——, 'Nationalizing the "Creative Industries"', *Contemporary Theatre Review* 13:1 (2003).

——, 'The real nation?: Michel Tremblay, Scotland, and cultural translatability', *Theatre Research in Canada* 16:1/2 (1995).

——, 'Robert Lepage', in Joseph Natoli and Hans Bertens (eds), *Postmodernism: The Key Figures*, Oxford: Blackwell, 2002.

——, 'Transnationalism, orientalism, cultural tourism: *La Trilogie des dragons* and *The Seven Streams of the River Ota*', in Joseph I. Donohoe and Jane M. Koustas (eds), *Theater sans Frontières: Essays on the Dramatic Universe of Robert Lepage*, East Lansing: Michigan State University Press, 2000.

——, and Erin Hurley, 'States of play: locating Québec in the performances of Robert Lepage, Ex Machina, and the Cirque du Soleil', *Theatre Journal* 51:3 (1999).

Haskell, Molly, *From Reverence to Rape: The Treatment of Women in the Movies*, Chicago: University of Chicago Press, 2nd edn, 1987.

Hawkins, Maureen S. G., 'Brenton's *The Romans in Britain* and Rudkin's *The Saxon Shore*: audience, purpose, and dramatic response to the conflict in Northern Ireland', in Harrington and Mitchell (eds), *Politics and Performance in Contemporary Northern Ireland*.

Haydon, Laura, 'Courthouse Interviews', in Byrne (ed.), *convictions*.

Hewison, Robert, *Culture and Consensus: England, Art and Politics since 1940*, London: Methuen, revised edn, 1997.

——, *In Anger: Culture in the Cold War, 1945–60*, London: Methuen, revised edn, 1988.

——, 'Public policy: corporate culture: public culture', in Olin Robison, Robert Freeman, and Charles A. Riley II (eds), *The Arts in the World Economy: Public Policy and Private Philanthropy for a Global Cultural Community*, Hanover, NH: University Press of New England, 1994.

Higgins, Vincent, 'Time well spent', *Fortnight* (December 2000).

Hill, John, and Pamela Church Gibson (eds), *World Cinema: Critical Approaches*, Oxford: Oxford University Press, 2000.

Hobsbawm, Eric, and Terence Ranger (eds), *The Invention of Tradition*, Cambridge: Cambridge University Press, 1983.

Hollis, Patricia, *Jennie Lee: A Life*, Oxford: Oxford University Press, 1997.

*Housing the Arts in Great Britain, Part I: London, Scotland, Wales*, London: Arts Council of Great Britain, 1959.

*Housing the Arts in Great Britain, Part II: The Needs of the English Provinces*, London: Arts Council of Great Britain, 1961.

Hughes, David, 'The Welsh National Theatre: the avant-garde in the diaspora', in Shank (ed.), *Contemporary British Theatre*.

Hutchison, Robert, *The Politics of the Arts Council*, London: Sinclair Browne, 1982.

*Independent/Rough Guide to Edinburgh 1993, The*, London: Rough Guides Ltd, 1993.

Jackson, Anthony, '1958–1983: renewal, growth and retrenchment', in Rowell and Jackson, *The Repertory Movement*.

Jacobs, Jane M., *Edge of Empire: Postcolonialism and the City*, London: Routledge, 1996.

——, 'Noir', in Steve Pile and Nigel Thrift (eds), *City A–Z*, London: Routledge, 2000.

Jacobs, Nicholas, and Prudence Ohlsen (eds), *Bertolt Brecht in Britain*, London: TQ Publications, 1977.

Jain, Madhu, 'Bollywood: next generation', in Joshi (ed.), *Bollywood*.

Jones, Calvin, 'Comparative disadvantage?: the industrial structure of Wales', in Jane Bryan and Calvin Jones (eds), *Wales in the 21st Century: An Economic Future*, Basingstoke: Macmillan, 2000.

Jones, Marie, 'Court No. 2', in Byrne (ed.), *convictions*.

Jordan, Stephanie, and Andrée Grau, Introduction, in Andrée Grau and Stephanie Jordan (eds), *Europe Dancing: Perspectives on Theatre Dance and Cultural Identity*, London: Routledge, 2000.

Joseph, May, *Nomadic Identities: The Performance of Citizenship*, Minneapolis: University of Minnesota Press, 1999.

Joshi, Abhijat, *A Shaft of Sunlight*, London: Nick Hern Books, 1999.

Joshi, Pratik, 'The classics and blockbusters', in Joshi (ed.), *Bollywood*.

Joshi, Pratik (ed.), *Bollywood*, London: Dakini, 2001.

Joughin, John J. (ed.), *Shakespeare and National Culture*, Manchester: Manchester University Press, 1997.

Kapur, Geeta, and Ashish Rajadhyaksha, 'Bombay/Mumbai, 1992–2001', in Iwona Blazwick (ed.), *Century City: Art and Culture in the Modern Metropolis*, London: Tate Publishing, 2001.

Kaye, Nick, *Art into Theatre: Performance Interviews and Documents*, Amsterdam: Harwood Academic Publishers, 1996.

——, *Site-specific Art: Performance, Place and Documentation*. London: Routledge, 2000.

Kazmi, Nikhat, *The Dream Merchants of Bollywood*, New Delhi: UBS Publishers' Distributors, 1998.

Kelly, Alexander, Borce Nikolovski, and Ken Foster, 'On show', *On Tour* 19 (2002).

Kennedy, Dennis, 'Shakespeare and cultural tourism', *Theatre Journal* 50:2 (1998).

Kershaw, Baz, 'Discouraging democracy: British theatres and economics, 1979–1999', *Theatre Journal* 51:3 (1999).

——, *The Radical in Performance: Between Brecht and Baudrillard*, London: Routledge, 1999.

Khan-Din, Ayub, *East Is East*, London: Nick Hern Books, 1997.

King, A. D., *Global Cities: Post-Imperialism and the Internationalisation of London*, London: Routledge, 1990.

King, Barnaby, 'Landscapes of fact and fiction: Asian theatre arts in Britain', *NTQ: New Theatre Quarterly*, 16:1 (61, 2000).

Klein, Herbert S., *The Atlantic Slave Trade*, Cambridge: Cambridge University Press, 1999.

Klein, Naomi, *No Logo*, London: Flamingo, 2000.

Knapper, Stephen, 'The theatre of memory: Theatre de Complicité's *Mnemonic*', *TheatreForum* 17 (2000).

Knowles, Ric, 'The Edinburgh Festival and Fringe: lessons for Canada?', *Canadian Theatre Review* 102 (2000).

Kruger, Loren, *The National Stage: Theatre and Cultural Legitimation in England, France, and America*, Chicago: University of Chicago Press, 1992.

Kwon, Miwon, 'One place after another: notes on site specificity', in Erika Suderburg (ed.), *Space, Site, Intervention: Situating Installation Art*, Minneapolis: University of Minnesota Press, 2000.

——, *One Place After Another: Site-specific Art and Locational Identity*, Cambridge, MA: MIT Press, 2002.

Labour Party, *New Labour New Britain: The Guide*, London: Labour Party, 1996.

Landy, Michael, *Break Down*, London: Artangel, n.d. [2001].

Leask, Josephine, 'The silence of the man: an essay on Lloyd Newson's physical theatre', *Ballett International* 8–9 (1995).

Lecoq, Jacques, in collaboration with Jean-Gabriel Carasso and Jean-Claude Lallias, *The Moving Body*, trans. David Bradby, London: Methuen, [1997] 2000.

Lefebvre, Henri, *The Production of Space*, trans. Donald Nicholson-Smith, Oxford: Blackwell, 1991.

Leggatt, Alexander (ed.), *The Cambridge Companion to Shakespearean Comedy*, Cambridge: Cambridge University Press, 2002.

Lewis, Justin, *Art, Culture, and Enterprise: The Politics of Art and Cultural Industries*, London: Routledge, 1990.

Ley, Graham, 'Theatre of migration and the search for a multicultural aesthetic: twenty years of Tara Arts', *NTQ: New Theatre Quarterly* 13 (52, 1997).

Lichtenstein, Rachel, *Rodinsky's Whitechapel*, London: Artangel, 1999.

Lingis, Alphonso, *The Community of Those Who Have Nothing in Common*, Bloomington and Indianapolis: Indiana University Press, 1994.

Littlewood, Joan, *Joan's Book: Joan Littlewood's Peculiar History as She Tells It*, London: Methuen, 1994.

Llewellyn-Jones, Margaret, *Contemporary Irish Drama and Cultural Identity*, Bristol: Intellect, 2002.

McBurney, Simon, interview, in Polly Irvin, *Directing for the Stage*, Mies, Switzerland: RotoVision SA, 2003.

McCartney, Nicola, 'Jury Room', in Byrne (ed.), *convictions*.

McCullough, Christopher, *Theatre and Europe: 1957–95*, Exeter: Intellect, 1996.

Mace, Rodney, *Trafalgar Square: Emblem of Empire*, London: Lawrence and Wishart, 1976.

McGrath, John, *The Cheviot, the Stag and the Black, Black Oil*, London: Eyre Methuen, 1981.

McKinnie, Michael, 'The state of this place: *Convictions*, the Courthouse, and the political geography of performance in Belfast', *Modern Drama* 46:4 (2004).

——, 'A sympathy for art: the sentimental economies of New Labour arts policy', in Deborah Lynn Steinberg and Richard Johnson (eds), *Labour's Passive Revolution: The Cultural Politics of Blairism*, London: Lawrence and Wishart, forthcoming.

MacKinnon, Kenneth, '"I keep wishing I were somewhere else": space and fantasies of freedom in the Hollywood musical', in Marshall and Stilwell (eds), *Musicals*.

McKittrick, David, and David McVea, *Making Sense of the Troubles*, Belfast: The Blackstaff Press, 2000.

Mackrell, Judith, *Reading Dance*, London: Michael Joseph, 1997.

McLucas, Cliff, and Mike Pearson (Brith Gof), interview, in Giannachi and Luckhurst, *On Directing*.

——, Interview, with Nick Kaye in Kaye, *Art into Theatre*.

McMillan, Joyce, *The Traverse Theatre Story*, London: Methuen, 1988.

McQueen, Steve, '*Caribs' Leap / Western Deep*', in van Noord (ed.), *Off Limits*.

——, Interview with Hans Ulrich Obrist and Angeline Scherf, in McQueen, *Speaking in Tongues*.

——, *Speaking in Tongues*, Paris: Paris-Musées, 2003.

Mäkinen, Helka, S. E. Wilmer, and W. B. Worthen (eds), *Theatre, History, and National Identities*, Helsinki: Helsinki University Press, 2001.

Malkin, Jeanette R., *Memory-Theater and Postmodern Drama*, Ann Arbor: University of Michigan Press, 1999.

Marshall, Bill, and Robynn Stilwell (eds), *Musicals: Hollywood and Beyond*, Exeter: Intellect Books, 2000.

Martin, Neil, 'The Crum', in Byrne (ed.), *convictions*.

Mason, Jeffrey D., and J. Ellen Gainor (eds), *Performing America: Cultural Nationalism in American Theatre*, Ann Arbor: University of Michigan Press, 1999.

Massey, Doreen, 'A global sense of place', *Marxism Today* (June 1991).

——, 'Places and their pasts', *History Workshop Journal* 39 (1995).

——, *Space, Place and Gender*, Cambridge: Polity Press, 1994.

Matthews, Peter, 'True confetti', *Modern Review* 1:15 (1994).

Maurin, Frédéric, 'Did Paris steal the show for American postmodern directors?', in David Bradby and Maria M. Delgado (eds), *The Paris Jigsaw: Internationalism and the City's Stages*, Manchester: Manchester University Press, 2002.

May, Alex, *Britain and Europe since 1945*, London: Longman, 1999.

Meisner, Nadine, Introduction to Newson, '*Strange Fish*: Lloyd Newson talks to *Dance and Dancers* about his new work'.

Mercer, Kobena, 'Diaspora culture and the dialogic imagination: the aesthetics of black independent film in Britain', in Mbye B. Cham and Claire Andrade-Watkins (eds), *Blackframes: Critical Perspectives on Black Independent Cinema*, Cambridge, MA: MIT Press, 1988.

Middleton, Peter, and Tim Woods, *Literatures of Memory: History, Time and Space in Postwar Writing*, Manchester: Manchester University Press, 2000.

Miller, Eileen, *The Edinburgh International Festival, 1947–1996*, Aldershot: Scolar Press, 1996.

Minihan, Janet, *The Nationalization of Culture: The Development of State Subsidies to the Arts in Great Britain*, London: Hamish Hamilton, 1977.

Mishra, Vijay, *Bollywood Cinema: Temples of Desire*, London: Routledge, 2002.

——, 'The diasporic imaginary: theorizing the Indian diaspora', *Textual Practice* 10:3 (1996).

Mitchell, Gary, 'Holding Room', in Byrne (ed.), *convictions*.

Moffat, Alistair, *The Edinburgh Fringe*, London: Johnston and Bacon, 1978.

Montgomery, Amanda, '*Convictions* at the Crumlin Road Courthouse', *Art Bulletin* 18:97 (2001).

——, '*convictions* visual art installations', in Byrne (ed.), *convictions*.

Morley, Sheridan, *Our Theatre in the Eighties*, London: Hodder and Stoughton, 1990.

Mouffe, Chantal, *The Democratic Paradox*, London: Verso, 2000.

Mulgan, Geoff, and Ken Worpole, *Saturday Night or Sunday Morning? From Arts to Industry – New Forms of Cultural Policy*, London: Commedia, 1988.

Murray, Christopher, *Twentieth-century Irish Drama: Mirror up to Nation*, Manchester: Manchester University Press, 1997.

Myerscough, John, *The Economic Importance of the Arts in Britain*, London: Policy Studies Institute, 1988.

Nancy, Jean-Luc, *Being Singular Plural*, trans. Robert D. Richardson and Anne E. O'Byrne, Stanford: Stanford University Press, (1996) 2000.

Newman, Barbara, '*Bombay Dreams* and *The Fairy Queen*: another opening, another show', *The Dancing Times* 92 (1004, 2002).

Newson, Lloyd, 'Dance *about* something', in *Enter Achilles* programme, 1995.

——, 'DV8: ten years on the edge' (partly based on an interview with Mary Luckhurst), in *Bound to Please* programme, 1997.

——, Interview, in Giannachi and Luckhurst, *On Directing*.

——, 'Lloyd Newson in interview with Jo Butterworth', in Butterworth and Gill Clarke (eds), *Dance Makers Portfolio: Conversations with Choreographers*, Bretton Hall: Centre for Dance and Theatre Studies, 1998.

——, '*Strange Fish*: Lloyd Newson talks to *Dance and Dancers* about his new work', *Dance and Dancers* (July 1992).

Nora, Pierre, 'Between memory and history: *Les Lieux de mémoire*', *Representations* 26 (1989).

Nora, Pierre (ed.), *Les Lieux de mémoire*, Paris: Editions Gallimard, 1984.

Orozco, Gabriel, *Empty Club*, London: Artangel, 1998.

Palmer, Richard H., *The Contemporary British History Play*, Westport, CT: Greenwood Press, 1998.

Palmowski, Jan, 'Democratic Republic of Congo (Zaïre)', *A Dictionary of Contemporary World History*, Oxford: Oxford University Press, 2003.

Parker, Martin, 'Nostalgia and mass culture: McDonaldization and cultural elitism', in Alfino *et al.* (eds), *McDonaldization Revisited*.

Peacock, D. Keith, *Radical Stages: Alternative History in Modern British Drama*, New York: Greenwood Press, 1991.

——, *Thatcher's Theatre: British Theatre and Drama in the Eighties*, New York: Greenwood Press, 1999.

Pearson, Mike, 'From memory: or other ways of telling', *New Welsh Review* 30 (1995).

——, 'Special worlds, secret maps: a poetics of performance', in Taylor (ed.), *Staging Wales*.

——, 'Theatre/archaeology', *The Drama Review*, 38:4 (T144, 1994).

Pearson, Mike, and Michael Shanks, *Theatre/Archaeology*, London: Routledge, 2001.

Pendakur, Manjunath, and Radha Subramanyam, 'India. Part 1: Indian cinema beyond national boundaries', in John Sinclair, Elizabeth Jacka, and Stuart Cunningham (eds), *New Patterns in Global Television: Peripheral Vision*, Oxford: Oxford University Press, 1996.

Petrie, Duncan (ed.), *Screening Europe: Image and Identity in Contemporary European Cinema*, London: BFI, 1992.

Phelan, Mark, 'A new light on Northern culture?', *Irish Theatre Magazine* 3:11 (2002).

Phelan, Peggy, 'Introduction: the ends of performance', in Peggy Phelan and Jill Lane (eds), *The Ends of Performance*, New York: New York University Press, 1998.

——, *Unmarked: The Politics of Performance*, London: Routledge, 1993.

Pieterse, Jan Nederveen, 'Unpacking the West: how European is Europe?', in Ali Rattansi and Sallie Westwood (eds), *Racism, Modernity and Identity: On the Western Front*, Cambridge: Polity Press, 1994.

Pilkington, Lionel, *Theatre and the State in Twentieth-Century Ireland*, London: Routledge, 2001.

Prece, Paul, and William A. Everett, 'The megamusical and beyond: the creation, internationalisation, and impact of a genre', in Everett and Paul R. Laird (eds), *The Cambridge Companion to the Musical*, Cambridge: Cambridge University Press, 2002.

'(P)Review', *On Tour* 19 (2002).

Prickett, Stacey, 'Profile: Lloyd Newson', *Dance Theatre Journal* 19:1 (2003).

Quine, Michael, 'The theatre system of the United Kingdom', in H. van Maanen and S. E. Wilmer (eds), *Theatre Worlds in Motion: Structures, Politics and Developments in the Countries of Western Europe*, Amsterdam: Rodopi, 1998.

Rajadhyaksha, Ashish, and Paul Willeman (eds), *Encyclopaedia of Indian Cinema*, London/New Delhi: British Film Institute/Oxford University Press, revised edn, 1997.

Ramade, Bénédicte, 'Steve McQueen, in focus', *L'Oeil* 544 (2003).

Rebellato, Dan, *1956 and All That: The Making of Modern British Drama*, London: Routledge, 1999.

Rehm, Rush, 'Lives of resistance: Theatre de Complicite, an appreciation', *TheatreForum* 6 (1995).

Reid, Donald, *Edinburgh: The Mini Rough Guide*, London: Rough Guides Ltd, 2000.

Reinelt, Janelle, *After Brecht: British Epic Theatre*, Ann Arbor: University of Michigan Press, 1994.

——, 'Performing Europe: identity formation for a "new" Europe', *Theatre Journal* 53:3 (2001).

——, Review of *Mnemonic*, Complicite, Riverside Studios, London, 1999, in *Theatre Journal* 52:4 (2000).

Rice, Alan, *Radical Narratives of the Black Atlantic*, London: Continuum, 2003.

Riddell, Mary, 'Helena Kennedy (Chair of British Council)', *New Statesman* (27 March 2000).

Ritchie, Rob (ed.), *The Joint Stock Book: The Making of a Theatre Collective*, London: Methuen, 1987.

Ritzer, George, *The McDonaldization of Society: An Investigation into the Changing Character of Contemporary Social Life*, Thousand Oaks, CA: Pine Forge Press, 2nd edn, 1996.

——, *The McDonaldization Thesis: Explorations and Extensions*, London: Sage, 1998.

Ritzer, George (ed.), *Mcdonaldization: The Reader*, Thousand Oaks, CA: Pine Forge Press, 2002.

Roddick, Nick, '*Four Weddings* and a final reckoning', *Sight and Sound* 5:1 (1995).

Rojek, Chris, and John Urry, 'Transformations of travel and theory', in Chris Rojek and John Urry (eds), *Touring Cultures: Transformations of Travel and Theory*, London: Routledge, 1997.

Rolfe, Heather, 'Arts festivals', *Cultural Trends* 15 (1992).

——, *Arts Festivals in the UK*, London: Policy Studies Institute, 1992.

Rowell, George, and Anthony Jackson, *The Repertory Movement: A History of Regional Theatre in Britain*, Cambridge: Cambridge University Press, 1984.

Rutherford, Jonathan, 'A place called home: identity and the cultural politics of difference', in Rutherford (ed.), *Identity: Community, Culture, Difference*, London: Lawrence and Wishart, 1990.

Said, Edward W., *Orientalism*, Harmondsworth: Penguin, 1985.

Sanchez-Colberg, Ana, 'Altered states and subliminal spaces: charting the road towards a physical theatre', *Performance Research* 1:2 (1996).

Savage, Roger, 'A Scottish National Theatre?', in Stevenson and Wallace (eds), *Scottish Theatre Since the Seventies*.

Savill, Charmian C., 'Brith Gof', in Taylor (ed.), *Staging Wales*.

——, 'Dismantling the wall', *Planet* 79 (1990).

Schwarz, Bill, 'Afterword: postcolonial times: the visible and the invisible', in Driver and Gilbert (eds), *Imperial Cities*.

——, 'Black metropolis, white England', in Mica Nava and Alan O'Shea (eds), *Modern Times: Reflections on a Century of English Modernity*, London: Routledge, 1996.

Schneer, Jonathan, 'Anti-imperial London: the Pan-African Conference of 1900', in Driver and Gilbert (eds), *Imperial Cities*.

Scottish Arts Council, *Response to the Consultation on National Cultural Strategy*, Glasgow: SAC, November 1999.

*Scottish Arts Council Annual Report, 1998–99*, Glasgow: SAC, 1999.

Scottish Executive, *Creating Our Future … Minding Our Past: Scotland's National Cultural Strategy*, Edinburgh: Scottish Executive, 2000.

——, *Scotland: A Global Connections Strategy*, Edinburgh: Scottish Executive, 2001.

——, *A Smart, Successful Scotland: Ambitions for the Enterprise Networks*, Edinburgh: Scottish Executive, 2001.

*Scottish National Theatre: Final Report of the Independent Working Group*, Glasgow: Scottish Arts Council, 2001.

Shank, Theodore, 'Preface to the 1996 reprint', in Shank (ed.), *Contemporary British Theatre*.

Shank, Theodore (ed.), *Contemporary British Theatre*, Basingstoke: Macmillan, revised edn, 1996.

Shellard, Dominic, *British Theatre since the War*, New Haven and London: Yale University Press, 1999.

Shepherd, Simon, and Peter Womack, *English Drama: a Cultural History*, Oxford: Blackwell, 1996.

Sierz, Aleks, 'British theatre in the 1990s: a brief political economy', *Media, Culture and Society* 19 (1997).

——, *In-Yer-Face Theatre: British Drama Today*, London: Faber and Faber, 2001.

Sinclair, Andrew, *Arts and Cultures: The History of the 50 Years of the Arts Council of Great Britain*, London: Sinclair-Stevenson, 1995.

Smith, Andy, '"Grass Roots": Eric Cantona, Jürgen Klinsmann and the Europeanisation of English football', in John Milfull (ed.), *Britain in Europe: Prospects for Change*, Aldershot: Ashgate Publishing Ltd, 1999.

Smith, Chris, *Creative Britain*, London: Faber and Faber, 1998.

Smith, Donald (ed.), *The Scottish Stage: A National Theatre Company for Scotland*, Edinburgh: Candlemaker Press, 1994.

Smith, Tori, '"A grand work of noble conception": the Victoria Memorial and imperial London', in Driver and Gilbert (eds), *Imperial Cities*.

Smoodin, Eric (ed.), *Disney Discourse: Producing the Magic Kingdom*, London: Routledge, 1994.

Snape, Libby, 'Lloyd on love: Lloyd Newson talks to Libby Snape', *Dance Theatre Journal* 15:2 (1999).

Sobieski, Lynn, 'Breaking the boundaries: the People Show, Lumiere & Son and Hesitate and Demonstrate', in Shank (ed.), *Contemporary British Theatre*.

Stallybrass, Peter, and Allon White, *The Politics and Poetics of Transgression*, London: Methuen, 1986.

Stelfox, Dawson, 'Conviction', in Byrne (ed.), *convictions*.

Stephens, Elan Closs, 'A century of Welsh drama', in Dafydd Johnston (ed.), *A Guide to Welsh Literature, c.1900–1996*, Cardiff: University of Wales Press, 1998.

Stevenson, Randall, and Gavin Wallace (eds), *Scottish Theatre Since the Seventies*, Edinburgh: Edinburgh University Press, 1996.

Syal, Meera, 'Bombay-Mumbai', in *Bombay Dreams* Programme.

Taylor, Anna-Marie (ed.), *Staging Wales*, Cardiff: University of Wales Press, 1997.

Taylor, Hilary, 'Language in their gesture: Théâtre de Complicité', *The European English Messenger* 2:2 (1993).

Terdiman, Richard, *Present Past: Modernity and the Memory Crisis*, Ithaca: Cornell University Press, 1993.

Thomas, Rosie, 'Indian cinema: pleasures and popularity' *Screen* 26:3/4 (1985).

*Time Out Edinburgh Guide*, London: Penguin Books, 1998.

Tompsett, A. Ruth (ed.), *Black Theatre in Britain* (*Performing Arts International* 1:2), Amsterdam: Harwood Academic, 1996.

Trussler, Simon, *The Cambridge Illustrated History of British Theatre*, Cambridge: Cambridge University Press, 1994.

Tushingham, David (ed.), *Live 1: Food for the Soul: A New Generation of British Theatremakers*, London: Methuen, 1994.

Tyrrell, Heather, 'Bollywood in Britain', *Sight and Sound* 8:8 (1998).

Tyszka, Juliusz, 'The school of being together: festivals as national therapy during the Polish "Period of Transition"', trans. Jolanta Cynkutis and Tom Randolph, *NTQ: New Theatre Quarterly* 13:50 (1997).

Uberoi, Patricia, 'The diaspora comes home: disciplining desire in *DDLJ*', *Contributions to Indian Sociology* 32:2 (1998).

——, 'Imagining the family: an ethnography of viewing *Hum aapke hain koun ...!*', in Rachel Dwyer and Christopher Pinney (eds), *Pleasure and the Nation: The History, Politics and Consumption of Popular Culture in India*, New Delhi: Oxford University Press, 2001.

Van Noord, Gerrie (ed.), *Off Limits: 40 Artangel Projects*, London: Merrell, 2002.

Vasudevan, Ravi S., 'The politics of cultural address in "transitional" cinema: a case study of Indian popular cinema', in Christine Gledhill and Linda Williams (eds), *Reinventing Film Studies*, London: Arnold, 2000.

Verhoef, Matty, *European Festivals*, trans. Sam A. Herman, Geneva: European Festivals Association, 1995.

Verma, Jatinder, 'Binglish: a *jungli* approach to multi-cultural theatre', *Studies in Theatre Production* 13 (1996).

——, '"Binglishing" the stage: a generation of Asian theatre in England', in Richard Boon and Jane Plastow (eds), *Theatre Matters: Performance and Culture on the World Stage*, Cambridge: Cambridge University Press, 1998.

——, 'The challenge of Binglish: analysing multi-cultural productions', in Patrick Campbell (ed.), *Analysing Performance*, Manchester: Manchester University Press, 1996.

——, 'Cultural transformations', in Shank (ed.), *Contemporary British Theatre*.

——, Interview, in Maria M. Delgado and Paul Heritage (eds), *In Contact with the Gods?: Directors Talk Theatre*, Manchester: Manchester University Press, 1996.

Visiting Arts, *Visiting Arts Guide to the Edinburgh Festivals 2000*, London: Visiting Arts, 2000.

Wade, Alan, 'A *Theatre Annual* interview with Theatre de Complicite's Lilo Baur and Marcello Magni', *Theatre Annual* 53 (2000).

Wallis, Brian, 'Selling nations: international exhibitions and cultural diplomacy', in Daniel J. Sherman and Irit Rogoff (eds), *Museum Culture: Histories, Discourses, Spectacles*, Minneapolis: University of Minnesota Press, 1994.

Walvin, James, *Britain's Slave Empire*, Stroud: Tempus, 2000.

Wandor, Michelene, *Post-war British Drama: Looking Back in Gender*, London: Routledge, 2001.

Waters, Malcolm, *Globalization*, London: Routledge, 2nd edn, 2001.

Watson, Keith, 'Under the influence', *Dance Theatre Journal* 18:1 (2002).

Whitfield, Sarah, 'London: Douglas Gordon/Steve McQueen', *The Burlington Magazine* 145:1198 (2003).

Wilkie, Fiona, 'Mapping the terrain: a survey of site-specific performance in Britain', *NTQ: New Theatre Quarterly* 18:2 (70, 2002).

Williams, David (ed.), *Peter Brook and* The Mahabharata: *Critical Perspectives*, London: Routledge, 1991.

Williams, Dawn Bastian, Robert W. Lesh, and Andrea L. Stamm, *Zaïre*, Oxford: Oxford University Press, 1995.

Wilmer, S. E., *Theatre, Society and the Nation: Staging American Identities*, Cambridge: Cambridge University Press, 2002.

Winter, Christopher, 'Love and language: or only connect the prose and the passion', *Dance Theatre Journal* 7:2 (1989).

Wolf, Stacey, *A Problem Like Maria: Gender and Sexuality in the American Musical*, Ann Arbor: University of Michigan Press, 2002.

Yarrow, Ralph, and Anthony Frost, 'Great Britain', in Yarrow (ed.), *European Theatre, 1960–1990: Cross-cultural Perspectives*, London: Routledge, 1992.

Young, John W., *Britain and European Unity, 1945–1999*, London: Macmillan, 2nd edn, 2000.

Young, Robert J. C., *Colonial Desire: Hybridity in Theory, Culture and Race*, London: Routledge, 1995.

## Select newspaper, Internet and radio articles

Arnot, Chris, 'Arts: theatre: stand by your nan', *Guardian* (5 January 2000).

Bhuchar, Sudha, 'Arts etc.; answer the questions!', *Independent* (30 September 2001).

Billington, Michael, 'Britain's theatrical chauvinism', *Guardian* (1 October 1977).

——, 'Why I hate the Fringe', *Guardian* (25 July 2002).

——, 'The year of living dangerously', *Guardian* (6 June 2001).

Black, Ian, 'Analysis: cultural diplomacy: no business like show business …,' *Guardian* (4 August 1998).

*Bombay Dreams* reviews, rpt in *Theatre Record* 22:13 (16 July 2002).

'*Bombay Dreams* week', *BBCi Asian Life Film* (20 June 2003), www.bbc.co.uk/asianlife/ film/indiansummer/bombaydreams/index.shtml.

Brooks, Libby, '"It's good to keep a clean head"', *Guardian* (30 September 2002).

Brooks, Richard, 'Cool Britain flops on the world stage', *Sunday Times* (21 November 1999).

Brown, Allan, 'Cash cow has finally leapt over the moon', *Sunday Times* (12 August 2001).

Chakravorty, Vinayak, 'Dancing to Bollywood's tune', *HindustanTimes.com* (n.d.), www.hindustantimes.com/2002/Nov/29/674_105475,00310006.htm.

Chrisafis, Angelique, 'Hollywood stars choose fringe for Sept 11 catharsis', *Guardian* (15 August 2002).

——, 'A performing duck, a badger, and 20,340 other events: it must be the fringe', *Guardian* (3 August 2002).

——, 'Sermons mounting at the fringe', *Guardian* (6 August 2002).

Church, Michael, 'Stand in line for a triumph of style over substance', *Observer* (17 May 1992).

Clark, Andrew, 'Maestro with a touch of prejudice', *Financial Times* (3 August 2002).

Clarke, Jocelyn, review of *convictions*, *Sunday Tribune* (26 November 2000).

Collard, James, 'Bollywood', *The Times* (6 April 2002).

Cornwell, Tim, "Dark horse lands top theatre job', *Scotsman* (30 July 2004).

——, 'Festival refuses to be sidelined', *Scotsman* (7 August 2004).

Ellis, Samantha, 'London calling', *Scotsman* (23 August 2002).

Espiner, Mark, 'All the world on stage', *Guardian Weekend* (23 February 2002).

'Exclusive: Fringe uses venue for 5000 and uplifting show for one', *Herald* (5 June 2002).

Ferguson, Brian, 'City says no to cash for Fringe', *Edinburgh Evening News* (27 August 2002).

Flynn, Bob, 'Bollywood meets Holyrood', *Guardian* (22 August 2002).

'Fringe tops record with £10.8m of tickets sold', *Edinburgh Evening News* (20 October 2004).

Gardner, Lyn, 'Life after debt', *Guardian* (6 August 2001).

——, 'Never mind the length, feel the quality', *Guardian* (30 July 2001).

——, 'Why I love the Fringe', *Guardian* (25 July 2002).

Gibbons, Fiachra, 'African play blocked by visa refusals', *Guardian* (7 August 2001).

——, 'Festival chiefs deny cash crisis: special report: the Edinburgh festival 2000', *Guardian* (19 August 2000).

——, 'Festival's buzz is back as 1m flock to shows', *Guardian* (21 August 2001).

Gooch, Adela, 'High-tech Britain is making an exhibition of itself abroad', *Independent on Sunday* (19 April 1992).

Greig, David, 'Reaping the harvest of Scottish theatre', *Independent* (9 August 2002).

Harlow, John, 'Cook sells Britain's new look abroad', *Sunday Times* (6 September 1998).

'Havergal urges more aid for Scottish theatre', *Herald* (21 August 2001).

Higgins, Charlotte, 'Continental drift', *Guardian* (17 April 2003).

Hobson, Harold, 'A French actor', *Sunday Times* (12 September 1948).

'Holyrood still on target', *BBC News* (26 January 2004), news.bbc.co.uk/2/hi/uk_news/scotland/3430963.stm.

Jamieson, Alastair, 'Record-breaking Fringe sales hit 918,000', *Scotsman* (27 August 2002).

Kemp, Arnold, 'Scottish National Theatre must wait in wings', *Observer* (3 February 2002).

Kieffer, John, 'Let's talk about art, maybe', *Observer* (28 March 1999).

Lawson, Mark, interview with Martin Lynch, *Front Row*, BBC Radio 4 (7 November 2000).

Lloyd, John, 'For the best of Britannia, go to Berlin', *The Times* (6 March 1998).

Logan, Brian, 'Show me the money', *Guardian* (26 August 2002).

McBurney, Simon, 'You must remember this', *Guardian* (1 January 2003).

McGlone, Jackie, 'Serious horseplay', *Scotsman* (23 August 2002).

McKittrick, David, 'Courthouse takes centre stage as actors revisit horrors of Belfast', *Independent* (15 November 2000).

McLean, Pauline, 'Funky beat in Bay as band backs Brith Gof', *Western Mail* (28 February 1996).

McMillan, Joyce, 'When Harrower met Fosse', *Scotsman* (22 March 2002).

Majumdar, Krishnendu, 'Theatre: Salaam Bombay', *Guardian* (21 February 2001).

Malvern, Jack, 'Festival's first couple attack Iraq war plans', *The Times* (17 August 2002).

Moroney, Mic, 'Court in the act', review of *convictions*, *Guardian* (1 November 2000).

Morrison, James, 'Welsh backs rival festival for locals', *Independent* (11 August 2002).

Moss, Stephen, 'Arts: the man behind Blair plc Michael Johnson is the design guru charged with selling the UK – and the government – to the people', *Guardian* (10 September 1998).

Mullaney, Andrea, 'High rents set to bring house down for Fringe', *Edinburgh Evening News* (23 August 2002).

'Outdoors at the Fringe' (1 May 2002), *Edinburgh Festival Fringe*, www.edfringe.com/story/html?id=125&area_id=35.

Owen, Edward, 'Expo 92 ends with late rush of visitors', *The Times* (12 October 1992).

Pais, Arthur J., '*Bombay Dreams* to come true in New York', *redriff.com* (8 September 2003), in.redriff.com/movies/2003/sep/08bd.htm

Peterkin, Tom, 'Holyrood's shadow puts paid to theatre building', *telegragh.co.uk* (25 July 2001), money.telegraph.co.uk/news/main.jhtml;sessionid= QEOFZRVH CURABQFIQMGCM54AVCBQUJVC?xml=/news/2001/07/25/nrood25. xml&secureRefresh=true&_requestid=123278 (accessed November 2004).

Powell, Kenneth 'Building up to a fiesta or siesta?' *Daily Telegraph* (16 April 1992).

'Record-breaking Fringe tops £7m in ticket sales', *Herald* (27 August 2002).

Scott, Kirsty, 'Fringe benefits outweighed by high prices', *Guardian* (24 August 2002).

Searle, Adrian, 'Into the unknown', *Guardian* (8 October 2002).

Shuttleworth, Ian, 'Escorted through the courthouse', review of *convictions*, *Financial Times* (20 November 2000).

Stenhouse, David, 'Edinburgh notebook', *The Times* (26 August 2002).

Sturges, Fiona, 'Edinburgh Festival: how I spent 12 hours showjumping at the Fringe', *Independent* (17 August 2002).

Taylor, Paul, 'Russia's new revolution', *Independent* (6 March 2002), p. 9.

'This job? It can change people's lives', *Scotsman* (18 March 2002).

Thorncroft, Tony, 'Corporates join in the party: Edinburgh sponsorship: the festivals would be a pale shadow without support from big companies', *Financial Times* (3 September 2001).

Thorpe, Vanessa, 'West End looks to East for next hit: Royal Opera House follows Lloyd Webber in bringing romance of Bollywood to Britain's stage and screen', *Observer* (5 November 2000).

Wade, Mike, 'Cash storm destroys theatre of dreams', *Scotsman* (28 November 2002).

Walker, Lynne, 'Edinburgh Festival: each night is an adventure in unknown territory', *Independent* (8 August 2002).

Wilson, Jamie, and Matthew Taylor, 'And down comes the statue ... but this time it's Trafalgar Square', *Guardian* (21 November 2003).

'A writer's report from the front', *Financial Times* (9 September 1998).

Young, Robin, 'Record ticket sales for Fringe', *The Times* (27 August 2002).

## Select website references

*Artangel*, www.artangel.org.uk

*BITE (Barbican International Theatre Event)*, www.barbican.org.uk/bite

*Bombay Dreams*, www.bombaydreamsthemusical.com

*British Council*, www.britishcouncil.org

*Bush Theatre*, www.bushtheatre.co.uk

*Complicite*, www.complicite.org

*DV8*, www.dv8.co.uk

*Edinburgh Festival Fringe*, www.edfringe.com

*Edinburgh Festivals*, www.edinburgh-festivals.com

*Edinburgh International Festival*, www.eif.co.uk

*Edinburgh Mela*, www.edinburgh-mela.co.uk

*European Parliament*, www.europarl.eu.int

*LIFT (London International Festival of Theatre)*, www.liftfest.org

*London International Mime Festival*, www.mimefest.co.uk

*Royal Court Theatre*, www.royalcourttheatre.com

*Scottish Arts Council*, www.sac.org.uk

*Scottish Executive*, www.scotland.gov.uk

*Scottish Executive, Creating Our Future ... Minding Our Past: Scotland's National Cultural Strategy*, www.scotland.gov.uk/nationalculturalstrategy

*Tamasha Theatre Company*, www.tamasha.org.uk

*Theatre Babel*, www.theatrebabel.co.uk

*Theatre in Wales*, www.theatre-wales.co.uk

*Tinderbox Theatre Company*, www.tinderbox.org.uk

*Tricycle*, www.tricycle.co.uk

# Index

Note: 'n.' after a page reference indicates the number of a note on that page. Page numbers in *italic* refer to illustrations. Performance, art, and literary works can usually be found under the name of their producing company, maker, or author.

7:84 (Scotland)
   *Cheviot, the Stag and the Black, Black Oil, The* 43

A B & C 88
Abbey Theatre 88, 100, 121–2
Actors' Studio Theatre 121
Albert Memorial 194, 196, 205
Aldwych Theatre 121–2
Americanisation 76, 79–80, 89–90
   *see also* 'Disneyfication';
      'McDonaldization'
Amin, Ash, Doreen Massey, and Nigel
   Thrift 192, 199
Anderson, Benedict 1–7, 16, 35n.3,
   113
   *Imagined Communities* 1, 13n.3
Anderson, Donald 96–8
Anderson, Lea 130
Anouilh, Jean 121
anti-theatricality 9, 114, 117–19, 144
Apollo Victoria Theatre 157, 176
Arden, Annabel 136
Arden, John 122
Armitstead, Claire 115, 126
Arrabal, Fernando 124
Artangel 43, 68n.13, 193, 201, 214n.2
Artaud, Antonin 122, 127–9
Arts Council of Great Britain 7, 10,
   18–22
Atkinson, Rowan *26*
Aurora Nova 87–9, 102
Austen, Jane 25
Avalon 86

BAC *see* Battersea Arts Centre
Baker, Bobby 28, 39n.65
   *Kitchen Show, The* 43
Bakhtin, Mikhail 9
   dialogism 54, 70n.56
   *see also* carnival
Barba, Eugenio 46, 127
Barbican International Theatre Event
   (BITE) 125–6
Barish, Jonas
   *Antitheatrical Prejudice, The* 117–18, 129
Barjatya, Sooraj 168
Barrault, Jean–Louis 120
Bartlett, Neil 145
Battersea Arts Centre (BAC) 126
Baudrillard, Jean 98
Baur, Lilo 137–8
Bausch, Pina 127–8, 130, 137, 151n.80
Beckett, Samuel 128
Belfast 1, 8, 28, 43–4, 53–61, 66
Belgrade Theatre (Coventry) 21
Berger, John 137, 142
Berkoff, Steven 39n.65, 88
Berliner Ensemble 120–2, 124
Beynon, John and David Dunkerley 76
B, Franko 39n.65
Bhabha, Homi K. 10
   mimicry 163, 175
Bharucha, Rustom 89, 169–70
Bhuchar, Sudha 167, 170–1, 174
Bieito, Calixto 100
Billig, Michael 1
Billington, Michael 74–6, 85, 117, 124
Binglish 175, 185

Birmingham Repertory Theatre 168, 172, 174
BITE *see* Barbican International Theatre Event
Black, Don 180
Blair, Tony 1, 17, 25
Blast Theory 145
Bollywood film 9, 11, 156–66, 182, 186n.2
  *Dilwale Dulhaniya Le Jayenge* 179
  *Hum Aapke Hain Koun …! (HAHK)* 161, 166, 168–72, 175
  Parsi theatre 161–2
*Bombay Dreams* 10, 156–7, 163, 166, 176–86, *177–8*
Bond, Edward 15, 122
Boniface, Priscilla 74, 92
Boyd, Jimmy 64
Brecht, Bertolt 42, 120–1, 137, 148n.37
Breth, Andrea 81
Bridie, James 124
Brith Gof 8, 44–53, 67, 68n.19
  *Disasters of War, The* 49
  *Gododdin* 8, 43, 45–53, *48*, 67, 69n.29
  scenography 47–9, *48*, 70n.43
British Asian 9, 156–9, 166–8, 171–6, 179–81, 184–5
British Council 8, 25–31, 35, 39n.73, 86, 100
  Edinburgh Showcase 27–9, 99–101
  posters *26 7*
  publications 27–8
British Library 196–7
British Museum 196–7
Broadway Theatre 186
Brook, Peter 122–3
  Charles Marowitz 122
  *Mahabharata, The* 123, 157
  *US* 123
Brown, Gordon 25, 112
Bryden, Bill
  *Ship, The* 43
Bryden, Ronald 120–2
Burke, Gregory
  *Gagarin Way* 95, *96*
Bush, George W. 200
Bush Theatre 125

Butler, Judith 3, 6
Byron (Lord) George Gordon 197

Cafédirect 87
Cameron, Alasdair 51
Cardiff 28, 43, 47–8, 50–2, 67
Carlson, Marvin 42, 45
carnival 9, 102–3
Cartlidge, Katrin 138, 143
Carville, Daragh
  'Male Toilets' 54, 57, 58
Caughie, John 146
CEMA *see* Council for the Encouragement of Music and the Arts
censorship 19, 116
Chambers, Colin 123
Charnock, Nigel 39n.65, 129, 131, 133, 135
Chaudhuri, Una 99
Chopra, Aditya 179
Christie, Julie *26*
Churchill, Caryl 39n.65
Circus Oz 88
Citizens Theatre 124–5
Clod Ensemble, The 145
Coetzee, J. M. 137
Comédie Française 120–2, 124
comedy 54, 84–5, 96, 131, 164, 168, 172, 174–5, 179
Commission for Racial Equality (CRE) 167
Communicado 28
community 2, 7, 10, 12, 14n.13, 16, 41–2, 45, 47, 53, 113, 118, 126, 164–5, 171–2, 179, 181
Compagnie Jouvet de Théâtre de l'Athénée 124
Compagnie Roger Planchon 124
Complicite 8, 127, 135–7, 142–3
  *Anything for a Quiet Life* 137
  *Caucasian Chalk Circle, The* 137
  *Chairs, The* 137
  *Elephant Vanishes, The* 136
  *Foe* 137
  *Light* 137, 140
  *Minute Too Late, A* 136

*Mnemonic* 9, 114, 136, 138–44, *139–40*, 153n.119
*Noise of Time, The* 137
*Out of a House Walked a Man* 137
*Please, Please, Please* 137
*Street of Crocodiles, The* 137
*Three Lives of Lucie Cabrol, The* 136, 140
*Visit, The* 137
Congo, Democratic Republic of 206
Congreve, William 115
Conservative Party 1, 134
Cool Britannia 17–18, 25–6, 30
Council for the Encouragement of Music and the Arts (CEMA) 18
Coveney, Michael 124–5
Crawford, Iain 97
Crawford, Mairtín 64
CRE *see* Commission for Racial Equality
creative industries *see* New Labour
Crumlin Road Courthouse 43–4, 53, 55–66, *56*, 72n.82
Cunningham, Merce 130

Dahl, Mary-Karen 158
Dale, Michael 105n.15
Daubeny, Peter 120–3
  World Theatre Seasons 121, 123
David Glass Ensemble 39n.65, 145
Davison, Peter J. 131
DCMS *see* Department for Culture, Media and Sport
democracy/democratic 3, 9, 11–12, 17, 19–22, 30, 35, 74–6, 78–82, 101, 192–3, 214
Department for Culture, Media and Sport (DCMS) 24–5
Department for National Heritage 24
Department of Trade and Industry 25
Derevo 88
Derrida, Jacques 146
Deschamps, Jérôme 136
Desperate Optimists 39n.65, 145
devised theatre 117
devolution 1, 4, 7–8, 17, 59
diaspora 7, 9–11, 157–8, 165, 168, 171, 174, 176, 184, 212

'Disneyfication' 8, 76, 92–4, 101, 109n.97
Dixit, Madhuri 170
Do/Fabrik 88
Doo Cot 145
Driver, Felix and David Gilbert 195
Dubbeljoint Theatre Company 39n.67
Dürrenmatt, Friedrich 137
DV8 Physical Theatre 39n.65, 127–30, 145
  *Can We Afford This* 129, 152n.105
  *Dead Dreams of Monochrome Men* 129
  *Enter Achilles* 129, 152n.105
  *Happiest Day of My Life, The* 129
  scenography 129–31
  *Strange Fish* 9, 114, 128, 130–5, *132–3*
Dyer, Richard 170, 172

Eade, John 198
Edgar, David
  *Pentecost* 144
Edinburgh 28, 32, 43, 74, 78, 85, 90–8, 100, 102, 168
  Castle Rock *93*
  Meadows, the *83*
  Royal Scottish Academy *84*
Edinburgh festivals 8–9, 11, 30, 74–103, 123–4, 192
  Edinburgh Book Festival 77
  Edinburgh Festival Fringe (Fringe) 9, 27, 78–80, 82–103, 105n.15
    British Council Edinburgh Showcase *see* British Council
    Festival Cavalcade 82, 94
    Festival Fringe Society 90–1, 105n.15
    Fringe First awards 88
    Fringe Sunday 82, *83*, 106n.36
    Perrier Awards 84
    sponsorship 87
    street performance 82–3, *84*
    venues 86–7, 90, 92
  Edinburgh International Festival (EIF) 8, 77–8, 80–2, 92–101, 105n.11, 120

Edinburgh International Film
Festival 77
Edinburgh International Jazz and
Blues Festival 77
Edinburgh Mela 95
Edinburgh Military Tattoo 77, 94
financial economies 96–8
Edwardes, Jane 117
EIF *see* Edinburgh festivals
Elgin Marbles 197
Eliot, T. S. 124
Elsom, John 123
entertainments tax 19, 36n.25
Ersatz 130
Europe/European 7–9, 11–12, 31,
44–6, 50–2, 67, 78, 80–1, 101,
113–27, 129–30, 133–8, 140–6,
211–12
Unification 1, 4, 105n.13, 112, 134
EXPO 92 134

Farrah 123
Featherstone, Vicky 34
Fenton, Rose 126
festivals 106n.32
Belfast at Queen's Festival 53, 61,
127
Brighton Festival 127
European Arts Festival 134
Festival d'Automne (Paris) 99
Mayfest (Glasgow) 127
Melas 179, 191n.88
Osterfestpiele (Salzburg) 81
*see also* Aurora Nova; Edinburgh
festivals; London International
Festival of Theatre; London
International Mime Festival
Feuer, Jane 162
Fo, Dario 88, 136
Forced Entertainment 39n.65, 145
*Nights in the City* 43
Foreign Office 25
Fosse, Jon
*Girl on the Sofa, The* 100
Foucault, Michel 112–13
*Four Weddings and a Funeral* 10, 175–6,
185, 190n.77

Fowler, John 33
Frantic Assembly 28, 88, 145
Freshwater, Helen 137, 139–41, 143
Fricker, Karen 63, 66, 99, 108n.71
Fringe *see* Edinburgh festivals
Fuchs, Anne 172, 174

Gardner, Lyn 74–5, 84–5, 88
Gate Theatre 124–5
Gaulier, Philippe 136
genealogy *see* historiography
Ghedia, Mala 170, *173*
Gibbons, Fiachra 84, 92
Gillis, John R. 41
Gilroy, Paul 211
black Atlantic 211–12
Giraudoux, Jean 121
Glasgow 32, 43, 50–1, 124–5, 127,
198
globalisation 1, 4, 8–9, 11, 74–82, 89,
98–103, 192
Gododdin 46, 48
*Gododdin, Y* 46
Goode, Chris 88
*Goodness Gracious Me* 179
Gordon, Fiona 136
Gorky, Maxim 124
Gorman, Damian
'Judge's Room' 54, 57–8
Graham, Martha 130
Grant, Hugh 176
Graver, David and Loren Kruger 98–9
Greig, David 88, 95–6
*Europe* 144
Grenada 202
Grid Iron 88, 145
Grotowski, Jerzy 46, 124, 127
Gupta, Tanika 180

Hall (Sir) Peter 115–16, 123
Hall, Stuart 146, 213
Hare, David 28
Harewood (Lord) George Lascelles 85
Harris, Zinnie and Marian Adamia
*Gravity* 81
Harrison, Ben 88
Harrower, David 100

Haque, Sophiya *178*, 179
Harvie, Jen 14n.14
Havergal, Giles 124
Hawkins, Maureen 41
Hawkins, Tim 87
Hesitate and Demonstrate 145
Hewison, Robert 19, 34
Higgins, Vincent 59
Hill, Benny *26*
Hirst, Damien 17
historicism 5
historiography 9, 10
    British theatre and drama 112–19
history plays 42
Hollis, Patricia 21
Hollywood musicals 162, 164–5
*Housing the Arts in Great Britain* 21
Houstoun, Wendy 129, 132–5, *132*
Hussein, Saddam 200
hybrid and hybridity 7, 9–12, 46, 50,
    52, 74, 100, 127, 132, 135,
    145–6, 157–8, 162–3, 166,
    174–5, 184–6, 192, 199, 213

imagined communities *see* national
    identity
Improbable Theatre 28, 39n.65, 145
Institute of Contemporary Arts (ICA)
    126
Ionesco, Eugène 127, 137

Jackson, Anthony 21
Jacobs, Jane M. 201
Jain, Madhu 171
Johnston, Adrian 132
Joint Stock 120
Jones, Lis Hughes 44, 47
Jones, Marie
    'Court No. 2' 54, 57–8
Jonson, Ben 118
Joseph, May 167–8
Julian, Isaac 215n.8

Kane, Sarah 28
Kantor, Tadeusz 46, 124, 137
Kapur, Geeta and Ashish Rajadhyaksha
    165

Kapur, Shekhar 179
Kaye, Nick 50
Kazmi, Nikhat 169–70
Kennedy, Dennis 102, 109n.98
Kennedy, (Baroness) Helena 25–6
Kershaw, Baz 36n.6, 51
Khan–Din, Ayub 180
Khan, Farah 179
Kharms, Daniil 137
Kieffer, John 30
King, Barnaby 174
Knapper, Stephen 142
Knowles, Ric 80, 87, 98–9, 106n.23
Komedia 87–9
*Kumars at No. 42, The* 159, 179
Kwon, Miwon 73n.110

Laast, Anthony Van 179
Landon–Smith, Kristine 167, 170–1
language 30, 45, 47, 64, 75, 89, 141,
    174, 179
Lawrence, Stephen 1
Lawson, Mark 56
Lecoq, Jacques 127, 136, 142
Lee, Jennie 21–2
Lefebvre, Henri 60–1, 72n.86
Lepage, Robert 99
LIFT *see* London International Festival
    of Theatre
Lindgren, Torgny 137
Lingis, Alphonso 14n.13
Littlewood, Joan 120, 148n.39
Livingstone, Ken 196
Loane, Tim 71n.61
local authorities 22
Lochhead, Liz
    *Medea* 99
London 1, 10–11, 18, 20–1, 28–9, 32,
    50, 59, 81, 86, 88, 95–6, 120–1,
    124–7, 134, 144, 156–7, 167,
    176, 193–201, 204–5, 211
    Tube, Underground, or Transport
        for 10, 195–9
    posters *196*, 197–8, *198–9*
London International Festival of
    Theatre (LIFT) 43, 68n.13,
    125–6

London International Mime Festival 125–7
Lumière Cinema 10, 193, 201, 204–6
Lumiere & Son 145
Lynch, Martin
  'Main Hall' 58, 62
Lynch, Susan 138, 143
Lyric Hammersmith 168

McBurney, Simon 136–9, *139*, 143–4
McCafferty, Owen
  'Court No. 1' 54
McCartney, Nicola
  'Jury Room' 58
Mace, Ronald 195
McCullough, Christopher 115, 117, 127
'McDonaldization' 8, 76, 90–2, 98, 101
MacDonald, Robert David 124
McGrory, Hugh 56
McGuinness, Frank 100
McKinnie, Michael 24, 33, 64
McKittrick, David 60
McLucas, Clifford 45, 47, 49–52
McMaster, Brian 80–1, 85
McMillan, Joyce 100
McPherson, Conor 39n.65
McQueen, Steve 208–10, 217n.35
  *Bear* 210
  *Caribs' Leap / Western Deep* 10, 193, 201–14, *203–4*
  *Deadpan* 210
  *Illuminer* 209
  *Speaking in Tongues* 209
Magni, Marcello 136
Major, John 24, 112, 128, 134
Malkin, Jeanette R. 65
Marber, Patrick 28, 39n.65
Marceau, Marcel 124
Martin, Neil 56, 61
Martinez, Ursula
  *Show Off* 29
Marx, Karl 92
Massey, Doreen 43, 212
materialism 5
Matthias, Sean 88
Maurin, Frédéric 99

Maxwell, Douglas
  *Decky Does a Bronco* 43
Meehan, Thomas 186
memory 4, 41–4, 46, 49, 52, 56, 60, 62, 64, 66–7, 100, 137–9, 143
metropolitanism 10, 17, 20, 22, 32, 35, 192–3
Meyerhold, Vsevolod 127, 137
mimicry, postcolonial 10
Mishra, Vijay 159, 161, 165
Mitchell, Gary
  'Holding Room' 54, 58
Moffatt, Alistair 105n.15
Molina, Jordi Cortes *133*, 135
Moncreiff, John Scott 40n.83
Montgomery, Amanda 61
  *convictions* installations 55–8, *55*, 62, *63*, 64–5, 71n.63
Morgan, Abi 88
Moscow Art Theatre 121
Moti Roti 29
Mottram, Stephen 28
Mouffe, Chantal 11
Mulgan, Geoff and Ken Worpole 22
Murakami, Haruki 137
Murphy, Mark 130
musicals 5
  *see also* Bollywood film; Hollywood musicals

Nagra, Parminder 170
Nancy, Jean-Luc 14n.13
national identity 1–8
National Theatre 21, 122, 144
National Theatre of Scotland 8, 18, 25, 31–4, 40n.85
Natural Theatre Company 28
Neal, Lucy 126
Negro Ensemble Company 121
Nelson, Anne
  *Guys, The* 83–4
neo-imperialism 18, 79, 162
neo-liberalism 3, 9, 24, 35, 82–3, 101–2
'New Britain' 1, 8, 24, 31, 35, 38n.46
Newell, Mike 175
New Labour 1, 4, 17, 22–3, 26–7, 32–5

creative industries 8, 11, 17, 23–4,
     27, 30–1, 33–4, 37n.37
Newson, Lloyd 127–8, 130–2, 134
Ninagawa, Yukio 124
NITRO 29
Nora, Pierre 42
Northern Ireland 17, 28, 44
     Good Friday Agreement 8, 43, 53,
        58–9
     Troubles, the 8, 56–8, 66,
        71n.74
Northern Stage 28
Nō Theatre 121–2
Nottingham Playhouse 39n.67
Notting Hill Carnival 186n.6
nva 28

Oasis 17
O'Donnell, Damien 168
O'Donnell, Mary 65
Old Vic 19
Opera House 19, 32, 156
Orientalism 10, 157, 171, 180
Osbourne, John 120, 122
Ostermeier, Thomas 100
Other Place, The (Stratford) 116
Out of Joint 28

Pagnieu, Monika 136
Paines Plough 34
Panel 2000 25
Pappenheim, Melanie 132, 135
Parmar, Pratibha 215n.8
Pearson, Mike 44–5, 47, 50, 52–3
People Show 145
performance art 30
performance studies 5
Phelan, Peggy 14n.9, 42
physical theatre 5, 9, 114, 129, 142
Piccolo Theatre 121, 124
Pimlott, Stephen 180
Pinter, Harold 115
Pit (Barbican) 116
Pook, Jocelyn 132
Potter, Lauren 132–3, 135
Protein 130
Prowse, Philip 124

Queen Victoria 62
     see also Victoria Memorial

Rahman, A. R. 179, 185
Rahman–Hughes, Stephen 177
Ravenhill, Mark 28, 39n.65
Really Useful Group 180
Rebellato, Dan 116, 118–19, 121
Reckless Sleepers 145
regionalism 35
regional theatre 18–22, 37n.36
Rehm, Rush 142
Reinelt, Janelle 120, 127, 140–5
remembering see memory
repertory theatre 20–1
Ridiculusmus 88, 145
Right Size, The 88
Ritzer, George 90–2, 98, 108n.81
Riverside Studios 144
Rolfe, Heather 106n.32
Rover car factory (Cardiff) 48, 52
Roy, Sanjay 101
Royal Court 28, 30, 125
     Upstairs 116
Royal Dramatic Theatre (Sweden)
     121
Royal Exchange Theatre 125
Royal National Theatre see National
     Theatre
Royal Opera House see Opera House
Royal Shakespeare Company (RSC)
     38n.65, 122–3, 126

SAC see Scotland
Sadler's Wells 19
Said, Edward 157, 180, 200
     see also Orientalism
Saint–Denis, Michel 123
St Martin's Lane Hotel 201–2, 206
Sanchez-Colberg, Ana 128
Sankofa Film Collective 215n.8
Sartre, Jean–Paul 124
Schaubühne Theatre (Berlin) 100
Schneer, Jonathan 199
Schrager, Ian 201
Schulz, Bruno 137
Schwarz, Bill 198, 201, 213

Scotland 17, 21, 28, 92, 95
  Holyrood (Scottish Parliament) 32
  newspapers 88, 95
  Scotland Europa 31
  Scotland the Brand 39n.77
  Scottish Arts Council (SAC) 18, 25,
    31, 40nn.78–80
  Scottish Enterprise 31
  Scottish Executive 8, 18, 25, 33
    *Creating Our Future ... Minding Our
    Past: Scotland's National Cultural
    Strategy* (2000) 31–2
  Scottish National Theatre
    *see* National Theatre of Scotland
  Scottish Screen 31
  Scottish Trade International 31
Shakespeare, William 25–6, *27*, 38n.65,
  115
Shank, Theodore 126
Shared Experience 28, 145
Shaw, George Bernard 115
Shellard, Dominic 10, 120, 122
Shelley, P. B.
  'Ozymandias' 200
Shepherd, Simon 118–19
Sierre Leone 89
Sierz, Aleks 114–15
Signal to Noise 88
site-specific theatre and performance 5,
  8, 42–67
  touring 44, 73n.110
  *see also* McQueen, Steve
slavery 211–12
Smith, Chris
  *Creative Britain* 23
Sobieski, Lynn 145
South Bank 21
Spymonkey 88
Stallybrass, Peter and Allon White 103
Stanislavski, Constantin 127
Stan's Cafe
  *It's Your Film* 29
Starck, Philippe 201, 206
Station House Opera 39n.65, 145
Stein, Peter 81
Stelfox, Dawson 61
Stoppard, Tom 26, *27*, 115

Stratford 19–20
Strehler, Giorgio 124
Strindberg, August 124
Suspect Culture 145
Svoboda, Josef 122
Syal, Meera 179, 183

Tamasha Theatre Company 29, 167,
  186n.39
  *Balti Kings* 167, 174
  *East Is East* 167–8, 174, 180
  *Fourteen Songs, Two Weddings and a
    Funeral* 157, 163, 166–8, 171–7,
    *173*
  *Ghostdancing* 167
  *House of the Sun* 167
  *Shaft of Sunlight, A* 167
  *Strictly Dandia* 167
  *Tainted Dawn, A* 167
  *Untouchable* 167
  *Women of the Dust* 167
  *Yearning, A* 167
Tanner, Dale *132*, 135
Tara Arts 29, 168, 188n.44
Teale, Polly 88
Teamworks
  *Yeh Hai Mumbai Meri Jaan* 99
Terdiman, Richard 41
Test Department 47, 50
Thatcher, Margaret 1, 49, 128
Théâtre de Complicité *see* Complicite
Théâtre National Populaire 121, 124
Theatre O 88, 145
Theatre Workshop 120
third cinema 160
Thomas, Rosie 160
Tinderbox Theatre Company 8, 70n.55
  *convictions* 8, 43, 53–67, *55*, *63*,
    70n.55
total theatre 128, 130, 136
touring 20, 27, 33, 45, 50–3, 100–1
tradition 67n.2
Trafalgar Square 194–6, 199–200
Tramway 50, 124
Transport for London *see* London
Traverse Theatre 96, 99, 124
Tricycle Theatre 125

Tron Theatre 125
Tyrrell, Heather 156

Uberoi, Patricia 169, 171
universalism 9, 137–43
Unlimited Theatre 88

Valle–Inclán, Ramón
    *Barbaric Comedies* 100
Vardimon, Jasmin 130
Vasudevan, Ravi S. 163–5
Verma, Deepak 167
Verma, Jatinder 174–5, 186n.5, 188n.44
Victoria and Albert Museum 194,
    196–7
Victoria Memorial 194, 205
Vilar, Jean 121
Volcano (Canada)
    *Lambton, Kent* 99
Volcano Theatre Company (Wales) 28,
    145
V-Tol 39n.65, 146

Wales 8, 17, 21, 28, 44, 49, 69n.24
Warner, Deborah 88

Watson, Keith 130
Webber (Sir) Andrew Lloyd 10, 156,
    179–81, 186
Webster, John 115
Weiss, Peter
    *Marat/Sade, The* 122
Welsh, Irvine 92, 94
    *Trainspotting* 92, 95
Western Deep, South Africa 11, 203
Wilde, Oscar 115
Wilkie, Fiona 68n.12, 70n.52
Williams, William Emrys 19–20
Wilson, Robert 99
Winslet, Kate *26*
Wolf, Naomi 86
Wood, Harvey 98
World Trade Center 212–13
World War Two 7
Wycherley, William 115

Yarrow, Ralph and Anthony Frost 122
Yellow Earth Theatre 29

Coventry University